DATE DUE

DEC 9 1991	
APR 27 1992	
NOV 4 1992	
MAR 22 1993	
JUN 20 1994	
FEB 10 1997	
MAY 08 1998	
MAY 08 1998	
AUG 11 1998	
DEC 01 2003	
SEP 06 2011	

PUBLIC OPINION
IN
AMERICAN
POLITICS

W. LANCE BENNETT
University of Washington

Under the General Editorship of
James David Barber
Duke University

HARCOURT BRACE JOVANOVICH, INC.
New York San Diego Chicago San Francisco Atlanta
London Sydney Toronto

To Walter D. and Anna J.

Preface

Public opinion has played a vital role in American history. The importance of public opinion to political processes is proclaimed explicitly in the Constitution and affirmed implicitly in the people's continuing expectations of their role in popular government. Even the most casual look at contemporary society shows that opinion is a powerful political force. The fortunes of parties, politicians, and policies depend on it, and through it individuals express their feelings about government and everyday life. Loss of public support for leaders or government can be a serious blow to the smooth functioning of the political system and the effectiveness of government policies.

For such pioneer theorists as Floyd Allport, Arthur Bently, V. O. Key, Jr., Harold Lasswell, Charles Merriam, and Walter Lippmann, public opinion was a major source of insight into the functioning of social and political processes in America, and they left to modern opinion researchers a heritage of rich ideas. Yet despite this great legacy, contemporary opinion research has produced a fragmented and politically anemic picture of opinion. Instead of formulating a general, integrated understanding of opinion and politics, opinion analysts tend to treat the various dimensions of opinion (for example, socialization, belief systems, opinion and personality, issue formation and agenda setting, mass communication, and policy making) as isolated topics. Analysts often oversimplify the political functions of opinion, reducing them to crude questions of whether or not public opinion causes public policy. This emphasis on the relationship between opinion and policy has led to a preoccupation with the failings of public opinion rather than with its contributions to the political system.

Public Opinion in American Politics presents a broad analytical framework that integrates opinion methodology with real-world political conditions and balances the shortcomings of opinion with the essential roles opinion plays in American politics. The expanded theoretical focus does not mean that existing opinion concepts and methods have been abandoned in favor of a new vocabulary and new topics; existing knowledge is organized in a way that lends coherence to the subject. Topics often isolated in standard opinion texts are discussed separately and then linked together to show how the various dimensions of opinion contribute to the workings of the larger political system. For example, individual-centered topics like socialization, belief systems, and personality and opinion are relevant to the larger processes of issue formation, mass communication, and agenda setting. The opinion that crystallizes in issue formation and mass communication processes feeds in turn into institutional and policy formation processes.

With this approach public opinion becomes a viable analytical tool for explaining why various things do or do not happen in different political situations. While traditional approaches regard public opinion as a more or less fixed state of mind with a limited political role, the emphasis here is on the ways public opinion can vary in its origin, formation, expression, and political impact. In keeping with this orientation, students are introduced to the concept of a public that is constantly shifting in its social composition and political motivation, reacting differently to different social and political circumstances.

Chapters 1 and 2 present analytical perspectives on public opinion, pointing out pitfalls as well as productive approaches. Chapter 3 introduces the methodology of opinion polling and measurement and applies it to the analysis of actual political situations. This review of opinion methods is more than just a guide for the beginner. Emphasis is placed on sources of error in research and on ways of correcting these errors. Chapter 3 concludes with an explanation of the importance of theories as foundations for survey methods and data-analysis techniques.

Chapter 4 continues the discussion of theories by outlining general opinion variables that enter into the working of the political system. This chapter has been designed as optional reading. It establishes a general model of opinion and politics that provides a theoretical framework for the sequential development of the rest of the book toward explanations of political integration, legitimation, stability, and change. If the instructor chooses to omit this chapter, the subsequent chapters stand independently as treatments of the conventional topics in public opinion. Chapters 5, 6, and 7 discuss socialization, belief systems, and opinion and personality. Chapters 8 through 11 address issue formation and agenda setting, symbolism and persuasion, and mass media and mass communication. Chapters 12, 13, and 14 present policy making, political institutions (courts, Congress, the presidency), opinion and voting behavior, and political legitimation.

This book could not have been written without the help, criticism, and moral support of many people. Perhaps the greatest debt goes to students who have contributed to the development of these ideas over the last several years. In addition to the important feedback provided by students, a number of colleagues have been kind enough to comment on the manuscript: James David Barber, Murray Edelman, Alex Edelstein, William Haltom, Michael Huspek, Robert Lane, Richard Niemi, Lee Scheingold, Stuart Scheingold, David Sears, and John Sullivan. I would also like to thank Richard Lamb for his support during an earlier stage of the project. Joanne Daniels has been the perfect editor. It was a delight to be able to exchange movie reviews and gardening hints before launching into serious business about the progress of the manuscript. Pat Herbst proved to be a remarkably diplomatic and skillful manuscript editor, and Juliana Koenig made the final stages of manuscript preparation an easy and painless process. Mary Pierce's infinite patience as a typist has at last been rewarded with the publication of this book.

W. L. B.

Contents

PART ONE

Concepts,
Methods,
and Theories

1
Public Opinion:
A Matter
of Perspective

THE ART OF INTERPRETING and influencing public opinion is the key to politics in a liberal democratic society like the United States. The legitimacy of government depends on the support of the people. Election to public office depends on the vote of the people. The priorities assigned to issues and policies depend on the concern of the people. Support, votes, and political concerns can arise through grassroots communications and common political experiences, or they can be purchased through the billions of dollars spent every year by government and private interests on public relations, mass communications, and propaganda. In either case, the political responses of the public are registered as public opinion, and public opinion is the key variable in American politics.

The workings of the political system are affected both by public opinion that arises from grassroots concerns and by public opinion that emerges in response to carefully designed political influence campaigns. The success of virtually every public political action depends on the strength of opinion behind it. In some cases, opinion is expressed in formal and focused ways—through voting, writing letters to representatives, contributing money to candidates and interest groups, or joining protest organizations. In other cases, opinion is registered in less formal and less direct ways—through the publication of opinion polls and the analyses of journalists and politicians about the "national mood."

Both formal and informal aspects of opinion are in play constantly as political actors come under public scrutiny and present their various causes to the public. The fates of actors and their issues often hinge on the delicate business of interpreting and mobilizing public opinion. There are few better examples of the political effects of public opinion than Jimmy Carter's stormy presidency.

In 1975, when Carter began his race for the presidency, he was an obscure political figure with little national following. Carter violated all the laws of presidential politics: He had little support in his party. He was an outsider in an insider's game. He was a Southerner. He had few credentials as a leader. He had no national visibility. He was not particularly glamorous or charismatic. However, Carter took advantage of a powerful resource: opinion polling.

From the earliest days of his campaign, Carter commissioned opinion polls to assess the national mood and the concerns of various groups of voters. By addressing his appeals to broad public concerns and specific group interests, Carter quickly separated himself from the other candidates. He was able to capitalize on being an outsider at a time when the public distrusted insiders. He escaped the stigma of not being an established leader by advocating a new kind of leadership that was responsive to the needs of the people. He compensated for his lack of experience with traditional issues by promoting new issues centered on trust, morality, and decency in government. In short, Carter ran his campaign with an attentive eye to the concerns of the public.

Following Carter's successful use of public opinion in his campaign, opinion polling became a primary activity in his administration. Patrick Caddell, the man whose brilliant reading of the public mind helped Carter get elected, became a central figure on the presidential team. The pulse of the public was monitored regularly by the President's pollster. Caddell conducted a dozen national surveys for the White House in 1977 alone.[1] The sensitivity of the Carter administration to public opinion was so apparent that "Doonesbury," a popular political comic strip, invented an "Office of Symbolism" as a parody of Carter's continuing efforts to mobilize public opinion.

Despite his preoccupation with public opinion and his efforts to harness it, Carter's popularity began to plummet. At the end of his first year in office, Carter's detractors outnumbered his supporters. His downhill slide began in 1977 with his first serious effort to rally the public behind a major policy program, a comprehensive energy plan. Carter's failure to win public support in this initial policy offensive (and his continuing inability to mobilize public opinion) illustrates a number of important points about opinion: Opinion is a crucial ingredient in leadership and agenda building. The concerns of the public are difficult to interpret. There are limits to the degree to which public opinion can be manipulated through symbolism and rhetoric alone. Finally, the failure to exert some influence over public opinion can mean disaster for leaders and their policies.

In his first major policy statement, Carter urged the American people to "wage the moral equivalent of war" against the energy problem. He proposed a sweeping energy program centered on conservation and cutbacks in the wasteful American life style. To the surprise of Carter and his advisers, the public did not respond positively to these proposals. In fact, public approval of Carter's handling of energy dropped nearly twenty points between March 1977 and March 1978.[2] The decline in public support for the energy program was paralleled by a similar drop in overall public approval of Carter's performance as President.[3]

The reason for Carter's disastrous failure to win popular support for his energy recommendations involved a serious misreading of public concerns. Major national pollsters, like Louis Harris and Carter's private pollster Caddell, all seemed to agree that the public favored energy conservation and resented aspects of the wasteful American life style. On the basis of this consensus about the public mood, Carter's appeal to the public emphasized conservation, sacrifice, and more modest economic expectations. The pollsters' interpretation of the public mood turned out to be much too simplistic, however. Subsequent polls by Caddell and George Gallup explained the public's resistance to Carter's proposals.

Although the public favored conservation and abhorred waste, the majority feared economic cutbacks and restricted life style even more strongly. The failure of Carter and his advisers to view public support for conservation in the context of larger concerns about the economy led to the construction of the wrong political appeals. In an effort to determine what went wrong with Carter's bid for public support, Gallup asked a national sample of American adults to respond to the following statement: "Some people think the Carter plan puts too much emphasis on conservation of energy and not enough on the development of new energy sources. Do you agree or disagree with this opinion?" Nearly 60 percent of the sample agreed that conservation was overemphasized.[4]

Carter's early errors in reading public opinion were compounded later in his presidency by his inability to appeal to the concerns of the public even when he did interpret them correctly. Despite some upturns in public support following his successful diplomacy in the Middle East, the general trend in popularity continued steadily downhill. By the middle of 1979, Carter's popularity had dropped below the record lows recorded by Richard Nixon shortly before he resigned from office as a result of the Watergate scandal. In short, Carter was in serious political trouble, and some miraculous reversal in the opinion polls was required in order to save his presidency.

A large-scale energy shortage struck the country in 1979. The price of gasoline at the pump went over $1 a gallon, and the cost of home heating oil followed closely behind. Carter promised the nation that he would deliver a major energy speech in early summer. He and his staff recognized that the critical moment of his political career was at hand. Instead of delivering the speech on the day it had been scheduled for, the President postponed the speech, withdrew to his Camp David retreat, and contemplated his political options. Perhaps chastened by his earlier energy campaign, he examined his proposals carefully and searched for some grander appeal to the public.

Once again Carter called on Patrick Caddell to forecast the public mood. Caddell said that his polls showed the public to be burdened with a deep malaise, a profound lack of confidence and optimism. He reportedly urged the President to shift the focus of his speech to the psychological problems confronting the public.[5] He recommended that the President adopt an uncharacteristic posture of strong and assertive leadership. According to his analysis, the public needed to be scolded for its self-absorption and urged to turn to broader concerns. Other advisers disagreed with the President's pollster. Vice President Walter Mondale reportedly agreed with Caddell's assessment about the national malaise but felt that the public did not need a scolding. He contended that the people were responding realistically to an uncertain economic situation and needed solid economic proposals to rally their spirit.[6]

Carter emerged from Camp David with a decision to adopt a mixture of the advice he had received. His July 1979 speech was a curious blend of an uncharacteristic leadership posture, abstract references to the public malaise, and concrete recommendations about energy. Carter's rhetorical style was aggressive and bold, punctuated with overdramatized hand gestures and forced voice intonations. He talked at length about the despair of the public. He urged the people to support his energy proposals as a means of reversing the mood of apathy and rebuilding public confidence in America.

Although most observers felt that Carter had assessed the public mood correctly, his speech produced only temporary increases in public approval of his leadership and popular support for his programs. Despite a more accurate assessment of public opinion, Carter had failed to make an effective political appeal. His momentous speech illustrated only too painfully the limits of political rhetoric and symbolism in mobilizing the public. Even the proper interpretation of public concerns does not guarantee that political actors can mobilize those concerns to their political advantage. Carter's inability to deliver promised economic improvements contributed to the continued erosion of his political position.

In the fall of 1979 on the eve of a hotly contested reelection campaign, Carter's political position could not have been much worse. A poll conducted for *Time* magazine by the opinion research firm of Yankelovich, Skelly and White revealed that only 10 percent of the public expressed confidence in Carter's ability to deal with the economy.[7] A slim 13 percent of those interviewed in the poll felt confident that Carter could handle the energy situation. Only 12 percent thought that the embattled President was a strong leader. Nearly two-thirds of the Democrats contacted in the national survey favored the nomination of Massachusetts Senator Edward M. Kennedy as the Democratic candidate for President in 1980. Only 24 percent wanted to see Carter return as their party's nominee. Perhaps most significant was the finding that Kennedy would fare better than Carter against any of the likely Republican candidates in 1980.[8]

This discussion of the political fortunes of Jimmy Carter is not intended as a listing of his failings as President; its purpose is to illustrate the integral role of public opinion in American national politics. The story of Jimmy Carter after nearly four years in office resembles, with a change of plot here and there, the stories of Harry Truman in 1952, Lyndon Johnson in 1968, Richard Nixon in 1974, and Gerald Ford in 1976.

A number of patterns running through Carter's experiences appear time and again in American politics. These characteristics of opinion that emerge from practical political situations raise important issues for opinion theory and research. Perhaps the most important lesson from Carter's early days in office is that public opinion is complex and must not be interpreted in simplistic ways. Carter's mistaken interpretation that the public favored strict energy conservation policies was not just the naive mistake of an inexperienced politician. Experienced pollsters like Louis Harris and Patrick Caddell made the same analysis of the situation. In fact, it is likely that Carter followed the judgment of such experts. This example points out the fact that a major concern about public opinion is the problem of how to measure and interpret it accurately. This concern is shared by politicians and opinion analysts alike.

A second important point about opinion that emerges from the Carter experience is that even when public opinion is interpreted correctly, it cannot always be manipulated at will. Simply knowing the moods or the needs of the public does not necessarily provide politicians or opinion analysts with the insights needed to channel public concerns in particular political directions. Carter seemed to diagnose the public mood accurately prior to his major energy speech of 1979, but he failed to convert his analysis into an effective political appeal. A major question for opinion research is to understand both the ways in which opinion can be shaped and the conditions under which people are resistant to political appeals.

The number of ways in which public opinion entered Carter's political calculations both before and after he became President illustrates the fact that opinion can operate politically in a variety of formal and informal ways and with a number of political effects. For example, public opinion expressed through the formal mechanism of the vote was responsible for electing Carter to office, yet subsequent informal expressions of opinion through the polls and press reports undermined Carter's leadership and damaged his political programs. Among the most challenging tasks facing opinion research is discovering the different forms in which opinion can be expressed and explaining the political effects that various expressions of opinion can have. It is a relatively simple matter to measure the vote in an election and determine the impact of the vote on the outcome of the election. However, it is another matter altogether to determine how various kinds of informal opinion expression affect a President's leadership or undermine his political programs.

Perhaps the most important lesson illustrated by experiences of the Carter presidency is that public opinion is an ever-present and powerful force in all institutional settings. Opinion can become both a volatile factor and a valuable resource in almost any political conflict. Public opinion is taken into account routinely by elected officials, hopeful candidates, interest groups, and the press. Sometimes opinion can be harnessed, and sometimes not. Whether opinion can be focused and channeled in particular ways often determines the outcomes of political processes.

In short, Jimmy Carter's troubled courtship of public opinion illustrates four important political characteristics of opinion. First, public opinion is often complex and difficult to interpret. Second, even when opinion is interpreted correctly, it is not always obvious how to present an effective political appeal to the public. Third, public opinion can be expressed in a variety of ways with a variety of political effects. Fourth, opinion can emerge as a key political factor in virtually any public political context.

These characteristics make public opinion both a powerful political force and a challenging subject to study. The excitement of opinion research comes from being able to explain problems of measurement and interpretation, processes of opinion formation and change, expressions and impacts of opinion, and the roles played by opinion in political institutions and the surrounding political system. The payoff from clarifying these and other aspects of opinion is not just the building of more sophisticated theories of opinion. The real payoff from opinion research is understanding the workings of the American political system. The goal of this book is to provide a sensible framework for thinking about public opinion in order to make public opinion a useful tool for political analysis.

DOMAINS OF PUBLIC OPINION

The study of public opinion is concerned with how people form and share judgments about problems, goals, and issues. Public opinion research explores complex processes of human understanding and communication, investigating how men and women respond to events and how their responses in turn shape events. These concerns make public opinion a fascinating subject with roots in individual belief systems, social relations, communication technologies, cultural traditions, and political processes. The central role of public opinion in society has made it a major topic of research in a number of fields, including psychology, sociology, political science, and communications. Few subjects have attracted such wide interest.

The apparent complexity of public opinion can be reduced by recognizing that most research and theorizing about opinion can be classified under one of the following three topics: (1) the individual and society, (2) issue formation and political communication processes, and (3) political institutions and culture. Although each area is often treated as a separate domain of opinion, a major aim of this book is to show how closely related they really are. Public opinion results when *individuals* seek expression through *mass communication channels* in order to participate meaningfully in *political and cultural affairs.* The defining characteristics of each domain of opinion and the relationships between the domains can be summarized easily.

The *domain of the individual and society* encompasses how men and women think about the world around them and how their opinions affect their social adjustment. People acquire stable patterns of belief and judgment as a result of socialization processes that begin in early childhood and continue throughout life. Differences in political socialization can explain why some people value equality more than wealth, why others emphasize security and authority over freedom, and why still others become life-long Republicans instead of Democrats. Changes in socialization experiences may explain why people sometimes undergo radical conversions in political philosophy, or become "born again" with new religious convictions, or alter their patterns of political behavior.

In addition to the long-term focus on socialization, the domain of the individual and society also concentrates on short-term opinion formation and change. How do people form and express opinions when they are exposed to new information, issues, candidates, and experiences? The psychological processes that govern the formation of opinion may differ from person to person; they also may lead people to react differently under different political circumstances. These differences help to explain why some people can be persuaded easily while others resist new information. They also may explain why some issues catch on and others do not, why some propaganda is effective and some is not, and why some candidates win popular support while others are rejected.

Studying the long-term effects of political socialization provides information about the basic values and beliefs in society and about the patterns of change that affect them. Socialization research also reveals how much support exists for political institutions and their procedures. Through the short-term processes of forming and expressing opinions, individuals are constantly aligning themselves with or against these dominant social values. This alignment affects both the social adjustment and the psychological well-being of every person. Opinions are not just abstract political forces; they are also intimate expressions of social acceptance, group pressure, membership, identity, and psychological needs.

The formation of opinions by individuals is the first step in the development of public opinion. The emergence of public opinion depends on the communication and the convergence of private concerns. This is accomplished through the workings of mass communication processes. In the *domain of issue formation and political communication* private concerns are transformed into public issues and positions. Mass communication takes place in election campaigns, public opinion polling, news and public affairs programming on television, information and editorial comments published by the press, and information campaigns run by interest groups and big business. In one way or another, the mass media dominate these channels of communication. Therefore, an understanding of political communication requires both an analysis of the content of political messages and an investigation of the media through which they are transmitted.

As a result of the political communication that takes place through various channels, the concerns of individuals gradually develop into a set of commonly agreed upon issues, goals, problems, and conflicts. This so-called political agenda begins as a loose and unfocused set of public moods and discontents. In the *domain of political institutions and culture* these emerging issues are converted into clear statements of policy, legitimate options for political action, and focused expressions of political values. Institutions shape the definitions of issues and create linkages between public opinion and the resolution of issues. Research in this domain addresses the problem of how opinion affects political decisions and policies and the question of how institutional procedures restrict the expression of opinion. Institutions do more than merely present policies and programs to the public for its approval. They also define policies and programs, and they regulate the expression of public responses in ways that tend to broaden areas of agreement, limit the intensity of conflict, and promote the acceptance of the outcomes.

Public opinion is more than just an "input" to the political system. As an object of institutional regulation and political control, it is also an important "output" of the political system. In order for the political system to work smoothly, the public must appear to accept day-to-day political outcomes and the procedures that produce them. Thus, the way in which public opinion is regulated by political institutions is as important a question as whether public opinion affects the outcomes of those institutions.

The dual focus on institutions and culture in the third domain of opinion is intended to highlight the idea that institutions are more than just arenas in which leaders are chosen and policies are made. Institutions also embody fundamental political principles and values. They endow special meaning to the issues that pass through them. When issues become part of the agenda of an institution, they represent more than narrow political outcomes. They also become symbols of individual concerns, group identities, and cultural values. For example, even a seemingly concrete issue like the energy shortage is wrapped up in questions about individual rights, social equality, and the national image. In the coming years the energy crisis will raise fundamental questions about whether individuals who can afford to purchase and waste energy should have the right to do so. In addition, the increasing costs of energy for transportation and private use will become volatile issues in the widening gap of social inequality. Perhaps the major symbolic concern will be the dependence of the United States on foreign sources of energy and the resulting economic damage of that position. This reliance is an abrasive force acting against traditional American values of independence and superiority.

In short, institutions are not just elaborate decision-making schemes. They are also the protectors of traditional social and political values. As issues pass through institutions on their way to resolution, various mechanisms ensure that the public will explore them for any implications they may have for traditional values and understandings. As a result, institutions can become forums for educating the public about social needs and for establishing priorities.

The educational and culture-maintaining functions of institutions have an important impact on socialization and opinion formation in the domain of the individual and society. Values and beliefs promoted in the day-to-day operations of political institutions become the basis of long-term socialization and short-term opinion formation processes. In the early stages of the public opinion process, the political concerns of individuals are channeled by the mass media into the operations of political institutions. Later, the political messages shaped by institutions are filtered back through mass communication processes to influence the way individuals think about themselves and their society. This two-way flow accounts for patterns of stability and change in public opinion. It also illustrates the constant interplay of individuals, communication processes, and institutions to transform private sentiment into public opinion and to make public opinion a powerful force in private life. In this framework, each domain of opinion serves a separate political function, but each is coordinated with the others to make public opinion the central regulating mechanism in the political system.

CLARIFYING THE CONCEPT
OF PUBLIC OPINION

In order to understand what happens in the three domains of opinion, the first order of business is to clarify the concept of public opinion. The perspective in this book is based on one fundamental idea: Public opinion is a diverse and ever-changing form of social expression. Because opinion has origins in different spheres of society it can take on different characteristics under different circumstances. Since it can play a variety of political roles, it can exhibit different forms of expression. Most importantly, since the objects of public opinion are so numerous and of such varying importance to individuals, the composition of "the public" changes constantly from one political situation to another.

All these things may seem obvious, but it is easy to oversimplify the concept and think of public opinion as a fixed state of consciousness that applies to the whole population of individuals under all circumstances. The misguided notion that public opinion is a constant force with permanent characteristics probably comes from classical notions of democracy, in which "the public" is treated as the group of all citizens who have the civic duty to express informed, consistent, and well-articulated political judgments about all political matters. This may be a noble ideal, but it simply does not square with reality. Moreover, since it focuses only on the classical concern with opinion as a causal force in policy formation, it ignores the other roles that opinion can play in the political system. In order to understand the range of public opinion expressions and their possible political impacts, it is necessary to define the concept in a more flexible and open way.

The major obstacle to a more flexible theory of opinion is the tendency to regard public opinion as the product of a permanent state of mind or collective consciousness. Implicit in this view, which may be called the *state-of-consciousness perspective*, is the idea that the public is a stable entity that changes little in composition or state of consciousness from one situation to another. The general public, in this view, is the totality of individuals in society who could conceivably react to an issue.

Because the state-of-consciousness perspective sets out to generalize about the public's state of mind, it assumes that public opinion is based on some fairly constant pattern of thinking. When public opinion is approached in this way, it makes sense to ask questions like these: Is public opinion informed? Is it sensitive to the range of issues that life in modern society raises? Is it stable and committed, or is it unpredictable and changing? Is there a common frame of reference or a set of collective understandings that gives public opinion obvious coherence and meaning?

The problem with this perspective is that attempts to study public opinion as a general concept have resulted only in confusion. Some studies seem to show that the public is ignorant and uninformed. Other studies indicate that the public is capable of making informed judgments and rational choices. Some research indicates that public opinion is unstable and changing, while other findings support the argument that opinion may be remarkably stable. If the assumption that there is a general state of consciousness underlying public opinion is valid, then all these findings cannot be right. Public opinion cannot be both informed and uninformed, stable and unstable, lacking in underlying principles of reasoning and at the same time displaying coherence.

A different view brings greater clarity to the study of public opinion. The *situational perspective* regards the public as the collection of individuals who actually form and express opinions on a specific issue at a particular time. From this perspective, the general public is simply the overall population of individuals or groups from which public opinion emerges in response to various issues and situations. Because conditions change and the population of actors shifts from situation to situation, the characteristics of opinion may vary from one context to another. From the situational view, public opinion may involve different individuals, different objects of interest, and different states of arousal and consciousness from one situation to another.

When the situational perspective is used, differences in the information, stability, or coherence of public opinion can be accounted for by the diversity of conditions affecting the formation and expression of opinion. Differences in the characteristics of opinion need not be regarded as contradictory if they are caused by different conditions in individual psychology, political communications, or institutional procedures. Instead of regarding public opinion as the product of a general state of consciousness, the situational perspective explains variations in public opinion as the result of interactions between the beliefs and values of individuals and social and political conditions. For example, issues pertaining to racial equality may trigger one sort of response when they are stated as general public policy problems or as questions of constitutional law. They may mean something else when they hit close to home in such contexts as the integration of schools through forced busing or the creation of employment opportunities through affirmative action programs in the work place. Such differences are hard to explain with theories based on the state-of-consciousness perspective.

The problems with the state-of-consciousness perspective were first pointed out by Allport more than forty years ago. In an argument that many experts still regard as the seminal discussion of the concept of public opinion, Allport showed that seven approaches to the definition of public opinion lead to dead ends.[9] Although each path has some appeal to common sense, each turns into a blind alley when pursued to its logical or empirical conclusion. Each of the seven blind alleys identified by Allport can be traced to an origin in the state-of-consciousness perspective.

One of the fallacies most often committed in defining public opinion is the assumption that some common principle or logic underlies the opinions of different individuals in the public and may inform or shape expressions of public opinion. This assumption leads to the easy conclusion that logical connections ought to exist between opinions on different issues. Although Allport admitted that such connections can be established between particular issues under particular circumstances, he pointed out that it is unreasonable to consider such states of mind as stable or as defining characteristics of public opinion. When research fails to reveal such connections, the state-of-consciousness perspective may lead researchers to draw the meaningless but rhetorically "loaded" conclusion that there is no coherence or logical order in the public's thinking. The state-of-consciousness fallacy can also make it difficult to understand changes in the public's reaction to an issue. For example, if the public is thought to be united by some common "soul" or set of fixed dispositions, then it is easy to talk about the public as though it were one person with a single mind. If this view is adopted, it is tempting to think that "the public has changed its mind" if differences are observed in public reactions to an issue. For instance, it would be easy to adopt such a conclusion if we found that the public was generally opposed to the idea of formal political relations with China in 1953 but generally favored the idea in 1980. Such an interpretation, however, would ignore so many changes in political context, the composition of the public, and the reasoning behind the opinions that on close inspection it would make no sense. More importantly, such an approach would tell us nothing about how opinion processes work, what issues mean to people, or why public opinion changes.

Specific opinion contexts can differ in important respects such as how issues are defined, the relation of issues to social values and institutions, the perceived consequences of issues, and the composition of the public. In light of this, Allport argued that it makes sense to think of public opinion only as the changing product of "groupings of specific individuals with a certain common agreement among them at one time and a different sort of agreement at another time."[10] To proceed in any other way can result only in overgeneralized and contradictory findings. As Allport observed, when public opinion is regarded as "an entity or a content to be discovered and then studied or analyzed, our efforts will meet with scant success."[11] These conclusions led Allport to adopt a flexible definition of the concept, which is consistent with the general theoretical orientation of this book (the italics are Allport's):

> The term *public opinion is given its meaning with reference to a multi-individual situation in which individuals are expressing themselves, as favoring or supporting (or else disfavoring or opposing) some definite condition, person, or proposal of widespread importance, in such a proportion of number, intensity, and constancy, as to give rise to the probability of affecting action, directly or indirectly, toward the object concerned.*[12]

This definition implies that any description or analysis of public opinion must take into account the composition of the public, the situation that the members of the public hold in common, the dominant objects of concern, the conditions that affect feelings about those objects, the manner in which the resulting opinions are expressed, and the impact of those opinions on the situation.

BELIEFS AND VALUES: THE BASES OF OPINION

Opinions can be based on a variety of factors. Sometimes people may go along with the crowd or make up something to say in order to please or impress the people they are with.[13] However, opinions that help individuals make sense out of a situation and respond meaningfully to it are based on underlying values and beliefs.

Values represent the things people find most important in life. They are the factors that seem, in the individual's view of things, to be necessary conditions for the good life. Some values may take the form of personal goals like success, wealth, or enlightenment. Other values, such as a strong national defense or respect for the law, may pertain to the conditions of social order. Still other values may include commitments to freedom, equality, and justice. Values like hard work, competition, and self-reliance may serve as measures of individual worth.

Beliefs are the facts people take for granted about the world. They are propositions regarded as true and real. Beliefs can operate independently from values as isolated bits of information, but they also can serve to connect values to the real world. Beliefs often provide understanding about how values are promoted or threatened in different situations. For example, a person who *values* self-reliance and hard work may come to *believe* that the welfare system undermines these important virtues by rewarding people who don't work. Such a person may evaluate new welfare programs or political candidates' statements on the issue according to this belief-value pair. This orientation may produce positive opinions about programs or candidates that promise to reduce payments and increase incentives to work. Negative opinions may emerge in response to plans to increase welfare allocations or ease the requirements for recipients.

Opinions are the result of complex value and belief calculations that establish a sensible fit between the outer world and life experiences. Opinions hold the world together for people. That is why people can become so concerned about an issue like welfare and why they can become so outraged by the few individuals who take advantage of the welfare system.

Consider the case of a Greek immigrant who worked as a janitor fourteen hours a day on two jobs. His statements to Sennett and Cobb show that values like hard work and self-reliance helped keep him going in the face of a hard, unrewarding, and demeaning existence:

> Well, you see . . . now I am what I am, a family man, a daddy, and . . . I feel I have a duty to them . . . a duty to make something of my-self here in America where the children are born . . . so that they can respect me, you see . . . now I am a cleaner . . . now there is nothing wrong with that, that is my lot . . . so what I have to do is make something of it.[14]

The values implied in a personal statement like that provide a context for judging concrete social problems and political issues, and they allow people to judge distant issues with reference to their own experiences and feelings. Sennett and Cobb observe that for individuals like the janitor, opinions play an important role in maintaining self-esteem. Values related to work and self-reliance and beliefs about welfare programs and their clients become means of shoring up personal existence against the ravages of poverty, frustration, indignity, and self-doubt. The creation of new welfare programs or the discovery of cheaters may challenge personal convictions. Opinions are means of responding to such challenges and reasserting personal worth. Under such circumstances a complex view of the welfare system is probably not useful or necessary. For many people like the janitor, the existence of one welfare cheater can be as upsetting as the existence of thousands. Sennett and Cobb concluded:

> If there are people who have refused to make sacrifices, yet are subsidized by the state, their very existence calls into question the meaning of acts of self-abnegation. Since sacrifice is a voluntary virtue, a meaning the sacrificer has created out of the material circumstances of his life, it takes only one "welfare chiseler," getting sympathy and help from the authorities without any show of self-sacrifice, to make that willed, that created meaning ever so vulnerable.[15]

People's opinions are like coded messages about their life experiences, and underlying systems of beliefs and values provide the keys to the code. However, opinions are more than just means of translating the outer world into familiar and manageable terms. They are also individual efforts to confirm personal experiences and understanding. When an individual's opinion merges with the sentiments of a larger group, the assumptions that support his or her life experience are reaffirmed. When the opinion of the group has some impact on the resolution of an issue, each individual's values and beliefs become institutionalized. Thus public opinion channels individual orientations into common expressions that can affect the development of a situation, and, by doing so, public opinion confirms the initial orientations of the individuals involved. Understanding of this two-way process requires a grasp of the interactions between individuals' beliefs and values and the properties of situations that focus the expression of common sentiments.

The simple idea of an interaction between individuals' values and beliefs and the objects of attention in situations can be developed into a useful set of terms for describing opinion. Later chapters will provide details about how situations vary and why particular patterns of opinion occur under certain circumstances. However, it is useful at the outset to have a sense of the general contours of opinion situations. Any opinion situation can be described in terms of the *scope*, *direction*, and *distribution* of opinion.

The *scope* of public opinion will vary in response to different issues, for some issues appeal to a broader range of beliefs and values than others. Any object of public attention will fall within the range of beliefs and values held by some individuals and beyond the range of others. The scope of opinion is simply the ratio of opinionated to nonopinionated individuals. Situations that generate a broad scope of opinion can be volatile. Thus political actors who want to increase the impact of their cause or enlist broader involvement may try to define issues in ways that connect with a wide range of public values and beliefs. For example, when the United States normalized relations with China in 1979, a major theme stressed by President Jimmy Carter was the economic advantage of the move. This emphasis made it possible to view the ation as more than just a foreign policy move. It may have increased the salience of the action in the eyes of many people who are more attentive to economic issues than to foreign policy questions.

Another political goal may also have been achieved by emphasizing the economic advantages of the new China policy. If the issue had been defined simply as establishing relations with a communist country and severing ties with a former ally, public opinion might have run in a strongly negative *direction*. However, defining the issue in economic and pragmatic terms established a connection with other values (such as economic prosperity) and beliefs (for exam-

FIGURE 1-1
Unimodal Distribution of Opinion

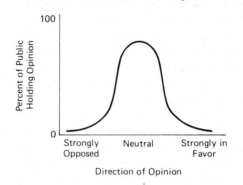

Direction of Opinion

ple, advantageous trade relations are important to economic prosperity), which pulled opinion in a more positive direction. The
economic emphasis may have produced a value conflict in some individuals who would have strongly opposed relations with China
under other circumstances. The resulting conflict between economic and political values may have neutralized some potential opposition and shifted the weight of public opinion in a more positive
direction. In this manner the distribution of opposing values and
beliefs in the public interacts with the way in which an object of attention is defined to determine the direction of opinion.

The overall scope and direction of opinion are important determinants of the priority of an issue, the level of conflict it generates,
and popular acceptance of its resolution. However, opinions of the
same scope and direction can be distributed differently over the
members of the public. The *distribution* of an opinion can provide
clues about what actions people might take on an issue, how volatile the situation is, and whether changes in the situation are likely
to produce changes in public opinion or action.

There are many different ways in which the opponents of an issue could balance out the proponents to produce a general tendency toward neutrality. In one case a "neutral" pattern of opinion
may have a distribution with a strong central tendency and a small
frequency of extreme responses. This is one type of *unimodal distribution* (see Figure 1-1). Some unimodal distributions are centered
around strong opposition or support positions. Neutral unimodal
distributions result when objects of opinion are ambiguous or
when they are only weakly related to individual orientations.

For example, in the 1960s when the government began talking about the possible cancer-producing agents in our food and in the environment, most people were unsure about the true danger or proliferation of such agents. Under such conditions certain special interests or groups with access to independent information formed strong opinions in one direction or another about government involvement in this area. However, most individuals probably had little basis for seeing that values involving the quality of health or consumers' freedom of choice were affected one way or another by government investigation and regulation. The expected result would be a heavy concentration of opinion in the center of the spectrum.

After years of research, more people were convinced that certain agents in air, water, and food constituted a general health hazard and that the government should take action to control them. Other people were still not sure they could believe the studies, and still others regarded the increasing level of government intervention as a greater threat to values than the continued exposure to health hazards. Some workers in chemical plants preferred to continue working in harmful environments rather than see the plants close down to comply with government standards. Similarly, some smokers preferred to take the health risk rather than give up the pleasure of smoking or undergo the pain of quitting. Under these circumstances questions about government intervention produced the same overall direction of opinion as before, but the distribution was relatively flat, or even (see Figure 1-2).

The *flat distribution* approximates the opinion situation in California in 1978 when a proposition to outlaw smoking in public places was placed on the ballot. At first, reactions to the proposition were distributed fairly evenly across the spectrum. Then the tobacco interests launched an expensive campaign to change the definition of the issue, thereby activating values and beliefs that would push individuals who remained in the center of the spectrum into the group that opposed the proposition. The main theme of the campaign was the claim that government intervention would be an intolerable attack on freedom and privacy. This definition provided an outlet for the expression of beliefs and values other than those related strictly to health and smoking.

The campaign worked. It had an effect on all three dimensions of opinion. The final scope of opinion was very broad. Almost as many people registered a vote on the antismoking proposition as voted for governor. The size of the vote on the issue was 99 per-

FIGURE 1-2
Flat Distribution of Opinion

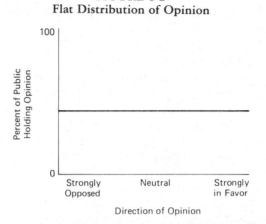

cent of the size of the vote for governor and approximately 1.2 times larger than the vote on ballot measures concerning the state public utilities commission and the status of surplus state-owned coastal property.[16] Over a million more votes were cast on the antismoking issue than on these other issues—even though the same total number of voters stood in the voting booths, were exposed to the whole list of propositions, and had the opportunity to pull all the voting levers. Even more important, of course, is the fact that the persuasion campaign shifted opinion on the issue in a negative direction. The majority of those who pulled the levers voted against the proposition. The shift in direction was accompanied by a change in distribution.

The change in the distribution of opinion was probably the most important factor in this situation because opinion in an election must be expressed through the vote in order to have a political impact. The vote registers the opinions only of people who have moved away from the center of the distribution. Those who remain neutral or undecided either do not vote at all or their votes tend to be distributed randomly to both sides. In either case, middle-of-the-road opinions do not affect the outcome of the election. That is why the opposing sides in elections work to define the issues or candidates in ways that push the center of the opinion distribution into their respective camps. In the case of the California antismoking proposition, the efforts of the tobacco interests paid off. The final expression of opinion was in a negative direction, with a *bimodal distribution* as shown in Figure 1-3.

FIGURE 1-3

Bimodal Distribution of the Vote on the Antismoking Proposition

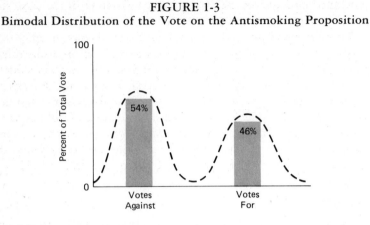

This example of the interplay of individual orientations, political communication processes, and institutional procedures shows why a flexible definition of public opinion is necessary. Public opinion research must focus on how opinion actually operates, and not on whether it conforms to narrow standards such as the doctrines of classical theories of democracy. Even if our interest is to explore democratic practices in a political system, such an investigation will be biased by a perspective that assumes that the responsibility for democracy lies with individual citizens who must approach all issues with a uniform level of consciousness. The state-of-consciousness perspective ignores variations in individual interests, the mind-altering effects of political communications, and the impact of institutions on individuals' thought and action. By focusing on the interplay of individual, communications, and institutional factors, a situational approach to public opinion casts a much wider net around the conditions that affect democratic practice and political outcomes in the American political system.

LOOKING AHEAD

The aim of this book is to develop a theory of politics and public opinion that both identifies the forces that shape opinion and explains the functions of public opinion in the political system. With this end in mind it should be clear why a state-of-consciousness conception of public opinion is overly limiting. It does not take into account the different foundations of public opinion, the different functions it serves, or the enormous variation in the ways that opinion is expressed.

An understanding of the situational determinants of opinion is really not a narrower conception of the subject, as the name might imply. To the contrary, recognizing the political forces at work in different situations makes it possible to expand the description of public opinion to encompass its multiple roles in the political system. The role of opinion in such diverse areas of politics as socialization, integration, agenda formation, policy making, legitimation, and change can be understood only by recognizing the changing faces of public opinion in different political contexts.

NOTES

1. Kevin P. Phillips, "The Energy Battle: Why the White House Misfired," *Public Opinion*, Vol. 1 (May–June, 1978), p. 11.
2. Ibid., p. 11.
3. Ibid., pp. 11–12.
4. Reported ibid., p. 11.
5. Reported in Elizabeth Drew, "Playing Presidential Politics with the National 'malaise,'" *Washington Post*, September 3, 1979, p. A11.
6. Ibid., p. A11.
7. Reported in *Time*, September 10, 1979, p. 10.
8. Ibid., p. 11.
9. Floyd H. Allport, "Toward a Science of Public Opinion," *Public Opinion Quarterly*, Vol. 1 (January 1937), pp. 7–23.
10. Ibid., p. 7.
11. Ibid., p. 22.
12. Ibid., p. 23.
13. See Philip Converse, "Attitudes and Non-Attitudes: Continuation of a Dialogue," in *The Quantitative Analysis of Social Problems*, ed. Edward R. Tufte (Reading, Mass: Addison-Wesley, 1970), pp. 168–89.
14. Quoted in Richard Sennett and Jonathan Cobb, *The Hidden Injuries of Class* (New York: Vintage Books, 1972), p. 49.
15. Ibid., p. 137.
16. The breakdown of votes on the antismoking proposition and the comparison ballot choices are as follows:

Governor:	6,835,951
Antismoking Proposition:	6,750,654
Surplus Coastal Property Proposition:	5,783,410
Public Utility Commission Proposition:	5,565,626

Source: Los Angeles Times, *November 9, 1978, p. 19.*

Competing Images
of the
American Public

A SITUATIONAL THEORY of public opinion rests on the assumption that the general factors that affect opinion can occur in different combinations in different political situations. Political situations may vary along such lines as the individuals in them; the values and beliefs shared by those individuals; the way the symbolic presentation of an issue, a candidate, or an event engages values and beliefs; and the ways opinion can be expressed. These and other factors can have a number of impacts on public opinion. All this is most obvious when opinion is considered as a practical political force operating within the context of political institutions, conflicts, and communication processes. In fact, when opinion is viewed in such contexts, it may be hard to imagine how the state-of-consciousness fallacy described in Chapter 1 could be a serious obstacle to the development of a general theory of opinion.

When the political context of opinion is defined in another way, however, sharp situational distinctions seem to melt away, and it becomes tempting to think of public opinion as the product of a general state of consciousness. The state-of-consciousness fallacy generally emerges when the public is described from the standpoint of classical theories of government—particularly theories about democratic government. Such theories (and the opinion research they have inspired) generally treat the public as an entity that must possess certain qualities of mind in order to be capable of self-government.

Most students of democracy agree that the success of a democratic political system depends on the quality of public opinion in it. Three general characteristics of opinion are normally cited as the minimum conditions for democracy. First, the opinion expressed about important matters of public policy must be well informed. Unless people are informed, so the argument goes, there is no basis for making sound choices, and leaders would be ill advised to listen to their (uninformed) constituents.

Second, the distribution of public opinion must remain fairly stable over time. If people are constantly changing their positions and thereby altering the distribution of public preferences, public policy cannot have a secure foundation. If people reject policies they formerly supported, leaders will have little way of knowing whether their constituents will continue to support their actions.

Third, it is often argued that strong and constant principles must underlie public thinking about different issues. Without such common principles to constrain the formation of opinion, leaders could never be sure whether opinion reflects the idiosyncratic thinking of thousands of individuals, or whether a thread of common meaning is underlying public opinion. Moreover, the classical view holds that unless the public understands the practical connections between clusters of issues, public opinion can provide little guidance for policy makers and leaders who must deal with issues.[1]

When public opinion is placed in the context of information, stability, and constraint, the state-of-consciousness perspective seems like a perfectly reasonable way of approaching public opinion. In fact, since it is part of every schoolchild's experience in learning about democracy, it may seem as legitimate as the situational perspective. Indeed, these different images of the public and public opinion slip in and out of our thinking much as the alternating images in an optical illusion slip in and out of our field of vision.

Even though the existence of the two views can be shown to complicate the explanation of opinion processes and the interpretation of opinion data, each perspective seems to occupy a natural place within a sensible domain of political inquiry. For example, it seems to make more sense to talk about the formation of opinion as a situational process when fluctuations in support for political leaders, public reactions to political events and crises, and political responses to persuasion and propaganda campaigns are being described. However, it appears to make sense to regard opinion as the product of a stable state of public consciousness when questions are being posed about whether the public is capable of self-government, whether it is capable of dealing with particular issues, and whether common political principles make the expression of opinion meaningful.

One solution to this state of affairs is merely to recognize that the two conceptions of public opinion exist and that they address different kinds of political questions. This might at least reduce the confusion produced when people engage in debates about "public opinion" but really mean quite different things by the concept.[2] However, as long as these competing perceptions persist, there will be serious disagreements about how to measure public opinion and how to interpret the results. For example, a situational perspective might try to explain differences in opinion on different issues (or on the same issue at different times) by looking at the way beliefs and values are affected by various political conditions or by changes in the way the issues are defined. A state-of-consciousness perspective, on the other hand, would not try to measure situational or definitional variations, for changes in the characteristics of opinion would be taken as some indication of an underlying structure of belief.

The two perspectives can produce quite different interpretations of important behavior. One group of researchers who studied the opinion characteristics of American voters found that the voting public displayed "widespread ignorance and indifference over matters of policy."[3] However, a situation-oriented investigation of the way candidates defined issues in an election led another team of researchers to hold out the possibility that factors external to the voter may "depress" the possibility of making a serious or informed choice about an issue:

> In this case, at least, the behavior of candidates seems to have inhibited the occurrence of policy voting. If similar candidates and ambiguous rhetoric are the rule in American elections, they may well have depressed voting on other issues, and in other elections as well. Our picture of the ignorant voter may be ... largely a reflection of the choices he is offered.[4]

The easy alternation of the two perspectives is likely to prolong confusion about public opinion. Unfortunately, we can hold both images of public opinion and slip back and forth from one to the other without thinking clearly about how our assumptions change each time we do so. Since the state-of-consciousness fallacy produces simplistic and unresearchable models of public opinion, it makes sense to translate general questions about opinion and democracy into a situational framework. If this is to be a convincing solution, however, we must show how the state-of-consciousness perspective introduces problems into general thinking about public opinion and democracy. Otherwise, the power that this familiar perspective holds on us will make abandoning it difficult.

THE STATE-OF-CONSCIOUSNESS FALLACY AND DEMOCRATIC THEORY

How can a perspective that most of us learn as fact contain a fallacy? A place to begin answering this question is to recognize something unique about the idea that the survival of democracy hinges on the state of public consciousness. This idea is both a theoretical formula and part of a broad set of beliefs that most Americans learn in school and reencounter throughout their lives as citizens. The state of the public mind is discussed by journalists, debated by editorialists, celebrated by politicians, and lamented by intellectuals. The idea that a minimum general level of public consciousness is necessary for democracy is as much a political myth as it is an academic theory. In fact, its status as a myth calls into question its adequacy as a theory.

The fact that ideas exist as powerful myths does not mean that they are false. The problem is almost just the opposite: Their formulation as myth makes them virtually impossible to disprove. Most people believe them, and this makes them a poor foundation for theory. Myths cast the real world in such general terms that they reduce complex relations to simple propositions anchored as much in faith as in serious reality testing. Moreover, myths so simplify the real world that it becomes easy to find confirming evidence for them and difficult to see the relevance of other information at all.

These properties of myth are important politically because they help legitimate political institutions and social values. The myth that the public must attain a particular state of consciousness in order to qualify for democracy serves a number of important political functions. It can be invoked to underscore the importance of "the people" in the American political system. Leaders, teachers, or fellow citizens can use it to inspire people to become better citizens through greater involvement or more education. In still other situations, the myth becomes a safety valve to take pressure off political institutions for their failings: The myth distributes the blame for poor policies or political negligence to all the members of the public who were uninformed or unconcerned about the issues in question. Generality, simplicity, and ambiguity enable myths to be used for many different and even contradictory purposes. The generality, simplicity, and ambiguity of myths explain their political effectiveness and, at the same time, account for their theoretical failings.

Two key problems illustrate the shortcomings of theories of opinion and democracy based on the state-of-consciousness perspective. First, the abstract idea that the public must display a certain level of consciousness in order to make democratic government possible forgets one important thing. The political consciousness of any "public" in the real world is shaped by real political conditions such as the form of government, the distribution of power, and the effects of laws and policies. These and other conditions can exert some systematic effects on the situations in which public opinion develops. If their impact is ignored, a systematic bias will emerge in thinking about opinion and democracy. Indications that the political system is not living up to its democratic ideals will almost always be attributed to failings of the public (rather than the other way around).[5] This manner of reasoning introduces a similar bias into thinking about political reform and institutional change. Even though the conditions that lead to reform and change almost always produce some disarray in public opinion, elites and intellectuals operating with the state-of-consciousness perspective usually interpret the disarray as a characteristic of public thinking rather than as a natural product of changing social and political conditions. This interpretation often supports the conclusion that radical reforms or open democratic institutions are unjustified because the public is incapable of operating sensibly within them.

That reasoning is, of course, circular. Since it is never clear how the public would have "behaved" under other conditions or under different institutional changes, whatever happens to public opinion after political reforms can be taken as a sign of the accurate analysis of the reformers. If opinion becomes more structured, the reforms can be called a success. If opinion remains unstructured and erratic, then the initial concerns about the public seem even more correct, and the reforms may be regarded as too radical. The state-of-consciousness bias in most theories of democracy thoroughly confuses such questions of cause and effect.

The second problem associated with the state-of-consciousness bias in democratic theory and myth stems from the failure to recognize that different situations are possible within the boundaries of a political system. This variety has several implications: The meaning and importance of issues may change as political situations develop. New ways of looking at issues may alter the values and beliefs that people use to form opinions. The movement of issues in and out of institutional settings (such as elections, the courts, and legislative bodies) can affect the focus of public attention and the acceptability of various ways of expressing opinion. These and other factors will affect the scope, direction, and distribution of opinion. However, if one accepts the state-of-consciousness perspective and searches for unchanging characteristics of opinion, the situational factors become impossible to contend with, and analysts are forced to define issues in rigid ways that are removed from specific contexts. The inevitable result is that opinion surveys produce different findings, depending on how the questions are asked, when the studies are done, and what real-world references the subjects use to think about the issues. This increases the chance that generalizations drawn from any set of data will be different from or in contradiction with conclusions drawn from other sets of data.

Since the demands for generalization imposed by the state-of-consciousness perspective lead observers to screen out the natural political contexts in which the public perceives issues, analysts who use that perspective must provide their own contexts for making sense of various expressions of public opinion. Once analysts fashion their own general interpretive contexts out of their suspicions about the nature of public consciousness, the resulting disagreements between analysts become virtually impossible to straighten out.[6] Different observers will see the same situations differently, and they will not be able to provide easily observable documentation to support their observations. The problems caused by the state-of-consciousness perspective suggest that this approach is, in Allport's terms, a "dead end." Its persistent appeal can be attributed to its roots in a powerful political myth. However, the properties of myth that favor the use of the state-of-consciousness perspective in the political world undermine its contributions to scientific explanations of public opinion.

This point can be illustratd powerfully by showing that the same problems of validation and disputed interpretations exist whether the perspective is employed in practical political situations or in scientific efforts to explain the objective characteristics of public opinion. There are certain advantages to the use of abstract and unprovable ideas in practical political situations, but such formulations only frustrate the goals of scientific inquiry. In the next section of this chapter, the debates among the framers of the U.S. Constitution show that the myth of public qualifications for democracy became a major issue in the analysis of public opinion and the justification for the limited representative government contained in the Constitution. In the section following that, the same notion is shown to be a source of confusion in contemporary scientific analysis of public opinion and American democracy.

IMAGES OF THE PUBLIC
AND
THE ORIGINS OF
AMERICAN GOVERNMENT

Seldom have there been such perceptive political analysts and such brilliant political theorists as Alexander Hamilton, James Madison, and Thomas Jefferson. These men played major roles in framing the Constitution and governing the new nation. All three agreed on the principle of popular government in America. They also agreed on a system of elected representatives, constitutional guarantees, and separate but equal branches of government to limit the influence of any single branch. However, when each of them looked at the public, he saw something different. As a result of their individual notions of the public resulting from their differing conceptions of public consciousness, each man advocated a different form of representative government.

Hamilton did not trust the general public. He saw them as being ignorant about the complex matters facing a government. More importantly, they were given to emotional and unstable responses on matters that affected their narrow interests. At the time of the debates about the Constitution, many farmers rose up in protest against the harsh treatment they were receiving from creditors and landlords. Hamilton saw these uprisings as a sign of the general state of public consciousness and pointed to them as proof that average folk are incapable of holding reasoned discussion based on stable political attitudes.

It is hard to separate the conception of public consciousness used to interpret these expressions of public opinion from Hamilton's own opinions about political interests and the future of America. Even though the American economy was based on agriculture, Hamilton did not favor the farming interests. He saw the future of America in an economy based on the expansion of trade, banking and credit, and manufacturing. Such interests required the assistance of the government. They also depended on protecting the interests of (and granting special rights to) a wealthy minority in the presence of a poor and propertyless majority. For all these reasons, the majority of citizens represented a threat to the stability of the state and the interests of the wealthy minority. According to Hamilton's image of the public, if the majority had a direct say in government, it would act on its whims and shift its opinions against whatever group had the greatest wealth at any time. Stable government under these circumstances would be impossible, not just because of divisive class conflict, but because of the constantly shifting nature of public opinion as the wealth of society passed from one group to another.

From Hamilton's standpoint a limited representative system would not only hold the majority in check, but it would ensure that representatives would not have to base policy on the narrow, unstable, and inconsistent opinions of the public. Moreover, since property requirements were widely imposed on voters, Hamilton felt safe in assuming that men of some wealth and wisdom would be elected to office and would best "represent" the general interests of the nation and its people. Not only would such people hold the most agreeable (from Hamilton's standpoint) opinions about the public interest, but their opinions were likely to be stable, informed, and consistent with some set of general principles. These men of secure means and greater education were surely the best judges of the common good.

Nowhere is Hamilton's analysis of the characteristics and sources of public opinion better revealed than in his remarks at the Constitutional Convention in 1787:

> All communities divide themselves into the few and the many. The first are the rich and the well born, the other the masses of people. The voice of the people has been said to be the voice of God; and however generally this maxim has been quoted and believed, it is not true in fact. The people are turbulent and changing; they seldom judge or determine right. Give therefore to the first class a distinct, permanent share in the government. They will check the unsteadiness of the second, and as they cannot receive any advantage by change, they therefore will ever maintain good government. Can a

democratic assembly who annually revolves in the mass of the people, be supposed steadily to pursue the public good? Nothing but a permanent body can check the imprudence of democracy.[7]

In short, Hamilton felt that the opinions of the general public on most issues were uninformed, inconsistent, and unstable. This belief supported his aristocratic notion that a few good men of wisdom and stable social position should judge the good of all. For Hamilton, a popular government (or government of the "many") was acceptable only as long as it was set up so that final judgments about the public interest could be made by the elite "few" who had the intelligence and common material interests necessary to make informed, stable, and internally consistent decisions.

As this example shows, the generality of the state-of-consciousness perspective invites people to use their own political interests and experiences as bases for thinking about the public. When such general ideas are put forward, they become very hard to prove or disprove. Moreover, the perspective permits the observer to screen out immediate contextual or situational factors when evaluating expressions of opinion as evidence for or against the general orientation. Thus, Hamilton was able to interpret the farmers' rebellions as characteristic products of public consciousness rather than as understandable responses to political instability, inadequate channels for the expression of opinion, or economic exploitation.

Madison essentially agreed with Hamilton about the wisdom of letting a political elite interpret the interests of the general public. He also applied a general context of property interest versus self-interest to support the notion that the consciousness of the general public lacked coherence and posed a threat to a political system responsive to the direct expression of public opinion. Madison painted a general picture of society divided into a few people who owned property and the many people who didn't. As a result of this division, "Those who hold and those who are without property have ever formed distinct interests in society."[8] Conflicts among classes would produce, between different groups, narrow and divided opinions based more on passion than on reason and reflecting self-interest rather than concern with the public good. In short, public opinion in Madison's view tended to be uninformed, and it lacked coherent unifying principles.

Madison, however, did not consider public opinion to be as unstable as Hamilton did. Madison perceived a recurring pattern to the opinions held by the public but believed the public was so divided on most important issues that to let the people make policy directly would be dangerous. Government, after all, was intended to provide smooth resolutions for conflicts, not to inflame them. Public opinion could be expressed directly in the election of representatives, but the representatives should then retire to conduct calm and reasoned discussions of volatile issues.

Thus, for Madison, public opinion existed in a natural state of conflict caused not just by property differences among people but also by human tendencies:

> A zeal for different opinions concerning religion, concerning government . . . ; an attachment to different leaders ambitiously contending for preeminence and power; or to persons of other descriptions whose fortunes have been interesting to the human passions, have, in turn, divided mankind into party, inflamed them with mutual animosity, and rendered them much more disposed to vex or oppress each other than to cooperate for their common good.[9]

A government that limited the power of factions was, Madison believed, a means of promoting cooperation among people who would not cooperate on their own. It was a way of appointing representatives to reach compromises when conflicts of opinion were too intense to be worked out directly among members of the public. The virtue of a representative democracy was that it would

> refine and enlarge the public views by passing them through the medium of a chosen body of citizens, whose wisdom may best discern the true interest of their country and whose patriotism and love of justice will be least likely to sacrifice it to temporary and partial considerations. Under such a regulation it may well happen that the public voice, pronounced by the representatives of the people, will be more consonant to the public good than if pronounced by the people themselves.[10]

The opinions of the public could not be used to settle each question of policy directly because the images of the common interest in society were too numerous and too opposed to one another. Madison (like Aristotle) believed that a true democracy, in which the people decide on each issue, would be a corruption of good government: "Democracies have ever been spectacles of turbulence and contention; have ever been found incompatible with personal security or the rights of property; and have in general been as short in their lives as they have been violent in their deaths."[11]

Largely as a result of these feelings, Madison also saw the farmers' rebellions against landlords and creditors as proof of his observations that the public was incapable of any reasonable resolution of its differences of opinion. However, unlike Hamilton, Madison felt that public opinion about issues like the rights of renters and debtors was stable enough to be interpreted by elected representatives. He felt that the representative system (called the "republican" form of government in those days) would make it possible to moderate the extremes of public opinion while taking some measure of popular feeling into account in making public policy. Madison's use of the state-of-consciousness perspective, like Hamilton's, allowed his political assumptions to be imposed on the public. In addition, the tendency to take specific expressions of opinion (like the farmers' rebellions) as evidence of general characteristics provided convincing support for his analysis and the political position that it implied.

Jefferson also agreed that a republican form of government was necessary. However, he favored a much more open, representative, system than the kind that Madison and Hamilton advocated. Feeling that the public had the capacity to make informed, stable, and consistent judgments about important issues, Jefferson did not consider the channeling of public opinion through elected representatives to be a cure for public ignorance or a check on destructive factions. He saw representative government simply as a practical solution for the technical problem of how to translate into policy the opinions of so many citizens. America was too large in territory and population to make direct democracy feasible.

Jefferson's departure from the viewpoints of Hamilton and Madison was the result of his imposing still another analytical context on the public. In place of Hamilton's vision of narrow self-interest, Jefferson saw Americans as a people uniquely blessed with equality of status and a common history that would give rise to shared beliefs and values. Where Hamilton feared the ignorance of the public, Jefferson saw in America the possibility for universal public education and the creation of an enlightened citizenry. Where Madison saw enduring social and economic conflicts forever dividing the opinions of different groups, Jefferson saw a nation of people who believed in the same god, who engaged overwhelmingly in the same economic activity (farming), and who placed the greatest value on the most abundant economic resource (land).

Jefferson felt that the agricultural economy and the abundance of land would lead to shared values and stable opinions. The farming life demanded that people be independent, honest, and unselfish. The political opinions of Americans would, therefore, be consistent with strong moral principles; these opinions would not be based on greed or shifting social position. In short, the public was capable of forming stable, informed, consistent positions on important issues. Public opinion would be constrained by the life experience itself in America. Not wealth or property, but the nature of work and the style of living would shape the values and beliefs on which public opinion rested. There was no conflict between the interests of the poor-but-proud agricultural majority and the wealthy minority in America. Public consciousness had a clear organizing force that would produce the most stable sort of opinion:

> We have now lands enough to employ an infinite number of people in their cultivation. Cultivators of the earth are the most valuable citizens. They are the most vigorous, the most independent, the most virtuous, and they are tied to their country, and wedded to its liberty and interests by the most lasting bonds.[12]

Jefferson's interpretation of the farmers' rebellions that followed the American Revolution was much different from Hamilton's and Madison's. He saw the uprisings as the natural response of a majority of citizens whose government did not represent their interests. If the government had paid attention to the clearly expressed opinions of the people, revolts like the one led by Daniel Shays in Massachusetts would never have happened. If direct institutional expression of popular opinion doesn't work, then the people have little alternative but to resort to direct noninstitutional ways of expressing their views.

Jefferson knew that Hamilton and Madison interpreted the rebellions differently. Since they were using the rebellions to support their arguments in favor of a government in which the representatives would not be bound by public opinion, Jefferson was moved to try to convince them of his interpretation. In a letter to Madison, Jefferson wrote:

> The late rebellion in Massachusetts has given more alarm than I think it should have done. Calculate that one rebellion in thirteen states in the course of eleven years, is but one for each state in a century and a half. No country should be so long without one. Nor will any degree of power in the hands of government, prevent insurrections. In England, where the hand of power is heavier than with us, there are seldom half a dozen years without an insurrection. In France, where it is still heavier . . . and where there are always two or three hundred thousand men ready to crush insurrections, there

have been three in the course of the three years I have been there.... [These and other cases raise the question of] whether peace is best preserved by giving energy to the government, or information to the people. This last is the most certain, and the most legitimate engine of government. Educate and inform the whole mass of the people.... They are the only sure reliance for the preservation of our liberty.[13]

Jefferson regarded the rebellions as deviant episodes. He interpreted them as the natural responses of people faced with an unresponsive government. Therefore, he concluded, limited political representation was the cause of, rather than the solution for, public unrest and conflict. This is why he believed an open representative government would be more consistent with the nature of public consciousness.

The use of generalized notions of public thinking leads to interpretations of opinion that cannot be proved or disproved easily. As the foregoing example shows, this proposition holds true even when observers with different interpretations of the public mind turn to the same real-world events and behaviors to support their interpretations.

In the real world, interpretations of public consciousness lead to specific political actions such as decisions to release public information, efforts to solicit or discourage public input, and various political reforms. The case of the debates about the U.S. Constitution shows that images of the public mind can even lead to the design of entire systems of government.

The institutional structure of American government was much more a response to Hamilton's and Madison's views of the public than it was an implementation of Jefferson's ideas. As suggested earlier, moreover, political institutions and patterns of political reaction to public input can affect the formation and expression of opinion itself. Thus images of the state of public consciousness, when introduced into practical political situations, may become self-fulfilling: The acceptance of particular ideas may set in motion the conditions that seem to confirm them. This self-fulfillment occurred when the untested (and untestable) assumptions about opinion shared by Hamilton and Madison became the basis of a government that molded opinion according to those assumptions. Some additional examples will clarify the concept.

If government officials believe that the opinions of the public are uninformed and unstable, they may be less concerned about determining the will of the people on matters of policy. They may not even bother to provide to the public the detailed information that is necessary for making rational choices about policy. If the government does not engage in two-way communication on important matters of policy, the public, in turn, will have a harder time gathering information, crystallizing clear positions on issues, and expressing opinions in meaningful ways. In short, the public may begin to act as if its opinions were not structured. On the other hand, if public officials believe that the public is capable of structured and coherent political thinking, the government might spend more time informing the public on questions of policy. It also might provide better ways for the public to focus and express its opinions. The result of this is likely to be a public that speaks with a more rational and coherent voice.

Throughout American history we have seen examples of how different images of public opinion have had self-fulfilling effects on the behavior of citizens and leaders alike. During the administrations of George Washington and John Adams, many of the Federalists (of whom Hamilton was the most influential) feared that a republican form of government would invite candidates and leaders to make political appeals to the irrational and emotional public and, thereby, win political power by manipulating the ignorant masses. In response to these fears, the Federalist-dominated Congress passed the Alien and Sedition Acts of 1798, which virtually prohibited opponents of the government (which was dominated by the Federalists) from speaking out in public and "inciting" the people against the government. Such laws, of course, are the best way to create the very conditions they are designed to prevent.

The Alien and Sedition Acts produced passionate public protest, and they broadened the base of the emerging "Republican" party, which soon would dominate the government. The Federalists saw these public reactions as justification for their laws. The Republicans, on the other hand, saw the laws as the cause (not the effect) of legitimate popular outrage. For them, the formation of a political party was not a way to use the voice of the people to win power for a few; it was a way to organize (structure) the opinions of the public to give the people a genuine share in political power. From the standpoint of Republican leaders, this is exactly what happened. In the next thirty years the system of competing parties was responsible for vast reforms in election laws and the incorporation of large numbers of people in national elections.

The pattern of self-fulfilling images thoroughly confuses any possibility of proving that characteristics of public opinion are the result of enduring states of consciousness. Such confusion of cause and effect is a defining characteristic of the state-of-consciousness fallacy. *It is meaningless to argue that a government can only be as democratic as the consciousness of the people allows, if the consciousness of the public depends in large part on how the structure of government affects opinion situations.* There is no way out of this blind alley. Sorting out the tangle of cause and effect would require an initial formulation that included some testable propositions about the impact of political situations on opinion and, ultimately, about the effects of general properties of the political system on opinion situations. Such a formulation, of course, would undermine the state-of-consciousness perspective.

Jefferson finally concluded that the institutionalization of particular images of the public could affect the very nature of public thinking and behavior. Toward the end of his life he lamented that the only way to unravel the twisted pattern of cause and effect in the relations between the government, the public, and the limits of democracy would be to conduct a controlled experiment, returning the nation once again to 1787 and introducing a new constitution. This would make it possible to compare public behavior under the chosen form of government and under alternative forms that were not chosen:

> Both of our political parties . . . agree conscientiously in the same object—the public good; but they differ essentially in what they deem the means of promoting that good. One side . . . fears most the ignorance of the people; the other, the selfishness of rulers independent of them. Which is right, time and experience will prove. We think that one side of this experiment has been long enough tried, and proved not to promote the good of the many; and that the other has not been fairly and sufficiently tried. Our opponents think the reverse.[14]

These remarks imply that Jefferson understood that if differences in opinion behavior can be attributed to the form of government or to the political system, then it makes no sense to treat public consciousness as a constant factor with enduring general characteristics.

In the absence of assumptions about general states of consciousness, the powerful myths we hold about public opinion and democracy fall apart under logical scrutiny. But, as suggested earlier, such myths may play an important (albeit disagreeable) role in the political world. Their circular logic and their abstract formulation of political relations may help to establish the legitimacy and inevitability of political arrangements that otherwise would be subject to constant challenge. When the same reasoning enters some branches of scientific research on politics and public opinion, however, the resulting confusion serves no function whatever. The state-of-consciousness fallacy causes serious problems for opinion theory and research.

THE STATE-OF-CONSCIOUSNESS FALLACY IN OPINION RESEARCH

It is tempting to think that the sophisticated methodologies used in modern opinion research would prevent the problems described in the preceding section. Of course, in many areas of opinion research the problems are under control. Generally, these are areas in which situational approaches have taken into account the interactions of individual political orientations and properties of political situations. However, when opinion research is aimed at general questions about public consciousness and American democracy, the confusions that characterized the practical political disagreements just outlined emerge once again. This suggests that the problem lies more in the way questions about opinion are framed than in the technical or methodological sophistication of opinion analysis.

In particular, the reappearance of the same confusions suggests that the state-of-consciousness fallacy tends to operate whenever the public is viewed as a general entity with an overall state of consciousness. Moreover, the fact that the fallacy emerges both in practical political situations and in the context of scientific research adds weight to the idea that the perspective's appeal stems from its origin in powerful myths about opinion and democracy. Only if the specific problems produced by the fallacy are pointed out will its appeal to common sense be shaken.

Before citing examples of the fallacy in contemporary opinion research, it is important to emphasize once again that the fallacy does not emerge in all, or even most, opinion research. However, there are a couple of reasons for beginning this book with the area of opinion and democratic government, in which the fallacy does appear frequently. First, this book advances a theoretical perspective on opinion and government that identifies public opinion as a major political force. In current views of opinion and democracy, the way in which the state-of-consciousness fallacy operates makes it seem that opinion plays a very modest role in American government. Moreover, current theories of opinion and government suggesting that opinion is not very coherent are hard to reconcile with situation-based opinion research, which has found sensible patterns in opinion when situational factors are considered. If a general theory of opinion and government is to be developed, and if this theory is to be reconciled with the large body of information generated by situation-oriented research on public opinion, it is necessary to move past the state-of-consciousness fallacy.

Second, even when we adopt a situational frame of reference to explain specific expressions of opinion, it is easy to shift back into a state-of-consciousness framework when thinking about general problems of opinion and government. The shifting back and forth makes it difficult to integrate general knowledge in the field. If the state-of-consciousness fallacy can be shown to operate in most research on general questions of opinion and government, avoiding it may be easier in the future. This would pave the way for general theories of opinion and politics that are more compatible with situational perspectives. Such a change in thinking would lead to much better integration of general knowledge about public opinion.

As explained earlier, the "classical" theory of opinion and democracy proposes that public opinion must be informed, stable, and constrained along some shared lines of reasoning or belief. In the absence of these characteristics, so the theory goes, an open, representative government would be given to wild swings in policies, irrational decisions, and poor communication between citizens and leaders. Opinion researchers who have adopted this perspective tend to regard opinion as the expression of more or less fixed states of consciousness.[15] Once these general indicators of public thinking have been measured on opinion surveys, judgments can be made about such things as whether the public is suited for more open governmental institutions and whether the government's failure to live up to some of our democratic ideals is justified.

The process of generalizing the indicators of public opinion beyond their specific contexts is precisely where the state-of-consciousness fallacy enters the picture. This is the means through which Hamilton, Madison, and Jefferson were able to impose their own interpretations of opinion on the public. A similar process operates in most opinion research on public consciousness and democracy.[16] Since the state-of-consciousness perspective views opinion as the product of factors more general than the conditions operating in any situation, it gives analysts great latitude in defining the contexts for thinking about the public mind. These contexts normally reflect the analysts' own ideal images of democracy and the public.

Just as the farmers' rebellions were lifted out of their immediate social, political, and economic contexts, so too are opinion data generalized beyond the specific questions, concepts, and response formats that generated them (not to mention the surrounding historical context at the time of the study). Although things like the wording of questions and the formats for responses on questionnaires have parallels to different factors that operate in real political contexts, they are treated as neutral, general representations of issues and responses. As long as this assumption is maintained, survey findings can be generalized beyond the limitations operating in any specific study.

Just as the state-of-consciousness perspective did not permit Hamilton, Madison, and Jefferson to explore the question of whether the farmers' rebellions were unique responses to isolated social, political, or economic circumstances, opinion analysts operating under this fallacy cannot adequately confront the issue of how general their findings really are. This makes their research a rather delicate business in which certain ways of wording questions and measuring concepts have become sacred. Even though it is impossible to show that any one way of defining an issue, eliciting a response, or wording a question reveals *the* way that all such stimuli appear in the real world, it is necessary for some opinion analysts to maintain such pretenses because the hope of uniformity in opinion data depends on them.

In the early days of opinion research it was possible for the rather small number of researchers using similar measures to generate fairly consistent findings about public consciousness. However, as the number of researchers increased, the historical contexts of surveys changed, and the measures of opinion became more diverse, conflicting findings about public consciousness became more numerous and more difficult to resolve.[17] A number of studies now show clearly that characteristics of opinion like information, stability, and constraint vary a great deal according to how concepts are defined, how questions are worded, and how responses are recorded.

As long as the analysts operate within the state-of-consciousness perspective, these differences cannot be acknowledged for what they are: evidence that different situational factors (as reflected in the wording of questions and in response-recording formats on questionnaires) affect the characteristics of opinion. Such a conclusion would shatter the state-of-consciousness perspective. But the power of the perspective is so strong that most analysts who have generated data that seem to contradict earlier findings argue either that the state of public consciousness has somehow changed or that more work needs to be done to figure out how general characteristics of public thinking can be measured most accurately. As a result, the tendency is to conclude that our picture of public consciousness is muddled, rather than conclude that there is no single picture of public consciousness to be had. The latter conclusion would make consistent sense out of all the data from the seemingly contradictory studies, and it would make possible more productive research on the conditions that affect information, stability, constraint, and other characteristics of opinion.

To return to an earlier metaphor, the resistance to the most obvious way out of the muddle created by the state-of-consciousness fallacy is similar to the way in which the mind works in the presence of some optical illusions.[18] If someone suggests a way of looking at an ambiguous visual stimulus, the suggestion may govern the perception of the stimulus even though other ways of seeing the image may provide more information about it. Often it is necessary to have the outlines of another image pointed out in order for a shift of attention out of the first perspective to be possible. In the case of opinion research, once a particular way of looking at the data has been adopted, the sheer force of intellectual determination may keep the perspective in play even when it becomes an inadequate and confusing means of organizing the data. It may be necessary to point out the outlines of another configuration before an initial framework can be abandoned. If it can be shown that certain contradictions and confusions dissolve when opinion data are viewed from a situational perspective, then perhaps the intellectual resistance to a shift in perspectives can be overcome.

It can be shown that research on information, stability, and constraint, as they relate to general questions about democratic government and opinion, has been riddled with the state-of-consciousness fallacy. The effects of the fallacy are easiest to grasp in generalizations about levels of information and constraint underlying public opinion. To understand the question of the stability of opinion requires somewhat more sophisticated methodological skills. Therefore, the discussion of stability will be reserved until Chapter 3, and the remainder of Chapter 2 will focus on the more straightforward research done on public information and the degree of consistency or constraint in public thinking.

Information and Public Consciousness

The problems that the state-of-consciousness perspective can cause are illustrated nicely by research on the concept of political information. When information is lifted out of specific political contexts and imagined as a general attribute of public consciousness, it is easy to adopt an idealized definition like the following: "The democratic citizen is expected to be well informed about political affairs. He is supposed to know what the issues are, what their history is, what the relevant facts are, what alternatives are proposed, what the party stands for, and what the likely consequences are."[19] This general notion is reminiscent of the lofty ideals that civics books prescribe for citizens in a democracy. These sentiments may bring to mind news stories that highlight the deficiencies of citizens' knowledge. According to one news report, for example, members of a high school civics class interviewed residents of their town and discovered that people thought the Declaration of Independence was a communist document. According to another news story, a college professor tested his government class and discovered that the majority didn't know how many justices sit on the Supreme Court.

From time to time pollsters bemoan the woeful ignorance of the public on a major national issue. The above-mentioned definition and incidents all reinforce the general myths that make up our common-sense understandings of political information. When we generalize about information and opinion within the framework of democratic myth, it seems obvious that "informed" people ought to know about the structure of government, the nature of public issues, the identities of major political figures, and other straightforward "facts of political life." When such generalized measures of political information are applied to the public, however, the public comes up far short of reasonable expectations.

The conclusion of study after study seems to be that one indelible characteristic of public consciousness is lack of information.[20] The most comon way to illustrate this conclusion is simply to let the polls speak for themselves. Even a casual overview of opinion poll data on public information reveals a shocking picture. The following examples of results from national surveys are typical of the overall trend:

- In 1944, only 38 percent of the public knew the length of the term served by a member of the U.S. House of Representatives.[21]
- In 1947, a poll showed that only 31 percent of the public knew the correct name of the national anthem.[22]
- In 1952, only 19 perent of the public could name the three branches of government. Another 27 perent could identify one or two of the branches correctly.[23]
- A 1954 poll showed that only 49 percent of the public knew how many U.S. Senators there were from each state.[24]
- In 1963, 70 percent of the public did not know what presidential hopefuls Barry Goldwater and Nelson Rockefeller stood for.[25]
- In 1964, only 58 percent of the public knew that the United States belonged to NATO, and 38 percent thought that the Soviet Union was a NATO member.[26]
- In 1970 only 49 percent of the public knew which political party held a majority of seats in Congress.[27]
- In 1977, less than a year after the presidential election, only 56 percent of the public could recall ever hearing anything about Robert Dole, the man who was the vice-presidential candidate of the Republican party.[28]

These and numerous other findings from polls and major opinion studies seem shocking. In fact, they provide a source of almost bitter humor in light of what the polls tell us about public information on other subjects. More people know their astrological sign (76 percent) than know the name of their congressperson.[29] In another poll it was discovered that 82 percent of the public could identify the advertising slogan of a leading toilet tissue ("Please don't squeeze the _____."); 79 percent could correctly identify the jingle for a major upset-stomach remedy ("Plop, plop, fizz, fizz. Oh, what a relief . . ."); 59 percent knew the slogan for a popular soft drink ("It's the real thing."); and 58 percent could identify the margarine that appeared in commercials with the punch line "It's not nice to fool Mother Nature."[30]
These comparisons make it tempting to agree with the early re-

searchers who concluded that the quality of public opinion is damaged by the "hard core of chronic know nothings" in the population.[31] Indeed, this conclusion gained even wider acceptance when it was confirmed by a pioneering voting study in which the public was accused of "widespread ignorance and indifference over matters of policy."[32]

However, the certainty and the meaning of these conclusions begin to melt away when we recognize that they are built on the classic flaws of the state-of-consciousness fallacy: the confusion of cause and effect, generalization beyond the context of the data, and the imposition of arbitrary definitions and analytical contexts.

The conclusion that a large portion of the public consists of a "hard core of chronic know nothings" assumes that relevant political information is equally available to citizens in any situation and that the supply of information does not vary significantly from one political situation to another. If these assumptions are not true, then we would have to acknowledge that there may be enduring political causes for low levels of information. If there are such causes, the attribution of ignorance to the failings of individual citizens is much too simplistic.

It has long been argued that there is a systematic bias in the political system against the free transmission of information to the public. Information is an important political resource, and candidates, government agencies, and leaders are not likely to distribute it unless doing so is to their political advantage. V. O. Key, Jr., was probably the first critic to argue that, when it comes to explaining low levels of public information, the arrow of causality probably points more in the direction of the political system than toward the citizen.[33] Key's position has been echoed by others, who have taken it close to a general hypothesis about the political sources of public ignorance. Stanley Kelley, a contemporary of Key's, observed:

> Anyone who examines the course of discussion in campaigns can hardly fail to conclude that it is as often designed to subvert as to facilitate rational voting behavior. What candidates say frequently lacks relevance to any decision voters face, exposes differences in the views of candidates imperfectly, and is filled with evasions, ambiguities and distortions.[34]

This general observation has been formalized into a "law" of candidate behavior by Page. He demonstrated that in the context of a normal election it is irrational for candidates to distribute clear information to voters about their positions.[35] The implication of this law is that we can expect voters to be informed only if candidates (and, by extension, other political actors) behave irrationally. This is fairly strong evidence for the proposition that there may be a systematic bias in the political system against the transmission of clear political information. The state-of-consciousness perspective is not equipped to consider this possibility, however. In fact, its standard formulation has no room for causal variables not related to the dispositions of individuals. As a result, the perspective forces a dangerous bias in thinking about questions like the nature of public information.

Related to this broad bias is a more specific problem generated by the state-of-consciousness perspective. It is clear that the level of public information about candidates, issues, or other political matters must vary from one situation to another. Some elections may be more issue oriented than others; some issues may be more salient than others; and some campaigns to inform the public may be more serious and effective than others. These common-sense assumptions need to be tested. But the state-of-consciousness perspective is not equipped to do so. Because the perspective is oriented toward generalizations about the public mind, it tends to reduce matters of situational variation to summary statements about general tendencies. In fact, the whole idea of searching for a general tendency may simply be meaningless and misleading. If acquisition of the information is as dependent on the situation as it is on the individual, it doesn't make sense to go beyond a simple description of the types and frequencies of situations in which the public expresses informed opinions. This more sensitive focus would increase the chances of discovering the areas of politics in which information is more available and more useful, and it would make it easier to discover what factors seem to account for these patterns.

The state-of-consciousness perspective strains against this solution because it undermines the simplicity of the idea that the public must display certain qualifications for democracy regardless of surrounding factors. However, the maintenance of the state-of-consciousness position increases friction in the theoretical approaches and empirical findings that point to the strong situational determinants of information. For example, in response to Hyman and Sheatsley's lament about the chronic know nothings in the public, Mendelsohn pointed out that the problem may have more to do with the way information is presented.[36]

Mendelsohn argued that most of the "know-a-lots" on any issue bring some prior interest or knowledge to bear on the information available to the public. Evidence shows that when an effort is made to present information in ways that alert people to the personal or group importance of an issue, the information tends to be incorporated in dramatic ways. Unless we wish to take the absurd position that every citizen must be equally interested in every issue (a position that adherents of the state-of-consciousness perspective must adopt), it makes little sense to blame individuals for not being informed about everything. As Mendelsohn argues, there is little to be gained from a stance that assumes "when the communications 'hypodermic needle' fails, the patient is to blame."[37]

An increasing body of evidence suggests that when useful information is not available, the public does not develop informed positions; but when information is present, people tend to incorporate it into their thinking. For example, Brody and Page concluded from their study of voting that in the 1968 election there was little difference between the major candidates' positions on the key issues. Not surprisingly, the voters seemed to have little relevant information about the issues underlying their voting choices.[38] In other elections, however, differences between the candidates have been sharper, and, as a consequence, there has been greater possession and use of information by the voters.[39]

In the face of such growing evidence it seems only reasonable to recast the implicit model of information and opinion so that assumptions about general states of consciousness are replaced by more precise statements about interactions between consciousness and situational factors in specific political contexts. Indeed, such a gradual shift from a state-of-consciousness perspective to a situational approach is under way. For example, Schulman and Pomper concluded from their study of elections that "voters are capable of a wide range of behaviors and are not 'inherently limited.' In the appropriate circumstances, such as the intense contests of 1964 and 1972, the electorate will respond to issue differences between the candidates."[40] Perhaps the most concise formulation is Niemi and Weisberg's conclusion: "Voters *can* take stands, perceive party differences, and vote on the basis of them. But whether they do or not depends heavily on the candidate and the parties."[41]

A few direct examples of the state-of-consciousness perspective continue to appear.[42] And some qualified versions continue to complicate analyses.[43] Nevertheless, the overwhelming trend in the specialized area of voting research is toward a reformulation of questions of information and public consciousness in situational terms. However, there is a painful time lag between the emergence of change in such frontier areas of research and change in the broad field of public opinion as a whole. Two of the more sophisticated contemporary texts on opinion contain these statements: "Though the 'informed citizen' is often claimed to be a necessary ingredient of democratic government, most citizens in our society are not very well informed."[44] And: "Opinion polls have long demonstrated that many citizens do not possess even the most elementary political knowledge."[45] The impact of the emerging situational perspective on the general field of public opinion will probably not be felt until a general reformulation of theories about opinion and government takes place. The theory to be presented in Chapter 4 is a small step in this direction.

The preliminary signs of a change in thinking about information and public consciousness are encouraging. They are consistent with a situational theory of opinion, and they offer hope that the confusion produced by the state-of-consciousness fallacy can be sorted out. However, a good deal of work still needs to be done before a comprehensive situational theory can be developed.

The Constraint Controversy

In many respects the progression of work on opinion constraint has been similar to developments in research on information. Early studies agreed that public opinion demonstrates little underlying structure that might reflect broad areas of meaning behind expressions of opinion. The absence of constraint seemed to imply that issues that might be part of the same general policy area were often unrelated as far as the public was concerned. Recent studies have found higher levels of constraint operating in public opinion; however, the state-of-consciousness fallacy has made it difficult to determine what these new findings mean. As long as the fallacy continues to affect thinking about the problem, the confusion will continue to grow. When the sources of confusion are examined within a situational perspective, however, it becomes much easier to see what the problem is and how to resolve it.

Constraint refers to the underlying structure of a belief system. If beliefs about specific political matters rest on some fundamental beliefs and values, then opinions about specific objects in the political world will take on a pattern. The result for the individual is that the world will seem more coherent and connected. The result for an observer or analyst of the individual's opinions is that opinions will be more predictable and underlying political reasoning will be easier to interpret.

For example, a person who believes that equal opportunity programs, government aid to education, and subsidized public housing all contribute to the value of social equality may be likely to express opinions of similar direction and intensity when these general areas of government policy are raised as political issues. By contrast, a person who does not connect these three beliefs to the same value might express opinions of different direction and intensity on the issues of equal opportunity programs, federal aid to education, and increased funding of public housing. In other words, constraint refers to the degree to which basic elements of belief go together in a system of belief. As Converse put it, this determines, in turn, "what goes with what" in the political world.[46]

Although the concept of constraint is used in psychology to refer to the structure of individual beliefs, it has been adapted by political scientists to fit into the general theory of opinion and democracy. The argument is that some shared dimensions of belief constraint must be operating in the public in order for expressions of opinion to be coherent and in order for the relevance of issues to be clear. Constraint in this sense is a property of individual consciousness, and, because it is shared, it forms the basis for mass consciousness.

As pointed out earlier, the level of generalization invites the analyst to impose his or her idealized image of opinion concepts on the public. The idealized notions of constraint contained in myths about opinion and democracy tend to be of two sorts. In one view, responsible citizens should interpret political issues according to the way they relate to the general principles of democracy on which the country was founded. In another view, issues should be organized according to some general ideological perspective (such as economic liberalism or conservatism) that brings the political world in focus, permits careful reasoning about issues, and stimulates the acquisition of information. These bases of constraint are not at all exclusive. In an idealized conception of a democratic public, it is easy to imagine that issues first would be judged against the common democratic principles that everyone shares and then would be evaluated in terms of the ideological dimensions that reflect legitimate differences in public values.

Both images of constraint have been tested, and it appeared for a while that the public did not share either frame of reference for thinking about political issues. In the case of public adherence to general democratic principles, several studies compared levels of support for general democratic principles against levels of support for specific policy questions that seemed to refer to those principles. Time and again it was found that even though the public tended to express strong support for general principles such as equal rights and free speech, specific political proposals such as allowing communists to run for office or speak in public tended to gather only moderate support.[47] The conclusion from these studies seemed to be that most people did not satisfy the ideal of a shared commitment to democratic principles when it came to thinking about specific policy problems. This conclusion was summarized bluntly in Converse's claim that these studies showed that "the individual lacks the contextual grasp to understand that the specific case and the general principle belong in the same belief system."[48]

So much for the ideal of shared beliefs about democracy. What about the ideal of some broad ideological dimension underlying public thinking and reflecting a consensus of opinion about different issues? Converse undertook this investigation. He used a straightforward measure of the degree to which opinions expressed by individuals on one issue tended to be associated with the direction and intensity of opinions expressed on other issues. Although there seemed to be some underlying connection between opinions on issues like aid to education and federal programs to increase employment, only weak connections were drawn across a whole range of other issues.[49] This finding seemed to suggest that the public had struck out as dramatically on the second idealized dimension of belief organization as it had on the first.

However, the state-of-consciousness fallacy has begun to take its toll on these interpretations. The findings of low consensus on democratic principles have drawn criticism to the effect that the analysts simply imposed their own logic on the connections between specific policy issues and the general principles.[50] It has been suggested that there are other ways in which people could have made these connections in a consistent fashion. For example, consider the interpretation that low support for the idea of communists speaking in public indicates a confusion about how to apply the general democratic principle of free speech. Suppose that most people believe both in the general principle of free speech and in the principle that treason against our form of government should be prevented. Who is to say that the issue of communists speaking in public should be more relevant to the free speech principle than to the treason principle? The connection might go either way, thereby making the total level of support for the specific political issue lower than the level of support for either of the general principles. The possibility that people connected the specific issues to different principles is all the more likely when we consider that the studies were done in the 1950s, during the height of the cold war against foreign communist governments and the "witch hunts" conducted against alleged communists inside the United States. That was a period in which people were accused of treason for holding radical political beliefs and tried for treason for speaking about those beliefs in public.

The point here is not to establish the real logical connection between specific issues and general principles. The point is that we will never know what that connection was because the analysts did not bother to find out. They simply imposed their own interpretations on the data. The result is a situation analogous to the one that confronted Hamilton, Madison, and Jefferson in the political context described earlier. In both cases the opinion data used to test hypotheses about public consciousness were recorded with so little reference to situational factors that the observer had to supply the interpretive context. The result is that different analysts can look at the same data and draw different conclusions.

The only way out of such dilemmas is to assess the impact of situational factors on the expression of opinion. Studying the operation of democratic principles as bases of opinion involves the careful investigation of how specific issues are connected to underlying beliefs. It also involves the determination of the factors that affect these connections. For example, subtle changes in the wording of issues may change the way in which people "reference" an issue to different beliefs. Such changes in wording or definition may correspond, in turn, to real variations in practical political situations that affect judgments.

A good example of the clarification of patterns of constraint by taking situational factors into account comes from a study of racial prejudice by Williams. He concluded that prejudice is based on connections between specific issues or incidents and general beliefs, but that the patterns of connection depend on situational factors.[51] In fact, he called this the "situational variability" of prejudice.

Williams asked his subjects to respond to a number of hypothetical situations. In one example the subjects were told to imagine themselves as a customer in a restaurant in which a black person enters and is refused service. When this was the only reference to the situation, about 90 percent of the sample disapproved of such racial discrimination. However, in the next item on the questionnaire the story continued, and the restaurant manager explained to the rejected customer that he had no prejudice against blacks, but if he served him, the majority of his customers would object strongly. When the issue was put this way, more than half of those who opposed the discriminatory action in the first instance shifted their opinions to support the manager's action.

One interpretation of this shift would be that the people in the study were simply inconsistent in their thinking and showed no constraint in applying to the two cases the general principle of equal rights. However, in rejecting this interpretation, both Williams and another analyst, Schuman, point out that the two situations are different, and people cannot help but think about them in different ways. In the second situation people may think about general values of majority rule, social harmony, and economic success. In doing so, they must sort out the conflicts among these values. For some people (about half in this case) the value of equal rights still came out on top, and their opinions stayed the same. However, for the other half of the people, another value took precedence over the one they used to judge the initial situation, and their opinions changed.

In his discussion of these findings Schuman presented other data showing that changes in the description of a situation or the wording of an issue produced apparent changes in the principles that people incorporated in their opinions.[52] It is easy for the analysts to regard the general issues as unchanged from one version to another. But, Schuman argued, the subtle changes in wording on the questionnaire corresponded to the subtle pressures, conflicts, and compromises that people experience in different concrete situations. Thus the way a situation is defined can produce different "clashes of abstract values in concrete form." From this Schuman concluded: "Depending upon the exact phrasing of the question—the values involved and how they are operationalized—a respondent chooses one side or the other, though he can very likely appreciate both to some extent."[53]

This adds a whole new dimension to the idea of constraint. It suggests that constraint may operate in opinions on different issues; but the way the issue is defined may trigger different underlying principles, and the complexity or ambiguity of the issue may place some principles in conflict with others. Therefore, generalizations about which general principles ought to operate in judgments about particular issues are little more than the wishful thinking of analysts. These questions can be resolved only by understanding how situational factors do, in fact, trigger various belief principles and by determining how different ways of asking questions on opinion polls reflect those situational differences. The wording of questions plays a large part in the confusion that has developed over ideological constraint.

The study by Converse that found only the lowest level of ideological constraint operating in the public was accepted as fact for some period of time. This study was based on the responses of voters in 1956, 1958, and 1960. Some years later, a pair of researchers decided to bring the findings up-to-date by looking at patterns of voters' responses on issues in 1964, 1968, and 1972. What they found was startling. Beginning in 1964 there was a marked jump in the degree of association between the opinions that individuals expressed over a range of issues. Nie and Andersen concluded from their findings that the level of ideological thinking in the public had increased sharply.[54] They guessed that the increase was due to the politically turbulent years of the 1960s, in which dramatic political events such as the civil rights protests, the volatile election of 1964, the antiwar movement, and the presence of key domestic and foreign policy issues combined to "raise" the consciousness of the public.

Although Nie and Andersen allude to situational factors underlying this change in opinion constraint, the fact that they regard the change as a general alteration in the overall state of public consciousness indicates that they continued to operate within a state-of-consciousness perspective. This is where the trouble began. A number of critics pointed out that in 1964 there was a change more immediate than the increased level of national political activity. The way in which questions were worded in the national election surveys of 1964, 1968, and 1972 differed markedly from the way in which they had been worded in Converse's original studies. The pre-1964 questions were stated as one-sided policy proposals. They were followed with five-point scales on which the individual recorded his or her opinion, ranging from "strongly agree" to "strongly disagree." An example of these questions is the following item designed to tap opinions about employment policy:

> The government in Washington ought to see to it that everyone who wants to work can find a job.

In 1964, however, the wording and response format were changed. The questions all stated a pro and con position on the issues. The five-point response scale was replaced by a simple two-option response format in which people merely indicated their agreement with either the pro or the con position. The 1964 version of the employment issue looked like this:

> In general, some people feel that the government in Washington should see to it that every person has a job and a good standard of living. Others think the government should just let each person get ahead on his own.

Several interesting studies have been conducted to assess the possible effects of the changes in wording and response format on the structure of opinion found in these studies. One investigation was based on a national survey conducted in 1973. It exposed different groups of subjects to the three dominant question and response formats used in national surveys during the period in which the alleged change in public consciousness had been observed. Since this study was done at a much later date, if the same kinds of differences were observed between question formats, it would be hard to attribute them to genuine changes in public consciousness due to historical events. The problem with the data used by Bishop and his colleagues was that it was hard to sort out the effects of question wording from the effects of changing the response format. However, significant differences were found in the constraint levels of the different groups. A careful comparison of the questions indicated that some of the difference was clearly due to the change in response formats, though some was probably the result of changing the wording of the question. The conclusion reached by Bishop was that the observed change in public consciousness had little if anything to do with historical changes or raised public consciousness; the main factor was the change in question wording and response format.[55]

The fascinating thing about the Bishop study is that the authors chose to adopt the pre-1964 studies as the "real" indicators of opinion constraint. As a result, they concluded that the thinking of the public in 1973 continued to be as unsophisticated as it was when the early studies were done. There is, of course, no more basis for drawing this inference than for reaching the opposite conclusion—that the level of constraint really was as high as the post-1964 studies show and that the earlier studies had defined the issues improperly or measured responses inaccurately.

The most elegant study in the constraint controversy was conducted by Sullivan and his colleagues. They, like the Bishop group, reasoned that if pre- and post-1964 versions of the issues were presented to people at a later date (using the same response formats) a clear picture of the effects of question wording would emerge. If levels of constraint were about the same in response to the different questions, then it would be possible to conclude that question wording was not a factor and the change in constraint was genuine. But, if differences appeared at the later point in time, then question wording (not changes in the political system) would be responsible for the differences in constraint. The latter pattern emerged from this study.[56] The findings led to a conclusion similar to the one reached by Bishop and his colleagues: The general level of opinion constraint has not changed significantly in the past thirty years. However, Sullivan and company were less willing to say which set of findings reflected the real level of constraint. They wisely refrained from making a bold statement on this question beause, of course, it can't be resolved. At least it can't be resolved as long as the state-of-consciousness perspective leads researchers to look for one general measure of opinion constraint.

Each change in question wording and response format will produce a different level of constraint in opinion. More studies aimed at finding the "true" level of constraint will produce only more confusion. Consider the situation as it now stands:

- Converse claimed that the public has never displayed a high level of constraint.
- Nie and Andersen concluded that opinion constraint used to be low but has increased dramatically in the past decade.
- Bishop and his colleagues argued that the level of constraint has never changed and the public is as unsophisticated in its thinking today as it was in the 1950s.
- The Sullivan group agreed that the level of constraint had never changed but refrained from addressing the question of which level of constraint was the correct one.

To this already confusing list we can add the work of Achen, who showed that corrections for ambiguous questions and response formats dramatically increased the level of stability in opinion survey data.[57] (Recall that stability is the degree to which opinions tend to stay the same over time.) Achen's conclusions could be applied to the constraint controversy to suggest that the level of opinion constraint was probably always higher than the findings from Converse's study indicated. With the addition of this conclusion, all possible interpretations have been pretty well covered. Depending on whom one chooses to believe,[58] it is possible to conclude that the public

- never was constrained in its political judgments;
- always displayed constrained political judgments;
- changed its level of constraint in the 1960s;
- never changed in the 1960s and always displayed low constraint;
- never changed and may or may not have displayed low levels of constraint.

If all this is beginning to seem confusing, that is because it is confusing. This is precisely the kind of confusion that results when the state-of-consciousness perspective leads people to try to generalize about the overall nature of public opinion. As long as analysts try to find the *one* general state of consciousness operating in the public, they cannot acknowledge the validity of each others' findings. Moreover, future studies can only add to the confusion. However, if a situational perspective could be brought into play, it would be possible to consider that different question and response formats correspond to differences in real-world situations that affect judgments about issues. The different findings would not have to be seen as mutually exclusive. They could be thought of as the range of constraint levels that the public is capable of displaying under different political conditions.

CONCLUSION

The constraint controversy is a particularly nice example of how the state-of-consciousness fallacy has inhibited the development of a general theory of opinion and politics. It shows how different analysts can draw different conclusions about the same thing and not be able to explore the reasons for their differences. It also demonstrates that as long as only one image of the public mind is imaginable, an increase in the number of studies trying to clarify the disagreements will only increase the confusion. Perhaps most importantly, the constraint controversy illustrates the powerful hold that a theoretical perspective can have on observers even when an alternative perspective would make much more sense out of the data.

It is interesting that research on opinion constraint seems to be moving in the direction in which the earlier research on opinion and information was headed when a shift toward a situational perspective finally began to occur. However, the concept of constraint is somewhat more complicated than the concept of information. In addition, it is necessary to show some external political variables that might affect the consistency of opinions, just as it has been demonstrated that external variables can affect the level of information underlying opinions.

A number of such factors come to mind. For example, it is clear that in some political situations opinion must be expressed within very structured response options, while other political situations provide more fluid opportunities for registering opinion. In an election, political preferences are usually limited to one of two responses. Voters generally have the option of voting either "yes" or "no" on ballot propositions, and they generally have to channel their candidate preferences into support for the candidate of one party or the other. Under these circumstances the level of constraint operating on opinions should be fairly high. In other political situations, by contrast, the range of options for registering political sentiments is much broader. In a protest movement, for example, a number of mechanisms may exist for expressing the direction and intensity of political feeling. People may write letters, demonstrate, participate in boycotts, join riots or other illegal actions, or suspend their activities altogether when the situation changes. In this kind of situation it is likely that opinions on different issues may be less constrained simply because the means of expression are so numerous and changing.

The matter of question wording also corresponds to a number of real-world political conditions. In some cases, political issues are presented to people in simple and direct form; in other cases, the mode of presentation is more complicated. In addition, some issues are defined in emotionally arousing or "loaded" language, while other issues tend to be defined in dry and unemotional terms. These and other factors probably affect the way in which people link issues together and the degree to which people form consistent opinions about groups of issues. For example, it is common for the wording of propositions on ballots to be complex and somewhat confusing. This complexity affects the way people see the issues in comparison to simpler versions of the same issues.[59] In other political contexts, issues may be presented in volatile language or in the emotional atmosphere of political crisis. These factors also may affect the public's perception of the connections between issues.

Current research has explored only a few of the issue formats that the public may encounter in real political situations. Thus current discrepancies in the findings on levels of opinion constraint may really be only a subset of the range of findings that should emerge when other ways of wording questions are tried out in opinion surveys.

The discrepancies cease to become confusing and turn into rich grounds for theory when a situational framework is substituted for the state-of-consciousness perspective. When the impact of various political conditions on political thinking is acknowledged, it becomes possible to talk about the range of opinion characteristics that the public *can* exhibit in any given political situation. Studies of information and opinion have already headed in this direction. The shift in perspective not only helps to resolve confusion about the general nature of public opinion, but it opens up questions about what political factors produce what effects on the characteristics of public opinion.

In no way does the shift in perspective prevent us from generalizing about public opinion. However, the generalizations drawn from the situational approach will no longer require thinking about members of the public as simple-minded beings with only one state of consciousness to bring to bear on political problems. More importantly, generalizations based on a situational perspective will not be forced to explain expressions of opinion exclusively as indicators of individual consciousness. *From a situational perspective, opinion is seen as having a range of possible characteristics, and this range depends in part on the psychological orientations of members of the public and in part on the political circumstances that affect their thinking.*

There are two important aspects to the shift in perspective. First, the idea of a range of opinion characteristics makes it possible to sort out the confusion in past research and begin to identify specific variables that explain the differences. Second, the inclusion of situational factors in the conception of public opinion makes it possible to break out of the pessimistic outlook created by the state-of-consciousness perspective. This perspective is based on myths about opinion and democracy that suggest that a political system can be no more democratic than the political consciousness of the public will allow. Serious moral dilemmas are associated with this position.

As the case of the constitutional debates showed, this approach does not take into account the effects of the political system on political thinking. No consideration is given to how sophisticated the thinking of the public *could* become. The state-of-consciousness perspective legitimizes the political status quo no matter how far short it falls from democratic ideals. Since this perspective attributes the characteristics of opinion to enduring psychological dispositions, very little can be done to change the nature of public opinion. The corporation of situational factors in a theory of opinion reopens the subject of political change.

Even the most extensive changes in the presentation of issues and the structuring of political responses would not make the political thinking of all citizens equally sophisticated. Such a result is not possible. Nor is it clear why we should expect uniform patterns of political thinking over a population as diverse as the American public. We must acknowledge inevitable differences among people in political interest, ease of political access, and political communication skills. Morever, political conflict and policy formation dictate that each political issue will be presented differently to different groups according to the way in which the groups may figure into the resolution of the issue.

Despite these necessary limitations of the uniformity of political consciousness, it is clear that the use of situational variables in descriptions of opinion opens up a much more hopeful avenue for political reform. It also provides the more acceptable moral position of not blaming individuals for the shortcomings of political arrangements they did not create. This, along with the empirical considerations already described, makes a situational perspective a solid foundation for a general theory of public opinion and American politics.

NOTES

1. Various summaries of these conceptions of public opinion abound in the literature. For illustrations, see Bernard C. Hennessey, *Public Opinion*, 3rd ed. (Belmont, Calif.: Wadsworth, 1975), ch. 2; and Robert Weissberg, *Public Opinion and Popular Government* (Englewood Cliffs, N.J.: Prentice-Hall, 1976), ch. 3.
2. For a discussion of this and other problems related to the study of

public opinion and the belief systems of mass publics, see W. Lance Bennett, "The Growth of Knowledge in Mass Belief Studies: An Epistemological Critique," *American Journal of Political Science*, Vol. 21 (August 1977), pp. 465–500.

3. Angus Campbell, Philip E. Converse, Warren E. Miller, and Donald E. Stokes, *The American Voter* (New York: Wiley, 1960), p. 186.

4. Benjamin I. Page and Richard A. Brody, "Policy Voting and the Electoral Process: The Vietnam War Issue," *American Political Science Review*, Vol. 66 (September 1972), p. 995.

5. See V. O. Key, Jr., "Public Opinion and the Decay of Democracy," *Virginia Quarterly Review*, Vol. 37 (Autumn 1961), pp. 481–94.

6. For an excellent discussion of the difference between looking at opinions from the context of the individuals who form them as opposed to the context imposed by the analyst, see Robert E. Lane, "Patterns of Political Belief," in *Handbook of Political Psychology*, ed. Jeanne Knutson (San Francisco: Jossey-Bass, 1973), pp. 98–105. See also Bennett, "The Growth of Knowledge in Mass Belief Studies."

7. From Max Farrand, ed., *The Records of the Federal Convention of 1787*, Vol. 1 (New Haven: Yale University Press, 1937), pp. 299–300.

8. *The Federalist Papers*, No. 10 (New York: Mentor Books, 1961), p. 79.

9. Ibid., p. 79.

10. Ibid., p. 82.

11. Ibid., p. 81.

12. Saul K. Podover, ed., *Thomas Jefferson on Democracy* (New York: Mentor Books, 1939), p. 68.

13. Ibid., p. 23.

14. Ibid., p. 44.

15. For a more detailed discussion of the state-of-consciousness theory of democracy, see Bernard R. Berelson, Paul F. Lazarsfeld, and William N. McPhee, *Voting* (Chicago: University of Chicago Press, 1954). For an excellent critique that goes well beyond the scope of the present discussion on public opinion, see Carole Pateman, *Participation and Democratic Theory* (London: Cambridge University Press, 1970).

16. See Lane, "Patterns of Political Belief." Also see W. Lance Bennett, "Public Opinion: Problems of Description and Inference," in *Public Opinion: Its Formation, Measurement, and Impact*, ed. Susan Welch and John Comer (Palo Alto, Calif.: Mayfield, 1975), pp. 117–31.

17. See Bennett, "The Growth of Knowledge in Mass Belief Studies."

18. Actually, this metaphor may not be far from a literal description. In a fascinating discussion of thinking and perception, R. L. Gregory points out the similarities between fallacies in scientific perspectives and fallacies in visual perception. See R. L. Gregory, "The Confounded Eye," in *Illusion in Nature and Art*, ed. R. L. Gregory and E. H. Gombrich (New York: Scribner, 1974), pp. 49–95.

19. Berelson, Lazarsfeld, and McPhee, *Voting*, p. 308.

20. For just a few of the studies that reach this conclusion, see Hazel G. Erskine, "The Polls: The Informed Public," *Public Opinion Quarterly*, Vol. 26 (Winter 1962), pp. 669–77; Hazel G. Erskine, "The Polls:

COMPETING IMAGES OF THE AMERICAN PUBLIC

Textbook Knowledge," *Public Opinion Quarterly*, Vol. 27 (Spring 1963), pp. 133–41; Hazel G. Erskine, "The Polls: Exposure to Information," *Public Opinion Quarterly*, Vol. 27 (Fall 1963), pp. 491–500; M. Patchen, *The American Public's View of U.S. Policy Toward China* (New York: Council on Foreign Relations, 1964); and Don D. Smith, "Dark Areas of Ignorance Revisited: Current Knowledge About Asian Affairs," in *Political Attitudes and Public Opinion*, ed. Dan D. Nimmo and Charles M. Bonjean (New York: McKay, 1972), pp. 267–72.

21. Gallup Poll 336-K, question 3a, polling date: December 2–7, 1944.

22. Gallup Poll 399-K, question 13a, polling date: June 20–25, 1947.

23. Gallup Poll 491-TPS, question 18, polling date: April 27, 1952, to May 2, 1952.

24. Gallup Poll 526, question 14a, polling date: January 28, 1954, to February 2, 1954.

25. Gallup Poll 678-K, question 8, polling date: October 11–16, 1963.

26. Reported in Lloyd A. Free and Hadley Cantril, *The Political Beliefs of Americans* (New York: Simon and Schuster, 1968), p. 199.

27. Survey Research Center, University of Michigan National Election Study, 1970.

28. From a Gallup Poll reported in *Current Opinion*, Vol. 5 (October 1977), p. 117.

29. From a Gallup Poll reported in *Current Opinion*, Vol. 4 (October 1976), p. 110.

30. From an R. H. Bruskin Associates marketing survey reported in *Current Opinion*, Vol. 5 (July 1977), p. 82.

31. Herbert B. Hyman and Paul B. Sheatsley, "Some Reasons Why Information Campaigns Fail," *Public Opinion Quarterly*, Vol. 11 (Fall 1947), pp. 412–23.

32. Campbell, Converse, Miller, and Stokes, *The American Voter*, p. 186.

33. V. O. Key, Jr., *The Responsible Electorate* (Cambridge, Mass.: Harvard University Press, 1966).

34. Stanley Kelley, Jr., *Political Campaigning: Problems in Creating an Informed Electorate* (Washington, D.C.: Brookings Institution, 1960), p. 51.

35. Benjamin I. Page, "The Theory of Political Ambiguity," *American Political Science Review*, Vol. 70 (September 1976), pp. 742–52.

36. Harold Mendelsohn, "Some Reasons Why Information Campaigns Can Succeed," *Public Opinion Quarterly*, Vol. 37 (Spring 1973), pp. 50–61.

37. Ibid., p. 50.

38. See Page and Brody, "Policy Voting and the Electoral Process." See also Richard A. Brody and Benjamin I. Page, "The Assessment of Policy Voting," *American Political Science Review*, Vol. 66 (June, 1972), pp. 450–58.

39. See, for example, David E. RePass, "Issue Salience and Party Choice," *American Political Science Review*, Vol. 65 (June 1971), pp. 389–400; John E. Jackson, "Issues, Party Choices, and Presidential Votes," *American Journal of Political Science*, Vol. 19 (May 1975), pp.

161–85; and Mark A. Schulman and Gerald M. Pomper, "Variability in Electoral Behavior: Longitudinal Perspectives from Causal Modeling," *American Journal of Political Science*, Vol. 19 (February 1975), pp. 1–18.

40. Schulman and Pomper, "Variability in Electoral Behavior," p. 17.
41. Richard G. Niemi and Herbert F. Weisberg, *Controversies in American Voting Behavior* (San Francisco: Freeman, 1976), p. 168.
42. See, for example, Michael Margolis, "From Confusion to Confusion: Issues and the American Voter (1952–1976)," *American Political Science Review*, Vol. 71 (March 1977), pp.31–43.
43. See, for example, Philip E. Converse, Warren E. Miller, Jerrold G. Rusk, and Arthur C. Wolfe, "Continuity and Change in American Politics: Parties and Issues in the 1968 Election," *American Political Science Review*, Vol. 63 (December 1969), pp. 1095–1101.
44. Stuart Oskamp, *Attitudes and Opinions* (Englewood Cliffs, N.J.: Prentice-Hall, 1977), p. 117.
45. Weissberg, *Public Opinion and Popular Government*, p. 33.
46. Philip E. Converse, "The Nature of Belief Systems in Mass Publics," in *Ideology and Discontent*, ed. David E. Apter (New York: Free Press, 1964), pp. 206–61. See also Philip E. Converse, "Public Opinion and Voting Behavior," in *Handbook of Political Science*, Vol. 4, ed. Fred I. Greenstein and Nelson W. Polsby (Reading, Mass.: Addison-Wesley, 1975), pp. 75–169.
47. See, for example, Samuel A. Stouffer, *Communism, Conformity, and Civil Liberties* (Garden City, N.Y.: Doubleday, 1955); James W. Prothro and Charles M. Grigg, "Fundamental Principles of Democracy: Bases of Agreement and Disagreement," *Journal of Politics*, Vol. 22 (May 1960), pp. 276–94; and Herbert McClosky, "Consensus and Ideology in American Politics," *American Political Science Review*, Vol. 58 (June 1964), pp. 361–82.
48. Converse, "The Nature of Belief Systems in Mass Publics," p. 30.
49. Ibid., pp. 228–29.
50. See, for example, Steven R. Brown, "Consistency and the Persistence of Ideology: Some Experimental Results," *Public Opinion Quarterly*, Vol. 34 (Spring 1970), pp. 60–68; Norman R. Luttbeg, "The Structure of Beliefs Among Leaders and the Public," *Public Opinion Quarterly*, Vol. 32 (Fall 1968), pp. 398–409; Bennett, "Public Opinion: Problems of Description and Inference"; and Lane, "Patterns of Political Belief."
51. Robin M. Williams, Jr., *Strangers Next Door: Ethnic Relations in American Communities* (Englewood Cliffs, N.J.: Prentice-Hall, 1964).
52. See Howard Schuman, "Attitudes vs. Actions Versus Attitudes vs. Attitudes," *Public Opinion Quarterly*, Vol. 36 (Fall 1972), pp. 347–54.
53. Ibid., p. 353.
54. Norman H. Nie with Kristi Andersen, "Mass Belief Systems Revisited: Political Change and Attitude Structure," *Journal of Politics*, Vol. 36 (August 1974), pp. 540–87. See also Norman H. Nie, Sidney Verba, and John R. Petrocik, *The Changing American Voter* (Cambridge, Mass.: Harvard University Press, 1976), ch. 7.

COMPETING IMAGES OF THE AMERICAN PUBLIC

55. See George F. Bishop, Robert W. Oldendick, and Alfred Tuchfarber, "Effects of Question Wording and Format on Political Attitude Consistency," *Public Opinion Quarterly,* Vol. 42 (Spring 1978), pp. 81–92; see also George F. Bishop, Alfred J. Tuchfarber and Robert W. Oldendick, "Change in the Structure of American Political Attitudes: The Nagging Question of Question Wording," *American Journal of Political Science,* Vol. 22 (May 1978), pp. 250–69.

56. See John L. Sullivan, James E. Piereson, and George E. Marcus, "Ideological Constraint in the Mass Public: A Methodological Critique and Some New Findings," *American Journal of Political Science,* Vol. 22 (May 1978), pp. 233–49.

57. Christopher H. Achen, "Mass Attitudes and the Survey Response," *American Political Science Review,* Vol. 69 (December 1975), pp. 1218–31.

58. Recent exchanges of comments among these researchers indicate that none of them can clearly "disprove" the claims of the others, yet none is prepared to give up the position that it is possible to produce a general description of the state of public consciousness. The result is that each claims to be right, but none can prove it. See, for example, Sullivan, Piereson, and Marcus, "Ideological Constraint in the Mass Public"; and Bishop, Tuchfarber, and Oldendick, "Change in the Structure of American Political Attitudes."

59. There is, of course, a serious question about whether the simple and complex versions of an issue are really the "same" issue at all. Research on racial prejudice has shown that more complex cases of racial discrimination tended to be perceived as involving different issues entirely. However, for an interesting argument about the impact of the wording of ballot propositions on public opinion, see David Magleby, "Voting on Statewide Propositions" (Paper presented at the Annual Meeting of the Western Political Science Association, 1979).

3
Theory and Method
in
Opinion Research

IT IS IMPORTANT to understand the basic techniques of opinion research before turning to theoretical questions. Opinion polling and survey research are central aspects of the field. Moreover, the area of opinion research is especially relevant to the development of theory: It is crucial to know where questions of methodology end and where questions of theory begin. It is all too easy to search for *methodological* solutions to problems that require *theoretical* attention—particularly when the state-of-consciousness perspective is at work.

As the constraint controversy discussed in Chapter 2 showed, when a general state of consciousness is presumed to exist, different findings about the same characteristics of opinion cannot be interpreted as meaningful expressions of opinion. They tend to be labeled as "artifacts" of the methods used to measure and analyze data. This labeling leads in turn to an (unproductive) effort to discover the "correct" way of measuring opinion responses. Different research methods are not necessarily free of error. Some corrections for poor data collection or opinion measurement practices may be called for in many studies. However, different research methods may correspond to variations in real political situations. As a result, a theoretical framework is needed to point out areas of meaningful difference in research methods and to put the problem of error in proper perspective.

An overview of opinion research techniques helps to differentiate errors due to the misuse of methods from areas of uncertainty resulting from the absence of theories to guide the use and interpretation of methods. In this discussion, *error* will be defined broadly to refer to bias in the results of opinion research due to the improper construction or use of research methods. Errors can occur at a number of points—from drawing a sample, to gathering the data, to wording a question, to recording the response. Error at any step simply means that the method used to represent a real dimension of opinion distorted that dimension. For example, opinion surveys are based on studies of small groups of people called *samples*. These small groups are chosen so that they reflect the overall composition of some larger group, or *population*, about which the researcher wants to generalize. As the forthcoming discussion will show, different ways of selecting a sample will introduce different levels of sampling error into a study. The degree of sampling error indicates the extent to which the sample can be taken as truly representative of the larger population.

In some areas of opinion research (like sampling), the relationship between theory and method is pretty obvious. For example, a researcher generally knows what population he or she wants to study and how to go about drawing a sample that represents that population within a known margin of error. However, in other areas it is not so easy to decide where errors of representation stop and meaningful measures of opinion start. For example, there is room to debate whether a particular question on a survey is ambiguous (and, thereby, generates confusion from people responding to it), or whether it reflects some political stimuli that people encounter in the real world. Such questions may never be resolved completely, but a grasp of basic research problems and a sound theoretical framework will make it possible to think more sensibly about them.

The following overview of opinion research practices is divided into four general areas: sampling, data collection, measurement, and analysis. If an opinion survey is supposed to tell us something about the thinking of a larger population of individuals (like the entire American public), then we must be able to judge whether it really represents that general population. In the opinion research business, this is known as a question about *sampling*. However, even if the sample of people drawn for a study seems to represent some larger population pretty well, the findings may not always be valid. We also need to know how many members of the sample were contacted, what was done about "missing respondents," and how the respondents communicated their views to the researcher. These are questions about *data collection practices*.

Sometimes a sample is a good one and the data collection is done properly, but the questions people are asked are confusing or ambiguous. Sometimes the way answers are recorded loses too much information or produces outright misinterpretation. When these things happen, the data are not good indicators of what the researcher really wanted to study. These are problems of *measurement*. Even when the data are accurate measures of what the researcher wants to study, they still must be manipulated mathematically and interpreted according to some standards of comparison or judgment. It is possible for the data to be organized in ways that don't resemble the way they operate in the real world. It is also possible to apply such loose or vague standards of interpretation that the data don't really tell us anything conclusive. These are problems of *analysis* and *inference*.

SAMPLING

If we want to study a group of people as large as all Americans over the age of eighteen, it is obvious that we can't study every individual member of that population. Even if we had the time, we certainly wouldn't have the money. A pollster may spend anywhere from $20,000 to $50,000 to do a simple study with a national sample of only fifteen hundred people. Even if costs were not important, there would probably be less accuracy in a study that tried to contact all members of a large population than in a study that settled for a small, but carefully selected, sample of that population.[1] About the only researchers who try to study all members of large populations are the demographers at the U.S. Census Bureau. Their main reason for trying to round everyone up every ten years is to ascertain the exact size of the total population and the various groups in it. This is different from the goal of opinion researchers, who are interested in the distribution of various attitudes and beliefs in the population.

Common sense tells us that if we are going to learn anything about a large group by studying a relatively small number of its members, it matters which members we choose to study. If we want to predict the outcome of an upcoming election, we need to find a group that is fairly representative of all the people who might vote. Unfortunately, common sense may not be much help in figuring out how to find such a group. This point is illustrated nicely by the legendary example of the *Literary Digest*'s prediction that Alf Landon would win a landslide victory over Franklin D. Roosevelt in the 1936 presidential election. The magazine had attracted a good deal of national attention every four years by taking a poll and accurately predicting the results of the presidential election. In 1936 the magazine announced that Landon would win by a large margin. However, the voters overturned this prediction, electing Roosevelt. FDR won 60 percent of the popular vote. What went wrong with the magazine's sampling procedures?

The magazine credited the past successes of its polls to the large number of people it reached with its straw ballot. In an average election year, *Literary Digest* sent out from 10 to 15 million ballots and received anywhere from 2 to 3 million of them back in the mail. An impressive record, indeed. The year 1936 was no exception to this pattern. Over 2 million potential voters responded to the poll. How could a study of so many people have been so far off? The only explanation is that unintentionally the magazine must have contacted a group of people who were much more inclined to vote Republican than was the average voter. A look at *Literary Digest*'s methods for selecting the sample shows how this happened.

Most of the sample was drawn from three sources: subscribers to *Literary Digest*, registered automobile owners, and persons listed in telephone directories. At the peak of the Great Depression, what sorts of people would these have been? Only the relatively wealthy could afford to subscribe to magazines, own (or register) cars, or pay for a telephone. Such people, not hurt economically by the Depression, were the core of Republican-party voting support for its economic programs. Had *Literary Digest* recognized the economic bias in its sample, it might have predicted accurately how the upper classes were going to vote, but there clearly was no basis for generalizing about the whole voting public.

Two lessons emerge from this case. (Unfortunately, neither lesson helped the *Digest*, which went out of business in 1937 under a cloud of bad publicity about its fiasco.) First, in opinion research there is no safety in large numbers. After a certain point, an increase in the size of a sample does not make it more representative, more credible, or more scientific. Second, the most important thing about a sample is how it is drawn—that is, how the people in it are selected. In 1936, the reputation of the infant science of opinion research was saved by the presence on the scene of three pollsters who recognized these things.

Archibald Crossley, Elmo Roper, and George Gallup predicted the 1936 election correctly. From their prior experience in advertising and market research, each of them knew that an *unbiased sample* had to contain a mix of people that mirrored the composition of the larger population. Although their samples were much larger than they needed to be (Gallup contacted sixty thousand people in 1936), the techniques they established have been refined to provide the basis for opinion polling as we know it today.

Modern samples are called *probability samples*. This simply means that we know how likely it is that any member of the general population will be drawn in the sample. With this information we can estimate with great accuracy how close the sample is to the larger population. The most common form of probability sampling is the *random sample*. In a random sample every member of the general population has (at least in theory) an equal chance of turning up in the sample. The reason for drawing probability samples in general and random samples in particular is so that fairly exact calculations can be made about how close the sample comes to being a scale model of the general population. It is obvious that if we want to generalize about what the larger population thinks or how it may behave, we must know how close the sample comes to representing the population. Otherwise, cases like the *Literary Digest* debacle can occur in which generalizations are drawn from samples that contain large margins of error.

Probability sampling makes it possible to calculate the margin of error in a sample. It is possible to estimate the probability that some defining characteristic of the population will appear in a sample of a particular size. Suppose that we are interested in estimating the division of popular support between two presidential candidates. Since it is not possible to contact all the voters in America, we must design a sampling procedure that gives every voter an approximately equal chance of appearing in the sample. With such a procedure, the laws of probability tell us how close a sample of a particular size is likely to come to representing the actual population. For the most part, the laws of probability appeal to common sense. If the sample is very small, there is a greater chance that it will give us a biased estimate of the population. The extreme cases illustrate this point simply.

Suppose that the actual level of popular support is evenly divided between the two candidates. Half of the population supports

Candidate X and half supports Candidate Y. If our sample consisted of only two people, we would run an enormous risk of error. This is because if we took repeated samples from the population, we would expect half of those samples to contain either two X supporters or two Y supporters, and only half of the time would they contain the representative portion of one X supporter and one Y supporter. As the size of the sample increases, the chances of drawing such an unrepresentative mix decrease. The chance that a sample of one thousand would contain all X supporters or all Y supporters (drawn from an evenly divided population) is so small that the number of zeroes following the decimal point in the probability expression would run off the page.

Estimating the error of a sample of a given size rests on the principle that, on the average, repeated samples of that size can be expected to fall within a particular distance of the actual population distribution a certain percentage of the time. Suppose that we take a sample of five hundred people from the population of all American voters and discover that 52 percent of the sample supports Candidate X. We want to determine how close this percentage comes to the actual level of support in the population. Since this estimate is based on the average of all samples of this size in the population, we must first understand that our estimate will hold true only some percentage of the time. Probability theory allows us to calculate the strength of the estimate for different levels of reliability or confidence.

Suppose that we are willing to settle for a 95 percent chance of being correct in our estimate. For a sample of size 500, the probability coefficient for calculating sampling error with 95 percent confidence is 1.96. The equation[2] for calculating the error of this sample is

$$SE = .52 \pm 1.96 \sqrt{.52(1 - .48)/(500 - 1)} = \pm .044$$

This means that we can be 95 percent confident that the real support in the population for Candidate X is somewhere between 56.4 percent (52% + 4.4%) and 47.6 percent (52% − 4.4%). In a close election, this finding might not give us enough confidence to predict who is going to win. We can build more confidence into our estimates by increasing the size of the sample.

It happens to be the case that quadrupling the sample size reduces the margin of error by half. Suppose that we drew another random sample from our population. This time the chosen sample size is two thousand. On this occasion suppose that 53 percent of the sample supports Candidate X. This means that we can be 95 percent confident that the real level of support in the population lies somewhere between .53 $\pm$ .022, or between 55.2 percent and 50.8 percent. We could be very confident in predicting that if the election were held on that day, Candidate X would win.

Most national surveys are based on samples of somewhere between five hundred and two thousand people. The actual size of the sample within that range depends on the researcher's judgments about how much money can be spent on the study, how reliable the estimate has to be, and how evenly distributed the opinions probably are in the real population. If a pollster has a large budget, feels that his or her reputation is on the line, and guesses that support in the population is fairly evenly divided between two candidates, then a large sample may seem in order.

The laws of probability on which calculations of sampling error are based require that samples be randomly drawn. In a true random sample, every individual in the population must be identified somehow so that he or she can be included in the sample. This is possible to do in some cases, such as when a sample of the voting population of a city is drawn from the voting lists in that city. However, identifying the individual members of a population becomes difficult when a population as large and diffuse as the American public is being sampled. When faced with such a task, most pollsters and survey researchers use an alternative sampling method that by-passes the problem of individual identification and still produces a reliable sample in which levels of error can be estimated accurately.

The most common alternative is called *multistage sampling*. Instead of selecting individuals, multistage sampling selects a precise physical location (such as a house or an apartment) in which an individual might be found. Multistage samples begin with a sample of geographical regions matched according to population size. Each region is divided into smaller regions, also matched for population size. The division and subdivision continue until neighborhoods, blocks, and, finally, dwelling units are included in the sample. This method produces a slight increase in the level of sampling error, but the increase is offset by the tremendous savings of time and expense that accompany the procedure. Table 3-1 compares the margins of error for different sizes of random and multistage samples.

TABLE 3-1
Maximum Margins of Error for
Different Sample Sizes and Sampling Procedures

Sample Size	Maximum Error in a Random Sample*	Maximum Error in a Typical Multistage Sample*
94	±10.4%	±12%
375	5.1	6
1,500	2.5	3
6,000	1.3	1.5
24,000	.6	.75
96,000	.32	.375

*These ranges of error can be expected to hold 95 percent of the time.

Samples in which all members of populations have equal chances of being drawn are suited to some theoretical questions but not to others. It would be appropriate to draw a simple random sample[3] for a study designed to estimate the political opinions of the American adult population on various issues. However, suppose that the research question is somewhat more specialized. For example, it might be interesting to assess the effects of variables such as age and race on opinions about militant civil rights activism in America. It is reasonable to hypothesize that the civil rights views of older people might be more conservative than the views of people who grew up during the period of civil rights activism. It also seems likely that blacks would be more positive about radical civil rights activities than whites.

It would be interesting to see whether these two variables interact with each other. It could be argued that intense political activity and organization in the black population in the 1950s and 1960s rearranged the general distribution of values and beliefs related to civil rights issues more in the black population than in the white population. By contrast, the absence of much civil rights activity in the 1920s and 1930s might make the distribution of these values and beliefs more similar for black and white members of the two populations in those age brackets. If such an interaction emerged, it would tell us that political socialization in one era can have a much more polarizing effect on social groups than socializiation in

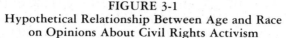

FIGURE 3-1
Hypothetical Relationship Between Age and Race on Opinions About Civil Rights Activism

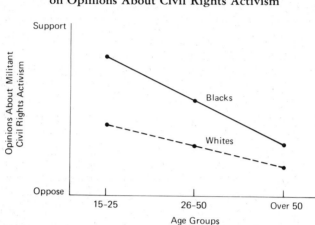

Testing such a hypothesis would require including in the age groups a larger number of blacks than would turn up in a simple random sample.

another era. (This finding would be another reason to avoid over-generalized state-of-consciousness approaches to public opinion.)

The hypothetical interaction shown in Figure 3-1 might be difficult to test with data from a simple random sample. This is because a sample as small as five hundred or one thousand people might not contain enough blacks in the various age groups to make statistical tests reliable. Blacks simply do not constitute a large proportion of the general population, and, as a result, they would turn up in very small numbers in a small random sample. The raw numbers would be even smaller within each age category chosen to test the hypothesis.

The solution to this sampling problem is to divide, or stratify, the larger population into groups defined by age categories and racial status. This procedure, called *stratified random sampling*, would allow larger numbers of blacks to be drawn randomly from each age bracket. As long as the groups that are "oversampled" are sampled randomly, valid statistical comparisons can be made between the groups. The entire sample, of course, will not be representative of the general population because certain groups are overrepresented. However, since the overrepresented groups were drawn randomly and their true proportion in the population can be estimated, it is a simple matter to transform a stratified random sample back into a simple random sample. This can be accomplished by dropping a random number of cases from the over-sampled groups until those groups reach the same proportions in the sample as they hold in the population. This makes it possible to use the sample to generalize about the overall population.

These examples cover the general outlines of sampling procedures in public opinion research.[4] They also suggest that sampling methods are probably not responsible for much of the conceptual confusion about public opinion. Once a group or a population has been identified as a research target, sampling it is a fairly routine matter. The problems of sampling have less to do with a lack of theoretical guidance than with the execution of well-designed strategies that make it possible to calculate the level of error in a sample. As long as the margins of error due to sampling procedures are known and reliable, determining how much of the difference in research findings may be due to differences in sampling techniques becomes a simple matter. Sampling is probably the most sophisticated technique of opinion research. Margins of error are straightforward and easy to calculate, and the relationship between theory and sampling procedures is easy to determine.

DATA COLLECTION PRACTICES

Once a sample has been drawn, the desired opinion data must be gathered. This means that the individuals in the sample must be contacted. Like sampling procedures, data-gathering practices are not complicated by serious theoretical problems. The central issue in data gathering is the problem of maintaining the integrity of the sample by trying to get all the members of it to participate in the study. A carefully designed sample is of little use if most of its members do not contribute to the data base of the study. Various data collection practices can bring error to a study because of how they affect the response rate of the sample and how they handle individuals who do not participate. Although data-gathering techniques are similar to sampling procedures in the sense that they do not raise theoretical questions, they differ from sampling procedures in an important respect: It is possible to estimate sampling error fairly accurately, but the error introduced into the representativeness of opinion data by data-gathering practices is often very difficult to assess.

Some opinion surveys are done over the telephone or through the mails, but most are conducted by face-to-face interviews. Personal contact increases the chances that a member of a sample will agree to participate in the study. (Personal interviews also improve communication with respondents and make the context in which a questionnaire is answered more uniform.) However, even the face-to-face interview does not solve all the problems. Several sources of error can be introduced in the interview stage of an opinion study.

The first difficulty is simply contacting all the members of the sample (or someone who is at home at each of the addresses on a multistage sampling list). What do you suppose would happen if you knocked on fifteen hundred doors in your area? How many people would be at home at ten in the morning, or three in the afternoon, or seven in the evening? No matter what time you chose, a good number of people would be away. Why not just call on the house next door? Samples as small as the ones used by most pollsters are reliable (that is, the error rate is small and predictable) only if all the people targeted in the sample actually end up in the study. For this reason, pollsters go to great expense, and interviewers are instructed to go to great effort, to make follow-up visits to households in which no one responded the first time. An interviewer may make four or five return visits to a large number of households; but despite these efforts many people are never contacted, and new persons must be added to the sample. In fact, a pollster is lucky to contact 80 percent of an original sample. In some cases, as much as 30 or 40 percent of the originally targeted subjects may be lost.

People who are seldom at home are not just like people who are often at home. If the hard-to-contact people belong to social groups with any important political characteristics, their loss may bias the study. It is pretty clear that some groups are overrepresented in many public opinion studies just because they happen to be at home when the interviewers call. Women are home more than men. Housewives stay home more than career women. Old people more than young people. Retired people more than working people. The unemployed more than the employed. And so on. Some of the "missing people" may live in quite different political worlds than people who spend much of their time at home.

This problem is compounded by the fact that many people who are contacted simply refuse to be interviewed. Interviewers tend to be persuasive, but some people refuse to tell their political views to a stranger at the door. These individuals may be special political cases also. The difficulty with both the "missing persons" and the "nontalkers" is that we cannot study them to find out how they differ from the people whom we can study. Since most pollsters do not know how this problem affects their findings, and since they take every possible step to minimize it, they tend not to talk about it very much. The findings from most public opinion studies should not be dismissed because of this gap, but it is important to be aware that the problem exists.

Another data collection difficulty of unknown proportions is the occasional practice of interviewers either to make up their interviews or to substitute easy-to-contact individuals for members of the sample who are difficult to reach. This is not to suggest that interviewers are dishonest. It is reasonable to suspect, however, that most of them are human. When confronted with bad weather, sinister neighborhoods, "beware of dog" signs, or hard-to-find addresses, they may be tempted to pick another person to interview. Since these matters are locked in the conscience of the interviewer, we will never know how serious an effect they have on opinion research. However, the discovery of an occasional fabricated study should make us think a bit. One particularly embarrassing case is reported by Wheeler:

> In 1968 the *New York Times* commissioned Gallup to do an intensive survey of attitudes of Harlem residents. The information was collected, tabulated, and submitted to the *Times* for publication. An editor was so pleased with the poll that he decided to play it up by sending a reporter and a photographer to get a story about some of those who had supposedly been interviewed. At seven of the twenty-three addresses Gallup had given them, the newsmen could not even find a dwelling! Moreover, five other people who had allegedly been polled could not be traced—the addresses existed but apparently the people did not. Not even all the remaining interviews were legitimate. In one case the *Times* reporter learned that the interviewer had talked to four people playing cards and incorporated all their answers into one interview.[5]

The point here is not to suggest that the hallowed science of public opinion is based on phony data. These examples simply tell us that even in areas of research over which the researcher has a great deal of control, there is probably more error than we would care to imagine. Since these problems of data collection are seldom discovered, we can't worry too much about them in any given study (except in those rare cases when they are detected). However, they are reminders that we should not take too much for granted when thinking about opinion research.

OPINION MEASUREMENT

Sampling procedures and data collection practices are important aspects of opinion research, but the means of eliciting and recording responses are the real heart of an opinion study. As suggested in Chapter 2, the ways in which questions are worded and responses are recorded are the most sensitive matters in contemporary opinion research. They are such difficult methodological areas because it is not always clear when there is theoretical justification for wording a question or recording a response in a particular way and when the chosen method simply introduces error or unreliability into the data. In short, the distinctions between theoretical and methodological guidelines are not as clear in the area of measurement as in the areas of sampling and data collection.

These problems are compounded when the state-of-consciousness fallacy leads researchers to overgeneralize about the opinion characteristics that emerge from their studies. The discovery of different findings in different studies makes it easy to blame particular measures for inflating or deflating the "real" response to an issue. For example, it has been argued that some ways of constructing questions make the issues ambiguous and some ways of constructing response scales give respondents too many or too few categories in which to express their opinions.[6] These may be valid objections to some measures, but they may unwittingly discourage the use of measures that reflect the ways in which political stimuli and opinion responses are structured in real political situations. It may never be possible to say how much of the difference in findings about opinion characteristics such as information, direction, intensity, constraint, and stability is due to poor measurement and how much is due to the use of different but theoretically defensible measures. However, it is possible to offer some general observations both about areas in which error may be present because of measurement problems and about cases in which differences in opinion data may result from valid measures that simply need better theoretical interpretation.

The major source of measurement error is probably questions that make it difficult for a respondent to say what he or she really feels about an issue. In some cases, the language used may not fit very well into the respondent's world, making it hard to determine what the question is about. In other cases, questions may contain logical premises that interfere with the logic of the subject's own beliefs. The logical trap forces the individual to state a position that is unrelated to his or her true feelings. The latter difficulty is easier to demonstrate with an example than to describe in abstract terms.

A good example comes from Wheeler's firsthand observations about what happens when a respondent has to react to a poorly constructed question. In one of the interviews that Wheeler observed, a woman was asked to register agreement or disagreement with a statement about former Secretary of State Henry Kissinger's efforts to make peace between Egypt and Israel in the early 1970s. The statement was worded in the following way: "Since Henry Kissinger failed to make peace between Egypt and Israel, it looks as though he is losing his touch as a peacemaker."[7] The woman was thrown by this question. Since she had never liked Kissinger and had never thought he was much of a peacemaker, his failure in this situation did not change her opinion of him. She didn't think he was losing his touch because she felt that he never had skills as a peacemaker in the first place. However, if she answered "no" to the question, her real feelings would not be understood because the pollster would interpret her response as supporting Kissinger. She was also reluctant to say "yes," because it would suggest that she had supported Kissinger in the past but had withdrawn her support when his latest diplomatic efforts failed.

The interviewer simply told the woman to respond as best she could. She was advised to pick the response that represented the lesser of two evils. However, the woman did not want her views misinterpreted and said that neither of the response options was adequate. The interviewer recorded her opinion as "not sure." This was a serious loss of information, for the woman had a clear opinion on the issue. Wheeler concluded that the logic of the question combined with the limited response options to completely distort the woman's true feelings: "No analyst, no matter how sophisticated, could divine the woman's real views from the 'not sure' recorded by [the interviewer]."[8]

These sorts of problem have led some opinion analysts to advocate the use of stimuli generated by the subjects themselves. One method is simply to ask a general question and leave the response format open-ended so that the subject can fill in his or her own answer.[9] For example, the woman's true feelings might have been easier to assess if she had been asked "How do you feel about Henry Kissinger as a peacemaker?" and had been allowed to give her own response. Another approach is to provide subjects with a general stimulus (such as "Henry Kissinger") and let them generate the dimensions they use to judge it.[10] With this method, the woman could have offered both her opinion of Kissinger and her reason for holding that opinion. This would have eliminated the logical confusion caused by the reference to Egypt and Israel in the pollster's statement. These methods make opinion data more difficult to gather and analyze, but they may reduce the level of ambiguity in the stimuli used in opinion surveys.

Although these solutions to measurement problems are not used often in large-scale studies, several rules of thumb are used by survey researchers to try to minimize errors and still maintain normal question-and-response formats on surveys. The most obvious maxim is to keep the questions simple. Most questions are written at about a fourth-grade reading level, which makes their vocabulary and sentence structure very simple. However, even the most basic ways of asking a question can produce unforeseen and undetected error in subjects' responses.

A classic example is the finding from a study conducted some years ago that a large number of blacks living in rural areas of the South were strongly opposed to "government control of profits." There was no doubt about the direction and intensity of opinions expressed on this issue. However, why these poor rural people would be oppposed to the government regulation of profits was a mystery. Their economic situation seemed to dictate just the opposite opinion. Some follow-up interviews solved the mystery. Many of the respondents were deeply religious individuals who belonged to fundamentalist churches. They thought that the interviewers were asking a question about politics and religion. The kind of "profits" they understood the question to be about had nothing to do with big business. The "prophets" that they were thinking about were controlled by the Lord, not by the government. If the government controlled prophets, it would violate the principle of the separation of church and state![11]

Another common solution to the problems of generating valid responses is to ask a series of follow-up questions about an issue. This practice often helps to clarify the issue of the respondents, and it provides a broader context in which to interpret their responses.

TABLE 3-2
A Sequence of Follow-up Questions
Illustrating the Difficulty of Using Follow-up
Techniques to Clarify Opinion Responses

Question	*Response*	
1. What is your opinion of Senator Joseph McCarthy—is it favorable or unfavorable?	Favorable	50%
	Unfavorable	29%
	No opinion	21%
2. In your opinion is Senator McCarthy helping or hurting the U.S. in its relations with our allies?	Helping	24%
	Hurting	41%
	Neither	17%
	No opinion	18%
3. Can you identify Joseph McCarthy?	Correctly identified	80%
	Incorrect or don't know	20%
4. Asked only of those who identified McCarthy correctly: In general, do you approve or disapprove of the methods used by Senator McCarthy?	Approve	38%
	Disapprove	47%
	No opinion	15%

Source: Gallup Poll 524-K; questions 12c, 18a, 18b, and 22; polling date: December 11–16, 1953.

However, follow-up questions can produce just the opposite effect if the issue is complicated. In such instances an attempt to probe beneath the surface may stir up a sequence of ambiguous responses. This is what happened when Gallup set out to measure popular support for Senator Joseph McCarthy in 1953.

McCarthy was one of the most controversial figures in modern American politics. He had waged a bitter propaganda campaign through speeches and Senate hearings that dramatized the claim that a massive infiltration of communists had occurred in many areas of American life. It might seem like a simple matter to determine what various segments of the public thought about such a well-known and controversial figure. Table 3-2 shows how difficult it can be to get a clear picture of public opinion even with a well-designed set of follow-up questions. Perhaps Gallup would have been better off stopping with the first question. That would have made it easy to generalize about public opinion on Senator McCarthy. Each additional question only complicated the picture.

We would probably discover the same to hold true if members of the public were probed beyond their surface reactions on many issues and personalities. The "confusion" that can result from such efforts to clarify public opinion probably reflects the true state of opinion on many subjects—complex, based on different individual perspectives, anchored in different levels of knowledge and interest, aimed at different political goals and values, and expressed with different skills in thinking and communication.

Such a realization brings focus to the problem of where measurement error stops and theoretically defensible measures of opinion begin. It is important to try to word questions and record responses in ways that minimize ambiguity for the respondents and prevent the loss of information for the analyst. However, it is important to recognize that some variability in responses may be theoretically meaningful and, as a result, should not be treated as a problem that necessarily calls for standardization in the use of opinion measures.

A good example of response differences that probably have little to do with measurement error comes from two opinion polls conducted by Harris and Gallup toward the end of the Vietnam War. These polls were designed to measure public reaction to President Richard Nixon's decision to bomb enemy positions in Cambodia—a risky move that threatened a new escalation of a war that was becoming increasingly unpopular with the American people. In light of the salience of this political action it would seem simple to obtain a clear reading of popular sentiment about it. However, each of the major pollsters asked a slightly different question, and each obtained a different finding about public support.

George Gallup decided that a simple description of the government's action would produce the most realistic response. His survey asked this question: "As you know, U.S. planes are bombing communist positions in Cambodia and Laos. Do you approve or disapprove of this action?" Fifty-seven percent disapproved and 29 percent approved. This represented a 2-to-1 margin of opinion against the government's policy.

Louis Harris reasoned a bit differently than Gallup. He felt that people probably take into account why the government is doing something when they evaluate an action. He asked this question: "The U.S. has used B-52 bombers in Cambodia in the fighting that has gone on there, because it is felt that the peace in Vietnam is threatened. Do you approve or disapprove of the bombings by U.S. planes in Cambodia?" When respondents considered the "official reasoning" behind the policy, only 49 percent opposed it and

33 percent favored it. In the Harris Poll the margin of opposition dropped to 3 to 2.[12]

Which was the "real" measure of public opinion about the issue? Rather than pose that question, it may be more useful to consider both versions of the issue as valid. The Gallup question is in a form that people might be more likely to encounter in an abstract discussion of the issue, whereas the Harris version probably resembles the way in which the government posed the issue in its efforts to stir up public support. Both questions are valid statements of the issue, for they reflect real political formulations. These kinds of findings are strong reasons to recognize the situational variables that can affect opinion. They also suggest that any abstract issue can generate a range of meaningful opinions, depending on the situational variables that surround the issue in a specific political context.

The measurement of opinion cannot be a mechanical process governed by rigid guidelines for reducing error and standardizing measures. Even the most obvious guidelines for reducing error and bias can run up against good theoretical reasons for selecting other measurement strategies. For example, it may seem completely obvious that "loaded" language should not be used in survey questions. This guideline may lead us to doubt the validity of a question like the following one asked by Gallup toward the end of World War II: "The Japs say that they will execute any American bomber pilots forced to land in Japan. If the Japs do this, should we use poison gas against Japanese cities?"[13] The use of the derogatory term "Jap" would seem to encourage the introduction of prejudice into thinking about a serious human question. However, we must remember that in 1944 most Americans probably referred to Japanese citizens as "Japs." It is questionable whether Gallup would have generated more "realisitic" opinions by using less emotional language.

Such problems make opinion research a fascinating field in which challenging questions about how to measure things must be weighed against both methodological and theoretical considerations. However, methodological guidelines have been developed much more fully than theoretical ones. This is why general theories of opinion, society, and politics stand as high-priority items in the field. The lack of well-formulated theory creates problems in the analysis of opinion that are as serious as the ones outlined in this discussion of measurement.

ANALYZING OPINION DATA

After the results of a survey are in, the difficult task of analyzing and interpreting the data begins. This stage of opinion research demands a great deal of creativity and sensitivity from the analyst. Even though there are sophisticated methods of analyzing data, it is necessary to develop better guidelines to figure out which analytical method ought to be used in a particular situation. We also need better theoretical standards for judging what the results of an analysis really mean.

Even fairly simple questions can create problems of interpretation. President Lyndon Johnson spent years worrying about how the public really felt about his conduct of the Vietnam War. He once commented on the frustrations of "reading" public opinion. He said that if Patrick Henry had taken a poll after his "Give me liberty or give me death" speech, the results would have been

Liberty	46%
Death	29%
Don't know	25%

Various methods of analyzing data can help analysts find patterns or structure in survey responses. These patterns can become the bases of stronger and clearer interpretations of public thinking.

Some analysis problems are fairly straightforward and probably do not require the theoretical guidance demanded by others. For example, a good opinion analyst would have been able to help Patrick Henry out of his hypothetical dilemma without much difficulty. This can be shown easily by turning Lyndon Johnson's humorous lament into a whimsical example. Perhaps an enterprising pollster on the scene at the time of the American Revolution would have recognized Henry's remarks as a good measure of support for or against breaking ties with Britain. A heated debate was raging through the colonies on this issue. Some people favored continued peaceful relations with England. Others demanded revolution. Henry's speech to the Virginia assembly in 1775 seemed to crystallize this national debate. He rose to his feet and said to his fellow citizens:

> The war is inevitable—let it come! I repeat . . . let it come. . . . Gentlemen may cry, peace, peace, but there is no peace. The war is actually begun! . . . Our brethren are already in the field! Why stand we

FIGURE 3-2
Hypothetical Trend in Public Reaction
to Patrick Henry's Speech

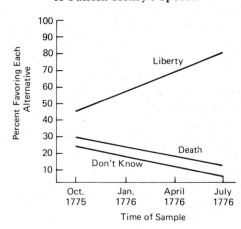

here idle? . . . Is life so dear or peace so sweet to be purchased at the price of chains and slavery? Forbid it, Almighty God—I know not what course others may take; but as for me, give me liberty or give me death!

This was such a timely and important speech that public response to these sentiments could be regarded as a good indicator of popular support for a revolution. However, the situation was so complex and things were changing so rapidly that it might be hard to interpret public feeling at any one point in time. The best way to analyze support would be to chart public reaction to the statement over a period of time. We might find, for example, that calculating reactions at several points in time would clarify things, as shown in the hypothetical graph in Figure 3-2. Perhaps it would clarify things even more to know where the growing trend of public support for "Liberty" was coming from.

It is reasonable to argue that a revolution will be more successful if support for it is shared by all kinds of people rather than by just one or two special groups. This idea could be explored by organizing the data so that the opinions of political, economic, and military leaders (call them the "elite") could be compared with the opinions of laborers, farmers, and craftspeople (call them the "mass public"). Even if public opinion ran strongly in favor of

Henry's sentiments, we might not give the revolution much chance if we discovered this pattern in the data:

	Liberty	Death	
Elite	30%	70%	100%
Mass	80%	20%	100%

However, we might be more optimistic in our interpretation if our analysis revealed this pattern:

	Liberty	Death	
Elite	70%	30%	100%
Mass	80%	20%	100%

This example indicates that some problems in opinion analysis can be handled with simple common sense and modest theoretical guidelines. However, other analytical strategies are more difficult to choose and evaluate because the methods of analysis are more complex and opinion theories are not well formulated. A good example of this problem is the research that has been done on the stability of opinions.

Recall from Chapter 2 that the classical perspective on opinion and democracy requires that individuals hold fairly stable opinions in order for their interests to be expressed clearly. The early research on stability was consistent with the early conclusions about information and constraint reported in Chapter 2. Converse found that most individuals change their opinions in an almost random pattern over time. This seemed to seal the case against the democratic qualifications of the general public. However, in recent years Converse's finding has been challenged in two ways. One criticism is that ambiguities in the wording of questions and the format of responses simply made the data unreliable, and the real level of stability may be much higher than Converse's analysis would indicate.[14] The other criticism is that the method used to analyze the data affected the results, and Converse used a very demanding method without a convincing theoretical reason for doing so.[15]

The latter criticism introduces the important point that the choice of a method for analyzing data is based on certain assumptions that the analyst makes about the real world. If the assumptions are not well specified in theoretical terms, it is difficult to judge how reasonable they are. Sometimes, on close inspection, they may appear questionable. This, in turn, may cast doubt on the chosen method of analysis.

Converse assumed that everybody organizes opinions along the same general liberal-conservative lines. This assumption led him to organize his data to see whether the responses of the entire sample tended to be stable or unstable on each issue. His analysis showed that attitudes were not very stable on most issues. However, it is possible to make the rather different assumption that individuals organize their beliefs in various ways or understand different things by "liberalism" and "conservatism." If that is the case, it would be possible for the attitudes of most individuals to be fairly stable about a whole set of issues, even though the attitudes of a whole group (or sample) of individuals might appear unstable on each particular issue.

Explaining the technical reasons for this would require a complicated methodological discussion. However, it is possible to illustrate the general idea with a simple example. Suppose we ask people to express their opinions on a group of political issues. Since we want to know whether their opinions are stable, we must interview them now, and we must return to ask them the same questions at some time in the future. To simplify things, let's say that we interview four people about four political issues. Things can be simplified even further by giving people a plus (+) for each issue on which they express the same opinion both times and a minus (−) each time they express an opinion different from the one they gave during the first interview. We might organize these data as shown in Table 3-3.

Now we have to decide how to analyze the data. If we assume that everyone has a common frame of reference, then we would want to calculate the level of stability across the whole group of individuals on each issue. One way of doing this might be to calculate a *stability ratio* by dividing the number of stable responses by the number of unstable responses. Using this procedure, the stability ratios for the four issues are 1, 1, 1, and 1.

On the other hand, we might assume that even if there is some kind of liberal-conservative dimension in public opinion, each indi-

TABLE 3-3
Hypothetical Opinion Stability Scores

	Issue 1	Issue 2	Issue 3	Issue 4
Person 1	+	+	+	−
Person 2	+	−	+	+
Person 3	−	−	−	−
Person 4	−	+	−	+

vidual may use it differently or make different calculations when forming his or her opinions. If this is true, then it would not make much sense to look at the stability across the group on each issue. We would want to analyze the degree of stability in each individual's thinking on the issues. If we compute each person's ratio of stable responses to unstable ones, we find that the stability ratios for the four individuals are 3, 3, 0, and 1. By any comparison, this way of analyzing the data produces much higher levels of stability (see Table 3-4).

If we decide that it makes just as much sense to look for the ways individuals organize their opinions as it does to analyze the thinking of groups, then we would have to change our interpretation of

TABLE 3-4
Alternative Ways of Analyzing Stability Data

	Issue 1	Issue 2	Issue 3	Issue 4	Individual Stability Level
Person 1	+	+	+	−	3
Person 2	+	−	+	+	3
Person 3	−	−	−	−	0
Person 4	−	+	−	+	1
Group Stability Level	1	1	1	1	

the group data. We can't really conclude that the political thinking of the public is unstable. All we can say is that members of the general public do not think within the same framework. This is much different from concluding that they do not think coherently at all. If analysts were more careful to show how their assumptions guide their analysis and influence their interpretations, it might be possible to clear up many of the confusions about public opinion.

THE ROLE OF THEORY IN OPINION RESEARCH

The development of theories about opinion, society, and politics will accomplish two important things in the field of public opinion. First, the specification of concrete, testable variables that affect the formation and expression of opinion will reduce the tendency to overgeneralize about the nature of public opinion. This check on the state-of-consciousness perspective should make it easier to determine when differences in research findings merely reflect a realistic variation in opinion responses to different situations. It should also discourage the unproductive tendency to debate which findings reflect the true state of public consciousness. Second, the development of better theory about the factors that affect the formation and expression of opinion will provide clearer guidelines for the construction of measures of opinion and the choice of analytical methods.

Theories are simply general statements of knowledge about a subject. They are collections of definitions and explanations that allow us to make educated guesses about what the findings and interpretations of research add up to. We can think of individual studies and their findings as separate pieces in a large and complicated jigsaw puzzle. In solving most social puzzles, we don't know what the big picture looks like when we begin; but as we learn things about the subject, we can make guesses about the big picture. When the findings are few in number and their connections are unclear, the guesses are pretty crude and often misguided. As the findings from research become more plentiful, we have more to work with. We can try different configurations and make better guesses. As the guesses improve, they begin to simplify the search for particular missing pieces. The more complete a theoretical picture becomes, the more accurate are our guesses, or *hypotheses*, about what to look for and how to find it. As hypotheses are confirmed or rejected, the theory becomes more complete. We begin solving our theoretical puzzles with crude guesswork and many false starts, and we generally end up with a sure sense of what we are doing and how to fit the remaining pieces together. This process continues until we reach the final piece of the puzzle and know exactly where it goes, how it fits in, and what the completed picture represents.

The concept of theory has been introduced here in a metaphor that compares theorizing to solving jigsaw puzzles. It is important to understand the limits of the metaphor because there are important differences between theorizing and puzzle solving. In solving a jigsaw puzzle, we can gain a tremendous advantage by looking at the picture on the box and using it as a guide. We do not have such helpful clues in solving social puzzles. Also, social puzzles are almost always too complicated to be solved down to the last piece. We generally have to tolerate some guesswork and speculation in interpreting an almost complete picture. Social concepts like public opinion do not come with all their parts packaged in neat boxes; thus even the best theories may leave out part of the picture. It is also easy to reach a dead end with a theory as a result of making a bad guess about how the parts fit together or by trying to assemble the parts of different puzzles in the same framework.

Even partial theories can be helpful, however. They can help us see general relationships among research findings. They also can help to establish the significance of concepts. Even a simple theory of public opinion might give us a better sense of how concepts matter to society and to the people in society. Rough theories can also point out general causes and effects of concepts. They can clarify how something like public opinion changes and what its various social forms are.

The best way to appreciate the importance of theory is to see how it might enter our thinking about particular questions of public opinion. Let's suppose that you decide to accept the group of studies that show public opinion on the whole to be uninformed, unconstrained, and unstable. As a result of reading this chapter, you have a better sense of the limitations of these findings. You are also aware that there might be other ways to think about how political attitudes are organized and used. For example, it might make sense to pay more attention to the way individuals, instead of groups, are oriented to politics. Despite these concerns, you decide that it is reasonable to conclude that the opinions of the public as a whole do not have much in the way of common organization. This sounds like an important finding.

Now, ask yourself what this conclusion really means and why it is important. On the one hand you might assume it means that Americans have failed to live up to their responsibilities as citizens in a democracy. On the other hand you might assume it means that the American democracy has failed in its responsibility to provide adequate citizenship training and meaningful political experiences. These are quite different understandings about the findings. We need some clear basis for comparing them and deciding which one makes the most sense. The first step is to begin defining terms.

Even though the two explanations use the same terms, they probably have different meanings. For example, "democracy" as it is used in the first explanation probably refers to some classical definition of democracy—perhaps in the sense that democracy was practiced in ancient Greece or as it was described by Rousseau. In the second explanation, the term probably refers to the practical political arrangements that operate in the United States. Similarly, the concept of responsibility means different things in the two explanations.

When we begin defining terms clearly, we take the first step toward developing theories of public opinion. As the theories become better defined, we will see that each one provides a different explanation for such characteristics of public opinion as information, stability, and consistency. Each will generate different hypotheses about the causes, the effects, and the overall importance of these things. If we expanded the theories by testing the hypotheses, we would develop a better sense of which theory makes the most sense of certain findings. Perhaps we would even conclude that each theory explains some things pretty well, and parts of each explanation could be combined into a more general theory. In this fashion, theories of public opinion could help us understand the significance of our findings and see how they fit together. As theories clarify these important problems, we can begin to use them to guide research. Better explanations of how concepts actually work in the real world will lead to much better ideas about how to measure those concepts and how to analyze and interpret the data.

Many of the basic concepts in public opinion research have been developed and studied on the basis of little more than the common sense of pollsters and social scientists. This makes it difficult to understand new findings or to resolve conflicts between competing findings. The development of research in the area of political information, discussed in Chapter 2, is a good example of this. Only after an accumulation of studies showed that levels of information seemed to vary from one election to another did situational variables begin to enter thinking about information and opinion. However, this advance represents just one step toward understanding the relationships among information, opinion, and political context. In order to investigate these relationships in other cases of politics, it is necessary to have a better understanding of the nature of political information. In place of simple common-sense definitions there is a need for a precise theoretical formulation of what political information is. Such a framework might address the questions of when people become informed, what political conditions promote information seeking, and what kind of information is relevant to different political circumstances.

Even the obvious question of what constitutes real or meaningful political information is far from being resolved. Most studies about how "informed" the public is have used simplistic common-sense measures, such as knowing the differences between the Republican and Democratic parties, being able to identify various public officials, and knowing the particulars about current political issues and government programs. On the face of it, these seem like reasonable measures of "political information." The trouble is, we have never really studied what kinds of information people actually use in their daily political lives.[16] As a result, it is not clear what the findings about an "uninformed" public really mean.

For all we know, knowing the names of members of Congress, governors, cabinet officers, or Supreme Court justices may be no more useful politically than knowing such trivia as who costarred with Ronald Reagan in *Bedtime for Bonzo* or knowing the names of the horses ridden by Roy Rogers, Hopalong Cassidy, and the Lone Ranger. In fact, more people probably know social trivia than political trivia. Gallup once asked a sample of Americans this question: "Can you tell me what famous people, living or dead, made the following statements well known?"[17] The statements and the percentage of correct guesses are as follows:

Come up and see me sometime.	61%
The only thing we have to fear is fear itself.	37%
Speak softly and carry a big stick.	33%
The world must be made safe for democracy.	14%

At first it may seem shocking that only 14 percent of the public could place Woodrow Wilson's statement, while a clear majority recognized Mae West's famous line. However, the question remains whether this bit of political information is any less trivial than Ms. West's invitation. It could be argued that just the opposite is the case: The greater social relevance of "Come up and see me sometime" accounts for its higher recognition among the public. In the end, common-sense arguments supported by "shocking" findings are poor substitutes for careful definitions and sensitive measures.

The case is overstated here to make a point. We need to start building theories of public opinion if we are going to be able to judge how realistic our measures are and what our findings really mean. Knowing the names of public officials may be a less realistic measure of political information than something like knowing how to express political preferences effectively in different situations or knowing how to petition the government on various matters. (It is possible to know what public official to contact without knowing his or her name.) Unless we begin developing some simple but specific theories of public opinion and politics, we will never have a basis for making convincing judgments about what explanations make the most sense of findings from opinion research. Neither will we be in a good position to ask the right questions or to make the right guesses to guide future research.

A full-blown theory of public opinion is beyond the scope of this book. However, it is possible to make a start on it. The place to begin building theory is with what we already know and with the partial theories and hypotheses that already exist. The field of public opinion is rich with findings about the origins of opinions, the factors that cause opinions to change, the uses of political opinions, the connections between opinions and public policy, the role of interest groups in politics, the effect of information and political interest on the formation and expression of opinion, the role of the mass media in public opinion processes, and on and on and on. There are also the beginnings of simple hypotheses and theories about many of these things. In Chapter 4 will be presented the outlines of a simple theoretical framework that can be used to organize and interpret many of the existing scattered perspectives and, at the same time, chart some productive new approaches for the future.

NOTES

1. It is difficult to locate all the members of a large and diverse population. A carefully designed sampling procedure is more likely to produce a representative slice of the population. Also, the human errors involved in organizing a massive study (getting enough reliable interviewers, keeping track of the questionnaires, covering all the geo-

graphical areas, scoring the questionnaires properly) would probably
be greater than the errors that result from studying a scientific sample
of the population.
2. The general form of this equation is

$$\pm t \sqrt{p(1-p)/N-1}$$

where $t =$ the t statistic corresponding to the desired confidence
level of the estimate.

$p =$ the proportion of the relevant characteristic (such as
support for Candidate X) in the sample.

$N =$ the size of the sample.
3. For discussion purposes it is convenient to call alternative techniques
such as multistage and cluster sampling *random sampling techniques*.
4. For more detailed discussions of these procedures, the interested
reader should consult any of the numerous good books on survey research methods. Among the best are Charles H. Backstrom and Gerald D. Hursh, *Survey Research* (Evanston, Ill.: Northwestern
University Press, 1963); and Herbert F. Weisberg and Bruce D.
Bowen, *An Introduction to Survey Research and Data Analysis* (San Francisco: Freeman, 1977).
5. Michael Wheeler, *Lies, Damn Lies, and Statistics: The Manipulation of
Public Opinion in America* (New York: Liveright, 1976), p. 96.
6. See, for example, Christopher H. Achen, "Mass Political Attitudes
and the Survey Response," *American Political Science Review*, Vol. 69
(December 1975), pp. 1218–31; and Herbert B. Asher, "Some Consequences of Measurement Error in Survey Data," *American Journal of
Political Science*, Vol. 18 (May 1974), pp. 469–85.
7. Wheeler, *Lies, Damn Lies, and Statistics*, p. 92.
8. Ibid., p. 93.
9. See, for example, Alex Edelstein, *The Uses of Communication in Decision-making: A Comparative Study of Yugoslavia and the United States*
(New York: Praeger, 1974).
10. See, for example, Steven R. Brown and John D. Ellithorpe, "Emotional Experiences in Political Groups: The Case of the McCarthy Phenomenon," *American Political Science Review*, Vol. 64 (June 1970), pp.
349–66.
11. Backstrom and Hursh, *Survey Research*, p. 87.
12. Reported in Wheeler, *Lies, Damn Lies, and Statistics*, p. 140.
13. Gallup Poll 337-K, question 1, polling date: December 14–19, 1944.
14. See, among others, Achen, "Mass Political Attitudes and the Survey
Response"; and Asher, "Some Consequences of Measurement Error
in Survey Data."
15. See, for example, W. Lance Bennett, *The Political Mind and the Political
Environment: An Investigation of Public Opinion and Political Consciousness* (Lexington, Mass.: Heath, Lexington Books, 1975), ch. 2; and W.
Lance Bennett, "Public Opinion Problems of Description and Inference," in *Public Opinion: Its Measurement, Meaning and Impact*, ed. Susan Welch and John Comer (Palo Alto, Calif.: Mayfield, 1975), pp.
117–31.

16. For an excellent related discussion of the problems of deciding what is "real" about ideology and how to study it, see Steven R. Brown and Richard W. Taylor, "Perspective in Concept Formation," *Social Science Quarterly*, Vol. 52 (March 1972), pp. 852–60.

17. The authors of the statements are, in order, Mae West, Franklin D. Roosevelt, Theodore Roosevelt, and Woodrow Wilson. Source: Gallup Polls 577-K and 578-K2, questions 2 and 20, polling date: January 17–22, 1957, and February 7–12, 1957.

4

A Theory
of
Public Opinion

A THEORY OF PUBLIC OPINION and American politics must achieve several goals. First, a good theory should be stated in a way that minimizes the state-of-consciousness fallacy. It must take into account changes both in the public and in the political context in different situations. Such a formulation will help analysts avoid the tendency to regard opinion as the product of general states of consciousness, and it will also enable them to think about meaningful ranges of opinion and the degree to which differences in research findings have theoretical or methodological explanations.

Second, a good theory of opinion should guide the use of research methods. The fators that affect the formation and expression of opinion need to be defined well enough to convey clearly information about how to construct questions, record responses, and analyze data. The connections between opinion research methods and real political variables should be apparent, to aid the interpretation of different findings that emerge from different methods and measures.

A somewhat different requirement for a political theory of opinion is that it should address existing literature and research as much as possible. Little will be gained from a theory that turns its back on what we already know. The fact that there are disputes about the meaning of findings means not that different findings are wrong, but that they need to be interpreted. Similarly, the fact that different perspectives on public opinion are scattered through several academic fields does not mean that some of these perspectives cannot be incorporated in one way or another into a general framework. In fact, the framework in this book will be useful if it does nothing other than provide a sensible way to integrate diverse perspectives.

Finally, a good theory should be simple—not just because this is an introductory book, but because little is to be gained by an overly complex picture of opinion and politics. A theory is helpful only if it gives people a grasp of basic principles. If the principles are adequate, they can be extended quickly into more complex areas.

COMPONENTS OF
AN OPINION SITUATION

An opinion situation is composed of three parts: (1) the belief systems of individuals, (2) the object (that is, the issue, candidate, event, etc.) that people are judging, and (3) the way in which the situation itself channels and limits the expression of opinion. Common sense should tell us that opinion must be affected by some combination of what the public believes and values, how the issue (or other object of opinion) is defined, and how the expression of opinion is limited by the situation.

Individual Beliefs

Men and women can bring to bear many different beliefs, values, and levels of concern when they judge issues and other objects of opinion. The stronget beliefs can affect the scope, direction, intensity, and distribution of opinion. The impact of beliefs is well illustrated by changes in public opinion during the energy crisis of 1979.

Since the energy crisis of 1973–1974, the American public had been skeptical about how real the energy shortage was. Most people believed that the shortage was due either to manipulation by the oil companies or to the failure of the government and the oil companies to develop domestic energy sources properly. In spite of the widespread disbelief, however, all three American Presidents from 1973 to 1979 acted as though the shortage was genuine. Nixon, Ford, and Carter proposed similar programs to deal with the energy problem, and their main proposals were based on the assumption that the oil shortage was real and permanent. Because only a small percentage of the public shared this belief, it is not surprising that the energy programs generated little favorable opinion. In the spring of 1979, for example, only 16 percent of the public approved of the way in which President Carter was handling the energy problem.[1]

During the first half of 1979, Carter made two major speeches about the energy problem. At the time of these speeches the country was suffering the effects of a severe gasoline shortage and rapid price increases that were sending the price of gasoline over a dollar a gallon. Economists were citing the energy situation as a major factor in their predictions for a gloomy economic future. Carter's public rating as President had dropped almost perfectly in keeping with the steep decline in approval for his handling of the economy.[2] In the spring of 1979, his overall approval rating was even lower than Richard Nixon's popularity had been in the last days of the Watergate crisis.

Carter's second energy speech, in July 1979, was widely regarded as the most critical moment in his political career. The speech was acclaimed as his most powerful and convincing political performance. Cater's opinion advisers had interpreted the public mood as one that called for firm action on energy. Moreover, Carter's analysis saw a connection in the public mind between energy, the economy, and the loss of public confidence in national leadership. In the speech Carter emphasized the seriousness of these three problems and asserted that they required a common solution:

> Energy will be the immediate test of our ability to unite this nation. . . . On the battlefield of energy we can win for our nation a new confidence, and we can seize control again of our common destiny. . . . Our excessive dependence on OPEC has already taken a tremendous toll on our economy and our people. This is the direct cause of the long lines that have made millions of you spend aggravating hours waiting for gasoline. It's a cause of the increased inflation and unemployment that we now face. . . . The energy crisis is real. It is worldwide. It is a clear and present danger to our nation. These are the facts and we simply must face them.[3]

This appeal did not produce just a temporary surge in public approval (as almost any presidential performance will do); it produced a change in public beliefs about the oil shortage. Prior to the speech only 26 percent of the public believed that the energy shortage was real. After the speech a national poll showed that 35 percent of the public believed in the existence of an energy shortage.[4] This surge in belief was accompanied by an equally dramatic increase in support (from 16 percent to 34 percent) for Carter's proposals for handling the energy problem, even though those proposals were similar to his earlier recommendations in their reference to a real and enduring energy shortage. As pointed out in Chapter 1, Carter's earlier efforts to sell the public his energy program had been dismal failures. Compared to the earlier speeches, Carter's last energy speech in July of 1979 was an improvement. However, the level of support this speech generated for his energy program still fell far short of majority approval. More importantly, as explained in Chapter 1, the speech failed in its major goal: mobilizing general public support for Carter's overall leadership. This example shows that even when leaders read public opinion accurately enough to produce some changes in individual beliefs about specific issues, other factors in the opinion situation may work against desired political expressions of opinion.

The Definition of the Issue*

It is important to bear in mind that beliefs are not the only variables operating in opinion situations. The way in which issues and other objects of opinion are defined also has an important effect on the formation of opinion. For example, Carter presented the issue of the energy shortage in the context of a unique set of factors. Not only did inflation, gas prices, and inconvenience affect the probable meaning of the issue at that time, but Carter defined the issue in a special way. Throughout his speech he equated the energy issue with larger issues concerning the economy and national morale. In a case like this, the definitional context surrounding the issue may produce changes in public opinion. New social conditions can give rise to new beliefs, and new connections with other issues can lead people to use a broader set of beliefs and values when they think about an issue. Carter's attempt to equate energy with the economy and the national spirit may have induced people to think about the energy problem in terms of beliefs and values normally used in thinking about the economy or the state of the nation.

---

*Since issues are the objects most often associated with public opinion, in this chapter "issue" may be taken to refer to all objects of opinion. In Chapters 8, 9, 10, and 11, distinctions will be made between issues and other objects such as candidates, leaders, political organizations, symbols of authority, and events.

The real-world effects of redefining an object of opinion are parallel to the effects (discussed in Chapters 2 and 3) of changing the wording of a question on opinion surveys. Similarly, the real-world impact of creating new connections between one issue and other issues can be similar to the effects on opinion surveys of changing the circumstances surrounding the presentation of an issue. This was illustrated in Chapter 3 by the surveys in which different circumstances were cited in the survey questions about issues of racial discrimination and government policies during the Vietnam War.

The impact on opinion of both issue definition and the circumstances surrounding the issue is illustrated dramatically by the public's reaction to a nuclear accident near Harrisburg, Pennsylvania, in March 1979. The trouble at the Three Mile Island power plant was the most serious disaster ever to strike a nuclear energy facility. Mechanical malfunction and human error resulted in the escape of large amounts of radioactive gas into the atmosphere. The nuclear reactor came very close to a meltdown, which could have damaged the containment building and released deadly quantities of radioactive matter into the air and water. The potential danger of such an event to the lives and health of millions of people was grave. The actual damage done by the accident was both costly and frightening in terms of its unknown future effects.

The drama that unfolded over the course of two weeks at Three Mile Island was one of the most powerful news stories in years. A Gallup Poll showed that a full 96 percent of the public knew about the trouble at Three Mile Island. This high level of familiarity held true for all the demographic groups in the sample, including age, sex, race, education, income, occupation, and region.[5] The events at Three Mile Island undermined public confidence in the reliability of nuclear power. Seventy-five percent of those surveyed felt that a similar accident was likely to happen again at some future date.[6] In response to such concerns, 62 percent of the sample expressed opposition to the idea of a nuclear plant being built within five miles of their homes. In a survey taken before the Three Mile Island accident, the sentiment against living near a nuclear power plant had been only 45 percent.[7]

These responses to the incident at Three Mile Island would lead one to expect a sharp increase in opinion against the development of more nuclear energy. However, opinion on this crucial issue did not change much at all. In 1976, 34 percent of the public felt that it was "extremely important" to develop more nuclear power to meet the energy needs of the country. The week after the accident in Pennsylvania, the level of support dropped only five points, to 29 percent. Similarly, the 1976 Gallup Poll showed that 37 percent felt that the development of more nuclear power was "somewhat important." The week after the disaster near Harrisburg, the numbers in this group dropped only three points to 34 percent. Despite the costly and dangerous accident at Three Mile Island, support for the development of more nuclear power dropped only eight points, from 71 percent to 63 percent.[8]

In order to understand the relative stability of opinion in the face of a catastrophic event, it is important to understand how the issue of nuclear energy became defined in the wake of the Harrisburg disaster. The first important factor affecting the definition of the issue was that the country was already experiencing an energy crisis caused by dependence on foreign oil and a shortage of domestic sources of energy. When the Three Mile Island disaster struck, the issue of nuclear energy had immediate reference both to the human dangers raised by the incident and to the clear need to develop domestic energy sources. Had the accident not occurred in the midst of the energy crisis, the social context of the issue might have been dominated less by the energy problem and more by concerns about human risks.

The second crucial factor affecting the definition of the issue was the effort of the Carter administration to emphasize the linkage between nuclear energy and the solution to the energy shortage. In the weeks during and after the accident, Secretary of Energy James Schlesinger made numerous speeches, held press conferences, and appeared on news interview programs. He stressed the need for nuclear energy as the only near-term solution for America's dependence on foreign oil. He argued that the risks of nuclear energy had to be weighed against the needs of the nation. This linkage of nuclear energy with a larger national issue reinforced conditions operating in the immediate social context—rising fuel prices, long lines at gas stations, and a sluggish but inflation-ridden economy. Opinion polls taken immediately after the Three Mile Island accident show that these aspects of the definition of the issue had strong effects on the formation of opinion about nuclear energy.

The most dramatic result from the polls was the response to the Gallup question asking people, "Which do you think presents the greater risk to the nation—the presence of nuclear plants or the energy shortage that might result if these plants were eliminated?"

The majority of the public (56 percent) felt that an energy short-age was a greater national risk than the presence of nuclear power plants (31 percent).[9] Another item from this survey revealed how much the thinking about nuclear energy was affected by economic considerations. When asked if they were willing to pay higher prices for energy in order to reduce dependence on nuclear ener-gy, 50 percent of the public said "no."[10] These underlying dynam-ics of the public's reaction to the Three Mile Island accident indicate how much opinion can be affected by the definition of an issue in a specific situation. At another time, in another place, and beset by other concerns, public opinion about nuclear energy might have been much different.

Situational Constraints

The third component of an opinion situation is the way in which the norms and the structure of the situation itself channel and limit the expression of opinion. In some situations powerful norms in-hibit the expression of some opinions and encourage the expres-sion of others. Opinion situations also may contain formal rules for selecting and defining the issues and candidates that become the objects of opinion. In Chapter 1, for example, it was shown how the emergence of "yes" or "no" voting options affected the distri-bution and intensity of opinion. Many of the political processes of Congress, the courts, and government bureaucracy limit the defini-tion of issues and regulate the ways in which the public can re-spond to them.

Situational limits on issue definitions and the formal regulation of responses can affect virtually every characteristic of opinion. The real-world structuring of opinion has parallels in survey re-search—most notably in the construction of response formats and the choice of methods for eliciting responses. In order to explain the formation, expression, and impact of opinion it is necessary to understand how situational constraints operate. It is equally impor-tant to learn how to duplicate these constraints on opinion with survey research techniques.

The action of official government agencies in the aftermath of the Three Mile Island incident provides a good illustration of situa-tional constraints on the expression of opinion. At every step of the way from the initial accident to the follow-up investigation, various state, local, and federal agencies controlled the presentation of information to the public and provided channels for public responses to the events. The official procedures used by these agencies exerted as much effect on opinion about nuclear power as did the beliefs of the public or the issue definitions put forward by interested politicians.

The capacity of the officials in charge of the situation to regulate the flow of information undoubtedly softened the intensity of the public's reaction to the disaster. The first news stories reported a small leak and a cooling problem at the plant. Later stories implied that the situation was under control and not serious. Not until several days after the original accident was the public informed of the dangerously high temperatures and potentially explosive gases inside the reactor. Many of the most significant bits of information were not disclosed until after the incident was over—even though later investigations revealed that state and federal (and utility company) officials recognized the magnitude of the problem soon after the first signs of trouble.

It was argued by some of the officials in charge (such as the Governor of Pennsylvania) that the control, the delay, and the distortion of information were all necessary in order to prevent panic. Indeed, this goal was accomplished by the way in which information management techniques limited the scope and intensity of opinion and minimized the level of public outrage toward the government and the utility company. However, it could be argued that this management of information also prevented people in the area from making rational choices about whether to evacuate their homes and when to return to them. Moreover, the failure to disclose certain facts at the time that public attention was riveted on the developing events may have altered the direction and intensity of opinions formed about the true risks and dangers of nuclear energy.

After the crisis at the plant had been brought under control, another set of official procedures shaped the way in which the situation was concluded and public responses were registered. President Carter appointed an official commission to investigate the incident, receive testimony, and determine the causes. The commission also received input from concerned citizens and made public recommendations about safety procedures at nuclear plants.

As Lipsky and Olson pointed out in their study of commissions appointed to investigate the urban riots in the 1960s, official panels can affect public opinion about an issue in a number of ways.[11]

The simple act of extending the discussion of an issue over a long period of time in tedious hearings distracts public interest and breaks up any focused expression of opinion. The use of commissions as forums for communication with the public diverts opinion into official institutional channels, where its expression is likely to be less volatile and less threatening to official interests. Perhaps most importantly, commissions produce official versions of what happened and what to do about it. These official positions become lightning rods, attracting public debate and keeping public opinion away from dangerous topics and extreme positions.

THE SEEDS OF A GENERAL THEORY OF OPINION

Situational constraints, as well as individual beliefs and issue definitions, have been described in a general way so far. They have not yet been defined precisely enough to permit solid explanations of actual opinion situations. Each can take different forms and produce different effects in different situations. For example, many persuasion techniques may be used to define issues, and the impact of each technique may vary, depending on how it is communicated to the public. Thus the discussion of issue definition needs to be enlarged to include specific variables that can shape the definition of political issues (and other objects) and affect opinion. Similarly, it is necessary to identify the specific factors that shape individual beliefs and situational constraints. In Chapter 1, three domains of opinion were mentioned: (1) the domain of the individual and society, (2) the domain of issue formation and political communication, and (3) the domain of political institutions and culture. Each of these domains contains a set of factors that explain the workings of a different component of an opinion situation.

Variables at work in the domain of the individual and society affect individual beliefs. Most important are political socialization, opinion formation routines, and personality. Each of them affects the individual's response to the political world.

Issue definition is the result of issue formation and political communication. Thus, explaining issue definition in a particular situation requires a familiarity with variables in the domain of issue formation and political communication. It is important to understand where issues come from and what role the public plays in creating the issues that occupy the agendas of political institutions. It is also necessary to identify the techniques of persuasion and symbolization that shape the definitions of issues. Finally, the way in which political messages are transmitted to the public by the news media plays a major role in the definition of issues.

Factors in the domain of political institutions and culture explain how constraints on the expression of opinion operate in real political situations. Every political institution regulates the expression of opinion. Moreover, institutions operate in ways that maintain the basic values of the culture; thus issues that develop within institutions invariably take on familiar forms and reflect traditional values. These cultural patterns also limit the ways in which opinion operates politically.

The theoretical framework of this book will take root from discussions of the specific factors in each domain of opinion. The emphasis will be on how those variables affect opinion and how they work together in the political system. The remainder of Chapter 4 provides an overview of the key variables in the three domains of opinion, leading to the formulation of a general theory.

THE DOMAIN OF THE
INDIVIDUAL AND SOCIETY

As suggested in Chapter 1, values give meaning to life experiences when they are connected to the world through beliefs. Beliefs tell us how the world works, why people do what they do, why values are relevant, and how to apply values to the world. For example, the value of self-reliance may be supported and applied to the world through a system of beliefs about people and society: People are resourceful; people will take care of themselves if they have to; self-reliance builds character; "getting a handout" from the government destroys pride and self-respect. Perhaps the value of self-reliance is buttressed and applied through beliefs about who can be trusted and why it is unwise to turn to outsiders for help.

A second-generation Italian who grew up in Little Italy in New York learned the value of self-reliance in the context of a set of beliefs about who could be trusted in times of need:

> Pop used to talk to Joe and me on how important it was . . . to make sure that we had friends who we could trust. If he told us once, he told us a thousand times that you couldn't trust the judges and the politicians to do anything for you because they didn't understand the way things worked in the Italian district. Judges did everything

by the book or even worse, they did what they were told by the politicians who were out to get all they could from hardworking souls. The only protection was to take care of yourself and to make sure you had friends you could count on when the time came. Pop always said he trusted Italians more than Americans, Sicilians more than Italians, his *paisani* more than other Sicilians but most of all he trusted his family.[12]

That is a miniature prescription for living. Each of us holds on to a number of social values and related beliefs that connect the values to real life. These enduring dispositions and understandings are known as *systems of belief*. They guide us in selecting the everyday events that we pay attention to and in judging these events as they occur. In short, belief systems shape our daily concerns and provide the basis for our opinions on specific matters. For example, a person who places a high value on self-reliance and is struggling to maintain dignity in a marginal existence may find some issues much more important or troubling than others. Such a person is more likely to express concern about the welfare problem than about a question like how America is going to solve its future energy needs. The opinions that this person forms on the welfare question will have certain characteristics that follow from the nature of his or her belief system and life experiences.

The most important and fascinating question about public opinion is how large numbers of individual orientations become transformed into a smaller array of opinion about an issue. In order to explain this process, three variables in the domain of the individual and society must be understood. These areas (to be explored fully in Chapters 5, 6, and 7) are: (1) political socialization, (2) opinion formation routines, and (3) personality. Each factor accounts for important features of the political beliefs of individuals, and each links the individual to the general public in a significant way.

Political Socialization

The learning processes through which individuals acquire political beliefs and values are known collectively as *socialization*. However, the study of socialization is not just the study of individuals. It is also the investigation of common sources of political learning and the analysis of similarities and differences in the political experiences of different groups. As a result of the latter concern, the study of political socialization can tell us about the distribution of basic values and beliefs across the population.[13] Perhaps most importantly, the study of socialization offers clues about how to measure the pattern of values and beliefs operating in a public in any given opinion situation.

Opinion Formation Routines

Simply knowing the distribution of values and beliefs does not guarantee a sure understanding of the opinions that will emerge. It is also necessary to know what kinds of thinking go into the formation of opinion. Values and beliefs can become connected to an object of opinion in a variety of ways.[14] For example, individuals can form opinions by exploring the logic of an issue, by evaluating issues according to the views of social reference groups, and by weighing an issue against all the various values and beliefs it brings to mind. To some degree these routines are idiosyncratic—that is, their use depends on the psychological make-up of each individual. But even if the formation of opinion were entirely idiosyncratic, it would still be important to know how individuals form their political judgments. There is increasing evidence that people use different routines under different circumstances.[15] This finding suggests that the way an issue is presented and the social and emotional atmosphere of an opinion situation can affect the routines that will be employed. Thus an understanding of opinion formation is essential for explaining patterns of public opinion in different situations.

Personality

The domain of the individual and society is not governed by purely rational forces. In the most immediate sense, politics itself is not a rational business. It deals with the give and take of values that may lie at the center of individual personalities. For example, when court rulings increase protection for the rights of defendants or restrict the activities of police, people may get upset for reasons that have little to do with formal philosophies of law and justice. Some individuals may be comfortable with the idea of strict law and order because it appeals to deep security needs that have little to do with the impact of court decisions on crime rates or real-life experiences. Other individuals may find that the idea that a criminal is "getting off easy" threatens their own efforts to control aggressive impulses or leads them to project their fears that, in the absence of harsh punishment, other men and women will be unable to control their antisocial impulses.

There is a second sense in which the emotional undercurrents of opinion are important. Political events are distant from the life experiences of most of the public. Economic policies, international affairs, and court decisions involve issues and occur in arenas that have little immediate reference for most people.[16] Moreover, the impact of opinion on the resolution of political affairs is often not clear. These factors, taken together, invite people to use the actors, the dramas, and the powerful forces in the political world as objects onto which private fears, hopes, conflicts, and fantasies can be projected.[17] Much of what goes on in the political realm may become a target for personal imaginings and emotional release. This possibility has led to the idea that opinions—besides being a socially effective means of promoting one's beliefs and values by reacting to ongoing political issues—may serve a number of powerful emotional functions, ranging from simple reality orientation, to emotional release, to social adjustment.

The simple act of forming an opinion becomes a reassuring means of staying in touch with the outer world. Through this process, termed the *object appraisal function* of opinions,[18] people create a sense of a stable, objective world around them. In addition, opinion serves an *externalization function*, permitting individuals to express their personal doubts, conflicts, and hopes. For example, opinions about the importance of self-sufficiency and the kind of people who would accept welfare instead of a job may make it possible for some people to deal with their own frustrations and find a measure of sanity and satisfaction in an otherwise troubling existence. As Lane suggests, opinion may provide "an explanation for their situation in life; it helps explain things to their wives, who take their status from them; it permits their growing children to account for relative social status in school; it offers to each man the satisfactions of social identity and a measure of social worth."[19] The object appraisal function of opinion brings the outer world into personal focus; the externalization function gives personal concerns an external or objective meaning. In this sense, opinion brings the outer world in and carries the inner world out.

Opinion also has something to do with social adjustment. The formation and expression of opinion does not go on in isolation from other people. Opinions are social statements in response to social experiences. They may be influenced by other people, and the way we express them may depend on who our audience is and how its members figure into our lives. It is difficult to be confident about the objectivity of a judgment, or to find satisfaction in it, if it is rejected by those who hear it—particularly if they are people whom we like and respect. Moreover, it is hard to continue to like and respect people (and for them to respond similarly) if there is constant disagreement about important matters.

The *social adjustment function* of opinion has a direct impact on our relations with other people. Our opinions have a lot to do with whom we get along with and whom we don't. They may influence our decisions about joining some groups and leaving others. Opinions may even help us form a picture of society by providing a basis for identifying with or becoming antagonistic toward distant groups concerned about the things that matter to us. Opinions are the invisible membership cards of society. They tell us who is like us and who is different. They are clues about who may be with us and who may be against us. Opinions held in common are powerful bonds. We may have lots of minor disagreements with our friends, family, and associates, but the chances are pretty good that we will agree with them on basic issues. If basic agreement does not exist, it is hard to maintain close relationships. So strong is the social bonding-power of opinion that people may change their opinions (and perhaps their underlying beliefs and values) when they make major changes in life, such as moving, leaving home, starting a new job, going away to college, or getting married.

These underlying psychological factors can help explain why groups, as well as individuals, with similar values and beliefs may form different opinions about an issue. Various conditions in the political world can affect the emotional orientations of a public. Periods of social change and unrest can increase social adjustment concerns. Under such circumstances the expression of opinions can become both a means of advocating new social values and an invitation to join forces with others who may need social support. In other cases, the fears, threats, and crises that occur in the political world may both stimulate efforts to bring the world into better focus (object appraisal) and increase the desire to express personal concerns and anxieties through opinions. Arnold,[20] Edelman,[21] and Lasswell[22] have shown how important such conditions can be for arousing public emotions and how various definitions of issues can channel the resulting opinions into powerful political forces. A better understanding of the conditions that arouse, channel, and satisfy various emotional orientations will represent a major breakthrough in opinion analysis.[23]

THE POLITICAL SIGNIFICANCE OF POLITICAL BELIEFS

Not only do the various belief system variables in the domain of the individual and society explain important patterns in opinion situations, but they provide insights about the political impact of public opinion. When public opinion is viewed from a single general perspective, it is easy to think that its only major role is as an input to policy making. That is how public opinion is defined in the classical theory of opinion and democracy, and that is the most obvious place to start thinking about the political significance of opinion. However, breaking opinion down into its various domains and reducing the domains to their basic elements makes it clear that opinion has numerous political functions, which operate both in specific situations and in the political system as a whole.

It is helpful to consider the specific political functions of the variables in the domain of the individual and society before turning to their general impact on the political system. The values and beliefs produced by socialization and distributed over a population of citizens account for the range of political orientations present in each opinion situation. The presence of particular groups will indicate the potential existence of certain values underlying opinion. Socialization patterns also explain the existence of both particular broadly shared political outlooks and narrow and divisive perspectives. The degree to which relevant values and beliefs are shared helps to explain why particular issues may trigger widespread consensus while others may evoke intense group conflicts. In short, the distribution of values and beliefs in a public sets the outer limits on the possible expressions of public opinion in a situation.

The operation of various opinion formation routines can affect the development of an opinion situation. The existence of particular states of mind and habits in a group in a given situation makes that group more susceptible to certain kinds of political appeal than to others. For example, if the beliefs of a group tend to be based on logical considerations about a particular issue and the political context is not very emotional, emotion-based propaganda techniques may have little impact on the formation of opinion about the issue.

The existence of various opinion formation routines may have a strong effect on opinion when particular political conditions are present. For example, we know that some people base their voting decisions primarily on social references such as identification with a political party (resulting in a tendency to vote for the party's candidates) and reliance on information from respected labor, religious, or political groups (resulting in a tendency to vote for candidates endorsed by such groups). These voters can experience serious conflicts when a candidate endorsed by a reference group runs under the banner of the opposing party.

That sort of cross-pressure may have been experienced in the 1976 election by many "born again" Christians who were loyal Republicans. In some cases they may have resolved the conflict by shifting their votes to the Democratic candidate, Jimmy Carter, who also was a "born again" Christian; while in other cases, the conflict may have led people to refrain from voting at all.

Personality and emotional arousal also have important effects on the outcomes of opinion situations. Unless opinions satisfy deep psychological needs such as reality orientation and social adjustment, participation in politics will become a very empty matter. If the underlying psychological satisfactions are absent, people may form opinions only when an issue has some direct and major impact on their private lives. The larger emotional functions of opinion explain a great deal about what motivates people to become interested in issues and to regard their own judgments as important. Broad emotional feedback from opinions helps determine the scope of opinion and the meaning and satisfaction of political involvement.

Each factor in the domain of the individual and society has a place in every opinion situation. We can generalize about the patterns of values and beliefs that recur in various situations, the opinion formation routines used by different individuals and groups in different contexts, and the levels of emotional satisfaction present in various political contexts. These generalizations become important indicators of a major feature of a political system—its political integration.

Political integration refers to the presence of common bonds and the absence of enduring opposition and withdrawal among groups in the population. One aspect of integration is the degree of value consensus that is likely to emerge in most opinion situations. Such consensus increases the chances for the stable and effective resolution of conflicts. Another aspect of political integration is the de-

TABLE 4-1
The Domain of the Individual and Society

Variables	*Specific Political Consequences*	*General System Consequences*
Political socialization	Distribution of values and beliefs	
	Limitations on opinion formation	
Opinion formation routines	Susceptibility to various appeals	Political integration
	Opinion change	Stability
Personality	Limitations on political involvement	
	Political satisfaction	

gree to which the opinion formation processes operating in different groups are able to respond to (or utilize) common issues and concerns. When the same issues and symbols can be assimilated meaningfully by diverse groups, the levels of mutual understanding and clear political communication are increased. Finally, to the extent that individuals tend to find meaning in a broad range of issues, the composition of groups will tend to be diverse and broad rather than homogeneous and narrow. This diversity enhances the sense of common interest and promotes the value of political involvement.

The specific and general political consequences of variables in the domain of the individual and society are itemized in Table 4-1. It is important to notice that these variables are often overlooked in general perspectives that focus on public policy as the main political outcome of the opinion process. It will become clear that the relationship between opinion and policy is important. However, it is also important to recognize that the opinion expressed in any political situation can serve political functions in addition to, and sometimes instead of, policy making. This recognition opens up a much broader understanding of the role of opinion in the overall workings of the political system.

THE DOMAIN OF ISSUE FORMATION AND POLITICAL COMMUNICATION

The variables in the domain of the individual and society alone are not sufficient to explain what kinds of opinion will emerge in particular situations or what the political effects of opinion will be. In order to understand such things it is necessary to explore issues (and other objects of opinion) and their impact on beliefs.

Three general questions pertain to the impact of issues on opinion. The first question will be addressed in Chapter 8: How do issues rise to the public's attention? This concern with the origin of political issues directs attention to the political actors who are responsible for promoting an issue and the circumstances in which an issue enters the field of public awareness. The second question about the formation and communication of issues has to do with definition and persuasion: How are issues defined and symbolized, and how do they mesh with opinion formation routines? These concerns will be addressed in Chapters 9 and 10. The third question will be raised in Chapter 11, which is about the political uses of the mass communications media: How are political definitions and images transmitted to the public, and what impact do the news media have on the political message received by the public?

The Origin of the Issue

It is helpful to know what partisan groups or actors were instrumental in bringing an issue to the public's attention. Some issues can be traced to the efforts of special interest groups. Others seem to emerge in response to broad, grassroots concerns. Still others appear to be the work of powerful elites who have the resources, credibility, and public exposure to single-handedly place a political question before the public. The social origin of an issue can affect the perceived importance of the issue, the legitimacy of proposed solutions, and the scope of public involvement.

The efforts of interest groups often produce a small but intensely committed core of public support for an issue. The stable and intense qualities of public opinion on many interest group issues help to keep these matters alive on the public agenda over long periods of time. The issues supported by environmental groups like the Sierra Club are good examples of interest group activity accompanied by committed but narrow public involvement.

A contrasting pattern often occurs with grassroots issues. Concerns that seem to capture broad-based public interest often result in bursts of massive public involvement followed by the break-up of support and loss of interest. Such episodes may give birth to interest organizations that keep the issues alive on a smaller scale, but the scope and intensity of opinion may fluctuate drastically.

For example, in 1978 the country was swept with the spirit of a taxpayers' revolt. Enough grassroots support existed in California to put an initiative on the state ballot calling for a dramatic reduction in the property tax rate. The measure (Proposition 13) passed overwhelmingly. This strong showing of public opinion led news analysts to speculate about the possibility of a taxpayers' revolt sweeping the nation. Politicians began to incorporate the tax issue into their speeches. However, after the election, the issue seemed to drop from prominence almost as quickly as it had emerged. Several special interest organizations were left behind to keep the issue alive and to work for its reappearance in the next election. But the massive display of public opinion that had emerged during the brief election period subsided after the voters won a preliminary victory at the ballot box.

The introduction of issues by elites can affect opinion in a number of ways. Prominent political officials who control information about an issue and who have the resources to create public exposure can virtually determine the nature of public reaction. The case of defense policy during the cold war is a classic example. In the 1950s the military, the Congress, and the President exposed the public to a fairly steady diet of frightening estimates of Soviet military strength and political intentions. The reports were often terrifying, and the recommendations seemed inescapable: If the United States was to survive in the race with the Soviet Union, serious commitments would have to be made to build up America's military arsenal. The official, informed, and highly visible origins of the issue galvanized broad-based public support for high levels of defense spending. In the early 1960s, when President John Kennedy proposed to ease tensions between the Soviet Union and the United States by signing a treaty limiting the development and testing of nuclear weapons, many high-level military and State Department officials were alarmed. The suggestion that the two nations were moving toward peaceful reconciliation would make it more difficult for the military elite to control perceptions of national defense issues. The chair of the Joint Chiefs of Staff reported in testimony to a Senate committee that a treaty would lull the public into complacency and produce a "euphoria" that might "reduce our vigilance."[24]

Not only do issues originate from different sectors of the political population, but they also emerge under different circumstances. Some are anchored in more or less enduring life experiences. Economic issues are good examples of *structural issues*—political concerns that are embedded in the social and economic structure of society and that touch broad life experiences directly over long periods of time. In contrast to them are many issues that confront the public primarily because they occupy a place on the policy agenda of government. The government may make special efforts to make these issues visible and to shape public reaction to them. Insofar as these *agenda issues* are immediate and real, they are made so by the information campaigns and persuasion efforts of the government. A third sort of issue emerges through social, economic, or political crisis. When the country is threatened, or when civil violence breaks out, or when an energy shortage hits, the *crisis issues* involved rise to overnight prominence. The flow of information under such circumstances is unstable, and public opinion may be volatile.

FIGURE 4-1
Patterns of Opinion Reflecting Different Types of Political Issue

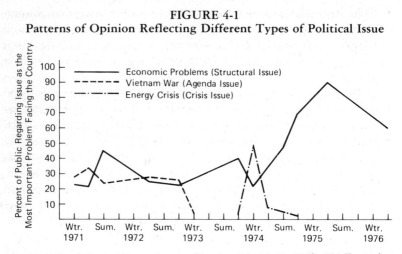

Source: Gallup Polls. 824-K, question 2, polling date: Feb. 19–22, 1971; 831-K, question 2A, polling date: June 4–7, 1971; 836-K, question 2A, polling date: Aug. 27–30, 1971.

These types of issue differ in important respects. Structural issues provide individuals a direct and independent basis for judgment. Concrete and stable exposure to these issues should make opinion fairly stable and constrained within various social and economic groups. Agenda issues are real because the government makes them real. Therefore, opinion characteristics in response to agenda issues are a function both of how the issues are presented in relation to other public concerns and of the frequency of shifts in government positions on them. Crisis issues are generally short-lived, unstable, and emotionally charged. Opinion during a crisis may depart radically from opinion about the same or similar issues in normal times.

Figure 4-1 indicates at least one dimension on which the three types of issue differ. The structural issue in the figure involves economic problems such as inflation, unemployment, and the cost of living. Notice that it generates a fairly substantial level of public concern across the entire time period covered by the chart. This *baseline effect*, which is characteristic of structural issues, emerges in public reactions to the importance of economic problems in poll data for the last thirty years. The increase in public concern departing from the baseline in 1974 reflects the serious economic downturn that began in that year.

The agenda issue involves public concerns about the situation in

Vietnam and the resolution of political problems in that country. As is typical of agenda questions, public concern about problems in Vietnam disappeared the moment the government dropped the issue from its agenda and stopped mobilizing public support for its policies.

The crisis issue shown in Figure 4-1 is the first major energy crisis, which struck the nation in late 1973 and early 1974. The pattern of public concern conforms to the typical pattern of crisis issues—an intense burst of concern followed by the almost complete disappearance of arousal when the surface conditions of the crisis disappear. It is clear that the energy problem was not resolved in 1974, yet increased supplies of fuel and government reassurances that the situation was under control effectively channeled public attention to other matters.

Issue Definition and
Persuasion Strategies

Whatever its origins, the meaning and impact of an issue will vary according to how it is defined. The energy crisis of 1973–1974 was not presented to the public in the same way as the energy crisis of 1979. The economic recession of 1975 was defined differently by the Ford administration than the economic troubles of 1979–1980 were handled by the Carter administration. The way in which an issue is defined and the persuasion strategies developed around that definition are crucial variables. The reason is simple: The variables in the domain of the individual and society (political socialization, opinion formation routines, and personality) respond differently to different kinds of input. Beliefs and values will be activated in different ways depending on how people perceive an issue. The public's perception depends in large part on the symbols that define the issue (and, of course, on the origins of the issue). This principle was illustrated in Chapter 1 with the example of the way in which the antismoking issue was defined by its opponents. The importance of issue definition was also demonstrated earlier in this chapter, by Carter's efforts to change public response to the energy problem by equating energy with other issues. As the more extensive discussion in Chapter 9 will show, there is increasing evidence that the way in which issues and other political objects are symbolized can have dynamic effects on the values and beliefs they engage and the opinions that result.[25]

The impact of a symbolic definition will depend to some degree on the persuasion strategy used to present it to an audience. People may use different psychological routines to establish the connections between values, beliefs, and political issues. Connections may be made in various ways, depending on whether the persuasion technique emphasizes an endorsement strategy (a social reference process), a rational choice strategy (an information and formal logic approach), or some other strategy.[26]

It is also clear that the degree to which definition and persuasion strategies arouse emotional responses will affect the formation and expression of opinion. Personality and emotional considerations are not projected onto political issues indiscriminately. The symbolic definition of an object of opinion can determine how deeper emotional concerns enter into the opinion process. In this respect political communication is less involved with the control of public emotions than with channeling the expression of those emotions.[27]

The Use of Mass Communications Media

The means of transmitting an issue to the public can have important effects on opinion. Radio, television, and newspapers are the most obvious public communications media. They differ in important ways in the amount and kind of political information they transmit and the type of audience they reach. It is also important to differentiate between information that reaches the public in the form of political advertising and information campaigns and issues that gain public exposure primarily through news reporting. Finally, the impact of communications media on opinion varies, depending on the political image being transmitted. For example, a candidate's image of personal style or character may be transmitted most effectively by television; serious political proposals may have a greater impact through radio or the newspapers.

It is interesting that there is a great deal of controversy about how much impact the mass media really have on the perceived importance of issues, the make-up of the public agenda, and the shape of public opinion.[28] Part of the controversy stems from the array of theoretical approaches and the diversity of measures used to assess media impact.[29] In Chapter 11 will be presented a way of thinking about the media that explains why some of these controversies exist and illustrates the important political uses of the mass media.

THE POLITICAL IMPACT OF
ISSUE FORMATION
AND POLITICAL COMMUNICATION

The political consequences of issue formation and political communication processes differ from the consequences that flow from the domain of the individual and society. In specific situations the origin, definition, and communication of an issue all affect the formation and the political consequences of opinion. An issue's origin can affect the duration of public interest in the issue and the characteristics of opinion expressed about it. These effects help shape the political role that opinion will play in a situation. Issue origins also determine the important matter of who controls political information. The locus of control may determine whether opinion is an independent political force or whether it is subject to political manipulation as a means of justifying narrow policies. The definition of issues and the use of persuasion techniques affect the way in which members of a group use their beliefs and values to form opinions. Therefore, the definition of an issue can directly affect the distribution of political support and opposition.

The fact that the way issues are defined affects political responses raises interesting chicken-and-egg questions about public opinion as a political force. The classical model of opinion and democracy regards issues as fixed entities that emerge in response to public demands. However, the idea that issues may be fluid and changing political objects suggests that opinion may be as much a response to issues as the other way around—particularly when issues originate in crisis situations or emerge from the agendas of the government, elites, and interest groups. The abilities of such sources to shape the public definitions of issues and to employ sophisticated persuasion techniques make it important to understand the political role of opinion when it is the effect rather than the cause of a political issue. As the discussions in Chapters 8, 9, and 10 will show, public opinion can be a major factor in altering the balance in political conflicts and establishing political support for policy options.

Mass communications can enter the resolution of a political conflict in a number of ways. Two are especially important. First, political groups' access to mass media can determine the issue definitions that will dominate public thinking. Second, even groups with access to media will fail to stir public opinion unless

TABLE 4-2
The Domain of Issue Formation and Political Communication

Variables	Specific Political Consequences	General System Consequences
Issue origins	Limitations on the scope and duration of public involvement	
	Partisan control of information	Distribution of control over the political agenda
Issue definition and persuasion strategies	Distribution of political support and opposition	
The use of mass communications media	Exposure of the public to issues	Mobilization of popular support for the political agenda
	Creation of dominant images of political reality	

they know how to use the media effectively. Particular persuasion strategies and political performances are necessary to transmit convincing political images through different media. Many voters felt that Richard Nixon was shifty and uncomfortable in his television appearances in 1960. However, when he ran for President again in 1968, his carefully staged and rehearsed performances were very effective.

Issue origins, definitions, and communication strategies tell us something important about the distribution of political power. In fact, a simple definition of the structure of political power could be fashioned out of these questions: Who introduces what political issues, and who exerts what degree of influence over public opinion on those issues? In short, the introduction, definition, and communication of political issues affect both the composition of the political agenda and the degree of public support for the items on the political agenda. How the agenda is formed and whether the public supports it are among the most important aspects of a political system. The specific and general political consequences of variables in the domain of issue formation and political communication are itemized in Table 4-2.

THE DOMAIN OF POLITICAL
INSTITUTIONS AND CULTURE

Issues (and other objects of opinion) do not reach the public agenda or become resolved by the sheer force of definition and mass communication alone. They are channeled through political institutions—elections, courts, investigative commissions, legislative hearings—which make unique contributions to their definition and provide outlets and structures for public responses. For example, the numerous questions raised by urban riots in the 1960s were passed on to official riot commissions.[30] These investigative bodies heard testimony from all sides, isolated the issues from more volatile public conflict, introduced a variety of myths about justice and social relations in America, and reassured the public that the situation was under control.

Even the most volatile issues are eventually "processed" in institutional settings, which shape the public's perception and involve the public either directly or vicariously in the resolution of the situation. Thus institutional variables—linkage mechanisms, cultural themes, and rituals—must be considered along with issue formation and belief system variables. Each opinion situation must be understood as part of an overall political process.

As the discussion in Chapters 12, 13, and 14 will show, institutional contexts affect public opinion in a number of ways, and public opinion serves several important functions as it is channeled through institutional settings.

Mechanisms Linking Opinion and Policy

The most obvious relationship between institutions and opinion involves the impact of opinion on policy. The traditional concern in this area has been whether constituents influence the decisions of elected representatives such as the President and members of Congress. Institutions do provide linkage mechanisms through which public opinion can have an impact on policy making. Elections, for example, provide a direct means of registering public opinion, although (with the exceptions of initiative and referendum voting) the vote is usually a method of selecting leaders, not a means of choosing policies. The courts also provide for direct public input, though that input is restricted to narrow legal channels and limited forms of expression. In addition to direct input through litigation, however, the courts tend to take public concerns into account in the indirect sense that their decisions speak for "the people" on matters of broad social concern.

The mechanisms that link opinion and policy also structure the expression of opinion. As mentioned earlier, elections generally force opinion into "yes" and "no" expressions. The registering of opinion about congressional legislation, however, may require more ingenuity from individuals and permit a greater range of responses. Differences in response structuring across institutions should affect such characteristics of opinion as scope, direction, intensity, and constraint. Thus the institutional context of an issue must be explored alongside the belief characteristics of the public and the definition and communication strategies of partisan political groups.

Cultural Themes

Although linkage mechanisms are the most obvious institutional factors relating policy to opinion, they are not the only ones. Institutions are the repositories of national history, values, and political understandings. They embody the nation's political goals, and they provide models for political action. As issues are processed by institutions, they become associated with the powerful cultural themes, or political myths, that the institution is empowered by law and custom to protect. The expression of opinion in highly structured institutional rituals becomes a means of affirming basic political values.

Sometimes institutions introduce the myths of political culture to the public in a systematic way, as in the case of legal ceremonies that embody fairness and dramatize the due process of law. Sometimes the themes emerge by implication: A court decision may select one social myth over another to explain a problem, or a political candidate may favor one traditional interpretation of an issue over others. Whether cultural themes are introduced mechanically or selectively, one thing is certain: Whenever the public is an audience to institutional procedures, the specific issues at hand will invariably become linked to enduring cultural themes and symbols. This institutional contribution to the definition of an issue may have important effects on the crystallization of opinion and the coherence of public thinking. It also increases the level of support for policy proposals as issues pass through institutional settings.

Rituals

If the introduction of cultural themes is a regular feature of the interaction of the public and political institutions, each institution must have some routine way of integrating specific political concerns with general cultural understandings. This integration of policy and culture is accomplished by what anthropologists refer to as the ritualistic aspects of institutions. Rituals are simply routine methods of applying important cultural principles to everyday problems.

Rituals differ from the mechanisms that link opinion and policy in an important sense. Opinion-policy linkage mechanisms are isolated parts of larger rituals. They serve the specific purpose of connecting public demands to political outputs. Rituals are broader patterns of behavior; they link policies and other outputs to enduring cultural themes. The themes, or myths, are presented to the public, and the public's ritualistic response becomes a reaffirmation of cultural principles.

For example, the vote (the linkage mechanism in an election) translates opinion into a measurable political output such as the passage of a ballot proposition or the election of a candidate. The ritual surrounding the vote is much more elaborate and serves other political functions. In an election candidates and citizens routinely behave in ways that dramatize the myth of popular choice, express common concerns about the future, and display the competition for leadership in a democratic society. These aspects of the ritual turn specific issues into illustrations of the democratic process. In an effort to simplify this idea, it is possible to think of opinion-policy linkage mechanisms (such as the vote) as specific outlets for public opinion, while the broader rituals of an institution (such as the familiar interactions of candidates and voters) serve as symbolic outlets through which opinion affirms cultural principles and endorses the institution itself.

Rituals that integrate policy and culture should produce some interesting effects on opinion. As issues pass through institutional settings, their association with general cultural themes should broaden the scope of interest in them and at the same time produce a consensus about their underlying meaning and importance. If we chart opinion trends as an issue develops, the issue should capture its broadest base of opinion and highest levels of consensus when it passes through its institutional phase.

The integration of policy and cultural principles in an institutional setting also provides an explanation for some of the findings on opinion constraint discussed in Chapter 2. Several of those studies found that the public displayed high levels of agreement about general cultural principles such as freedom of speech, but there was a serious division of opinion when it came to applying the principles to specific political issues.[31] These findings make sense when we recognize that the opinions generated by issues passing through institutions have two levels of reference: A specific policy proposal may divide the public, but rituals tend to generate support for the general cultural principles that the issue illustrates. Thus, it is not at all surprising to find a difference of opinion on specific issues and general principles.

THE POLITICAL IMPACT OF POLITICAL INSTITUTIONS AND CULTURE

The nature of institutional linkages between opinion and policy has been a major area of research on politics and public opinion. As the discussion in Chapter 12 will show, the findings are mixed. It seems clear that there are links between public opinion and the political positions of elected representatives on salient and controversial political issues. However, research indicates that the linkages are weak or nonexistent on the vast majority of less salient issues.[32] One explanation for weak opinion-policy linkages is the classical thesis that opinion on most issues is not coherent enough to serve as a guide to policy formation. An alternative explanation is that elected representatives pay close attention to the opinions of their constituents only when an issue is sensitive enough to affect their support in the next election.[33]

Much more conceptual work needs to be done on linkages. Most are probably much less direct and more difficult to measure than the ones explored in the early studies of representatives and their constituencies. Nevertheless, existing evidence supports the tentative conclusion that opinion is not a direct causal force in policy formation on most issues. However, this should not lead to the conclusion that opinion is an unimportant factor in the working of political institutions. If opinion did not matter, there would not be such elaborate efforts to capture, shape, and direct it.

A key aspect of opinion involves the public's response to the cultural themes associated with issues passing through institutional settings. These themes give issues a cloak of familiarity, and they grant legitimacy to the procedures used to resolve them. Even when opinion is not a causal force in policy making, it is often a key factor in promoting the acceptance of political outcomes. The question of whether the public accepts political policy is as important as whether the public initiated the policy. Similarly, the rituals through which general political principles become associated with specific political issues make the expression of opinion both a statement about specific policies and an affirmation of the institutions that produced them.

Different myths can become attached to specific issues or conflicts as they are processed by institutions. Some myths are statements about the political system. For example, the rhetoric and actions of candidates in elections inevitably address the myths of popular sovereignty, choice, and the strength of the democratic process. In like fashion, the way in which a case is handled in a legal trial invariably introduces themes of the rule of law, the importance of due process, and the fairness of the legal procedures. Other myths that become linked to specific concerns may have less to do with the virtues of the political system than with traditional understandings of social problems. Just as there are myths about democracy and justice, there are also enduring cultural understandings about things like America's role in world affairs, the causes of poverty and unemployment, and the conditions for social harmony.

Because these broad social understandings simplify and justify institutional behavior, they regularly emerge in the way institutions handle problems. For example, Piven and Cloward describe how myths about the causes of unemployment and poverty become routine parts of the scripts in public hearings on welfare reform and public relief legislation.[34] Since the days of Horatio Alger, pervasive beliefs about the causes of poverty have attributed it to lack of effort, poor self-discipline, and low moral standards. The introduction of these myths into institutional procedures designed to address the issue tend to justify current efforts, inhibit substantial redefinition of the problem, and mobilize support for institutions and political actors. Piven and Cloward conclude that the introduction of standard social formulas in institutional settings reinforces particular public definitions of the issues and vindicates dominant policies:

> It is partly by such public spectacles that popular definitions of relief are formed. Several years ago in Newburgh, New York, city officials made wholesale accusations of illegitimacy and fraud among recipients and proposed the not especially novel remedy of forcing mothers into the labor market and removing illegitimate children from their "unsuitable" homes. A similar spectacle was staged in 1962 by Senator Byrd, who forced District of Columbia welfare officials to acquire nearly as many "fraud investigators" as "social investigators." The fraud investigators . . . "proved" a year later that close to 60 per cent were "ineligible" for benefits, chiefly because they appeared to have contact with men. These allegations of immorality were, of course, highly publicized.[35]

The general functions that linkages, myths, and rituals serve in the political system are fairly obvious. First, although direct linkage mechanisms are weak, there is clearly some degree of direct public input to policy formation. Even when the public is not the moving force behind policy, it is generally involved in at least one key stage of the policy process: legitimation. Without the mobilization of opinion through political rituals, the high degree of support for institutions and the consensus on policies that has been a characteristic of American politics would be lacking. The capacity of institutional rituals to shape public perceptions and transform issues and problems into familiar formulas also serves as an important

TABLE 4-3
The Domain of Political Institutions and Culture

Variables	Specific Political Consequences	General System Consequences
Opinion-policy linkage mechanisms	Political outlets for opinion	Policy formation
	Opinion as a causal force in policy making	
Cultural themes (myths)	Limitations on the interpretation of issues	Political legitimation
	Acceptance of political outcomes	System maintenance and change
Rituals	Policies that illustrate political principles	
	Consensus and institutional support	

TABLE 4-4
A General Model of Opinion and Politics

Domain of Opinion	Variables	Specific Political Consequences	General System Consequences
The individual and society	Socialization	Distribution of values and beliefs	Political integration
		Limitations on opinion formation	Stability
	Opinion formation routines	Susceptibility to various appeals	
		Opinion change	
	Personality	Limitations on political involvement	
		Political satisfaction	
Issue formation and political communication	Issue origins	Limitations on the scope and duration of public involvement	Distribution of control over the political agenda
		Partisan control of information	Mobilization of support for the political agenda
	Issue definition and persuasion strategies	Distribution of political support and opposition	
	The uses of mass communications media	Exposure of the public to issues	
		Creation of dominant images of political reality	

Political institutions and culture

- Opinion-policy linkage mechanisms
  - Political outlets for opinion
  - Opinion as a causal force in policy making

- Cultural themes (myths)
  - Limitation on the interpretation of issues
  - Acceptance of political outcomes

- Rituals
  - Policies that illustrate political principles
  - Consensus and institutional support

Policy formation

Political legitimation

System maintenance and change

regulator of politial change. Even the most intense demands on the political system tend to become moderated as they pass through institutional settings. The variables in the domain of political institutions and culture are itemized in Table 4-3 along with their specific and general political consequences.

A GENERAL THEORY OF OPINION

The preceding discussion of political belief, issue formation, and institutions and culture contains the basic elements of a general theory of public opinion. Table 4-4 combines the separate domains into a general framework. This overview of the general theory brings out two important features. First, it is a theory based on a broad integration of existing approaches to public opinion. A glance down the second column of the table reveals the topics that compose the field of public opinion across the disciplines of psychology, sociology, communications, and political science. However, this framework does not simply list topics in an arbitrary fashion, as often happens when they are grouped loosely under such headings as "individual" versus "social" variables or "micro" versus "macro" levels of analysis. This framework shows how each component of opinion relates to the others, and how each enters the process of opinion formation and expression.

Second, this way of integrating the traditional approaches to opinion makes it possible to show how opinion operates in specific political situations and why it works as it does. Perhaps more importantly, the distinctions among different domains of opinion and the patterns that recur across various opinion situations make it possible to explain the broad role played by opinion in the political system. It is clear that opinion is involved in much more than just policy making. Each key dimension of the political system (integration and stability, control of and support for the political agenda, policy formation, legitimation, and political change) depends on basic opinion processes. This broad political relevance helps to demonstrate the importance of different aspects of opinion, and the spectrum of opinion domains provides, in turn, a general framework for understanding the political system.

This perspective satisfies the general theoretical requirements outlined in the beginning of the chapter. It integrates existing perspectives and shows how they operate together to affect political processes. The combination of different elements of opinion also makes it possible to explain differences in research findings that were difficult to resolve. Finally, the situational perspective of Table 4-4 escapes the trap of the state-of-consciousness fallacy without removing the possibility of generalizing about the characteristics of opinion. Not only are generalizations about the impact of opinion on the political system possible within this framework, but it is possible to talk about general patterns in opinion characteristics. The difference, of course, is that these generalizations will link the characteristics of opinion to the various social, psychological, and political forces that produce them, instead of removing them from their natural contexts. The task of describing the domains of opinion and developing their political significance is the challenge that lies ahead in the remainder of the book.

NOTES

1. Based on a New York Times/CBS News Poll of voting-age Americans. Reported in the *New York Times,* July 18, 1979, p. 1.
2. From an ABC News/Louis Harris Survey reported in *Public Opinion,* Vol. 2 (March–May 1979), p. 29.
3. From the text of Carter's speech of July 15, 1979, reported in the *New York Times,* July 17, 1979, p. A15.
4. Based on a New York Times/CBS News Poll reported in the *New York Times,* July 18, 1979, p. 1.
5. *The Gallup Opinion Index,* Report No. 165 (April 1979), p. 3.
6. Ibid., p. 2.
7. Ibid., p. 2.
8. Ibid., p. 2.
9. Ibid., p. 14.
10. Ibid., p. 12.
11. Michael Lipsky and David J. Olson, *Commission Politics* (New Brunswick, N.J.: Transaction, 1977).
12. Francis A. J. Ianni and Elizabeth Reuss Ianni, *A Family Business* (New York: Mentor Books, 1973), p. 80.
13. Some illustrative works on the distribution of political values and beliefs include Donald J. Devine, *The Political Culture of the United States* (Boston: Little, Brown, 1972); Lloyd A. Free and Hadley Cantril, *The Political Beliefs of Americans* (New Brunswick, N.J.: Rutgers University Press, 1967); Harmon Ziegler and C. Wayne Peale, *Interest Groups in American Society* (Englewood Cliffs, N.J.: Prentice-Hall, 1972); and David J. Elazar, *American Federalism* (New York: Thomas Y. Crowell, 1966).
14. For a good review of opinion formation and change processes, see Martin Fishbein and Isaac Ajzen, *Belief, Attitude, Intention, and Behavior: An Introduction to Theory and Research* (Reading, Mass.: Addison-

Wesley, 1975); Charles A. Kiesler, Barry E. Collins, and Neal Miller, *Attitude Change: A Critical Analysis of Theoretical Approaches* (New York: Wiley, 1969); and Daryl J. Bem, *Beliefs, Attitudes, and Human Affairs* (Belmont, Calif.: Wadsworth, 1970).

15. For various demonstrations of this principle, see, among others, Daryl J. Bem, "Inducing Belief in False Confessions," *Journal of Personality and Social Psychology*, Vol. 3 (June 1966), pp. 707–10; Daniel Kahneman and Amos Tversky, "On the Psychology of Prediction," *Psychological Review*, Vol. 80 (July 1973), pp. 237–51; and Daniel Kahneman and Amos Tversky, "Subjective Probability: A Judgment of Representativeness," *Cognitive Psychology*, Vol. 3 (July 1972), pp. 430–54.

16. For the classic discussion of the psychological implications of the "distant" world of politics, see Walter Lippmann, *Public Opinion* (New York: Free Press, 1922).

17. As evidence that even the most sophisticated and ideological members of the public may be prone to this kind of mental activity, see Lloyd S. Etheredge's study of the foreign policy attitudes of State Department officers: *A World of Men: The Private Sources of American Foreign Policy* (Cambridge, Mass.: M.I.T. Press, 1978).

18. The concepts of object appraisal, externalization, and social adjustment are from the pioneering study by M. Brewster Smith, Jerome Bruner, and Ralph W. White, *Opinions and Personality* (New York: Wiley, 1956).

19. Robert E. Lane, *Political Ideology* (New York: Free Press, 1962), p. 43.

20. Thurman Arnold, *The Symbols of Government* (New York: Harcourt Brace Jovanovich, 1962).

21. Murray Edelman, *Politics as Symbolic Action* (Chicago: Markham, 1971).

22. Harold Lasswell, *World Politics and Personal Insecurity.* (New York: Free Press 1965).

23. A promising step in this direction is the typology formulated by Daniel Katz in "Attitude Formation and Public Opinion," in *Political Attitudes and Public Opinion*, ed. Dan D. Nimmo and Charles M. Bonjean (New York: McKay, 1972), pp. 13–26.

24. Reported in Richard J. Barnet, *The Roots of War* (Baltimore: Penguin Books, 1972), p. 288.

25. Two studies that confirm the effects of stimulus composition on opinion are Solomon Asch, "The Doctrine of Suggestion, Prestige, and Imitation in Social Psychology," *Psychological Review*, Vol. 55 (September 1948), pp. 250–76; and W. Lance Bennett, *The Political Mind and the Political Environment: An Investigation of Public Opinion and Political Consciousness* (Lexington, Mass.: Heath, Lexington Books, 1975), ch. 5.

26. Recent reviews indicate some confusion in the persuasion literature about whether most persuasion techniques have any systematic impact. See, for example, David O. Sears and Richard E. Whitney, *Political Persuasion* (Morristown, N.J.: General Learning Press, 1973). However, it is interesting to note that very few persuasion studies have explored the link between persuasion methods and the corre-

sponding attitude change processes present or absent in individual belief systems.

27. For a variety of different perspectives on this, see Edelman, *Politics as Symbolic Action*; Katz, "Attitude Formation and Public Opinion"; and Lasswell, *World Politics and Personal Insecurity*.

28. See, for example, James C. Strouse, *The Mass Media, Public Opinion, and Public Policy Analysis* (Columbus, Ohio: Bobbs-Merrill, 1975); Denis McQuail, ed., *Sociology of Mass Communications* (Baltimore: Penguin Books, 1972); and Thomas E. Patterson and Robert D. McClure, *The Unseeing Eye* (New York: Putnam, 1976).

29. For an excellent overview of different perspectives on mass communication, see Dan Nimmo, *Political Communication and Public Opinion in America* (Santa Monica, Calif.: Goodyear, 1978), ch. 5.

30. See Lipsky and Olson, "The Processing of Racial Crisis in America." *Politics and Society*, Vol. 6, Winter 1976, pp. 79–103.

31. These findings appeared in Samuel Stouffer, *Communism, Conformity, and Civil Liberties* (Garden City, N.Y.: Doubleday, 1955); James W. Prothro and Charles M. Grigg, "Fundamental Principles of Democracy: Bases of Agreement and Disagreement," *Journal of Politics*, Vol. 22 (May 1960), pp. 276–94; and Herbert McClosky, "Consensus and Ideology in American Politics," *American Political Science Review*, Vol. 58 (June 1964), pp. 361–82.

32. See, among others, Charles F. Cnudde and Donald J. McCrone, "The Linkage Between Constituency Attitudes and Congressional Voting Behavior: A Causal Model," *American Political Science Review*, Vol. 60 (March 1966), pp. 66–72; and Warren E. Miller and Donald E. Stokes, "Constituency Influence in Congress," *American Political Science Review*, Vol. 57 (March 1963), pp. 45–56.

33. See David Mayhew, *Congress: The Electoral Connection* (New Haven: Yale University Press, 1974).

34. It should be pointed out once again that the term "myth" does not refer to a falsehood. It simply refers to widely accepted beliefs about society. Myths may be false in an empirical sense, but they are accepted as fundamental truth by the people who hold them. The fact that they are so deeply embedded in consciousness that they are not subject to disproof makes their empirical status irrelevant for understanding their social uses. These aspects of myth will be explained fully in Chapter 13.

35. Frances Fox Piven and Richard A. Cloward, *Regulating the Poor: The Functions of Public Welfare* (New York: Vintage Books, 1971), p. 169.

PART TWO

The
Domain of
the Individual
and Society

5

Political
Socialization

INDIVIDUALS acquire political values and beliefs through socialization, which is the foundation of the domain of the individual and society. Not only does the study of socialization address the origins of individual opinions, but it also explains a good deal about patterns of public opinion, political conflict, and support for the political system. Although socialization operates on individuals, it affects them through their memberships in groups. The norms to which individuals are exposed in the family, the school, the church, the peer group, and the work place form the basis of their political thinking. To some extent, of course, each individual has a unique personality and a unique set of social memberships, making it unlikely that any two people will respond to the political world in exactly the same way. However, the social experiences of some individuals may be so similar that they give rise to common political concerns and opinions. For example, blacks may agree among themselves but differ with whites on issues pertaining to social equality. The rich and the poor may see different causes of economic instability.

Two of the most important questions about a political system are whether the same groups line up time and again on different sides of issues and whether the underlying distribution of beliefs and values is likely to produce consensus or conflict in times of social strain. In order to answer such questions it is necessary first to understand how socialization works on individuals and then to explore its broad social effects.

SOCIALIZATION AND THE INDIVIDUAL

Socialization involves an interaction between psychological and social variables. Social factors such as group norms, social pressure, and the consistency of social experience determine the content, salience, and coherence of the political orientations acquired by the individual. The psychology of each individual's learning and thinking affects the way in which the individual assimilates and organizes political orientations. Although the interaction of social factors and psychological factors makes them hard to separate, it is important to recognize that each type of factor contributes differently to the political development of the individual.

Psychological Aspects
of Socialization:
Learning and Cognitive Development

Socialization studies have found that people begin to develop political orientations at a very early age. Children as young as five or six years old have strong feelings about their country and what it stands for.[1] Over 95 percent of the children in a national sample agreed that "America is the best country in the world" and "the American flag is the best flag in the world."[2] Long before children understand the meaning of elections or the technicalities of candidate selection, they overwhelmingly endorse voting as the primary symbol of American democracy.[3] These and other early signs of political development are the products of one of the most important human characteristics: the capacity to learn.

From early infancy most children demonstrate the capacity to learn concrete ideas through two processes. Some political ideas are learned by associating them with positive or negative images that have been established already. This is called *classical conditioning*. Other ideas are learned through a trial and error process in which the child is reinforced for proper behaviors. This is called *operant conditioning*. The simple association of what parents and teachers say and do with the love and trust most children have for these authority figures is enough to transmit most basic beliefs about government from adult to child through classical conditioning. It is not surprising that these generalized positive feelings about government are the first orientations to emerge. Other orientations will take hold somewhat more slowly as a result of learning by trial and error. For example, very young children develop positive feelings about political leaders, the police, and other authority figures. However, they lack the ability to distinguish among authority figures. One study showed that nearly 30 percent of second-graders believe that milkmen work for the government (and, therefore, presumably are authority figures).[4] Not until the sixth, seventh, and eighth grades does this erroneous association become extinguished. This extended learning period is probably due to the association of the milkman's uniform with the uniforms of government employees.

Most children develop attitudes about people and symbols in politics before they demonstrate a grasp of the procedures and processes that form the real substance of politics. The reason for this order of development is that the ideas behind political procedures and processes are more complex than simple beliefs about the government. Procedures need to be connected both to abstract principles and to concrete situations in order to be understood. For example, in order to understand the idea of voting it is necessary to understand the principle of citizen control of government and the specific situations or decisions that are suited to this principle. Trust in the President, by contrast, can be built into the child's world merely by associating the chief executive with parents, teachers, and other authority figures. That is a simple learning operation. In contrast, understanding ideas like voting or the role of complex political organizations like Congress and the Supreme Court requires certain thinking skills in addition to the capacity to learn. The skills of abstraction and discrimination (between, say, the functions of voting and the functions of Supreme Court decisions) are acquired as part of a psychological process known as *cognitive development*.

From late elementary school through adolescence, children exposed to normal intellectual stimulation (such as that available in most schools) learn to handle abstract ideas and to think with them. Over this period, an interesting thing happens to the child's image of government. As the young citizen begins to understand political procedures like voting and justice processes like trials, he or she increasingly identifies the government with them. For example, when second-graders were asked to pick two pictures that best showed what the American government is, 39 percent picked George Washington and 46 percent picked President John Kennedy (the study was done in 1962). When eighth-graders were instructed to do the same thing, only 2 percent picked George Washington and only 23 percent selected President Kennedy. The older students instead chose voting (47 percent) and Congress (49 percent) as elements most representative of American government.[5] Cognitive development may explain why the overwhelming majority of adults (generally from 80 to 90 percent) support abstract procedural ideas such as majority rule, minority rights, and due process.[6] Cognitive development also enables people to think in more sophisticated ways with the political ideas they learned in earlier stages of socialization.[7]

By adolescence, learning and cognitive development permit most individuals to comprehend the political system and its procedures. The power of early learning experiences also endows the majority of citizens with a strong level of support for the political system. In most cases, these political orientations are pretty stable. Many people are willing to support the government through thick and thin. Even when that faith is challenged, as it was in the mid-1970s during the Watergate era, individuals tend to look to the system itself for new laws and new leaders to restore their faith. Most people agree that the basic institutions and procedures of American government are the best ways to express political concerns and resolve differences. When these beliefs are challenged, the dominant response is to fix what is wrong with the system rather than to turn away from it.[8]

Although the majority of citizens learn these basic orientations, some groups are politically cynical and disaffected. In order to understand the reasons for these differences, it is necessary to consider the social variables that affect socialization. Differences in group memberships, life experiences, and exposure to political information can affect what people learn and how they think about politics.

Social Determinants of Socialization

The outcome of learning and cognitive development depends to an important degree on various social conditions operating on individuals. These conditions can affect the content of political beliefs, the intensity of political concerns, and the similarity of political orientations in various social groups. Certain conditions may be nearly universal, such as the young child's exposure, at home or in school, to positive reinforcement about government and authority. Other conditions, such as powerful politicizing events, different generational experiences, or contradictory political input, may produce important differences from group to group. The major social conditions that affect socialization are politicizing events and social changes, the political orientations of agents of socialization, and patterns of exposure to political stimuli.

Events

It is tempting to think of socialization as the slow and steady transmission of political outlooks from authority figures to new members of the political system. Although such transmission is a large part of the socialization process, it is important to recognize that individuals can be affected directly by events that have an impact on their lives at crucial stages of their personal development. For example, the assassination of a powerful leader such as John F. Kennedy or Martin Luther King, Jr., can crush the hopes and trust of young citizens.[9] Periods of rapid social change and turmoil can alter personal values and people's perception of government. Keniston cited the Vietnam War, the trauma of the draft, and the alienating university environment as factors that helped shape the "protest generation" of the 1960s.[10] Other research indicates that every major period of social or economic upheaval in America has produced massive changes in political identifications and patterns of participation.[11] It is difficult to predict whether the effects of powerful events will be enduring or short-lived, but it is clear that they can shape the outlooks and behaviors of the members of a political generation faced with common issues.

Agents of Socialization:
Family, School, Reference Groups

The most familiar aspect of socialization is the impact of influential individuals and groups on the developing person. Respected and authoritative figures such as parents and teachers can contribute heavily to the beliefs and values of receptive young people. Studies have shown that children tend to imitate the attitudes of their parents in important areas such as social prejudice and respect for authority.[12] It was once assumed that early socialization in the family virtually molded a person's political outlook for life.[13] However, new research has thrown open the question of how enduring the effects of primary socialization really are.

Important research on adolescents has shown relatively little correlation between the political outlooks of young adults and the political leanings of their parents.[14] Although one of the developments during adolescence is increasing cognitive sophistication, it is unlikely that this factor alone accounts for the withering away of parental influence. More research is required to clarify the processes at work.[15] However, the existing research on the effects of agents of socialization strongly implies that as an individual's social accordingly.

Political orientations reflect social position and life experiences. Changes in those will expose people to new, authoritative sources of political information. For example, a move from home to college, or from college to a job, often brings exposure to new political ideas. The result is likely to be a change in political perspective. This explanation is consistent with social reference theories of opinion formation that will be discussed in Chapter 6.[16] Until future research suggests evidence to the contrary, it is probably safe to say that agents of socialization such as family, teachers, reference groups, and work associates have powerful effects on the political development of individuals, but the effects fade when the agents cease to occupy a central position in the individual's social world.

Exposure to Political Ideas

The persistence of political ideas and the centrality of political orientations depend on more than the efforts of various agents of socialization. Individuals exist in complex environments in which they are exposed to ideas from different sources, with different intensities, and with different frequencies of reinforcement. Two aspects of political exposure are particularly important: (1) consistency and (2) reinforcement. The political orientations to which an individual is exposed may be more or less consistent across social experiences. Political ideas may be reinforced over time, or they may run up against increasingly negative input. The consistency of exposure at any point in time and the reinforcement of orientations over time have interesting implications both for individuals and for society.

The divergence between the thinking of parents and the thinking of their adolescent children, for example, may be explained by both factors. The trend in contemporary society for young people to leave home, seek diverse careers, and explore alternate life styles undoubtedly exposes them to conflicting political ideas during crucial stages of their development. This inconsistency, in combination with distance from parental reinforcement, may weaken the political bonds between generations.

Although a person's specific political outlooks may change as her or his socialization environment changes, research suggests the presence of some enduring, consistent, and increasingly reinforced political dispositions. General support for government and belief in American political procedures seem to register consistently across age groups and, in some cases, to increase over time. One study found that by the third grade 80 percent of children agree that "the government usually knows what is best for the people."[17] By the fourth grade, 95 percent of children think the government "knows more than many people," and 59 percent feel that it knows either more than most people or more than anyone.[18] A full 25 percent of fourth-graders feel that the government would *always* help them if they needed it, and 93 percent believe that they can count on the government to help them at least some of the time.[19]

Many of these beliefs grow stronger, perhaps as a result of the young citizen's relative isolation from the real political world, accompanied by regular reinforcement of positive images of government through story books, school books, parents, teachers, and the media. A group of fifth-graders in one study expressed a 46 percent agreement with this statement: "Democracy is the best form of government." (Thirty-six percent didn't know.) By the eleventh grade, however, 74 percent of the students in the same school system agreed with that idea (and only 18 percent didn't know).[20] These findings suggest that some fundamental political perspectives extend consistently across the life spaces of most individuals and are reinforced over time. However, even these perspectives are not distributed universally across society.

Evidence suggests that certain social and economic groups are likely to be exposed to contradictory political inputs and to have their early positive feelings about the political system damaged by the harsh realities of life. Black children start out having about the same level of support for the government as white children have; but as they grow older, black children agree much less often with statements like these: "The government is very helpful." "The government cares about us." "The government can be trusted."[21]

The same pattern has been found in the attitudes of Chicano children toward the President.[22] And a team of investigators who went into Appalachia in the late 1960s discovered that 41 percent of poor children from the Kentucky hills felt that the President does not work as hard as most men, while 27 percent believed that the President is less honest than most men.[23] These negative feelings are shared by only a tiny portion (only 1 or 2 percent) of average American white children.[24] Deviant "political support" groups are a small and isolated segment of the total population. Their opinions may depart from the general feelings of the public, but their voices are seldom heard above the crowd except when their frustrations boil over into riot or civil unrest.

The socialization patterns that emerge here are interesting. Certain minority groups tend to be split off from the majority both in terms of specific values and beliefs and with respect to general support for the political system. However, the majority of citizens seem to be anchored in a firm commitment to the political system and its principles. Within the context of general support for the system, there seems to be plenty of room for individuals to change specific opinions and beliefs over the course of their lives. Agents of socialization are important at each stage of a person's growth, but their impact is only as enduring as the individual's life experiences are stable. The intervention of traumatic events, inconsistent input, or change in reinforcement patterns may disrupt specific political orientations and weaken the influence of old socializing agents. The persistence of fundamental support for the political system is probably less the result of early parental influence than the consequence of consistent exposure and continuing reinforcement.

SOCIALIZATION AND POLITICAL INTEGRATION

The most obvious explanation for the relative stability and integration of the American political system is broad support for the institutions and principles that form the heart of the system.[25] Within this framework, changes in the specific political beliefs of individuals can be viewed as social adjustments rather than as sources of political tension. Moreover, even though individuals may change specific political views, there is no reason to think that the changes are random. They may be regulated by some deep structure within political belief systems. The discovery of an underlying structure would explain a good deal about the development of individual political orientations and the patterns of change in public opinion. Although some of the following discussion is speculative, it is consistent with long-standing observations about American society and culture that provide sensible explanations for previously puzzling opinion data. The basic proposition is a simple one: The belief systems of individuals tend to be organized internally and patterned socially through the workings of two core social values. These pervasive values are the competing forces of *individualism* and *equality*.[26] Some individuals may acquire a strong commitment to one or the other and build a systematic belief system around it; such persons are commonly known as *ideologues*. However, most people, during socialization, probably become attached in varying degrees to both core values. The presence of two competing values at the base of a system of political belief lets people develop different, but personally coherent and sensible, political orientations as their social experiences and immediate value concerns change.

This hypothesis about the belief structures of individuals not only suggests that there may be previously unrecognized patterns in individual political change, but it also argues that most individuals are not simply political chameleons who change political colors in perfect response to their surroundings. Changes are to some degree limited and predictable responses based on the relations between the core values in an individual's belief system. If most individuals have some commitment to equality and individualism, then it also becomes possible to explain broad patterns of political realignment and policy change in society.

Some periods in American history seem to be characterized by conservative political coalitions and an emphasis on laissez-faire social and economic policies with few social reforms or liberal policies. These periods of emphasis on individualism tend to be followed by liberal coalitions, which shift the policy emphasis in the direction of economic regulation and social redistribution. This broad value cycle in American politics may contain important clues about mass belief systems and the workings of individual opinion. A so-called pendulum effect both in individual thinking and in patterns of public opinion may also explain the limits of political change in America and the role of public opinion as a moderating influence during periods of change. The following discussion offers some evidence for the existence of this value cycle in American politics.

The Social Orientations
of Americans

Equality has been a theme in America since the beginning. The abundance of land and resources made it possible for a higher proportion of people to live well, to own property, and to advance socially and economically than in any of the traditional societies of Europe. The fact that America was a new land with no traditions or history of social discrimination permitted the development of a comparatively classless and status-free society. Reinforcing these patterns was the fact that many of the earliest settlers were members of persecuted religious groups whose beliefs called into question the values on which the European aristocracy had based its social and political domination. Finally, at the time of the American Revolution the thinking of many of the key political figures was influenced by the spirit of equality that was bursting forth in European intellectual circles.

The ideal that "all men are created equal," which inspired the American Revolution, continued to grow in nineteenth-century American society as property qualifications for voting were reduced, the party system became increasingly responsive to the people, and the grassroots power of the new American West celebrated its emergence with the election and tumultuous reign of Andrew Jackson as President. In the midst of this period of democratic celebration, America was visited by perceptive European observers such as Alexis de Tocqueville, James Bryce, and Harriet Martineau. They all proclaimed the intense equality of American social relations (although not all of them considered equality desirable).[27]

How can it be said that America was inspired by the value of equality when Americans practiced slavery, drove the Native Americans from their lands, denied the vote to women and to those without property, and tolerated huge fortunes to be amassed in the presence of great suffering and misery during the development of the West and the industrial revolution? Must one be blind to these things in order to believe that equality is a basic American value? It must be remembered that prior to the American Revolution no stable government in modern times had ever acknowledged the ideal of equality. Never before had there been so large a population in which so many could expect to lead such comfortable lives. In other words, *any* degree of equality was (and still is) a rare achievement in a world in which the dominant tendency was (and still is) for governments to be run by a few individuals with enough power to impose their notions of "the good" on the many. All these reasons aside, there is a more important reason for saying that equality is one of the core social orientations of Americans (while still acknowledging the serious shortcomings of American society): Acting alongside the value of equality is the equally powerful, though opposing, value of individualism.

America is the land of "the rugged individual," both by design and by chance. By design, because those who first settled and remained were individuals whose religious beliefs emphasized the development of qualities that would make them worthy in the eyes of God: courage, self-reliance, persistence, confidence, and strength of will. By chance, because at every stage of America's development—from the initial settlement, to the Revolution, to the formation of the Union, to the defense and settlement of the West, to the Civil War, to the industrial revolution and beyond—Americans were subjected to severe tests of endurance, self-reliance, and will. Growth and survival depended on the firm grasp of the idea of individualism.

This ideal passed from the early Puritans to the bankers, traders, manufacturers, and ultimately the workers of the new economy. It emerged in the aggressive competition, personal accumulation and ownership, and private enterprise on which the economic system was developed. These and other values mediated between the general value of individualism and specific life experiences and justified thinking of slaves as "property" rather than as human beings "created equal." Mediating values justified the accumulation of huge fortunes from banking and credit, speculation on Western lands, and the development of industry, while debtors, small Western farmers, and workers lived poor and unrewarding lives. Mediating values continue to justify the overwhelming feeling that there are limits to any effort to wipe out poverty, unemployment, sickness, and hunger in contemporary America, because social reform eventually threatens the values of self-reliance and personal achievement on which so many Americans take the measure of themselves. Values such as competition, hard work, and ownership even support the ever-present suspicion that people who are poor, unemployed, hungry, and outcast are suffering those plights as a result of some failure of character—some lack of inner strength or effort.

The seemingly contradictory values of individualism and equality live side by side in almost every area of Americans' lives. For example, most people believe in a free and equal education for all citizens. Yet within the schools it is common to encourage intense competition for grades, to make painful distinctions between different types of students, and to regard knowledge as an instrument for the individual's personal advancement in a career. American families tend to be remarkably egalitarian. Children are encouraged to express themselves, and family activities often are organized around the interests of the children. Yet children are often pressured to prove themselves in the eyes of their parents through individual competitive achievements in school, sports, and youth groups. The public has supported equal opportunity programs in education and employment. Yet it tends to draw the line when it comes to giving an individual from a disadvantaged group an edge over better-qualified individuals from groups that are not disadvantaged. Most people want their leaders to be like them in the sense that they might have come from immigrant stock or have grown up on a farm or have started out from a typical middle-class background. However, they also want their leaders to show that they have exercised greater individual initiative than most people by becoming wealthier, more successful, or more powerful.

In short, the two core values of equality and individualism have grown together to the point that it is possible to see the very means to equality in competition. Yet within this competitive equality lie the seeds of inequalities—inequalities that are hard to resolve because they are tolerable to most people if they seem to result from fair competition among individuals using their own skills, talents, wealth, or brains.

If individualism and equality are the basis of the social orientations of most Americans, we should find them reflected in public opinion about social problems and political solutions, and, indeed, they are. In a fascinating study of how Americans understand their social problems and what solutions they favored, Free and Cantril discovered that most people tend to explain social problems like poverty and unemployment in conservative terms, yet they favor fairly liberal solutions. In general, people tend to blame individuals for their problems, yet favor political solutions that adjust things in the direction of social equality.[28]

The impact of the value of individualism on opinions about some social problems is shown in Table 5-1. In addition to the re-

TABLE 5-1
Impact of the Value of Individualism
on Opinions About Social Problems

Social Issue Statement	Percent of Sample Who:		
	Agree	Disagree	Don't Know
Generally speaking, any able-bodied person who really wants to work in this country can find a job and earn a living.	76	21	3
The relief roles are loaded with chiselers and people who just don't want to work.	66	23	11
We should rely more on individual initiative and not so much on governmental welfare programs.	79	12	9

Source: The Political Beliefs of Americans: A Study of Public Opinion by Lloyd A. Free and Hadley Cantril. Copyright © 1967 by Rutgers, the State University. Reprinted by permission of Rutgers University Press.

sponses shown in Table 5-1, 72 percent of the sample expressed the opinion that lack of effort (or lack of effort in combination with circumstances) explained why a person was poor. The strength of the individualism value is reflected further in the fact that this was the overwhelming opinion of rich people and poor people alike. Sixty-eight percent of those whose family incomes were under $5,000 a year felt that lack of effort played some part in explaining poverty, while 74 percent of those earning between $5,000 and $10,000 a year felt this way, and 76 percent of those earning over $10,000 a year expressed this opinion.[29] From the richest to the poorest groups in society there was only an 8 percent drop in those who felt that lack of effort was either the sole cause of or a major contribution to poverty.

If Americans are this taken with the value of individualism, then surely they must oppose efforts of the government to step in and try to adjust serious cases of social inequality? If people's belief systems were logical, that would seem to be the logical conclusion. However, they are not logical (there is no reason why they should be); they reflect patterns of social and cultural experience. An understanding of the equality value shared by most Americans makes it possible to explain why people accept fairly liberal solutions to problems that they understand in conservative terms. Whereas Ta-

TABLE 5-2
Impact of the Value of Equality on Opinions
About Solutions to Social Problems

Solution to Social Problem	Percent of Sample Who:		
	Approve	Disapprove	Don't Know
A broad general program of federal aid to education is under consideration, which would include federal grants to help pay teachers' salaries.	63	28	10
Congress has been considering a compulsory medical insurance program covering hospital and nursing-home care for the elderly. This Medicare program would be financed out of increased social security taxes.	63	30	7
The federal government has a responsibility to try to reduce unemployment.	75	18	7
The federal government has a responsibility to try to do away with poverty in this country.	72	20	8

Source: The Political Beliefs of Americans: A Study of Public Opinion by Lloyd A. Free and Hadley Cantril. Copyright © 1967 by Rutgers, the State University. Reprinted by permission of Rutgers University Press.

ble 5-1 makes most Americans seem pretty conservative in their opinions about social problems, Table 5-2 shows that Americans are fairly liberal in their opinions about solutions to these problems. In addition to the seemingly liberal sentiments in Table 5-2, the majority of the sample favored continued funding of such redistributive federal programs as urban renewal, government-subsidized housing, head-start educational programs, and community-based poverty programs.[30]

Some analysts might regard the connection between seemingly conservative understandings and liberal solutions as contradictory or inconsistent. Such a conclusion would be consistent with many of the studies discussed in Chapters 2 and 3. Indeed, Free and Cantril conclude that their findings reflect a "schizoid" pattern underlying the public opinion of Americans. They think that the social understandings of Americans (based on individualism) are out of line with the social programs the public really wants. The solution they call for is to restate the American "ideology" more clearly so that the public can think more consistently about society. Just who is to restate the American ideology is never made clear:

> There is little doubt that the time has come for a restatement of American ideology to bring it in line with what the great majority of people want and approve. Such a statement . . . would focus people's wants, hopes, and beliefs, and provide a guide and platform to enable the American people to implement their political desires in a more intelligent, direct, and consistent manner.[31]

That conclusion seems to imply that Americans' opinions about social problems are not related to their opinions about political solutions to problems. It supposes that the public ought to be simple and strictly logical in its political thinking, but just what logic people should employ is not mentioned. Finally, it ignores the fact that Americans have always held these competing values. The country was built on them. And if this is the case, how can we say that these orientations are inconsistent or that they don't make sense?

A more reasonable explanation is that most Americans are socialized into accepting two competing values as the basis of their social thought. This acceptance produces for most people a certain tension, which may create political dilemmas on occasion but certainly does not produce random or meaningless political ideas. Far from it. The tension between equality and individuality accounts for many of the obvious patterns of American politics: the regular outbursts of social reform, followed by periods of private concern and public neglect; the clear limits placed on both the engineering of social equality and the abuses of private power; and the remarkable stability of the political system in the face of periods of intense social conflict. It just happens that during the 1960s, when Free and Cantril did their study, the policy focus of the public was on equality. However, at times America has been preoccupied with private concerns to the exclusion of concern about equality and the public good. As Tocqueville observed, individualism can sometimes shade into selfishness, which may dampen the spirit of equality. In a society that still clings to ideals of equality, however, the growth of selfish individualism will trigger outbursts of social reform and the celebration of equality. Such was the state of affairs when Tocqueville visited America during the Age of Jackson and observed:

> Democratic nations are at all times fond of equality, but there are certain epochs at which the passion they entertain for it swells to a

height of fury. This occurs at the moment when the . . . barriers of rank are . . . thrown down. At such times men pounce upon equality as their booty, and they cling to it as to some precious treasure which they fear to lose.[32]

Each swing from equality to individualism is usually held in check by the presence of the other value. In "normal" times these opposing forces come to rest in a balance between the common desire for individual gain and the shared willingness to sacrifice a small portion of that gain for the public good (through things like tax-supported programs, support for liberal political candidates, and tolerance for opposing political views). The integration of equality and individualism depends on what Tocqueville called "the principle of self-interest rightly understood." This principle allows that "every man may follow his own interest, but . . . it is in the interest of every man to be virtuous."[33]

The even distribution of these social orientations is a great stabilizing force in the American political system. The fact that the basic values are somewhat opposing leads inevitably to conflict on most questions of social policy. However, the fact that most individuals are capable of understanding the opposing viewpoint (and even adopting it in some cases) places limits on how far conflicts usually go. These limits result from two factors. First, as already mentioned, the fact that most people share the opposing value to some degree reduces the extremity of conflict and provides a basis for compromise. Second, the tension between the social orientations underlying public opinion on most issues fairly well limits the ways in which issues are defined and the range of opinion expressed about them.

An Expanded Model of
Socialization

The recognition that most individuals become attached to competing cultural values in varying degrees provides important insights about the political development of individuals and patterns of public opinion. The powerful political role of values makes it important to include the acquisition of competing cultural values in any general model of socialization. An important step in this direction has been taken by Edelman. In a fascinating discussion of socialization and its political impact, he proposes that most people learn competing explanations for most major social problems. Although

Edelman does not use the terms "individualism" and "equality" explicitly, the kinds of explanation he talks about revolve around values.

For example, Edelman describes what can be called the "individualist" explanation of poverty as one in which the poor are seen as "responsible for their own plight and in need of control to compensate for their inadequacies, greed, lack of self-discipline, immorality, pathology, or criminal tendencies, while authorities . . . cope more or less competently with the deviant and protect a basically sound social structure from the threat they pose."[34] The "egalitarian" reaction to poverty, on the other hand, regards the poor as "victims of exploitative economic, social, and political institutions; people deprived by circumstances (not by their personal defects) . . . while authorities . . . serve the interests of other elite groups."[35]

Edelman's major point about these explanations is in keeping with our argument about the distribution of basic social orientations in America:

> Though each person's social orientation is likely to make one or the other of these perspectives his or her dominant one, everybody learns both of them, for they are stock explanations of a universal phenomenon. The poor and the affluent, like everyone else, learn to perceive poverty in both ways and to emphasize one or the other view as necessary to justify their roles, to account for developments in the news, and to adjust to changing social situations. . . . The availability of both views makes possible a wide spectrum of ambivalent postures for each individual and a similarly large set of contradictions in political rhetoric and in public policy.[36]

This perspective on socialization points up some of the costs of political integration and stability. The presence of competing social values makes ambivalent Americans' opinions about major political problems. It allows people to deplore problems but to tolerate their continued existence. It encourages politicians to define issues for the public according to explanations that appeal to the standard value orientations, thereby short-circuiting new conceptions of problems that might yield serious solutions. This perspective also adds to our understanding of the political impact of the social orientations that underlie public opinion. Although public opinion in America tends to have a stabilizing effect on the political system, it limits the possibilities for significant social change and real solutions to many of the most pressing social problems.

SOCIALIZING EFFECTS OF
PUBLIC OPINION

The idea that people may support competing values suggests that many cases where people seem to have acquired *new* political orientations may simply involve the activation of latent values. Individuals may follow the lead of new agents of socialization not just because they want to imitate them, but out of a genuine capacity to understand and relate to their ideas. The development of competing values during early socialization may produce in later life a responsiveness to the value emphasis present in different social environments. An important implication of this responsiveness is that public opinion is not only shaped by patterns of socialization but is also a powerful agent of socialization.

The power of public opinion to activate latent values brings a special meaning to the long-standing observation that Americans tend to be unusually sensitive to the opinions of others. Consider some of these observations made by European visitors to America in the nineteenth century:

> The worship of Opinion is, at this day, the established religion of the United States.[37]

> [Americans display a] self-distrust, a despondency, a disposition to fall into line, to acquiesce in the dominant opinion.[38]

> In Europe, the men in the pit of the theatre stand up between acts, face the house, and examine the audience at leisure. The American dares not do this. He cannot stand the isolation nor the publicity.[39]

Over one hundred years after those observations were made, the sociologist David Riesman labeled this phenomenon "other-directedness."[40] Riesman argued that the other-directed American was a product of alienation, rapid social change, and a national obsession with social status and advancement. His analysis of America in the twentieth century echoed the sentiments of an obscure nineteenth-century study of the mental health of Americans:

> The population of the United States is beyond that of other countries an anxious one. All classes are either striving after wealth or endeavoring to keep up its appearance. From the principle of imitation which is implanted in all of us, sharpened perhaps by the existing equality of conditions, the poor follow as closely as they are able the habits and manner of living of the rich. . . . From these causes,

and perhaps from the nature of our political institutions, and the effects arising from them, we are an anxious, care-worn people.[41]

Tocqueville added to the history of early writing on other-directedness by arguing that the ideal of equality in America also produced a sensitivity to the opinions of others:

> Whenever social conditions are equal, public opinion presses with enormous weight upon the minds of each individual; it surrounds, directs, and oppresses him; and this arises from the very constitution of society much more than from its political laws. As men grow more alike, each man feels himself weaker in regard to all the rest as he discerns nothing by which he is considerably raised above them or distinguished from them; he mistrusts himself as soon as they assail him. Not only does he mistrust his strength, but he even doubts of his right; and he is very near acknowledging that he is in the wrong, when the greater number of his countrymen assert that he is so. The majority do not need to force him, they convince him.[42]

Long before Riesman pronounced Americans other-directed, a nineteenth-century commentator observed that in a fluid society in which social class is weak, advancement is guaranteed not by one's social position but by courting the favor of others:

> In a democracy every one at least hopes to get on and up. This ascent depends not upon the favor of a class, but upon the good-will of the whole. This social whole has to be conciliated. . . . To make one's self conspicuous and disagreeable, is to arouse enmities that block one's way.[43]

Whether or not we think that the devotion of Americans to the opinions of others takes on religious proportions, it is clear that there are conditions under which even the most self-reliant people will bend to the views of others. Certain opinions are almost badges of membership in particular groups. The fastest way to become accepted as a member is to adopt the dominant opinions of established members.

The operation of opinions as the membership cards of society may account for many of the peculiar characteristics of American public opinion. For example, it provides a clue about why individuals can be committed to a way of thinking, yet change their views drastically when they change their circle of friends, shift careers, or attain a new social status. It also explains why people are reluctant to discuss their social and political views with strangers or with people who are unlikely to share them. People tend to reserve their opinions for situations in which their expression will pose no threat to existing or future social relationships. When they are doubtful about the social impact of expressing an opinion, people tend to hide behind a façade of professed ignorance or unconcern. That tendency suggests a paradox about the private significance of public opinion. Even though some opinions are serious and important social membership devices for those who hold them, there is a tendency to downplay their significance and reserve their use precisely because they can be so volatile socially. Perhaps this generalization can be made even stronger: The private importance of an opinion tends to vary inversely with the degree to which an individual will acknowledge it in settings in which there is not some clear social support for that opinion.

As he did with so many aspects of social life in America, Mark Twain perfectly captured the paradox between private opinions and their public expression. A friend of his had published a controversial book on law and human nature. Twain agreed with her opinions, but he refused to defend her ideas in public. When she asked him to write something in her defense, he refused by saying:

> No, such a thing is unthinkable. . . . If I, or any otherwise intelligent and experienced person, should suddenly throw down the walls that protect and conceal his *real* opinions on almost any subject under the sun, it would at once be perceived that he had lost his intelligence and his wisdom and ought to be sent to the asylum. I said that I had been revealing to her my private sentiments, *not* my public ones; that I, like all other human beings, expose to the world only my trimmed and perfumed and carefully barbered public opinions and conceal carefully, cautiously, wisely, my private ones.[44]

The applications of this principle are everywhere in American social life, particularly with respect to the expression of political opinions. For example, an interviewer asked workers at the General Motors plant in Lordstown, Ohio, about their social relations. The time was the early 1970s. The workers consisted of small groups of blacks and local whites and a large percentage of whites who had migrated from the South. Even though both white groups tended to be young and wore their hair long, the Northerners shared opinions and life styles that earned them the stereotype "hippies," while the Southerners were labeled "hillbillies." One of the hippies remarked about the dangers of expressing political views in the wrong company:

> I have a rule not to rap about politics. Once I almost got the s——t kicked out of me. I went up to these dudes who had long hair and s——t. Thought they were hippies. They turned out to be hillbillies.

I started to rap about the [Vietnam] war and s——t. They began to call me Commie and I almost got my ass whipped.[45]

It is, of course, possible to work out these differences of opinion and still maintain good social relations. However, as the "hippie" implied in the statement just quoted, the most obvious solution is simply to adopt Mark Twain's rule and not express private sentiments in public. The irony of this solution is that it probably increases sensitivity to the opinions of others and reinforces the power of certain opinions as the keys to membership in particular groups.

As suggested at the beginning of this section, the socializing influence of public opinion is probably due to more than just a sensitivity to social pressure (although fear of isolation and social imitation are powerful factors, as writers from Tocqueville to Riesman have pointed out). Some of the socializing effects of opinion must be attributed to the existence in the public of latent values and beliefs that are activated by changes in social experience and exposure to corresponding social input. Without some prior attachment to newly reinforced perspectives, individuals might experience more conflict and trauma when they change their political views. More importantly, entire populations could not experience such easy shifts in political mood or such regular cycles in political outlooks. In cases like the rise of Nazism in Germany, the swings in political perspective can be so extreme that the seeds of various orientations must exist in order for the drastic change and the return to normality to occur so rapidly and un-self-consciously.

One of the most intriguing formulations of this hypothesis is contained in the work of Noelle-Neumann. She argues that individuals constantly compare their private feelings with the perceived dominant sentiments of the general public. When certain views appear to be in popular disfavor, individuals become increasingly reluctant to express them and increasingly anxious to locate feelings that are more compatible with "public opinion." As a result of this process, groundswells of support may arise for particular views and force other viewpoints out of circulation, creating the popular impression that the displaced opinions have disappeared altogether. However, when the dominant opinion recedes, the "silent" individuals are more likely to make their private feelings public once again.[46] Although the reemerging opinion may seem to be a new trend or a change in public outlook, it is often the simple product of suppressed private opinions that have regained enough social support to become public again.

Two implications of this view for public opinion as a social force are interesting. Perhaps the most obvious concern is the possibility that small but intense groups could monopolize channels of mass communication and distort people's perception of the distribution of public opinion on an issue. Such distortion could lead to the suppression of viewpoints that are numerically dominant but perceived as unpopular or numerically small.

The most important implication for understanding political socialization is the possibility that a cycle of recurring effects operates between the belief systems of individuals and public opinion. Patterns of socialization generate individual belief systems capable of supporting a range of opinions on various subjects. Certain social conditions may lead to a particular pattern of public expression. The way in which opinion is expressed, in turn, becomes a force operating on individual beliefs in a way that engages some and suppresses others. In this fashion, socialization can produce a range of public moods or climates of opinion, and particular climates of opinion can have short- or long-term socializing effects. The inclusion of competing values and the socializing effects of opinion in the analysis of political socialization both clarifies the link between individual opinion and public opinion and brings the impact of socialization on the political system into sharper focus.

NOTES

1. See, for example, David Easton and Jack Dennis, *Children in the Political System: Origins of Political Legitimacy* (New York: McGraw-Hill, 1969); and Fred I. Greenstein, *Children and Politics* (New Haven: Yale University Press, 1965).
2. Robert D. Hess and Judith V. Torney, *The Development of Political Attitudes in Children* (Chicago: Aldine Publishers, 1967), p. 26.
3. Ibid., p. 75.
4. David Easton and Jack Dennis, "The Child's Image of Government," in *Socialization to Politics*, ed. Jack Dennis (New York: Wiley, 1973), p. 71.
5. Ibid., p. 66.
6. See James W. Prothro and Charles M. Grigg, "Fundamental Principles of Democracy: Bases of Agreement and Disagreement," *Journal of Politics*, Vol. 22 (May 1960), pp. 276–94; and Herbert McClosky, "Consensus and Ideology in American Politics," *American Political Science Review*, Vol. 58 (June 1964), pp. 361–82.
7. See Joseph Adelson, "The Political Imagination of the Young Adoles-

cent," *Daedalus*, Vol. 100 (Fall 1971), pp. 1013–50; and M. Kent Jennings and Richard G. Niemi, *The Political Character of Adolescence* (Princeton, N.J.: Princeton University Press, 1974).

8. Several studies conducted during the Watergate years indicate increased levels of political cynicism and disrespect for authority. See, for example, F. Christopher Arterton, "The Impact of Watergate on Children's Attitudes Toward Political Authority," *Political Science Quarterly*, Vol. 89 (June 1974), pp. 269–88. However, it is too early to tell whether these changes are going to persist. In the absence of recurring political scandal and crisis, normal levels of political support are likely to return.

9. See, for example, Fred I. Greenstein, "Young Men and the Death of a Young President," in *Children and the Death of a President*, ed. Martha Wolfenstein and Gilbert Kliman (Garden City, N.Y.: Doubleday, Anchor Books, 1965), pp. 193–216.

10. See Kenneth Keniston, *Young Radicals* (New York: Harcourt Brace Jovanovich, 1968).

11. See Walter Dean Burnham, *Critical Elections and the Mainsprings of American Politics* (New York: Norton, 1970).

12. See, for example, H. C. Triandis and L. M. Triandis, "A Cross Cultural Study of Social Distance," *Psychological Monographs Series*, Vol. 76, No. 21 (1962); and Theodore W. Adorno, Else Frenkel-Brunswik, Daniel J. Levinson, and R. Nevitt Sanford, *The Authoritarian Personality* (New York: Harper, 1950).

13. See, for example, Herbert H. Hyman, *Political Socialization* (New York: Free Press, 1959).

14. M. Kent Jennings and Richard G. Niemi, "The Transmission of Political Values from Parent to Child," *American Political Science Review*, Vol. 62 (March 1968), pp. 169–84; and Jennings and Niemi, *The Political Character of Adolescence.*

15. The call for more research on adolescence is stated strongly in Richard G. Niemi and Barbara I. Sobieszek, "Political Socialization," *Annual Review of Sociology*, Vol. 3 (1977) pp. 209–33.

16. See Theodore M. Newcomb, K. E. Koenig, Richard Flacks, and D. P. Warwick, *Persistence and Change: Bennington College and Its Students After 25 Years* (New York: Wiley, 1967).

17. Easton and Dennis, "The Child's Image of Government," p. 75.

18. Ibid., p. 77.

19. Ibid., p. 78.

20. Jack Dennis, Leon Lindberg, Donald McCrone, and Rodney Stiefbold, "Political Socialization to Democratic Orientations in Four Western Systems," in *Socialization to Politics,* Dennis, p. 187.

21. Edward S. Greenberg, "Black Children and the Political System," *Public Opinion Quarterly*, Vol. 34 (Fall 1970), pp. 333–45.

22. F. Chris Garcia, *Political Socialization of Chicano Children* (New York: Praeger, 1973).

23. Dean Jaros, Herbert Hirsch, and Frederic J. Fleron, Jr., "The Malevolent Leader: Political Socialization in an American Subculture," *American Political Science Review*, Vol. 62 (June 1968), pp. 564–75.

24. See, for example, Robert D. Hess and David Easton, "The Child's

Changing Image of the President," *Public Opinion Quarterly*, Vol. 24 (Winter 1960), pp. 632–42.

25. See, for example, Gabriel A. Almond and Sidney Verba, *The Civic Culture* (Princeton, N.J.: Princeton University Press, 1963); and Jack Dennis, "Support of the Institution of Elections by the Mass Public," *American Political Science Review*, Vol. 64 (September 1970), pp. 819–35.

26. This value pair has also been referred to as competition-cooperation, achievement-equality, and acquisition-redistribution, and public versus private regardingness. See, among others, Louis Hartz, *The Liberal Tradition in America* (New York: Harcourt Brace Jovanovich, 1955); Seymour M. Lipset, *The First New Nation* (Garden City, N.Y.: Doubleday, Anchor Books, 1963); and Rush Welter, *The Mind of America: 1820–1860* (New York: Columbia University Press, 1975).

27. Alexis de Tocqueville, *Democracy in America* (London: Saunders and Otley, 1835); James Bryce, *The American Commonwealth* (New York: Macmillan, 1912); and Harriet Martineau, *Society in America* (New York: Saunders and Otley, 1837).

28. Lloyd A. Free and Hadley Cantril, *The Political Beliefs of Americans: A Study of Public Opinion* (New York: Simon and Schuster, 1968).

29. Ibid., pp. 28–29.

30. Ibid., pp. 11–14.

31. Ibid., pp. 180–81.

32. Alexis de Tocqueville, *Democracy in America*, Vol. 2 (New York: Vintage Books, 1945), p. 102.

33. Ibid., p. 130.

34. Murray Edelman, *Political Language: Words That Succeed and Policies That Fail* (New York: Academic Press, 1977), p. 6.

35. Ibid., p. 6.

36. Ibid., pp. 6–7.

37. Martineau, *Society in America*, p. 7.

38. Bryce, *The American Commonwealth* Vol. 2, p. 351.

39. John Jay Chapman in *The Selected Writings of John Jay Chapman*, ed. Jacques Barzun (Garden City, N.Y.: Doubleday, Anchor Books, 1959), p. 278.

40. David Riesman, *The Lonely Crowd* (New Haven: Yale University Press, 1950).

41. Quoted from Benjamin McCready, "On the Influence of Trades, Professions, and Occupations in the United States, in the Production of Disease," in Lipset, *The First New Nation*, p. 130.

42. Tocqueville, *Democracy in America*, Vol. 2, pp. 275–76.

43. Quoted from John Graham Brooks, *As Others See Us*, in Lipset, *The First New Nation*, p. 131.

44. Mark Twain, *The Autobiography of Mark Twain*, ed. Charles Neider (New York: Harper and Row, 1959), p. 386.

45. From Stanley Aronowitz, *False Promises: The Shaping of American Working Class Consciousness* (New York: McGraw-Hill, 1973), p. 30.

46. See Elisabeth Noelle-Neumann, "The Spiral of Silence: A Theory of Public Opinion," *Journal of Communication*, Vol. 24 (Spring 1974), pp. 43–51.

6

Belief Systems
and
Opinion Formation

belief

SOCIALIZATION explains the origins of individual belief systems and the broad trends in public opinion. However, socialization operates at a step removed from the immediate, day-to-day business of opinion formation and change. The belief systems brought into being by socialization can operate differently under different circumstances. Two general factors affect the formation of opinions about specific political issues. One is the structure of the individual's belief system. In some systems beliefs and values are linked in ways that make individuals open and flexible in their thinking and capable of forming a wide range of opinions. In other belief systems relatively few beliefs and values are connected in rigid ways that produce narrow-minded and mechanical political thinking.

The second factor affecting opinion formation is the specific way in which a political issue or other object of opinion strikes the individual and engages his or her thinking. Belief systems can be governed by a number of cognitive processes. Some individuals may rely heavily on particular opinion formation routines, but most people are capable of using a variety of methods to form their opinions, depending on how the political issue is perceived. In order to explain how particular opinions emerge, the structure of belief systems and the nature of various opinion formation routines must be understood.

STRUCTURES OF BELIEF

In Chapter 5 it was suggested that the social orientations of most Americans center around the core values of individualism and equality. Consider the hypothetical case of a woman who has developed a dominant commitment to individualism. As she applies this value to various areas of her life, it may take on specific forms. For example, when she thinks about matters related to welfare and relief policies, the individualism value may take the form of concerns about personal independence, integrity, the dignity of work, or the pride of accomplishment. Those specific values, in turn, become relevant to real situations as the woman develops beliefs about the social conditions that will promote or destroy the values. On the basis of these value-belief linkages, the woman forms specific opinions about practical political issues. Different individuals, on the basis of their socialization experiences in politics, will develop different ranges of values and beliefs and different connections among them.

For purposes of discussion, let's suppose the hypothetical woman's structure of belief about welfare issues resembles Figure 6-1. A person with a belief structure like this might be expected to form systematically negative and fairly intense opinions about welfare programs. For example, we might expect the kind of intense reaction given by a bricklayer interviewed by Sennett and Cobb. When asked about the welfare question, he snapped: "Welfare! Those lazy sluts having kids like it was a factory. . . . You don't work, you don't live, right?" This man felt that people on welfare have given up their respect and, worse yet, have "gotten away with it."[1] Or, we might hear something like this reaction from a factory worker interviewed by Lane: "But then you get a lot of people who don't want to work; you got welfare—they're happier than hell. Why should they work if the city will support them."[2]

The particular value and belief linkages that give rise to an opinion can be termed the *vertical structure* of the opinion. For example, the remarks of the factory worker quoted by Lane seem to be based on a belief about the impact of welfare on work incentives—a belief that may have been anchored in a strong value of free enterprise. The vertical structure can be thought of as a direct pillar of support for an opinion. The vertical structure accounts for the intensity of an opinion and its importance to the individual.

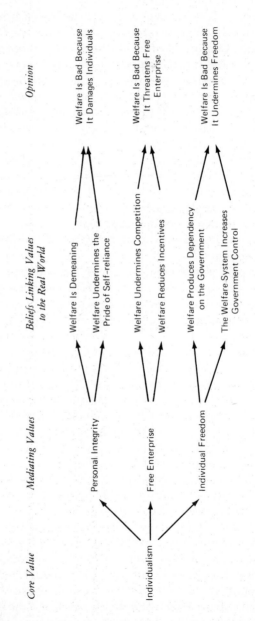

FIGURE 6-1
Hypothetical Belief Structure
Underlying Opinions About Welfare

Core Value   *Mediating Values*   *Beliefs Linking Values to the Real World*   *Opinion*

Individualism

Personal Integrity

Welfare Is Demeaning

Welfare Undermines the Pride of Self-reliance

Welfare Is Bad Because It Damages Individuals

Free Enterprise

Welfare Undermines Competition

Welfare Reduces Incentives

Welfare Is Bad Because It Threatens Free Enterprise

Individual Freedom

Welfare Produces Dependency on the Government

The Welfare System Increases Government Control

Welfare Is Bad Because It Undermines Freedom

In addition, an opinion might be supported indirectly or reinforced by other belief-value linkages. For example, the woman whose structure of belief is shown in Figure 6-1 holds a wide range of beliefs and values that all support essentially the same negative opinion about welfare. The breadth of beliefs and values that tend to be consistent with a particular opinion has been called the *horizontal structure* of a belief system.[3] The horizontal structure affects the stability of an opinion and its resistance to arguments and personal doubt. The vertical and horizontal structures of belief systems can account for such important characteristics of opinion as intensity, stability, direction, and the range of meaningful opinions that can be formed in response to different issues.

Some people may have separate belief systems pertaining to issues such as civil rights, economic problems, welfare policy, and foreign policy.[4] However, common values and beliefs connect these areas for many individuals. For example, vertical structures underlying opinions about civil rights and welfare may rest on the same values. Or the same beliefs may be part of the horizontal structures of different opinions. A steelworker who was asked about welfare and the economy based his opinions on the value of individual integrity and a belief in hard work as a means to achieving that end. This same base of opinion was part of the horizontal structure of his thinking about issues related to social and political equality:

> on the black thing . . . I can't really hate the colored fella that's working with me all day. The black intellectual I got no respect for. The white intellectual I got no use for. I got no use for the black militant who's gonna scream three hundred years of slavery to me while I'm busting my ass. You know what I mean? . . . I have one answer for that guy: go see Rockefeller. See Harriman. Don't bother me. We're in the same cotton field. So just don't bug me.[5]

Even though the steelworker is not an ideologue, it is clear that there is some coherence and continuity in his belief system. He is capable of seeing relationships between different issues and imposing some sort of analytical context on political problems. Lane has referred to this pattern of thinking as "contextualizing."[6] A person who contextualizes opinions displays less formal and systematic thinking than an ideologue but has a much more powerful grasp of political ideas than people who have completely fragmented or atomized belief structures. "Contextualizers" tend to see issues in relation to general political themes, recurring historical trends, or similarities to other issues and events. The steelworker placed the political demands of blacks in the context of general beliefs about work and social groups in America. By using this context, he not only related the political demands of blacks to his own experiences, but he concluded that other people in America are a more appropriate audience for these demands. This allowed him to form the understanding that the white working person is not responsible for the oppression of blacks. The poor working person is in the same boat as the black person. If anyone is responsible (and has the power to do something), it is the upper class.

This pattern of thinking is much different from the pattern we would find in someone who sees no connection between her or his life experiences and those of some black people, or someone who does not think that the upper classes have a role to play in society. Such a person might be inclined to generalize about all black people, taking the political demands of blacks as general personal threats without a specific reference. Such a person would find the world less coherent and events more difficult to explain.

Opinions on specific subjects (like the demands of political groups) might be anchored strictly in beliefs about the subjects themselves. For example, intensely negative opinions about the political behavior of blacks could be based on beliefs about the inferiority or undesirable qualities of black people. When opinions are not connected to general themes or to broad pictures of the world, people are forced to defend them more with emotion than with reason. This is simply because the structure of beliefs and values necessary for reasoning does not exist. Lane calls this pattern of thinking "morselizing."[7]

The continuum of belief patterns ranging from morselizing to contextualizing to ideology can be thought of as the dimension of belief system *integration*. The integration of a belief system simply refers to the existence of general rules or categories of belief that make it possible for an individual to draw on a range of beliefs and values when thinking about a variety of subjects. A second dimension of a belief system derives from the vertical and horizontal structures mentioned earlier. A belief system that contains a broad horizontal structure can be said to be differentiated. *Differentiation* gives people more than one way of thinking about a political problem, and it provides the capacity to think about many different kinds of problem. Belief systems that are integrated and differentiated can be thought of as *complex* belief systems; fragmented and undifferentiated systems can be regarded as *simple*. Research on cognitive complexity and simplicity shows that individuals with complex belief systems tend to produce more informed and stable opinions, and they are less swayed by political propaganda and persuasion techniques. By contrast, cognitively simple belief structures are more receptive to external pressures and produce less consistent and less far-ranging opinions.[8]

In light of our earlier discussion of the state-of-consciousness fallacy, it should be pointed out that these generalizations are applied to individuals and not to groups. Moreover, the political conditions operating in any particular political situation can affect information, emotion, perception, or response options to the point that cognitive differences in opinion formation may be washed out.

OPINION FORMATION ROUTINES

The structure of a belief system explains something about the general tendencies that an individual may display in his or her political thinking. However, it is important to remember that no opinion is completely determined by the structure or the content of a belief system. People may use different routines to apply their beliefs and values to objects in the real world of politics. The choice of one process or another to connect beliefs with objects of opinion and to resolve conflicting beliefs depends to some degree on the personal style and social experiences of each individual. The selection of an operation is also always somewhat dependent on the conditions present in the opinion situation.

For example, the hypothetical individual in Figure 6-1 can be expected to oppose welfare programs in most instances because of the consistently negative alignment of her beliefs and values in this area. However, suppose that the simple practice of adding up the positive and negative weights, or *valences*, of relevant beliefs and values isn't the only opinion formation method that this person can use. On some occasions she may weigh her feelings about an issue against those of friends or respected political leaders. If a well-respected person comes out strongly in favor of a new welfare policy, this support might produce an adjustment in our hypothetical woman's normal thinking about the issue—especially if the position of the reference person is based on a value that she already holds. For example, a new welfare program may contain a work-incentive plan that requires welfare recipients to seek work or receive job training in order to be eligible for welfare benefits. The reference person may argue that the work-incentive aspect of the program is consistent with such values as personal integrity or free enterprise, which are central to the political thinking shown in Figure 6-1. As a result, the woman may form a different opinion about welfare and perhaps even add a new belief to the horizontal structure in this area of her belief system.

This example shows how different circumstances can engage different opinion formation routines and how changes in opinion can even affect the underlying structure of belief. Because different opinion formation processes can affect the way in which people think about an issue, it is important to understand alternative models of opinion formation and change. These models provide direct insights about the patterns of opinion that emerge in various political situations. In fact, the opinion formation routines that are activated within a group in a political situation may be among the most significant determinants of the public support and opposition that emerge around the political issues at stake. If opinions about issues were simply the mechanical products of rigid belief structures, political actors could calculate public support for their issues from the outset. However, it is virtually impossible for political actors or groups to be certain of the levels of public interest and support that will materialize around a political cause. Public involvement will depend on who endorses an issue, how the definition of the issue becomes associated with various values and beliefs, and how these factors fit into different opinion formation routines that individuals have at their disposal.

This discussion suggests that opinion formation processes are important for understanding both the thinking of individuals and the dynamics of public opinion in political situations. Different models of opinion formation are often discussed as though they were mutually exclusive explanations for the way in which underlying beliefs and values become involved in the making of political judgments. The impression that different models are competing with one another to explain the same psychological processes is due largely to the desires of the authors of the various models to claim the maximum possible generality for their efforts. However, if these debates are examined from a distance, it becomes increasingly clear that no single model of opinion change is capable of explaining all the psychological operations that individuals are capable of using to form political judgments. Moreover, each model of opinion formation seems to have some empirical support, and it explains a plausible aspect of opinion formation. In this light, it makes more sense to discuss the various approaches to opinion formation as separate routines used by individuals according to their psychological dispositions and the limiting conditions of political situations.

Social Reference Theories

The earliest models of opinion formation were based on assumptions about social pressure and influence. The basic idea in social reference theories is that opinions are the most direct bonds of identification between people and, as such, become a basis for membership in groups. Once these bonds are established, people tend to maintain them by looking to influential group members for cues about how to think about new issues and problems. The pioneering work on social reference processes was done by Thomas and Znaniecki, who studied the political and social adjustment of Polish immigrants to America in the early part of this century.[9]

In addition to providing psychological reassurance through social membership and acceptance, social reference processes also simplify the task of forming opinions. An individual who trusts the judgment of someone else greatly reduces the complexity of his or her own thinking and lowers the so-called information costs of forming an opinion. As Tocqueville observed a century and a half ago:

> If man were forced to demonstrate for himself all the truths of which he makes daily use, his task would never end. . . . As from the shortness of his life, he has not the time, nor from the limits of his intelligence, the capacity to act in this way. He is reduced to take on trust a host of facts and opinions which he has not had either the time or the power to verify for himself, but which men of greater ability have found out, or which the crowd adopts.[10]

Newcomb's study of attitude change among a group of Bennington College students during the Great Depression is widely regarded as the classic illustration of the role of political opinions as social membership devices. Bennington, an exclusive women's college in Vermont, has had a very liberal faculty for several decades. The school now attracts students from fairly liberal families. During the Depression, however, its liberal reputation had not yet been established, and in the 1930s the families that could afford to send their daughters to an expensive private college tended to be conservative Republicans. The result was that women whose parents identified with the Republican party and voted for Alf Landon in 1936 were exposed to a faculty who were by and large Roosevelt Democrats.

With each year of residence at the college, each successive class of students became more liberal and identified more strongly with Franklin D. Roosevelt than the class behind it. Whereas the freshmen tended to be about as opposed to Roosevelt as their parents were (by about a two-thirds majority), only about 40 percent of the sophomores and 15 percent of the juniors and seniors opposed Roosevelt in the 1936 election.[11] Thus, prolonged exposure to new opinions held by respected sources (in this case, college faculty) in a supportive environment can produce significant change of opinions along with changes in social and political identifications.

Such changes can be lasting. People of the sort who go to wealthy private schools have (as a result of family money, career potential, and college contacts) greater choices about what to do with their lives than many other groups in society have. This was the case with many of the Bennington women. In a follow-up study done twenty-five years later, Newcomb and his associates found that the majority of the women in the original study had maintained their liberal beliefs. For example, about 60 percent of the Bennington graduates voted for Kennedy in the 1960 election, compared with about half of that percentage among women nationally who came from similar backgrounds and maintained similar standards of living but were not graduates of liberal colleges.[12] This finding suggests that once people have formed strong group memberships and have adopted these groups as *reference groups* for their own opinion formation, they will try to maintain some consistency in future social affiliations if their life choices make this possible. Most of the Bennington women, for example, married liberal professional men and maintained their residences in predominantly urban and liberal areas.

This discussion should not imply that anyone who is exposed to new opinions held by some powerful and immediate group will change the way he or she feels and thinks about the world. A number of the women in the Bennington study (about 15 percent of the juniors and seniors) maintained their conservative opinions. They tended to have very close family ties, and their families remained a stronger reference group than the college community of faculty and older, more liberal, students. However, these exceptions to the opinion change hypothesis tend to prove the rule about opinions and social membership. Most of the women who maintained their former political views did so only by self-consciously opting out of membership in the college community and by building elaborate psychological barriers between themselves and most of the faculty and their peers. As one of these holdouts put it: "I wanted to disagree with all the noisy liberals, but I was afraid that I couldn't. So I built up a wall inside me against what they said. I found I couldn't compete, so I decided to stick to my father's ideas. For the last two years I've been insulated against all college influences."[13] By almost any standards of membership in a group, the women who maintained their old political views never became real members of the college community. They seldom became involved in college activities. They were mentioned often by faculty and school health officials as students who seemed to have personality and adjustment problems. Finally, only the most liberal women at the college were mentioned by their peers when the researchers asked for the names of students whom they would like to have represent the college in outside affairs.

Reference group theories like Newcomb's give us a good idea about the importance of political opinions both for the psychological adjustment of individuals and for the social organization of groups. However, reference group theories give us only a general idea about how the psychological end of opinion change works. A number of models have been proposed to explain what goes on within a belief system during opinion change. Some of them combine social and psychological variables; others focus exclusively on cognitive processes. Each approach provides an understanding of some aspect of opinion formation under certain circumstances.

Balance Theory

One of the first attempts to explain the psychology of opinion change was Heider's balance theory.[14] The basic idea is that people try to bring new opinions into a balance with the opinions held by reference persons or groups. In many respects balance theory is a formal statement of the psychological aspects of social reference processes. Balance theory is often used to describe voting choice. For example, voters who considered themselves loyal Democrats in 1976 may have held mixed opinions of different Democratic candidates during the primary elections. However, when Jimmy Carter won the primary nomination at the convention, many strong Democrats formed positive opinions of him because of the endorsement of the party. The principle here is a simple one: If a person or group (such as the Democratic party) that people have positive feelings about expresses positive sentiments toward some object that they need to judge (such as Jimmy Carter), the chances are pretty good that they will try to bring this triangle of opinions into balance by forming a positive opinion of the object:

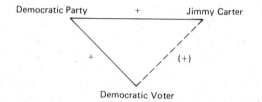

The converse of this balance principle also holds: If a group or person for whom people have little respect or positive feeling (call this a negative reference group) holds a positive view of an object, they will tend to bring their opinions into balance by forming a negative opinion of the object. Thus, balance theory would offer the following explanation for the opinions that many Republican voters formed about Jimmy Carter:

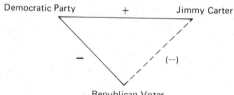

Balance theory becomes more interesting when it addresses the position of individuals who rely on multiple reference groups to form their opinions on certain matters. For example, consider the plight of the Republican voter who also belonged to an evangelical Christian church whose leadership felt that it was very important to put a "born again" Christian in the White House. This person's party affiliation would suggest a negative attachment to Carter, while his or her church affiliation would push toward a positive evaluation of the candidate:

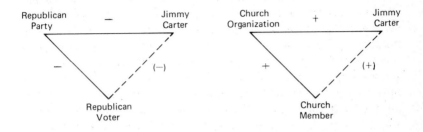

Balance theory would argue that there is a tendency to resolve the dilemma in favor of the reference group that the individual values most highly. In cases where the groups have nearly equal sway with the individual, he or she might withdraw from forming an opinion at all. In many cases in which voters are "cross-pressured," there is a tendency not to vote. If the cross-pressures become extreme, however, the individual may shift his or her reliance on the reference groups or change group affiliations altogether.

Models of Belief-Value Consistency

Not all efforts to evaluate new information involve reference to influential persons or groups. Sometimes a person may strive to form an opinion that simply promotes consistency (or minimizes conflicts) within his or her existing belief and value system. Many models of consistency do not rely directly (or exclusively) on social reference variables.[15] Most of these consistency theories share two common assumptions: First, people strive for a consistent set of beliefs and feelings toward any given object. Second, people develop some sort of private "psychologic" that governs the connection of beliefs and values to whole sets of objects. At the core of consistency theories is the idea that belief systems have structures or "logics" (no matter how idiosyncratic) that account for changes in opinions either when opinions on the same subject come into conflict or when a change in an opinion on one subject renders an opinion on another subject inconsistent or illogical. Thus, consistency theories recognize the possibility that people are aware of some logic in their opinions and are capable of changing their minds in ways that may seem almost rational.

There are too many consistency theories to permit an adequate review of them here. However, one example should illustrate the idea common to them all—namely, that opinion change results from resolving simple contradictions in feelings about an object, either through changing the perception of the object or by changing the underlying beliefs that are in conflict.

As earlier discussions have indicated, the simplest form of opinion organization is a vertical structure, which consists of an underlying value that a person wants to maximize, a belief about whether a particular object in the world has some impact on the value, and a resulting opinion about the object. Whether the opinion is positive, negative, or neutral depends on the object's impact on the value. Thus, a person who values individual freedom, and believes that the welfare system is undermining individual freedom, will probably hold a negative opinion of welfare. This is a simple example of an opinion that follows from (is consistent with) an underlying vertical value and belief structure.

One consistency theorist, Rosenberg, proposed that all stable opinions are connected to such vertical structures: "When a person has a relatively stable tendency to respond to a given object with either positive or negative affect, such a tendency is accompanied by a cognitive structure made up of beliefs about the potentialities of that object for attaining or blocking the realization of valued states."[16] According to Rosenberg, these opinion structures have a logic to them: They are governed by predictable psychological operations. People strive for consistency in the relations among the value that produces the affective (emotional) dimension of an opinion, the belief that represents the cognitive (rational) dimension of an opinion, and the resulting judgment about the object of opinion itself.

This assumption about consistency has some interesting implications. If it is true, a change in any element of the opinion structure should produce some changes in the other elements as well. This not only means that a change in beliefs or values should yield a change in opinions about certain issues, but it also implies that changes in certain opinions may lead to changes in underlying beliefs and values. This is a nice complement to reference group theories like Newcomb's. If opinions are social membership devices, we would expect that group pressures alone might account for some changes in the surface opinions of individuals. However, it is hard to explain the extent, the rate, and the character of subsequent changes in an individual's underlying beliefs and values by social pressure alone. Consistency theories predict that once an opinion change process has been triggered, the individual's own pattern of thinking and logic will direct the course of much of the subsequent change.

In order to test these ideas Rosenberg ran a fascinating, if ethically questionable, experiment. Subjects in the experiment were asked to express their opinions on the issue of whether communists should be allowed to speak in public places. The subjects were also given a list of values to be rated according to their importance. Finally, the subjects were asked to express the intensity of their beliefs that each value would be affected by allowing communists to speak in public. A score was computed for each value-belief pair. For example, if a person valued freedom a great deal and believed intensely that allowing communists to speak in public would promote this value, her or his score on this belief-value pair would be very high. On the other hand, if a person valued political stability a great deal and believed strongly that allowing communists to speak in public was a serious threat to political stability, the score on this pair would be negative.

Consistency theory predicts that the sum of underlying value-belief connections should be correlated with the opinion on the desirability of having communists speak in public. If a person believed that having communists speak in public would consistently promote a number of things that she or he valued, then opinion on this subject should be strongly positive. The belief that some values would be promoted and others damaged by this practice should render opinion neutral. Finally, if a person felt that most of the things she or he valued would be damaged by this practice, then opinion should be strongly negative. Rosenberg's experiment confirmed these predictions.

The confirmation was an impressive demonstration of his consistency theory, but Rosenberg carried the implications of the theory even further. He reasoned that if people change their opinions on a subject they probably experience some psychological pressure to change their underlying beliefs and values in order to make them consistent with the new opinion. (This would explain why the women in the Bennington study who changed some of their political opinions in response to social pressures later developed entire new belief systems on politics and social issues.) In order to test this hypothesis Rosenberg needed to find a way of inducing a genuine and comparable change in some important opinion held by each subject in the experiment. He hit upon the clever, if ethically dubious, idea of using hypnosis to implant the new opinions. He hypnotized each subject individually and induced a change in some opinion that the subject held strongly. For example, one subject was given this hypnotic suggestion:

> When you awake you will be very much in favor of Negroes moving into white neighborhoods. The mere idea of Negroes moving into white neighborhoods will give you a happy, exhilarated feeling. Although you will not remember this suggestion having been made, it will strongly influence your feelings after you have awakened.[17]

After they had received their new opinions, the subjects were sent out into the real world for a couple of weeks. At the end of this period they once again were asked to state their opinion on the relevant subject and to score their values and beliefs related to the subject. The results showed that the beliefs that linked opinions to values tended to change in correspondence to the direction and the degree of opinion change.

Dissonance Theory

The most famous of the consistency theories is Leon Festinger's theory of cognitive dissonance. Since it draws on more variables than any other consistency theory and has become the most famous theory of opinion formation, it deserves special mention. Moreover, dissonance theory differs somewhat from other consistency theories in the claim that it is not the striving for consistency but the desire to reduce psychological conflict, or *dissonance*, that governs opinion formation and change processes.

Dissonance is produced when elements of belief come into conflict either because the object of judgment adds new information to the belief system or because the individual has behaved in a way that is inconsistent with previous beliefs. Dissonance can be reduced by changing one of the beliefs in conflict, changing one's perception of the information or behavior that produced the dissonance, reducing the importance of the beliefs, or trying to find more support for one of the conflicting cognitions. The particular course of opinion change in a given situation will depend on such things as (1) the degree of dissonance aroused by the conflict, (2) the presence or absence of factors that permit the individual to rationalize the conflict away, and (3) the presence or absence of social support groups to bolster the initial opinion.[18] Dissonance theory is interesting because it covers a large number of variables, explains a wide range of cases, and makes some startling predictions. The logic of dissonance theory is best illustrated by a couple of studies that tend to bear out its central hypotheses.

A classic study took place at Yale University after a student riot that was put down with force by the local police department. Many students felt that the police overreacted and indulged in many incidents of brutality. The investigator, Arthur Cohen, selected students at random from the campus and asked them to write an essay that took the side of the police. They had to explain in their essays why the police actions were justified. Some students were paid comparatively large sums of money ($5 and $10) to write the essay, while other students were paid very small sums (50 cents and $1) to participate in the experiment. When the essay was finished, each student recorded his opinion of the police action. The opinions of the four groups were compared to the opinions of a control group selected at random from the student population. The members of the control group did not write an essay. This experiment induced the essay writers to behave in ways that in most cases were contrary to their prior feelings about the incident. Although most of them tended to have negative opinions about the police, they had written an essay in support of the police behavior. Such an action could be expected to arouse dissonance.

Common sense might tell us that those who received the most money would change their opinions most in favor of the police. However, dissonance theory predicts just the opposite. In terms of a dissonance explanation, those who received a large sum of money to take an action contrary to their prior opinions had an easy rationalization or excuse for what they did. They could maintain their original opinion and explain (rationalize) their discrepant behavior as a response to the money. However, those who received very little money for their actions had no such ready-made rationalization. As a result, they should have been more likely to change their opinions in the direction of a more favorable attitude toward the police. That is exactly what happened.

The attitudes of the groups that received $5 and $10 did not differ significantly from the attitudes of the control group—that is, they maintained their original attitudes. However, the group receiving $1 expressed opinions that were significantly more "pro police" than did the control group. The group that received 50 cents was even more favorable toward the police than the $1 group. The implication of dissonance theory here is that when behaviors contradict opinions and arouse dissonance, the dissonance will be resolved by bringing opinions in line with the behavior if no obvious factor can be used to rationalize the behavior away.[19] The outcome of this experiment might have been different if the subjects had been surrounded by people who continued to support their initial opinions even in the face of their discrepant behavior.

An illustration of this principle of dissonance theory was provided in the delightful study by Festinger and his associates of a crypto-religious flying-saucer cult whose members quit their jobs and in some cases left their families to wait with their leader for the end of the world. The cult leader had received a supposedly divine prophecy that the world would be destroyed on a particular date but she and her followers would be rescued in a spaceship shortly before the fateful event. When the appointed time came and went with no terrestrial upheaval, the dissonance of the loyal followers (who had quit jobs and left homes because they believed the prophecy) was compounded by the painful questions of the crowd of reporters and curiosity-seekers who gathered on the front lawn to witness the promised events. Some of the followers decided to return to families, homes, and jobs to await further word from their god from outer space. These members quickly resolved their dissonance by accepting the failure of the prophecy as proof that their beliefs had been misguided. This was the only resolution possible once they lost the support of their fellow "true believers" and encountered the skepticism of the real world. However, the followers who remained together with their leader bolstered their initial belief in the prophecy and resolved their dissonance by deciding that the failure of the prophecy was really just a test from their god to see whether they were loyal.[20]

Although dissonance theory is richer and more interesting than balance theory and other consistency theories, it should not be regarded as a more universal or reliable model of opinion formation. Dissonance is hard to measure, and it is not clear how much any individual can tolerate before he or she will set out to resolve it. Moreover, different individuals probably have different thresholds and tolerances for dissonance. Thus it is hard to know what the real individual impacts are of simple experimental manipulations like the ones used in the Yale study. Another problem is that dissonance theory is complex. It probably captures the elaborate psychological processes at work in some cases of opinion formation and change, but it may complicate needlessly many less exotic cases.[21]

Dissonance theory is not a universal theory of opinion formation. Nevertheless, it may have important applications in situations involving serious psychological tensions and the presence or absence of social support and opportunities to rationalize. For example, it is more likely that dissonance processes will operate during times of rapid social change, political crisis, or social upheaval than during periods of normality. In a similar fashion, it makes sense to look for social references and balance processes in political situations in which group membership is a relevant political variable. For example, in routine election contests, people who tend to vote along party, class, or social group lines may be expected to employ balance or reference processes in forming opinions about candidates and issues. In still other cases, people may have the information or the motivation to form political opinions along lines of rational self-interest. In these cases, it makes sense to explore various belief-value consistency models of opinion formation. As those examples suggest, each model of opinion formation has a place in the political thinking of different individuals under different circumstances. When viewed in this way, the proliferation of theories of opinion formation and change becomes a valuable resource for political analysis rather than a confusing assortment of competing perspectives.

Perceptual Theories

Each of the cognitive theories already discussed addresses internal belief processes aimed at consistency. It is reasonable to suspect that under certain circumstances certain individuals strive for consistency in their political orientations. However, it is also important to recognize that some opinions may not be governed directly by the forces of belief system consistency. In some cases, people may tolerate inconsistent responses to the world because they reflect the contradictions and complexities of the world itself. It has been said that consistency is the hobgoblin of small minds; many people probably regard some ambiguity as a sign of a healthy view of the world. Moreover, some situations seem to be more or less self-contained or laden with extenuating circumstances that make issues and other objects of opinion seem special. When people perceive a situation in a unique way, opinions may not engage the underlying logic of a belief system at all.

This principle is often made the center of persuasion and propaganda campaigns that attempt to change the image of a political object rather than to provide information or argumentation aimed at underlying beliefs and values. If people shift their perceptions of an object, opinions may not be constrained by values and beliefs that otherwise would have entered their thinking.[22] For example, the strategists who planned Richard Nixon's brilliant reelection campaign of 1968 decided not to address directly a whole cluster of long-standing voter concerns about Nixon's past political practices, his hawkish foreign policy record, or his earlier social policy views. Attempting to shape voters opinions through such direct appeals to firmly established and socially supported beliefs and values might have run directly against the forces of cognitive consistency. As an alternative approach, his campaign managers packaged the candidate as the "New Nixon," with new ideas, updated social values, broad-ranging concerns, and even a new political style.[23] Voters attracted to the image of the "New Nixon" were able to form supportive opinions based on values and beliefs other than the ones that might have clouded their judgments of the "Old Nixon."

Several models explain different ways in which perception can directly affect the formation of opinions. One of the most challenging explanations of perception is Daryl Bem's theory of self-perception. Bem argues that one of the most important psychological forces acting on opinions is the requirement to make sense of immediate behaviors and the surrounding social contexts in which they occur.[24] Most situations are complex. They bombard us with thousands of subtle stimuli of which we may not be aware, but to which we respond emotionally and behaviorally. In order to understand what we are doing and how we are feeling in response to these cues, we monitor our reactions and try to interpret them in the most sensible way under the given circumstances. We strive for an interpretation that makes the most sense out of the ongoing situation. This is not always an interpretation that is consistent with prior feelings or past behaviors.

For example, most of us have been in a situation in which we are with someone whom we like very much, yet we discover that the person is getting on our nerves. Perhaps our irritable response has little or nothing to do with the person. We may simply be tired, hungry, or preoccupied with something else. Yet the chances are pretty good that if the person is interacting with us and we snap at the person, we will perceive that something the person did was responsible for our negative feelings. For the duration of that situation we may even get mad at (hold a negative opinion of) that person, although we genuinely like him or her.

In other words, self-perception theory suggests that people monitor their ongoing responses to a situation and try to build the most sensible interpretation of the situation around those responses. Thus, people may find themselves "acting out of character," or expressing new opinions in a particular situation, simply because the actions or opinions are the most sensible ways of making the situation seem coherent. The interesting implication of self-perception theory is that opinions may not always be accurate expressions of what people really feel or actually believe. They may be their best guesses about what they must feel or believe in order to be doing what they are doing in the situation.

The major contribution of self-perception theory is the idea that some of our fomal thinking is the result of observing our own behavior and trying to make the best sense out of it in a given situation. This idea goes back to the psychologist William James, who suggested that many of our thoughts and opinions are the product of reconstructing our actions in ways that make situations credible, intense, and genuine. James posed the hypothetical question of what would account for our fright if we encountered a bear in the woods and ran away. Would we flee because we were afraid, or would we feel frightened because we had run away? James argued that most people would form the impression that they were frightened and that their fear had caused them to flee. This impression would be based on the perception that the bear "caused" their reaction. In fact, certain properties of the situation (for example, a menacing gesture, the discovery of an escape route, the shout of a friend to run) might have triggered the flight response, which in turn would produce physiological responses such as the release of adrenalin and an increase in heart rate. In the context of the situation, the most obvious interpretation of these bodily responses would be fear. From here it would be a simple reconstruction to assume that we were frightened by the bear and this fear caused us to run away. In fact, just the opposite is more likely to be the case, because the emotion (fear) was actually aroused by the behavioral response (running).

The monitoring of responses and relating them to dominant objects of perception in ways that produce sensible interpretations of a situation is illustrated nicely by an experiment conducted by Schachter and Singer.[25] The subjects were given a drug that produced physiological responses similar to those caused by adrenalin (increased heart rate, rapid breathing, and a sense of emotional arousal). After the injection, the subjects were placed in a waiting room to fill out a questionnaire prior to the beginning of the next phase of the experiment. Another person was already in the room. He was introduced as another participant in the experiment. In fact, he was an accomplice of the experimenter.

With one group of subjects the accomplice pretended to be happy. He joked, moved about the room, shot paper wads into the waste basket, and tried to engage the subjects in playful behavior. With a second group the accomplice pretended to be angry. He complained about the experiment, wadded up his questionnaire and threw it in the waste basket, and finally stormed out of the room. The subjects were asked later to describe their moods. Those who had waited with the happy accomplice described themselves as happy or euphoric. Those who were confined with the angry accomplice said they were upset or angry. The drug had produced the same physiological response in both groups of subjects, but the different circumstances surrounding their behavior led members of the two groups to completely different perceptions of their feelings. By contrast, a control group that received a placebo injection reported no unusual reactions to being with either the happy or the angry accomplice.

Self-perception theory may apply to many important political situations. For example, individuals who are unexpectedly swept up in crowds, protests, riots, or demonstrations may find themselves in confrontations with authorities, or they may find themselves imitating the behavior of other demonstrators. Some individuals may become "politicized" if they cannot locate some obvious excuse to rationalize away their new behavior.

In another context, individuals exposed to political campaign advertising may be receptive to the subliminal appeals of jingles, visual images, slogans, or dominant symbols. In an effort to interpret this positive feeling about the experience, the individual may construct a positive opinion of the candidate, even though the favorable feeling has nothing to do with the intrinsic qualities of the candidate.

To cite a final example, Bem argues that if people who have racial prejudices are allowed to choose whether they will associate with members of the other racial group, they will probably opt for segregation. However, if members of antagonistic racial groups can be brought together naturally (that is, not by force or threat) in situations in which they will feel obligated to interact in civilized ways (such as in churches, clubs, restaurants, public transportation, and neighborhoods), the chances are pretty good that they will begin to interpret their harmonious interactions as the result of more favorable opinions about members of the opposite group.[26] They will monitor their own behavior and attribute it to perceived attributes of the other group. Thus, self-perception theory adds a new wrinkle to the old hypothesis that opinions cause behaviors: In some cases it seems that behaviors produce opinions.

TOWARD A GENERAL MODEL OF OPINION FORMATION: ATTRIBUTION THEORY

Most of the models just described started as attempts to provide general explanations of opinion formation and change. As the discussion has indicated, competition among these perspectives has reduced the scope of each of them to cover a specific set of variables and a particular mix of situational factors. In many respects the obvious conclusion from this history is that a general theory of opinion formation is neither necessary nor desirable because individuals are sufficiently complex and political situations are sufficiently different to require several models to explain opinion formation. Nevertheless, there have been efforts to build general models of the process.

Dissonance theory is a fairly general model: It incorporates principles from social reference theories, balance theory, and models of value-belief consistency. However, the most general perspective on opinion formation is attribution theory. Within its framework it incorporates principles of cognitive consistency and perception. Like dissonance theory, attribution theory has been criticized for not being specific enough about when its principles come into play or how they operate together systematically.[27] Although attribution theory may not satisfy a rigorous definition of a theory (and therefore does not represent a truly general explanation of opinion formation), it does provide a useful overview of some of the major factors in the opinion formation process. As such, it brings a helpful focus to the subject.

Attribution theory begins with the simple assumption that if an object, event, or person has a major impact on people in a situation over time, people will try to form stable judgments about that stimulus in order to respond to it more sensibly and effectively. People stabilize their judgments about an object of opinion by performing various perceptual, cognitive, and social tests on their reactions to it. These tests help to define the stimulus and isolate its effects.[28]

The most obvious test is simply the monitoring of reactions to see whether feelings about stimulus remain fairly constant. If they do not, people begin to search for factors that might be affecting their reactions. For example, people may have developed a high opinion of a particular political candidate but discover later that they react negatively to her when they meet her in person. They may conclude that the positive opinion was based on the fact that she came across very well on television, yet has little charm or magnetism in face-to-face situations.

People may also test to see whether their response to an object of opinion is the result of associating (categorizing) the object with other things that they hold in consistently high or low regard. For example, the candidate may have been categorized as a liberal because of her remarks in press conferences and on news interview shows. People who regard themselves as liberals may have found this labeling enough to stabilize their initial reactions. However, in their personal encounter they may have asked a question to which the candidate gave an unmistakably conservative response. This might shake previous opinions, for it makes the liberal categorization on which opinion was based less applicable. Uncertainty about how to label the candidate may lead to social reference processes through which people test and stabilize their opinions by sounding out the reactions of reference groups or individuals whose judgments on the subject are usually reliable. As a result of such a test, people might change their opinion about the hypothetical political candidate if a respected political observer tells them that she has changed her position on many issues simply to win the support of the audience she is addressing at the time. On the other hand, their friends may persuade them to give the candidate another chance on the grounds that her poor performance was due to fatigue or to an inadequate opportunity to go into enough depth on the question that produced the seemingly conservative response.

In short, attribution theory simply assumes that we seek to clarify and stabilize our reactions to important objects around us by submitting those reactions to a number of tests. The tests clarify both the nature of feelings and the properties of the object of opinion or the surrounding situation that account for those feelings.

What is interesting about attribution theory is that its assumptions about the psychology of opinion formation are less demanding and less complex than the assumptions underlying other theories, yet attribution theory brings together many of the psychological operations described in the other theories. For example, the idea that people can stabilize opinions by filtering them through the judgments of others occupies a major role in reference group and balance theories and a minor role in dissonance theory. Attribution theory is similar to self-perception theory: Both suggest that people often associate their feelings about stimuli with dominant features of the situation in which those stimuli operate. Finally, attribution theory, like consistency theories, assumes that people seek stable understandings of objects that loom large in their social worlds.

CONCLUSION

Each theory of opinion formation and change seems to explain how individuals respond to different circumstances. As a group, they cover a range of opinion formation routines. It is important to recognize that these operations are not simply the products of differing individual styles of thinking. Although some individuals may rely on one routine more than on others, most people are capable of utilizing any routine when the circumstances are right. Therefore, it is important to see the connections between political situations and opinion formation processes. The connections illuminate another stage in the transformation of individual opinion into public opinion.

Public opinion may be the result of different routines under different circumstances. The case of public support for Richard Nixon shows a number of operations at work. During the trauma of the Watergate crisis, trends in political support seemed to conform to a classic dissonance pattern. Many of the President's supporters in Congress made early public statements defending the chief executive against charges of wrongdoing. As revelations of Nixon's increasing Watergate involvement began to appear, these supporters must have experienced increasing dissonance. Some early supporters changed their opinions of Nixon by using the subsequent revelations as a rationalization. They claimed that they could not have known the extent of Nixon's involvement and that they had been deceived by their leader. Such claims reflect the dissonance operations of rationalization and changing the perception of the object. A closely knit group of supporters continued to support the President and speak in his behalf in public. Their mutual support seemed to lead them to deny the importance of the charges against Nixon and to underemphasize the weight of the evidence against him. This corresponds to the dissonance operation of denial. These two tendencies also emerged in the broad trends in public support for Nixon. Shortly after the damaging testimony delivered by John Dean before the Senate investigating committee, public support for the President began slipping steadily from around the 50 percent level until it reached a low of around 25 percent. However, once it reached this level, the decline halted, and a small percentage of diehard supporters held firm until Nixon left office.

This pattern in both elite and mass support suggests the dominance of opinion formation routines different from the ones that probably governed public opinion under other circumstances. For example, the earlier discussion of Nixon's 1968 election campaign pointed out that information was presented to the public in ways that encouraged people to change their perceptions of the candidate rather than to engage in the resolution of cognitive dilemmas. Under other circumstances, public opinion may have depended more heavily on balance and social reference processes.

These suggestions are, of course, only hypotheses. Further research is needed to establish how much of the structure of public opinion is the result of common opinion formation routines triggered by different political circumstances. However, it is clear that people can use different routines at different times, and it is reasonable to suspect that dominant political conditions may produce common responses within groups in the public.

NOTES

1. From Richard Sennett and Jonathan Cobb, *The Hidden Injuries of Class* (New York: Vintage Books, 1972), p. 135.
2. Robert E. Lane, *Political Ideology* (New York: Free Press, 1962), p. 72.
3. The ideas of vertical and horizontal belief structures are explained cogently in Daryl J. Bem, *Beliefs, Attitudes, and Human Affairs* (Belmont, Calif.: Wadsworth, 1970), ch. 2.
4. The extreme case of compartmentalized or fragmented belief systems results in what Abelson has called "opinion molecules," in which

each opinion is a self-contained entity cloaked in its own belief-value linkage and detached from other opinions. See Robert P. Abelson, "Computers, Polls, and Public Opinion—Some Puzzles and Paradoxes," *Transaction*, Vol. 5 (September 1968), pp. 20–27.

5. From Studs Terkel, *Working* (New York: Avon Books, 1972), p. 6.
6. See Lane, *Political Ideology*, pp. 350–53.
7. Ibid.
8. For a more extensive discussion of cognitive structure in belief systems, see W. Lance Bennett, *The Political Mind and the Political Environment: An Investigation of Public Opinion and Political Consciousness* (Lexington, Mass.: Heath, Lexington Books, 1975), ch. 3.
9. W. I. Thomas and Florian Znaniecki, *The Polish Peasant in Europe and America* (Boston: Badger, 1918).
10. Alexis de Tocqueville, *Democracy in America*, Vol. 2 (New York: Vintage Books, 1945), p. 9.
11. Theodore M. Newcomb, *Personality and Social Change* (New York: Dryden Press, 1943).
12. Theodore M. Newcomb, K. E. Koenig, R. Flacks, and D. P. Warwick, *Persistence and Change: Bennington College and Its Students After Twenty-Five Years* (New York: Wiley, 1967).
13. Newcomb, *Personality and Social Change*, p. 119.
14. Fritz Heider, *The Psychology of Interpersonal Relations* (New York: Wiley, 1958).
15. For a review of these theories, see Robert P. Abelson et al., eds. *Theories of Cognitive Dissonance: A Sourcebook* (Chicago: Rand McNally, 1968).
16. Milton J. Rosenberg, "An Analysis of Affective-Cognitive Consistency," in *Attitude Organization and Change*, eds. Milton J. Rosenberg et al. (New Haven: Yale University Press, 1960), p. 18.
17. Ibid., pp. 26–27.
18. Leon Festinger, *A Theory of Cognitive Dissonance* (Evanston, Ill.: Row-Peterson, 1957).
19. Jack W. Brehm and Arthur R. Cohen, *Explorations in Cognitive Dissonance* (New York: Wiley, 1962).
20. Leon Festinger, Henry Riecken, and Stanley Schachter, *When Prophecy Fails* (New York: Harper and Row, 1956).
21. Criticisms of dissonance theory have been raised by a number of psychologists. See, for example, N. P. Chapanis and A. Chapanis, "Cognitive Dissonance: Five Years Later," *Psychological Bulletin*, Vol. 61 (January 1964), pp. 1–22. For a general review, see Charles A. Kiesler and P. A. Munson, "Attitudes and Opinion," *Annual Review of Psychology*, Vol. 26 (1975), pp. 415–56.
22. The idea of a "perceptual shift" theory of opinion formation is developed more fully in Dan Nimmo, *The Political Persuaders* (Englewood Cliffs, N.J.: Prentice-Hall, 1970).
23. For an excellent account of how the "New Nixon" was packaged and presented to the voting public, see Joe McGinniss, *The Selling of the President: 1968* (New York: Trident, 1969).
24. See Daryl J. Bem, "Self-Perception: An Alternative Interpretation of

Cognitive Dissonance Phenomena," *Psychological Review*, Vol. 74 (May 1967), pp. 183–200.

25. Stanley Schachter and Jerome Singer, "Cognitive, Social, and Physiological Determinants of Emotional State," *Psychological Review*, Vol. 69 (November 1962), pp. 379–99.

26. Bem, *Beliefs, Attitudes, and Human Affairs*, pp. 66–69.

27. See Kiesler and Munson, "Attitudes and Opinions."

28. For a discussion of attribution theory more detailed than the description presented here, see Harold H. Kelley, "Attribution Theory in Social Psychology," in *Nebraska Symposium on Motivation, 1967*, ed. David Levine (Lincoln: University of Nebraska Press, 1967). See also Edward E. Jones, David E. Kanouse, Harold H. Kelley, Richard E. Nisbett, Stuart Valius, and Bernard Weiner, *Attribution: Perceiving the Causes of Behavior* (Morristown, N.J.: General Learning Press, 1972).

7

Opinions and Personality

THE OPINIONS that men and women express can become part of their self-image and may be regarded by others as aspects of their personality. Personality also affects the opinion formation routines that individuals use. For example, some personality types may emphasize the social adjustment functions of opinions and use primarily reference group or balance routines to form opinions. The characteristics, conflicts, and demands of personality can affect the way in which a person expresses (as well as forms) opinion. The resulting opinions determine the effectiveness of actions and the gratifications a person receives from those actions. In short, personality shapes opinions, and opinions in turn shape personality.

Like the other variables in the domain of the individual and society, personality can affect both individual opinion and public opinion. Some events may produce universal sensations of fear, anxiety, guilt, sorrow, or joy; under these conditions people may experience similar emotional reactions. In other cases, periods of dramatic social change can create problems of social adjustment and object appraisal; these conditions may also produce similarity in the operation of belief systems. The ability of political actors to control events and images in ways that produce common emotional responses can be a powerful means of manipulating public opinion. The following discussion illustrates how personality shapes the political behavior of both individuals and groups.

PERSONALITY:
THE CONCEPT AND A CASE STUDY

Personality is generally defined as the recurring pattern of thoughts, feelings, and behaviors that distinguish an individual's performance in social roles from the actions of others who occupy the same or similar roles. Personality consists of regular patterns of behavior that can't be accounted for exclusively by constraints in a situation or the role a person occupies in a situation. Personality-related behaviors occur when an individual uses his or her characteristic psychological strategies to cope with recurring personal strains, place new experiences in a comfortable perspective, establish consistent patterns for relating to other people, and gain gratification from the available reward structure in a situation. These basic strategies orient the individual in the world and make his or her social behavior seem real and coherent, both personally and to others.

It goes without saying that some people succeed better than others in adapting to situations in satisfying ways. Different situations affect adaptation by offering emotional stimuli that are more or less satisfying to different personalities. Each personality, in turn, will interpret and respond to aspects of a situation differently, according to the needs, coping behaviors, and ego defenses that define the personality. Analyzing how a person forms opinions in new situations is the key to understanding how adaptive the personality is, how emotionally accessible the situation is, and how different individuals within the same situation manage to work out their own perspectives. When viewed from a personality perspective, opinions can be considered the initial and the most personally controllable links between the enduring orientations of individuals and the shifting social reality that surrounds them.

If we know something about the personality of an individual and the situation in which he or she is operating, the characteristics (content, intensity, direction, stability, constraint) of the resulting opinions can be very revealing. For example, consider the case of a young woman named Alice, who was raised in a politically active family.[1] Her parents were active members of the local party organization, and her older brothers followed in their footsteps. The social life of the family revolved around political functions ranging from campaign work and fund raising to socializing with politicians and other party faithful. The everyday conversation in the family centered on politics, and the personal success of family members was measured largely in terms of political accomplishments. Despite living in an environment in which political stimuli were dominant and particular opinions about party, candidates, and social issues were the keys to membership, Alice remained apolitical during the entire time she lived at home. She formed few opinions about politics in particular and social issues in general. She seldom participated in political activities. Perhaps most significantly, she formed only a weak identification with her parents' political party, even though the party was the clear focus of family life. One indicator of the absence of political ties in Alice's life is the fact that she didn't vote until years after leaving home, despite the fact that her family campaigned actively for many candidates and she knew some of them personally as a result of meeting them at family social functions.

Why did Alice avoid forming intense and stable political opinions similar in content to those held by everyone else in this politics-dominated environment? Personality factors usually account for cases in which an individual departs from strong situational pressures to conform, rejects the dominant opinions of the most immediate reference group, or selects different features of situations around which to build an emotional life and express individuality. Alice grew up as a highly competitive, achievement-oriented individual in a family in which the love and respect of parents (and, indeed, self-respect as well) depended on one's tangible accomplishments in the outer world. In this context, the political world was far from representing an arena for personal accomplishment; in fact, the political world placed Alice at a disadvantage. First, it was a male-dominated world in which women seldom made major contributions or received great acknowledgment. This made the easy availability of objects of opinion such as parties, candidates, and issues more a cause of frustration than a source of emotional gratification for her. Second, by the time Alice was old enough to begin forming ties with the outer world, her older brothers had already established themselves as young politicians. This placed her on an uneasy footing in the established reward system of the family. Both these factors left her with serious handicaps in a group in which competition and measurable achievements were the keys to success and emotional support. The result was that Alice turned to other areas of achievement and self-expression to establish herself in the family. The most important forum in which she expressed her competitive disposition and accumulated recognized accomplishments was in school.

The interesting aspect of Alice's case is that everything changed dramatically some years after she left home. She went from being apolitical to being an intensely political person. She became active in party politics. She expanded her belief system into a highly constrained, intense, and stable set of opinions. Finally, she returned to her family on its own terms; she became the recognized dominant political force in the group. The reasons for this dramatic change are as complex as the explanations for her earlier rejection of politics. However, they once again had to do with her personality and how it operated to integrate her social experiences around a coherent and functional self-image.

The discussion of Alice's political transformation will be limited to an analysis of two major changes that affected her identity deeply—so deeply, in fact, that she was forced to reorganize her entire belief system in order to stabilize her emotional life. The two events were related. First, she fell in love with a man and later married him. This sort of emotional involvement requires significant emotional adjustments for anyone. However, Alice's basic coping strategies were challenged further by the fact that the man was a Catholic who insisted that they be married in the church. The decision to become a Catholic represented a major life change for Alice. It required the formation of a whole new belief system—a belief system that had profound implications for her own identity because of the new opinions that she had to adopt concerning her role as a woman, her understandings about family, and so forth. The change also required her to accept a new reference group and struggle with the formation of certain opinions that were necessary to establish her as a member. To complicate things further, her family disapproved of the conversion to Catholicism, which meant that all of these significant changes represented a potential threat to her immediate support group and the one part of her emotional world that had been relatively stable. Finally, she had to manage these crises and changes in a way that did not threaten the relationship with her new husband.

This is where politics enters the scene for the second time. These events in Alice's life took place in 1960, a year in which a Catholic (John F. Kennedy) was running for President. The three major elements in Alice's life were strongly associated with his campaign. Her family were avid Kennedy supporters, and they campaigned actively for him. Her new husband was also involved in the election effort. Finally, the church became identified with the candidate indirectly through the Catholic connection and directly through social groups who worked for his election and encouraged members like Alice to become involved. Under these circumstances the world of politics suddenly held a strong attraction for Alice. Most importantly, the formation of a new system of political opinions became the means of reintegrating her emotional life and her social world.

The involvement in the Kennedy campaign let Alice link her ties to family, husband, and church in ways that were acceptable to all concerned. Second, her new-found political activities provided a much-needed outlet for her achievement orientation in the church context, where she had felt pressured to accept a more passive role as a woman. Whereas politics formerly had been associated with limitations on women's possible achievements, it now became a path to liberation. Third, and related to this, politics offered Alice an opening to begin redefining her affiliation with the church. Instead of seeming to be a foreign and somewhat threatening environment, the church came to represent a social setting in which Alice could express herself in terms of behaviors she had observed in her own home as a child. This "familiarization" of a stressful environment literally involved the symbolic conversion of the church from a threatening religious organization to a supportive political group. Finally, this transformation provided Alice with a means of establishing herself firmly with her new husband on her own terms. Where the religious constraints on her behavior could have become a source of friction and frustration, the emergence of mutual political commitments out of the religious context enabled the relationship to begin on an equal footing.

Once this process of opinion change began, it continued to evolve. Alice eventually developed a highly constrained and stable liberal ideology. She became a prominent figure in Democratic party politics in her state. She and her husband and her family frequently participated together in party work and in social activities related to politics. In short, Alice formed a set of opinions and related behaviors that integrated her social worlds in a way that was most consistent with her personality.

This brief case study suggests that there are different levels on which to explain the formation and changing of opinion. On one level it is clear that the changes in Alice's social orientation and political behavior can be explained by various aspects of the theories presented in Chapter 6. Themes in her story trigger obvious associations with reference group, balance, dissonance, self-perception, consistency, and attribution perspectives. However, it is important to recognize that powerful personality factors can activate these specific opinion change processes and determine the course of their development. Recognizing the impact of personality on social and political consciousness also brings home the fact that we all have very personal and compelling reasons for holding opinions. The logic that connects abstract opinions to our basic personal dispositions may not always be simple or easy to discover. It is always important to bear in mind, however, that our social outlooks are seldom far removed from enduring private dispositions and personal reactions to immediate life circumstances.

Not only does personality give us a basis for understanding the origins, the structural characteristics, and the functions of our social views, but it offers important insights about the origins and the motives behind many of the stands that ordinary people and political actors take on public issues. It would be wrong to reduce all questions of morality, political consciousness, and political action to matters of personality. Nevertheless, personality can help unravel many of the mysteries surrounding the political issues with which people become associated, the intensity of their commitments, and their styles of political action.

An extension of this concern raises the interesting question of how we can expect various personality types to respond to different political issues in different situations. Personality may be an important variable for predicting and evaluating the behavior of politicians in public office. As mentioned earlier, personality also opens up new ways of thinking about public opinion and collective political behavior. Personality perspectives can help illuminate the impact of political events, government actions, social changes, and crises on mass political thinking and behavior. The world of politics is one of rapid change, uncertainty, threats, and life and death decisions. Political events and crises can affect the very foundations of our personalities. A threat of nuclear attack can arouse anxieties based on needs for security. A decision to cut back food stamps or public assistance programs can arouse the fears or aggressions of those who depend on them for basic nurturance and survival. The sudden loss of a leader with whom people have identified can undermine their sense of trust and community. Often these sorts of events have an impact on large numbers of people in ways that release mass political outpourings directed at particular political objects.

The fact that the precipitating events and the objects of mass political attention may be uniform often produces the perplexing question of how so many different people can become spontaneously involved politically in such similar ways. Personality explanations show how similar events can take on numerous private meanings and still produce uniform mass behavior. The remainder of this chapter will explore these three major areas: (1) how personality enters the opinion formation process, (2) how personality mediated by opinions affects the political behavior of individuals, and (3) how personality enters the complex realm of mass political behavior.

PERSONALITY AND
THE FORMATION OF OPINION

One of the classic statements on the role of personality in opinion formation is Harold Lasswell's simple description: p) d) $r = P$. This framework represents a process through which private dispositions (p) are displaced (d) onto public objects or political issues and rationalized (r) in terms of publicly acceptable motives or standard political opinions.[2] Lasswell was interested in individuals who organized the bulk of their private lives around politics. People who engage in this process of transferring private sentiments to political objects can be thought of as political personalities (P). However, the same psychological process through which political personalities are created applies to all of us to some lesser degree. Any opinion that we hold intensely over a long period of time reflects to some extent the efforts of our personalities to produce a stable and emotionally satisfying world in which to operate.

Although there are many different approaches to the study of personality, research on personality and public opinion has drawn overwhelmingly on three related perspectives: (1) Freudian theories, (2) human-potential theories, and (3) personality trait theories. Each approach focuses on a different aspect of personality and, as a result, offers a slightly different explanation for the impact of personality on political opinions. However, some of the most imaginative research on personality and opinion has borrowed compatible elements from the different perspectives. Following this precedent, and in keeping with the account of opinion formation routines in Chapter 6, the major perspectives on personality and opinion will be discussed as complementary rather than as competing viewpoints.

Freudian Theories

Sigmund Freud is the father of the modern conception of personality. Although many contemporary theorists disagree with Freud, and few scholars who study belief systems and the psychology of opinions are true Freudians, there is little that has been written about personality that does not owe a considerable debt to Freud. Lasswell's formulation, for example, makes use of a number of important Freudian concepts.

Freud saw the origins of personality in the fundamental conflict between our biological imperative to satisfy primary needs of sex, nutrition and comfort, and elimination, and the demands of society to defer some of these biological impulses, to place others on rigid schedules, and to deny still others. Personality emerges out of this painful conflict between the urgings of biological drives and the demands of civilization to subordinate these drives to the laws and customs of society, the limits of the environment, and the whims of others. Freud termed the tendency to satisfy biological uges the "pleasure principle"; the subordination of biological drives to social and environmental demands he termed the "reality principle." Freud observed that most societies bring the biological nature of individuals into line with social customs according to a clear developmental sequence. At each stage of this sequence the individual learns to control a major biological impulse by associating it with a pattern of behaviors that become his or her means of expressing that impulse in socially acceptable manners and trying to satisfy it within the limits tolerated by society.

The first stage of personality or ego development is the *oral stage*. The infant's primary need is for nutrition and physical comfort. If he or she is to succeed in satisfying these needs throughout life, they must be expressed in meaningful terms and controlled so that they fit into society's prescribed means of obtaining food, shelter, and comfort. The parent provides the infant with certain universal lessons about oral gratification such as the importance of asserting one's needs and accepting the fact that one is often dependent for gratification on the schedules of others and their assessments of how deserving of gratification the individual is.

Relations with parents also introduce a range of variables into the infant's developing character. For example, some parents may feed infants on demand, while others place the child on a strict schedule that may or may not coincide with hunger. Some parents may lavish attention on the child during nursing, while others may reduce feeding to a fairly sterile, clinical process. Such variations in parental behavior can leave deep impressions on human character. As a result of these things some people may feel more in control of the acquisition of creature comforts in later life. Others may develop the enduring impression that the world is harsh and arbitrary and that one can do little to affect one's level of personal satisfaction.

Some people may come to associate basic oral gratification with other important aspects of the social world. For example, those who were lavished with attention, love, and pleasurable contact during feeding may see the world as a supportive place and on the basis of feelings about their parents, regard significant authority figures as helpful, supportive, and positive. Others, because of childhood experiences with unresponsive or emotionally distant parents, may become suspicious of others and feel that they may deprive them of needed love and support. The important idea here is that the individual, while developing strategies for satisfying basic biological impulses, acquires a related set of orientations about other people and objects.

The development of a stable orientation to the world through the adjustment of biological drives to the demands of reality continues in the *anal stage*. In this stage the child must learn to control the natural urge to eliminate wastes whenever the urge arises. The child learns that there are certain standards of order and cleanliness that must be observed in society.

As in each stage of development, a wide range of new personality variables can be added in the anal stage, depending on how the parents train the child in personal habits. For example, most children tend to view the waste products they eliminate as having some value because they seem to be the objects of so much parental attention and concern. If parents place the child on a harsh schedule of punishment for improper toilet behavior, the child may become wary or fearful about giving things to others or sharing things as a result of painful associations developed during this stage. Alternately, the use of positive reinforcement and support during this training process may produce an individual who values giving things to others and receives personal satisfaction from acts of sharing and openness.

The next stage of development involves the critical problem of channeling sex drives in socially acceptable ways. During the *genital stage*, the child must learn how to express sexual desires in keeping with social custom. He or she must acquire a sexual identity, come to terms with social norms that favor particular sexual relationships (such as the dominant pattern of monogamous heterosexual relationships in American society), and accept taboos against incest, sexual expression in public, and so forth. The genital stage is, to say the least, a very delicate stage in the development of the personality. Depending on whom children are encouraged to identify with sexually (father, mother, uncle, etc.) and how they are permitted to express their sexual urges, they may or may not acquire comfortable ways of expressing sexual desires and effective means of seeking gratification from others. Moreover, depending on the sensitivity with which society's sexual norms are imposed by parents, children can easily acquire in later life unhealthy fears, self-doubts, and attitudes about authority. According to the Freudians, if sexual desires are punished harshly and labeled as undesirable in some family contexts, children may learn to fear this mysterious element in their biological make-ups and throughout life accept the need to submit to severe authority—all as a result of early experiences in which they were treated as though they were incapable of controlling their evil desires.

After the genital stage, children enter the world outside the family and face the problem of establishing meaningful social relationships on their own. They must learn how to engage others, express themselves effectively, and establish ways of channeling the right kind of emotions and behaviors into relationships. In this, the *phallic stage*, the child is presented with opportunities to form all sorts of relationships—sexual, romantic, friendly, hostile, loving, caring. Depending on the diversity of social contact in the adolescent environment and how well earlier personality development has equipped the child to express and share emotions with others, the result will be to see the social world either as an emotionally responsive and personally accepting place or as a limiting and rejecting place.

In each stage of development the individual acquires an enduring set of social dispositions. For our purposes it is less important that the person learn to adapt his or her biological make-up to the demands of social reality than it is to realize that during the adaptive process, various objects in the external world become associated with important personal needs, drives, or impulses. For example, the way in which people progress through the oral stage

TABLE 7-1
Sociopolitical Factors Corresponding to
Freudian Stages of Personality Development

Stage of Personality Development	Corresponding Sociopolitical Factor
Oral	Security
Anal	Order
Genital	Authority
Phallic	Community

will determine a great deal about their senses of security, well-being, and independence. The course of anal development contributes to our general sense of order, change, and chaos. The genital stage shapes our orientations to authority in the important areas of our desire to give up our personal control to others or our conviction that we can control our own impulses and make our own life choices. Finally, the pattern of development in the phallic stage shapes our sense of community—how we feel about others and how we identify with different types of people.

In short, personality is the basic orientation that anchors us emotionally and intellectually in life situations and organizes the stimuli in the environments around us in terms of how they fit into our basic feelings about *security, order, authority,* and *community.* The significance of personality for opinion formation should be obvious from this formulation. The social world and the political conflicts within it revolve almost exclusively around the problems of *security, order, authority,* and *community.* Virtually any opinion expressed on any subject can be reduced to a concern about one of these factors. The implication of a Freudian model of personality is that the worldly objects in which we take an interest and the ways in which we express our interest can be reduced to the general associations we make between patterns of experience in the stages of biological development and the larger social images that emerge from each stage. These linkages between personality development and political orientations are summarized in Table 7-1.

In this context we can see how Lasswell proposed that people form political attachments and opinions by transferring private dispositions to public objects and adopting publicly acceptable explanations for their interest in those objects. This emotional transformation is carried out through a psychological network of what Lasswell (following Freud) called *ego defense mechanisms.*

A person's sense of self (ego) consists of the collection of enduring psychological and behavioral orientations acquired during the long process of reconciling biological impulses with social demands. In addition to these psychological and behavioral orientations, people also acquire a set of strategies for applying these general orientations to ongoing life situations. This process involves learning how to translate aspects of specific social contexts into terms that suit personal dispositions. The translation makes life personally meaningful. Ego defense mechanisms link the outer world to the inner world of personality in ways that are consistent with basic personal concerns and that protect the ego from shock, embarrassment, or emotional frustration. These defense mechanisms include displacing emotion from objects that are unsatisfying or threatening to objects that represent acceptable outlets for emotion; transforming basic biological impulses into more acceptable forms of thought and action; producing intellectually defensible (for example, rationalized) accounts of significant behaviors or feelings; and denying the existence or importance of aspects of a situation that are emotionally threatening. Every person builds up a large repertoire of these and other ego defenses, which guide people in selecting objects of concern and in establishing emotional bonds with those objects.

Applications of Freudian Theories

There are many ways of linking the developmental patterns of individuals to political consciousness. For example, in his classic study of a small group of working-class men, Lane found that early childhood relations between the men and their fathers had profound effects on their world views and political opinions. De Angelo, one of the men in Lane's study, came from a broken home. When he was a young child, De Angelo's mother remarried. De Angelo recalled his stepfather:

> he was bad when he was drunk. I never had too much respect for him. . . . When he was drunk he wanted to argue, you know. But my mother was bigger than him—didn't have too much trouble taking care of him. After a while my mother left him, you know, and we were on our own.[3]

As we might expect from someone with this sort of background, De Angelo experienced a number of insecurities in later life and tended to see the outer world in generally unsupportive and negative terms. For example, when asked whether he thought America was moving closer to a perfect society, he replied: "I don't think we'll ever get any closer [to a more perfect society]. We are getting farther and farther away from it, I guess. All indications are we're moving away from it. There's not enough people trying to make the world perfect."[4] He then expressed a number of specific opinions to explain his general view of society, blaming the loss of religion and the rise of communism. This case illustrates nicely the personality correlates of social orientations and the ways in which personality can operate to provide structure within a set of horizontal beliefs (in this instance, the way De Angelo supports his opinions about the state of the world with beliefs about religion and communism).

Some analysts have generalized from case studies of individuals to report the discovery of common patterns of personality development that produce personality types, or *syndromes*. Some personality syndromes have clear implications for the development of political orientations. The most famous syndrome is the so-called authoritarian personality discovered by a group of researchers following World War II.[5] They were interested in the question of whether any personality link might explain the mass adoption of the powerful attitudes of anti-Semitism and pro-fascism that led to the tragedies of that era. According to the developmental profile of the authoritarian personality, childhood experiences were characterized by little affection, harsh punishment, the treatment of sex as a taboo subject, the severe punishment of sexual behaviors, and strict authority and discipline. As a result of these and other developmental experiences, the authoritarian personality develops a distrust of his or her and others' abilities to control their impulses and aggressions; a need for strict hierarchical authority in all situations; an inability to live with uncertainty, accompanied by a rigid "black and white" style of thinking; a tendency to hold conservative political views; and an intense hostility toward people who are "different" or "deviant" (racial, sexual, and religious minorities, the mentally handicapped, the physically disabled). To translate these dispositions into the four sociopolitical factors listed in Table 7-1, it is fair to say that the extreme authoritarian personality has been damaged at each stage of personality development, with the result that his or her social views are dominated by concerns for *security*, an extreme penchant for *order* in all matters, a dominant need for strict, hierarchical social and political *authority*, and a narrow sense of *community* that involves extreme dedication to his or her immediate group and equally extreme hostility toward and condemnation of out-groups.

Concepts such as the authoritarian personality have an intuitive appeal: We all probably know someone who fits the stereotype. However, use of personality concepts to explain political thinking and behavior is risky, as research on the authoritarian personality syndrome shows. Even though the concept of authoritarianism is still popular among some scholars and has such a sufficient ring of truth that it has found its way into popular usage, it has been subjected to harsh criticism for nearly thirty years. Some critics argue that the defining criteria are too vague and the methods of fitting people into them are too crude to label someone an authoritarian with any confidence.[6] Others argue that if authoritarianism is a personality syndrome or a state of consciousness, it ought to apply to liberals as well as to conservatives; because it does not, the concept is biased politically.[7] Perhaps the most compelling criticism is that no matter what their personalities or private needs, people are often forced to adapt or conform to the environments they live in. If we are interested in understanding the rise of fascism in Germany or the problems of widespread racism in America, we need to look not to individuals' personalities but to the institutional patterns, social pressures, and prevailing reference group opinions at work in particular sectors of society.[8]

When judging any personality-based analysis, we must remember that it cannot be asked to do too much. It should not be used to explain all the origins of political thinking, nor should it be used in ways that imply that individuals' moral and political stances are governed solely by unconscious childhood conflicts. Rather, we should turn the problem around and recognize the limits of the analysis from the outset. It is helpful to begin with the understanding that the satisfaction of personality demands is just one function of opinions. Opinions, as well as many other governing mechanisms (such as social memberships, moral codes, and the internal logic of beliefs) must fit with personality patterns. The integration of personality with other social variables places analyses like Lane's in a more meaningful perspective, and the fact that personality always operates in conjunction with other variables should caution us that personality syndromes like authoritarianism can oversimplify complex phenomena.

The examples thus far have illustrated the applications of Freud-

ian personality principles to the political thinking of ordinary individuals. One of the most active areas of opinion and personality
research is the analysis of political elites and leaders. In fact, it was
through the study of a number of political activists, bureaucrats,
and elected officials that Lasswell derived his famous explanation
of the role of personality in shaping political orientations. Lasswell
found the world of the professional politician intriguing. It is a
world of grand ideas, great causes, little time or space for privacy
or personal concerns, and great amounts of social contact and public display. Whereas most of us devote some attention to public issues, remote ideals, and public action, the politician is consumed
by these things. This, Lasswell reasoned, must imply that so-called
political personalities are uniquely attracted to public life and tend
to be emotionally unsatisfied by the concerns of the mundane
world in which most of us live. Lasswell explored the political lives
of a number of politicians and concluded that there are a number
of different political types, each with a characteristic pattern of personality development in which unresolved childhood conflicts continue to be played out in the drama of the political arena.

One of Lasswell's types is the "agitator," who adopts abstract
ideals and tries to stir up the interest of others in them. Most agita-
tors, according to Lasswell, develop their commitments to abstract
intellectual ideals in response to living in emotionally sterile families in which intimate emotional relations seldom emerged. The
absence of emotional satisfaction in interpersonal relations leads
the agitator to find comfort in the following he or she receives
from supporters. One particular agitator in Lasswell's study illustrates this pattern.[9]

The agitator had competed with his brother during childhood
for the love of a harsh and cruel father. As a result, he developed a
deep hatred of his brother and a strong sense of discomfort in close
interpersonal relationships. He had to suppress his hostilities toward his brother to protect himself against further abuse from the
father and to prevent the guilt associated with such feelings. Unable to develop intimate relationships and unable to live with the
anxiety of filial hostilities, he turned to the international communist movement. The ideals of communism represented distant and
impersonal objects of emotional attachment, while the ability to
arouse audiences for his cause offered him a substitute for his
needs to be loved. Lasswell proposed that the dominant theme of
the "brotherhood" of communist workers offered this agitator a

form of brotherly love to compensate for his guilt feelings about his own brother. Thus, the dominant thoughts and actions of this political type can be said to be the result of basic personality characteristics and unresolved developmental conflicts.

Such analyses of leaders are fascinating because they seem to provide complete explanations for the puzzling question of why people become involved in politics. They also confirm the popular suspicion that someone has to be a little crazy to want to become a politician. The primary danger of these explanations, or any personality-based analysis, lies in the tendency to reduce everything to personality. This oversimplifying can create the uncomfortable impression that people are always driven by forces they don't understand and are incapable of taking rational or principled stands that compete with their personal needs or dispositions. One solution to these shortcomings, of course, is to regard personality as simply one of a number of factors that account for political consciousness.

Classical Freudian approaches also have been criticized for not taking a broad enough view of personality. For example, Lasswell's work and the majority of research on the authoritarian personality tend to attribute virtually all personality characteristics to early childhood experiences. Many critics of the Freudians argue that personality is a dynamic, ever-changing system that responds to significant changes throughout the life cycle.

Freudian approaches also tend to emphasize the neurotic and maladaptive aspects of personality over its healthy and positive manifestations. This emphasis is evident in Freud's writings, which were based largely on observations of neurotic and psychotic patients. The same bias emerges in studies such as *The Authoritarian Personality* and Lasswell's *Psychopathology and Politics*. In the former study, the authoritarian type was regarded as a severely damaged individual. In the latter case, most of Lasswell's subjects were either hospitalized or severely disturbed individuals. The implication of both studies is that extreme political commitments reflect some sort of sickness or personality damage. Critics argue that other conceptions of personality might allow us to see positive forms of personality expression in politics.

Other personality theories that have been important for the study of political thinking and opinion do not contradict Freudian assumptions as much as they expand the scope of personality to include continuing personality development throughout life and to provide better ways of describing healthy personalities. For these reasons, a number of human-potential theories have become increasingly popular alternatives to classical Freudian perspectives.

Human-Potential Theories

The human-potential approach to personality covers a large and diverse group of theories that includes the work of Goldstein,[10] Maslow,[11] Allport,[12] Rogers,[13] and Erikson.[14] The discussion in this section will concentrate on Erikson's theory of identity formation, for it probably has had the broadest impact on political psychology in general and on the area of opinion and personality in particular. The choice of Erikson as a central example, however, does not imply that Goldstein, Maslow, Allport, and Rogers make the same assumptions about personality.

For example, even though Erikson significantly extends Freud's theories, he accepts the basic Freudian ideas concerning early childhood development, the nature of the unconscious, and, most importantly, the driving force of the conflict between the pleasure and reality principles. In contrast, the human-potential theories of Goldstein and Maslow place little emphasis on the conflict between biological nature and social reality. Goldstein stresses the idea of "self-actualization"—a concept later made famous by Maslow. The self-actualization perspective defines the individual as a continually changing and evolving organism stimulated by the pleasure of each new level of development to continue to grow as far as the limits of the environment will allow. In this scheme and in the more elaborate hierarchy of human needs and potentials developed by Maslow, the human being is capable of ever-increasing growth in the direction of reaching his or her biological and social potential as a loving, thinking, creative being. In place of the Freudian image of the personality as a static structure of ego defenses designed to protect the individual from various stresses and threats, Maslow saw the essence of personality in the dynamic potential "to become more and more what one is, to become everything that one is capable of becoming."[15]

Although the various human-potential theories differ in some basic assumptions, they all agree in one way or another with the general sentiments of Maslow. They are united even more strongly by a common set of solutions to the major criticisms of Freud. First, the human-potential theorists all agree that the personality can continue to change and develop over the entire life cycle as long as the individual is exposed to new experiences, challenges, and opportunities. Second, the human-potential theorists tend to concentrate on the development of healthy personalities. As a result, they provide a set of concepts that accommodates the analysis of both healthy and damaged individuals. Third, human-potential theories do not take a deterministic view of personality: They do not view later personality functioning as being rigidly determined by early developmental experiences. Changes in the mature personality are possible for several reasons: The individual is believed capable of overcoming earlier dispositions that may have limited his or her potential. Individuals are not driven entirely by unconscious forces and conflicts; each level of development brings with it an increasing awareness of self and the capacity to make conscious choices. Moreover, situations often play a significant role in shaping both personality responses and personality change itself.

The ideas of Erik Erikson are important because he has responded to the major criticisms of Freud without abandoning all the powerful elements of Freud's analytical framework. Erikson subscribes to Freud's basic ideas about early childhood development, the unconscious, ego defenses, and the sociobiological conflict. However, he added three important elements to Freud's formulation.[16]

Erikson's first major contribution was the idea that life presents the individual with a series of "identity crises" beginning in childhood and continuing well into adolescence and, in some cases, throughout adulthood. These crises are triggered by significant changes in life experience, which disrupt the individual's ability to cope with the world. Some of the crises are fairly predictable, as when an adolescent passes into the adult world and is confronted with issues of responsibility, morality, personal support, and career. Other crises may be triggered less predictably by historical upheavals like war or depression or by unforeseen private traumas like the death of loved ones, divorce, separation, or personal failure. The severity of an identity crisis depends on such things as the nature of the precipitating factor, the supportiveness of the individual's social environment, and the adaptive potential of the individual's personality. The severity of the crisis determines the degree to which the individual must alter his or her image of the world (through profound changes of opinions and social orientations) to better accommodate personal dispositions, alter his or her basic personality structure to better fit the new life conditions, or alter both world view and personality.

Erikson's second contribution involves the idea that individuals resolve their identity crises by formulating some sort of intellectual perspective on the world and their places in it. People are thus able to analyze their life crises and to try to correct the conditions that produced them. The implication of this idea is that people have some degree of conscious control over changes in their personalities at key junctures in their lives. The degree of control varies from person to person, and some people may engineer the reconstruction of their identities better than others. However, Erikson, unlike Freud, suggests that people have some margin of conscious control over the evolution of their mature identities.

The final component of Erikson's perspective is related to the process of understanding life changes. He argues that the philosophy through which the individual analyzes and directs the interaction of personality and life circumstances may be influenced by prominent themes in the surrounding culture or in the immediate historical period. For example, in his provocative analysis of Martin Luther, Erikson argued that Luther resolved a profound identity crisis by translating it into terms relevant to problems in his relationship with the Catholic church and its doctrine.[17] As a result of reformulating his relationship to God and to the church, Luther was not only able to alter his identity, but in the process he developed a new social and religious philosophy. This philosophy had sufficient popular appeal to change both the church and society in ways that better accommodated Luther's emerging identity.

The idea that our private lives can be caught up in the course of history and public events has powerful implications for politics and public opinion. The most obvious possibility is that groups of individuals undergoing personal crises may turn to particular social philosophies for common resolutions. For example, some generations of youth undergoing adolescent crises may identify key political events as the causal factors and work out ideological frameworks that alter the political situation, redefine the individual's relation to that situation, and, thereby, alleviate strain. At other times adolescents may gravitate toward available religious movements. When historical conditions do not offer social changes, climactic events, or compelling intellectual frameworks, generations in crises may work out their problems in much more diverse and private ways. It is also likely that in historical periods characterized by relatively few traumatic events, social changes, or new social philosophies, individuals may suffer less severe personal strain and less intense identity crises.

*Applications of
Human-Potential Theories*

A number of interesting applications of human-potential ideas to the analysis of political behavior are contained in studies of the antiwar political movement of the 1960s. The core of the opposition to the Vietnam War came from adolescent, middle-class college students. The question of what led these "children of plenty" to adopt radical political views and rebel against the system has been given interesting answers by several human-potential theorists.

For example, Flacks regarded student radicalism of the 1960s (the "revolt of the advantaged," as he called it) as the result of particularly severe adolescent crises. The intensity of the strains experienced by this generation of middle-class youth resulted in part from their upbringing in families that were comparatively more liberal, egalitarian, and tolerant of diverse values than the families of previous middle-class generations. When these young people entered the world of universities and jobs, they encountered large, impersonal, and undemocratic organizations. These conditions intensified normal adolescent crises by limiting the effectiveness of earlier-acquired personality strategies for coping with sharply contrasting new experiences.[18]

In another study of the youth protest phenomenon, Keniston argued that, social adjustment problems aside, the Vietnam War galvanized the attention of the entire generation. The war and the seemingly impersonal and unresponsive government came to represent personal conflicts on a grand scale. The adoption of available liberal and left ideologies concerning democracy and government responsibility offered young people a world view that permitted a conscious analysis of their private problems.[19]

Keniston's formulation well illustrates the convergence in many human-potential perspectives of some traditional Freudian assumptions with new assumptions concerning conscious choice and the individual's capacity to resolve life crises creatively and collectively. In Keniston's analysis, the war and the government represented distant objects onto which the political activists could displace private dispositions—in keeping with Lasswell's model, $p \,) \, d \,) \, r = P$. However, a major departure from this traditional perspective came in the idea that the resulting political world view was a means of integrating masses of individuals suffering similar strains into an active political force in society. The integrating power of common personality strains made possible certain changes in society to accommodate the needs of this generation, and it forced members of the generation to come to terms with certain strain-producing aspects of the real world.

Human-potential theories have also been used to explain the thought and behavior of political elites. For example, Barber employed a number of Erikson's ideas in his early study of Connecticut state legislators[20] and in his more recent investigation of American Presidents.[21] In both studies he emphasized the possibility that certain personalities might achieve a healthy adaptation to the demands of public office. He also introduced the idea that the way in which public figures handle their first independent political challenge or crisis can be a significant factor in molding their mature "political personalities." This idea is similar to Erikson's notion about the significance of identity crises in later life.

Within the framework of these general assumptions, Barber's analysis revolves around two key dimensions of personality that explain dominant patterns of political thought and behavior: (1) the political actor's overall energy or activity level directed at political goals and (2) the political actor's feelings (positive or negative) about his or her role, office, or immediate political environment. The reasoning behind the emphasis on these two characteristics of personality is straightforward. An effective politician must be capable of sustaining a high level of activity in the midst of high degrees of stress, challenge, conflict, and public scrutiny, and little privacy. In order to maximize satisfaction from the job and in order to be responsive to a demanding environment, politicians also must view their roles and the world in which they operate in positive terms. Otherwise, political activity (no matter how high the activity level) will be grudging and negative. Without these two dimensions of personality, political behavior will be defensive rather than liberating and personally restrictive rather than creative.

Extending these ideas to an analysis of the presidency of the United States, Barber has defined four relevant personality dimensions: (1) active-positive, (2) active-negative, (3) passive-positive, and (4) passive-negative. For example, Richard Nixon was an active-negative President. He was driven to achieve, to work tirelessly, and to deny himself activities that were not goal oriented. This pattern clearly established him as an active type. Nixon also operated in a political world that he saw in very negative terms. His environment was threatening and hostile. He approached political goals as if he were preparing for war or battle. The opposition (and for Nixon there was always an opposition) was the enemy; he believed they were out to get him personally. The things he fought for were burdens that he carried, not passionate ideals. Nixon seemed to get more gratification from his suffering than from the activity itself or from the thrill of victory.

In contrast to this, Barber labels John Kennedy an active-positive type. Kennedy was not only energetic and driven to achieve, but he enjoyed the game of politics. He viewed the political world as flexible, malleable, and rewarding. He valued discourse and persuasion. He saw relatively few permanent enemies in his world. One might go so far as to argue that many people regarded Kennedy as charismatic because his positive orientation was both strong and infectious. There was a genuine ring to such stirring oratory as "Ask not what your country can do for you. Ask what you can do for your country." Indeed the Kennedy years of the New Frontier seem in retrospect to be times of activity and optimism.

In contrast to both these types there is the passive-positive character typified by Warren Harding. Harding was a man who trusted almost everyone too much. He was handsome, of comfortable means; life had been easy for him. Although the political world was positive, he was not driven to it. He followed the urgings of others. He felt no obligation to act in the name of lofty ideals or important policies. His key political prerogatives were delegated to trusted friends and advisers. While this positive soul reposed in the White House, his political passivity led him to turn the running of the government over to a group of political cronies from Ohio who operated from the "little green house" down the street. The result was that no one was more surprised than Warren Harding when his administration and his trusted friends became involved in the most extensive high-level corruption (the Teapot Dome oil lease scandal) that the government had known (prior to Watergate).

The final type is the passive-negative. A classic case is Calvin Coolidge, who was rudely ushered into the presidency on Harding's death. Coolidge had always been a reluctant politican. Moreover, he saw the political world as rigid and negative. Coolidge spent a good deal of his time in office sleeping. He required from ten to twelve hours of sleep at night and took regular naps during the day. When he was not sleeping, he made a point of doing as little as possible. Another classic passive-negative was Eisenhower, whom Barber describes as follows:

> Eisenhower's tendency to move away from involvements, to avoid personal commitments, was supported by belief: "My personal convictions, no matter how strong, cannot be the final answer," he said. The definition of democracy he liked best was "simply the opportunity for self-discipline." As a military man he had detested and avoided politics at least since his first command, when a Congressman had pressed him for a favor. His beliefs were carved into epigrams:
>
> He that conquereth his own soul is greater than he who taketh a city.
>
> Forget yourself and personal fortunes.
>
> Belligerence is the hallmark of personal insecurity.
>
> Never lose your temper except intentionally.[22]

The dimensions of presidential character shown in Figure 7-1 represent important links between personality variables and political thought and action. Although much of the foundation for these character styles is provided in early childhood development, Barber emphasizes the importance of later personal crises and struggles associated with establishing a political career. In many cases, the episode that most affects the way in which personality becomes channeled into political style is the first serious political challenge or crisis that the young political actor resolves successfully. The coping strategies used to resolve the first major political test tend to become the basis for formulating future strategies throughout political life.

For example, Richard Nixon's first independent political success came in his first congressional race in California. Until that time, Nixon's significant adult achievements had been tied to the help of his parents. As Barber observes, the race for Congress was different:

> Nixon's success at this period was independent of his parents; it was his first clearly political commitment in a personal sense; it was then, he wrote later, than "the meaning of crisis [took] on a sharply expanded dimension": he had tried several times to make it into the big time in a big city away from home and now he had achieved that.[23]

The key events in his confrontation with his opponent (Jerry Voorhis) were to remain part of Nixon's political style for the rest of his

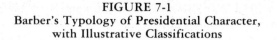

FIGURE 7-1
Barber's Typology of Presidential Character,
with Illustrative Classifications

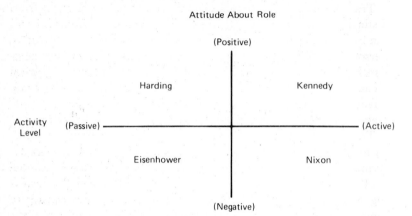

Source: Compiled from James David Barker, The Presidential Character, *2nd ed. (Engle-wood Cliffs, N.J.: Prentice-Hall, 1977), pp. 3–14.*

career. He saw the campaign as a personal crisis—a challenge to prove himself. The contest was bitter and hard fought. It escalated quickly into hostilities and name calling. Nixon saw himself alone. He had little outside help. He fought against an established foe. He made his own decisions, wrote his own speeches, and isolated himself from his campaign staff to make his judgments in solitude. Down to his final days in office, these characteristics of Nixon's earliest political venture emerged again and again in his political style. This process of working out a political world view in the midst of the first major challenge encountered in the real world of politics follows Erikson's thesis that identity crises are associated with significant life changes.

Trait Theories

Both Freudian and human-potential theories are rich sources of insight about human motivation and behavior. However, they require a comprehensive case study approach in order to provide convincing explanations. This requirement generally restricts their uses to small-scale studies of a few individuals. Although research on the authoritarian personality and Barber's analysis of Presidents suggest that broader uses are possible, many researchers have looked for a perspective that permits simpler measurement and wider applications. These advantages have been found (with some sacrifice of theoretical richness) in trait theories of personality.

Trait theories argue that particular types of behavior result from distinct personality traits, which govern the area of behavior and can be isolated from other traits for purposes of study. By breaking personality down into clusters of precisely defined traits, trait theorists have devised simple objective tests that yield precise empirical measures of each dimension of personality. The ability to generate quantitative measures of personality traits through simple tests makes it possible to compare individuals and to study large groups.

Trait theories have an intuitive appeal. They represent personality much as we conceptualize it in everyday life. People are not described in terms of their subconscious motives, developmental conflicts, stages of human potential, or their strategies for resolving identity crises. Rather, trait theories describe personality in much the same way that people judge personality in everyday situations: People are introverts, extroverts, dominant, sociable, tolerant, aggressive, conformist, flexible, rigid, controlled, impulsive, loving, hostile, and so on. Although some trait theories measure traits by observational techniques or clinical methods, most reduce each trait to a few general questions that tap some enduring disposition in the individual. Each trait, in turn, can be separated from the overall personality structure to determine its unique role in producing particular patterns of thought and behavior.

In order to avoid the impression that trait theories have solved the problems of research on personality and political consciousness, it must be pointed out that they have been criticized on several compelling grounds. They tend to offer less complete explanations of the origins and functions of personality. Their strength is in the description of personality-related behavior. Trait theorists defend the emphasis on description. Cattell, one of the leading trait theorists, argues that the description and measurement of individual behavior at a given point in time is the key problem for personality research. Other theoretical questions are irrelevant until this problem has been solved:

> To get some "practical" psychologists and psychiatrists to face the difficult theoretical issues of measurement, it has been necessary to reiterate that dependable laws about how personality grows, changes, and operates are to be found only after we can accurately refer to this "given personality at a given moment." Similarly, we are able to see the dynamic movement of people in a movie film

only because the instantaneous "frames" which rush through at sixteen a second are themselves descriptively intact.[24]

In addition to this unresolved debate between trait theorists and those more oriented toward psychiatric and psychoanalytical theories, there is concern that there is too little agreement among trait theorists about how many traits there are, what they are, or whether a trait identified by one analyst really is the same as a trait given the same name by another analyst. Some researchers claim that there are more than thirty stable personality traits, while others reduce the number of significant traits to as few as two.

In a related criticism, some of the questionnaire items used to measure particular traits seem to have little obvious connection to the trait. For example, one of the most established trait schemes is the California Personality Inventory, which measures eighteen different traits, one of which is called "capacity for status." This trait is described as a related cluster of personality qualities that lead an individual to achieve social status. The qualities include "ambitious, active, forceful, insightful, resourceful, and versatile . . . ascendant and self-seeking; effective in communication."[25] One of the more problematic items used to measure this trait is this true-false statement: "I think Lincoln was greater than Washington." A "true" response indicates greater capacity for status.[26]

Applications of Trait Theories

Despite criticisms, trait theories have been used in a wide range of research on public opinion and political consciousness. They are attractive for several reasons. They can be administered through questionnaires. They can be linked directly to a range of other measurable political variables, and they allow us to talk about the personality characteristics of large populations. For these reasons most research on questions of personality and political thinking in the mass public has been based on trait measures. Thus, for better or worse, trait approaches have opened up the "personality" of the mass public to intensive research.

A great deal of attention has been paid to the relationship between personality and alienation. The dimension of personality known as self-esteem seems to surface in many studies to explain alienation. One study found that low self-esteem leads to alienation from politics. The author argued that people who have a low estimate of their worth feel ineffective and withdraw from certain types of public activity, like politics.[27] Other studies have linked alienation to a personality syndrome that includes the traits of rigidity, anxiety, hostility, and low ego-strength (a trait related to self-esteem).[28]

In addition to explaining some of the sources of political apathy and withdrawal in the mass public, trait theories of personality have also been applied to the study of intense political involvement and activity. Following in the tradition of research on the authoritarian personality, many studies of extreme conservatives and right-wing activists have described these types in terms of clusters of rather undesirable personality traits.

For example, McClosky found extreme conservatives to possess traits that were characteristic of

> social isolates . . . who think poorly of themselves, who suffer personal disgruntlement and frustration, who are submissive, timid, and wanting in confidence, who lack a clear sense of direction and purpose, who are uncertain about their values, and who are generally bewildered by the alarming task of having to thread their way through a society which seems to them too complex to fathom.[29]

Although most scholars have been careful not to revert to obvious stereotypes for left-wing and right-wing political activists, most recent studies of left-wing political actors describe them in terms of personality traits that seem almost as stereotypical as those that emerge in most studies of the political right. For example, leftists have been found to be more intelligent, creative, emotionally stable, and higher in moral development than either rightists or average people.[30]

Although the personalities of individual numbers of political elites like Presidents and powerful leaders still tend to be analyzed through more classical approaches, trait theories have opened a new area of study about the political consciousness of elite groups. In recent years studies have emerged on samples of Democratic and Republican party politicians, party leaders, convention delegates, and even high officials in the United States Department of State. Most research shows that leaders of the major political parties are fairly similar in personality make-up,[31] although differences on the authoritarianism dimension show Republicans being somewhat more authoritarian than Democrats.[32] Related to this minor difference are the results of another study, which claimed that the leaders of the Republican party scored slightly higher than their Democratic counterparts on traits such as order, self-control, and personal endurance.[33]

The most interesting study thus far to come out of the use

of trait theory on groups of political elites is Etheredge's study of State Department officials. Etheredge drew a random sample of State Department foreign policy experts and asked them to give advice about how the United States should respond to a number of hypothetical international crises and incidents. His principal interest was in the degree to which these men would advocate the use of force. He reasoned that a recommendation for force would be determined in part by the personality traits of each individual. The world of high-level international intrigue and foreign policy is an abstract and ambiguous one, according to Etheredge. It is often hard to obtain information about events, and there is a great deal of uncertainty about the intentions of actors or the probable future patterns of their behaviors. All these things invite individuals who operate in this world to project their private concerns onto the actions of other countries and to identify privately with the preferred acts and policies of their own country.

Etheredge's theory tested out fairly well. He found that the tendency to advocate the use of force in foreign affairs was correlated with a cluster of personality traits that included the desire to dominate or hold power over others, competitiveness, and general mistrust.[34]

THE IMPACT OF PERSONALITY ON POLITICS: POLITICAL ELITES

Common to all approaches to opinion and personality is the idea that individuals with particular personal dispositions will, under the right circumstances, rely on those dispositions to perceive, interpret, and react to the political world. As several studies imply, some instances in which personality becomes the basis of political thinking and opinion formation can have a significant impact on political reality itself. When this is the case, we may want to consider the extent to which powerful individuals can (under some circumstances) create a world in their own private images. We also should think about the possible consequences on politics of interventions by powerful personalities. Finally, it is important to see whether remedies exist that would make political situations less distant or ambiguous in order to invite less private projection in the political realm. Reforms that would make political situations more structured in order to render them immune to being shaped according to the private wishes of individuals who operate in them should also be considered.

A good illustration of some of these general concerns about the impact of personality on political reality is Etheredge's State Department study. The central implication of his research is that American foreign policy is made by men whose personalities strongly affect their judgments, opinions, and actions. Moreover, the settings in which they operate and the sorts of problems and crises they confront reinforce the tendency to project private concerns onto crucial events in the real world of politics. There are several important considerations here. For example, it seems clear that the personality types in key decision-making posts will affect the course of events in the sphere of foreign policy. If private needs for power and competition lead officials to see the acts of the "enemy" in overly aggressive terms and to advocate the use of force, many foreign involvements of the United States may be shaped less by objective events or rational calculations than by the personalities of decision makers.

One solution would be to recruit policy makers who are less dominant on key traits. Another solution would be to structure the decision-making process in ways that would expose decision makers to more press scrutiny and public controls. It might be helpful to impose standards for the justification of high-level decisions. Bureaucratic processes should encourage mutual criticism and broader group participation in decisions. The last solution is similar to Janis' recommendations to alleviate the problem of "groupthink" in high-level decision making by a group. Groupthink reduces rational analysis, encourages projective and distorted thinking, and permits dominant personalities to control decision-making processes.[35]

Many early case studies of individual leaders pointed out instances in which dominant personalities unchecked by legal or procedural restraints affected the political world in important and often disturbing ways. For example in their classic study of Woodrow Wilson, Alexander and Juliette George demonstrated that unique features of Wilson's personality affected how he perceived the political world and formulated his political actions.[36] Some of these actions may have changed the course of history. The Georges' argument centered around Wilson's relations with his father, a harsh and demanding man toward whom Wilson must have felt intense hostility. The father imposed on Wilson a strict moral code, which led him to be overly demanding of himself and others. As a result, Wilson tended to transform his political battles into moral crusades in which his opponents became corrupt and immoral villains and Wilson assumed the role of self-styled savior. When opponents tried to thwart Wilson's political desires, he reacted to them with a vengeance that carried over from his feelings about the father who had often thwarted his childhood wishes. His political office allowed him to rationalize his private feelings of hostility and intense involvement in those struggles in terms of grand moral justifications.

On numerous occasions Wilson's behavior during World War I indicated that he took the resistance of the German government to his early peace overtures (and later the resistance of his own allies to his treaty proposals) as personal affronts, which he quickly translated into powerful questions about the moral bases of democracy and world freedom. Had he not been so rigid in his moral stands at key junctures in the war, the Germans might have surrendered much sooner, and the peace settlement might have been acceptable to all concerned, perhaps stabilizing some of the forces that led to the outbreak of World War II. Moreover, Wilson's solitary, stubborn, and moralistic posture concerning his plans for the League of Nations offended both the allies and the most powerful members of the U.S. Senate. Senate rejection of the treaty and the League of Nations set back the cause of an international peace organization thirty years.

One of the most interesting discussions of the potential impact of personality on political events is Barber's analysis of Richard Nixon. As mentioned in the preceding section, Barber classified Nixon as an active-negative type who was driven to act in the world but saw the political environment as hostile, threatening, out to get him, and governed by a continual and precarious struggle between the forces of good and evil. This active-negative character style, along with his reactions to his early independent political success, led Nixon to acquire a "crisis mentality" toward politics. He was constantly driven to act, and each action held the potential to trigger opposition and crisis. Barber's concern was not so much that Nixon saw the political world as a series of crises and potential crises, but that he might literally create disastrous crises out of situations in which he felt personally threatened. Barber speculated that

> if Nixon is ever threatened simultaneously with public disdain and loss of power, he may move into a crisis syndrome. In that case, the important resonances will be direct ones between character and the political environment. . . . The danger is that Nixon will commit himself irrevocably to some disastrous course of action.[37]

Indeed, such an episode occurred in the Watergate "crisis," in which Nixon's behavior conformed to the familiar pattern: He virtually isolated himself from the world, abandoned his concerns with other presidential problems, saw his critics and those on the various investigating committees as enemies out to get him, and contemplated a variety of potentially disastrous courses of action, including the possibility of ignoring an unfavorable Supreme Court decision on the Watergate tapes.

Fortunately the worst of all possible outcomes surrounding Nixon's behavior during the Watergate crisis never materialized. However, it is a bit worrisome to imagine the things that *could* have happened. These kinds of episodes in politics illustrate the impact that personality can have on perception, opinion formation, political behavior, and, ultimately, on the course of history. They also focus attention on alternative ways of structuring political situations to minimize the imposition of undesirable personal dispositions onto potentially volatile political realities. Perhaps one of the major contributions of personality approaches to the study of political consciousness is in paving the way for significant political reforms by identifying the conditions under which particular private dispositions will dominate the thinking and actions of key political actors.

The foregoing discussion has focused on the impact of elites' personalities on political situations. It is important to recognize that the personality characteristics of groups of individuals also can have important impacts on the political world. In many instances the private concerns of members of large groups have converged to produce awesome political consequences. For example, the authors of *The Authoritarian Personality* felt that personality strains shared by millions of citizens as a result of deteriorating social conditions in post–World War I Germany led to the popular appeal of Adolf Hitler and his fascist doctrines. The peasant rebellions in the Holy Roman Empire following the heroic deeds and writings of Martin Luther may have been due in part to mass personality dynamics. Sixteenth-century peasants were marginal people whose physical deprivations were greatly aggravated by an uncertain political order and a capricious church. The resulting frustrations and anxieties found expression in the popular attachment to Luther's doctrines.[38] In still another case, personality tensions in the mass public provide a partial explanation for the frenzied entry of the Western populace into the American political system during the

Age of Jackson. An even more complex set of personality conflicts has been identified to account for the broad-based popular support of the federal government's tragic program of Indian removal during the Jacksonian period—a program carried out with a crusading vengeance by Jackson himself.[39]

These and other examples suggest that the personality processes of individuals who share common social strains and tensions can produce powerful effects on the political world. They also suggest that political and social conditions can have important effects on individual personalities.

THE IMPACT OF POLITICS
ON PERSONALITY: THE MASS PUBLIC

Chaotic social conditions and economic crises can place the members of large populations under severe strains. These strains can undermine the normal personality defenses of individuals who lack a secure position in the changing social order. Under these circumstances, individuals often begin to search for reassuring explanations for their plight. In an effort to stabilize their emotional responses and to develop new intellectual perspectives, they become receptive to the formation of new opinions. As a result, mass fears and anxieties may be attracted to issues and other objects of opinion that capture emotions and represent satisfactory resolutions for private problems.

In times of turmoil and change, political symbols often dominate the mass communications channels. These symbols focus the attention of large numbers of people and are constructed so that they satisfy private concerns. Political formulations have this special capacity to satisfy private concerns and arouse mass involvement because they create the illusion that private concerns are really broadly shared problems created by political forces and amenable to political solutions. Political symbols do not arise by themselves. They are the product of the efforts of partisans, who seize the opportunity presented by social change and mass unrest to publicize their causes. Effective political appeals also depend on the skills of experts in the arts of persuasion and communication.

Important differences exist in the relationships between personality and politics in elite groups and in the mass public. In the elite case, dominant personalities operating in unstructured settings can have a direct impact on political events. In contrast, sustained interventions by mass publics in the political world generally require skillful groundwork by leaders and elites. Thus, although it is partly correct to acknowledge the impact of restless mass publics on the course of political events, it is probably more realistic to recognize that most incidents begin with some organized intervention from the distant political world into the private lives of ordinary citizens.

If the right political idea captures movies, books, major news events, or government information channels at the right time, it also may capture the attention and energies of distressed masses. For example, Lasswell points to the potential of economic crises to make the masses receptive to political symbols:

> Being thrown out of a job may be construed by the victim as the expression of the private malevolence of a hostile foreman; but such an interpretation does not survive indefinitely in competition with other interpretations when the army of the unemployed is swollen during depression. The deprivation now appears as an incident of one's relation to the whole social order, and when this degree of generalization is once accepted, the probability is increased that the person will seek to resolve almost any of his emotional problems by means of institutional symbols.[40]

The motivation for elite groups or the government to play on mass concerns is obvious. Political factions can often sway the outcomes of their causes by enlisting the moral support and participation of the larger mass audience. In other cases the government may favor particular policies over others and mobilize mass concerns to legitimize them. These motives for mobilizing public opinion need not imply an overly conspiratorial view of politics.

Several factors lessen the impression that the public is a puppet on a political string. For one thing, the mobilization of public opinion by an elite can be understood in part as a hard fact of mass communication. If large audiences are to respond coherently to an idea or an event, the stimulus that triggers the response must be constructed to ensure broad recognition and understanding, and then it must be transmitted uniformly to the audience. Effective mass political communication requires centralized broadcast media to condense and to distribute uniformly information to the public.

Cycles of crisis followed by political appeals that mobilize public support are routine aspects of daily life. We live in the midst of so many political crises that we tend to take them for granted. We routinely hear about economic crises, law and order crises, crises in military preparedness, energy crises, crises in confidence, and even moral crises. The fact that we can live in the midst of continual crisis and escape the conclusion that crisis is the normal or ordinary state of affairs attests to two things. First, crises are so routine that we tend to take them for granted. Second, any effectively managed crisis will be accompanied by political definitions that make it appear, as Edelman put it, that "this event is different from the political and social issues we routinely confront, different from other crises, and it occurs rarely."[41] Edelman's claim that crises are often carefully constructed by partisan political actors does not imply that they are unrelated to real problems and events. Indeed, they may be brought about by the conditions the actors point out. However, the definition of a situation as a crisis or serious problem encourages the public to suspend its long-term judgments about issues and operate more on the basis of emotion than intellect in forming opinions. Under these circumstances, people turn to the government and political groups for reassuring solutions, no matter how unrealistic the definition of the problem or the proposed solutions may be.

The sphere of politics that best illlustrates mass mobilization based on emotional arousal is national defense and foreign affairs. American involvement in world affairs can have profound effects on personal security and well-being. Government officials and political leaders have a great deal of control over the definition of the world situation and the dissemination of public information about it. The most salient symbol in this area of politics is "national security." As Barnet has observed, "There is an elusive connection between national purpose as articulated and promoted by the managers of foreign policy and individual purpose, between national security and personal security. For the average citizen, national security policy is a package of fears, dreams, and diversions."[42]

As Lippmann pointed out long ago, world leaders live in an isolated scene of private conferences, top-secret information, concealed objectives, and grand visions. They operate politically in the comfortable position of being able to (indeed, having to) conceal the reality of their dealings from the public. However, they also must win the support of the public for their actions. This is most often accomplished by transmitting simple, dramatic, stereotypical images of world affairs to the public.[43] These stereotypes are particularly effective when mass anxieties exist or when they can be manufactured by constructing political crises:

> In a time of anxiety, the politcal pressures mount to create stereotypes and to turn them into scapegoats. The picture Hitler drew for the German people of the six million Jews of Europe bore no rela-

tionship to reality, but it was powerful enough to incite a civilized nation to commit genocide. The German dictator was able to make the German people project self-doubt and self-hate onto an external "enemy" who became all the more "dangerous" because he was living in their very midst. For Americans in 1946, the stereotype of the Soviet Union, Stalin, and communism played a similar role. For many people these abstractions became convenient explanations of deep feelings of social and psychological distress. . . . For the American people, the immediate postwar years were marked by unprecedented feelings of insecurity. . . . This insecurity . . . had much less to do with the reality of Russian power . . . than with the bureaucratic revolution in the United States and the staggering social and political upheavals that accompanied World War II.[44]

The issue here is not whether the Soviet Union was a potential threat to the United States. The problem is that the government's dramatization of that threat probably bore little resemblance to the reality. As a result, many of the public tensions that were directed at the communists during the cold war were displaced from unrelated causes. This displacement distorted and exaggerated the popular reaction to an already dramatized situation. These public reactions may have conveniently fitted into the political scheme of various elites. It has often been observed that many instances in which public opinion was mobilized in this period were linked suspiciously to the announcements of new defense policies, the advancement of personal political careers, and pending U.S. international involvements.

Similar political treatments are often given to domestic issues. Among the various domestic issues, economic problems are probably the sources of the greatest emotional concern and the objects of the most concerted political attention. For example, every four years the voters hear a Republican candidate tell them that the Democrats are the party of inflation and reckless government spending. The Democrats can be expected to respond to this charge by labeling the Republicans the party of unemployment and favoritism to big business. Although these banal campaign appeals may not move the masses of voters, they may reach blocs of voters at both ends of the economic spectrum—from anxious business elites who live in a murky world of high finance, capricious markets, and risky investments to the unemployed and underemployed who may find consolation in the idea that one party may benefit the "little guy" with whatever leverage can be gained over the mysterious economy. In periods between elections, the economic situation shares the spotlight with foreign affairs as the staples of daily news. The public is exposed to a barrage of rapidly changing information about economic problems. One month the government may advocate public "belt tightening" to pave the way for higher unemployent, increases in the cost of living, or scarcity of credit. A short time later, in the hope of spurring investor confidence and consumer spending, the government may release optimistic news of promising growth indicators.

A fascinating aspect of the pattern of arousal and reassurance in economic and foreign policy issues is that foreign policy crises tend to dominate national attention during good economic times and recede from public concern when times get hard. Postwar polls show a strong tendency for public concern about foreign affairs to increase as economic prosperity increases and to decline as prosperity decreases. This relationship is shown in Figure 7-2. The measure of economic prosperity used is the one most directly relevant to the individual: the yearly percentage change in per capita income, controlling for the percentage change in inflation. This provides an estimate of how much the average person's real financial situation has changed (improved or worsened) from year to year.[45] The level of concern for foreign policy problems was obtained from postwar Gallup surveys that asked this question: "What do you think is the most important problem facing the country today?"

In part the relationship between economic prosperity and concern about foreign affairs may reflect the skill of leaders to mobilize public concern about one set of enduring (structural) issues when public concerns about another set of structural issues diminishes. It is also likely to expect that when two sets of concerns like foreign policy and the economy dominate day-to-day existence, crises in one area will drive out concerns in the other. This tendency may encourage elites to activate problems in one area when conditions in the other area improve. Whatever the reasons, the pattern of economic prosperity accompanied by foreign concern is one of the most obvious themes in contemporary American history. It has become commonplace to acknowledge that the economy tends to improve during periods of war or high productivity in the defense industry.

The connection between economic prosperity and foreign crises may be a driving force in the relationship between personality and mass political behavior. The linkage between the two issue areas may condition the public to anticipate foreign involvements during good times. This subtle conditioning may facilitate the government's capacity to mobilize attention around the world situation

FIGURE 7-2
Relationship Between Economic Prosperity and
Public Concern for Foreign Policy Problems

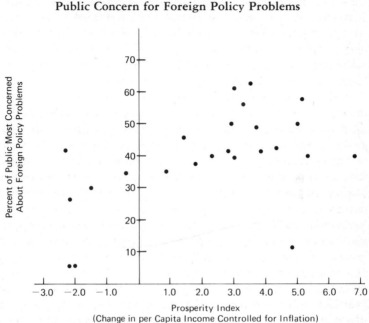

Prosperity Index
(Change in per Capita Income Controlled for Inflation)

whenever it chooses to do so. More importantly, this conditioning may leave the public in a virtually permanent state of low-level anxiety, associating even good times with considerable cause to worry; and it may produce a permanent reservoir of public distress to be mobilized at will. It also facilitates the shift in attention from foreign to economic concerns and back again because the two issue areas have become emotionally intertwined.

Perhaps the most significant implication of the deep, psychological connection between prosperity and foreign crisis is that it produces in the public a readiness to accept even drastic government moves in foreign policy because the moves represent both reassuring efforts to deal with uncertain situations and potential stimulation for the economy. As Henry has argued, this may even account for the seeming public willingness to go to war:

> since American industry expands and unemployment declines in the presence of a war atmosphere, the unusal economic and emotional deterrents to war do not exist for us. Thus, since *fear of war is anesthetized by heightened economic well-being*, we become accustomed to living comfortably under conditions of impending annihilation.

That is why a decision to go to war, or to the "brink," can be accepted much more readily than if the economy were placed in jeopardy by war. The fact that the Soviets are in the opposite situation has helped to save us, for since their way of life is threatened by war, they lack the temptations we have. . . . The fact that war-*fear* is partly narcotized by consumption-*euphoria* habituates us to living with the great fear.[46]

The shifting attention of elites from crises in one issue area to crises in another may provide a partial explanation for the seeming lack of constraint in mass opinion. If opinion is in part an emotional and personality-related phenomenon, then it follows that mass opinion will reflect whatever instabilities exist in the issue cycles of the political arena. This suggests that any measure of opinion structure such as stability or constraint ought to take into account changes in the political situation and shifts in the symbols used to define issues.

To the extent that public opinion appears random and the government appears unresponsive, it is convenient to impose the interpretation that the public displays no pattern in expressing its preferences and therefore the government cannot base its policies on public input. However, the idea that the public is emotionally involved with the changing political definitions of elites suggests that it makes as much sense to view public opinion as an output of the political system as it does to continue to define it as an input. Edelman presents this argument:

Americans have been taught to look upon government as a mechanism that is responsive to their wants and upon these in turn as rational reflections of their interests and their moral upbringing and therefore as stable and continuing. The American social scientist has been socialized to see individuals' political demands and attitudes as "inputs" of the political system. . . . The ready availability or opportunities for survey research on attitudes, moreover, places a premium upon the assumption that respondents' answers can be taken as "hard" data which have a clear, continuing, and systematic meaning. . . . Yet we have compelling evidence from a variety of kinds of observations that political beliefs, demands, and attitudes, far from being fixed and stable, are frequently sporadic in appearance, fluctuating in intensity, ambivalent in composition, and therefore logically inconsistent in pattern and structure. It is central to the explanation of political quiesence, arousal and violence both that attitudes potentially or actually have these unstable characteristics and that public policies and processes themselves move as cues that evoke particular changes in the direction and intensity of political cognitions. If this is the case, public policies and processes must be recognized not only or chiefly as the resultants of individuals' demands but also as the paramount source of particular attitudes and demands.[47]

The role of personality in opinion formation offers a fascinating perspective on public opinion. It leads us to think about a symbiotic relationship between the general public on the one hand and the government, interest groups, and political elites on the other. These political actors often need the support and attention of the general public in order to legitimize their causes, to pressure their opponents, or simply to maintain public order. The dramatization of issues in ways that arouse, channel, or soothe public anxieties becomes a means of achieving these political ends. As a result of this process, individuals in the public may experience politics as a world of drama, private release, hope, fantasy, and resolutions for the frustrations and anxieties of life.

NOTES

1. The basic data in this case study were gathered by Theresa Dunbar in a class project. I gratefully acknowledge her permission to publish these case materials. Since the basic analysis is mine, I also absolve her of any errors or distortion that may have entered the interpretation.

2. Harold Lasswell, *Psychopathology and Politics* (New York: Viking Press, 1960); and Harold Lasswell, *Power and Personality* (New York: Norton, 1948).

3. Robert E. Lane, "Fathers and Sons: Foundations of Political Belief," in *A Source Book for the Study of Personality and Politics*, eds. Fred I. Greenstein and Michael Lerner (Chicago: Markham, 1971), p. 164.

4. Ibid., p. 167.

5. Theodor W. Adorno, Else Frenkel-Brunswik, Daniel J. Levinson, and R. Nevitt Sanford, *The Authoritarian Personality* (New York: Harper and Row, 1950).

6. Richard Christie and Marie Jahoda, eds., *Studies in the Scope and Method of the Authoritarian Personality* (New York: Free Press, 1954).

7. Edward A. Shils, "Authoritarianism: 'Right' and 'Left,' "ibid., pp. 24–49.

8. Reinhard Bendix, "Compliant Behavior and Individual Personality," *American Journal of Sociology*, Vol. 58 (November 1952), pp. 292–303.

9. Lasswell, *Psychopathology and Politics*, pp. 78–126.

10. K. Goldstein, *The Organism* (New York: American Book, 1939).

11. Abraham H. Maslow, *Motivation and Personality* (New York: Harper and Row, 1954).

12. Gordon W. Allport, *Pattern and Growth in Personality* (New York: Holt, Rinehart and Winston, 1961).

13. Carl R. Rogers, "A Theory of Personality and Interpersonal Rela-

tionships, as Developed in the Client-centered Framework," in *Psychology: A Study of a Science*, Vol. 3, ed. S. Koch (New York: McGraw-Hill, 1959) pp. 184–256.

14. Erik H. Erikson, *Childhood and Society*, 2nd ed. (New York: Norton, 1963).
15. Maslow, *Motivation and Personality*, p. 92
16. See Erikson, *Childhood and Society*. See also Erik H. Erikson, *Young Man Luther* (New York: Norton, 1958).
17. Erikson, *Young Man Luther*.
18. Richard Flacks, "The Liberated Generation: An Exploration of the Roots of Student Protest," *Journal of Social Issues*, Vol. 23 (July 1967), pp. 52–75.
19. Kenneth Keniston, *Young Radicals* (New York: Harcourt Brace Jovanovich, 1968).
20. James David Barber, *The Lawmakers* (New Haven: Yale University Press, 1965).
21. James David Barber, *The Presidential Character*, 2nd ed. (Englewood Cliffs, N.J.: Prentice-Hall, 1977).
22. James David Barber, "The Interplay of Presidential Character and Style: A Paradigm and Five Illustrations," in *A Source Book for the Study of Personality and Politics*, eds. Greenstein and Lerner, pp. 397–98.
23. Ibid., p. 405.
24. Raymond B. Cattell, *The Scientific Analysis of Personality* (Baltimore: Penguin Books, 1965), p. 53.
25. Harrison G. Gough, *California Psychological Inventory Manual* (Palo Alto, Calif.: Consulting Psychologists Press, 1957), p. 10.
26. California Psychological Inventory test booklet and scoring manual.
27. Paul Sniderman, *Personality and Democratic Politics* (Berkeley: University of California Press, 1975).
28. Herbert McClosky and John Schaar, "Psychological Dimensions of Anomie," *American Sociological Review*, Vol. 30 (February 1965), pp. 14–40.
29. Herbert McClosky, "Conservatism and Personality," *American Political Science Review*, Vol. 52 (March 1958), pp. 27–45.
30. Among the works attributing these positive traits to leftists are Kenneth Keniston, *Radicals and Militants* (Lexington, Mass.: Heath, 1973); Norma Haan, M. Brewster Smith, and Jeanne Block, "The Moral Reasoning of Young Adults: Political-Social Behavior, Family Background and Personality Correlates," *Journal of Personality and Social Psychology*, Vol. 10 (November 1968), pp. 183–201; and the collection of articles edited by Edward E. Sampson in a special edition of the *Journal of Social Issues* devoted to "Student Activism and the Decade of Protest," Vol. 23 (July 1967).
31. See Sniderman, *Personality and Democratic Politics*.
32. Jeanne N. Knutson, *Psychological Variables in Political Recruitment: An Analysis of Party Activists* (Berkeley: Wright Institute, 1974).
33. Edmond Costantini and Kenneth Craik, "Women as Politicians: The Social Background, Personality, and Political Careers of Female Party Leaders," *Journal of Social Issues*, Vol. 28, No. 2 (1972), pp. 217–36.

34. Lloyd Etheredge, "Personality and Foreign Policy," *Psychology Today*, Vol. 8 (March 1975), p. 37–42. See also Lloyd Etheredge, *A World of Men* (Cambridge, Mass.: M.I.T. Press, 1978).

35. Irving Janis, *Victims of Groupthink* (Boston: Houghton Mifflin, 1972).

36. Alexander L. George and Juliette L. George, *Woodrow Wilson and Colonel House* (New York: Dover, 1964).

37. Barber, "The Interplay of Presidential Character and Style," p. 406.

38. See Erikson, *Young Man Luther*. Although Erikson's analysis is focused on Luther's impact on his times (and vice versa), evidence scattered throughout the book supports the peasant revolt thesis as well.

39. Michael Rogin, *Fathers and Children: Andrew Jackson and the Subjugation of the American Indian* (New York: Vintage Books, 1975).

40. Harold Lasswell, *World Politics and Personal Insecurity* (New York: Free Press, 1965), p. 118.

41. Murray Edelman, *Political Language: Words That Succeed and Policies That Fail* (New York: Academic Press, 1977), p. 44.

42. Richard J. Barnet, *The Roots of War* (Baltimore: Penguin Books, 1972), p. 253.

43. Walter Lippmann, *Public Opinion* (New York: Free Press, 1949).

44. Barnet, *The Roots of War*, pp. 253–54.

45. The sources for the per capita income and inflation statistics were U.S., Congress, House, *Historical Statistics of the United States: Colonial Times to 1970,* House Document No. 93–78, 93rd Cong., 1st sess., 1973; and U.S., Bureau of the Census, *Statistical Abstracts of the U.S.: 1976,* 97th ed., 1976.

46. Jules Henry, *Culture Against Man* (New York: Vintage Books, 1963), p. 102.

47. Murray Edelman, *Politics as Symbolic Action* (Chicago: Markham, 1971), pp. 3–4.

PART THREE

The Domain of Issue Formation and Political Communication

8

An Overview of
Public Opinion and
Issue Formation

THE EMPHASIS in Part Two was on the adjustive and integrating functions that opinions serve for individuals in the political system. The discussion in Part Three takes the next step—showing how opinion operates as a political force when individual opinions are transformed into public opinion.

It is important to understand how issues come into existence, how public involvement moves issues onto the agendas of political institutions, and how public opinion affects the legitimacy of public policy and government operations. It has been observed that many issues never reach the agendas of the Congress, the Supreme Court, or the executive branch unless they first occupy a prominent place on the broad public, or "systemic," agenda of the political system.[1] This preliminary agenda of politics consists of matters that come to the attention of the public because of media coverage and advocacy by elites or interest groups. The definitions that news stories and propaganda attach to political issues can shape the public's demands, expectations, and support for government policies.

Several factors affect the formation of issues and the level of public concern about them. Issues reach the systemic agenda when initiating groups define issues that become communicated through the mass media in ways that shape public reactions. This process of issue formation is diagrammed in Figure 8-1. As the figure shows, the dominant elements of the process can determine the importance of issues on the agenda of the political system and create pub-

FIGURE 8-1
A General Model of Public Opinion and Issue Formation

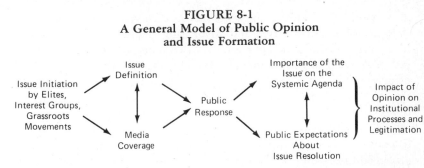

lic expectations about the resolution of those issues. The public expectations created by the issue formation process not only affect the way in which issues are resolved, but they also contribute to the public's willingness to regard institutional procedures and solutions as legitimate.

The general outlines of this process will be discussed in the remainder of this chapter. The crucial elements of symbolization and the mass media will be analyzed in greater detail in Chapters 9, 10, and 11.

THE INITIATION OF ISSUES

In the American political system different groups can play various roles as initiators of the issues on which government policies are eventually based. Some issues emerge from the so-called grassroots. This occurs when the life experiences, frustrations, or needs of large numbers of people converge to produce social movements, initiative campaigns, or a prevailing "public mood." An example is the taxpayers' revolt that swept the country in 1978. Following the landslide victory of an initiative to reduce property taxes that appeared on the California ballot in 1978, similar issues appeared on ballots and were introduced in state legislatures across the country. The press began to describe the public mood as one that was hostile to taxation and government spending. There was widespread talk about "restless taxpayers," "taxpayers' rebellions," and a national "tax revolt." In addition to petition campaigns, ballot initiatives, and lobbying efforts, many legislators introduced tax relief measures to court the favor of the voters and to try to head off the more drastic measures that might emerge out of grassroots efforts.

Although some public issues can be traced to broad popular action, the majority are brought into being by political elites and interest groups. (Even the taxpayers' revolt received heavy financial support for petition drives and advertising campaigns from landlords' associations and other groups of commercial-property owners, who stood to gain more from the tax cuts than did the masses of private-home owners.) It is only natural that most public issues should arise all or in part through the efforts of interest (sometimes called "pressure") groups or politicians, for they operate out of intense concerns, strong political commitments, or obligations to constituents and supporters. In a word, they are motivated to act. In addition, they tend to have the organization and skills necessary to develop an issue effectively. They also tend to have access to money and other political resources needed for mounting a sustained campaign. These characteristics of elites and interest groups stand in sharp contrast to the amorphous mass public, whose members may share concerns about a wide range of problems but lack the time, money, organization, or opportunity to convert their problems into viable political issues.

A simple rule of thumb in politics is that, for the most part, public issues originate with the politically powerful. In one of the classic theories of pressure groups in politics, Latham called organized groups "structures of power" because they "concentrate human wit, energy, and muscle for the achievement of received purposes."[2] Some theories of American politics, most notably James Madison's, argue that it is unreasonable to expect political issues to emerge consistently from the broad consensus of the general public. Politics almost always arises from the demands of special interests that find a common ground on which to organize themselves politically and express their preferences. Madison cautioned that care must be taken to hold the passions of special interests in check, but he saw the competition among groups as the ultimate guarantee against the unequal distribution of public resources or the domination of the government. In more recent times, those sentiments were echoed by a prominent member of Congress, who described interest groups as the ideal instruments of issue formation in a democracy:

> lobbying . . . includes all the messages by which citizens, individually or in groups—that is, in "interest" groups and "pressure" groups, business groups and labor groups, farm groups, and veterans' groups, women's groups and reformers' groups, liberal groups and conservative groups, religious groups and teachers' groups, statewide groups and regional groups—notify the Congress of their needs and wishes. After thirty-six years as a target of such messages,

I still regard them as the bloodstream of the democratic process and a *sine qua non* of effective legislation.[3]

There are, of course, numerous grounds for criticizing the role of interest groups as the initiators of public issues. For example, the politics of interest groups tends to promote the interests of the wealthy and advantaged over the interests of the poor and disadvantaged. Interest group politics also generates a disproportionate amount of public debate about the concerns of tiny segments of the public. Interest groups may stand between politicians and their constituents and make it difficult for the general public to receive sensitive or reliable representation. Finally, the dominance of interest groups may depress the overall level of democratic participation in the formation of issues. These and other objections to interest groups aside, however, the fact remains that pressure groups and political elites bring into being the majority of political issues.

Most pressure groups might be thought of as "materialistic" groups: They tend to form around particular issues of mutual interest, and they often have little basis for organization, association, or action beyond their narrow material concerns. Some—labor unions, manufacturers' associations, organizations of regional government, environmental groups—may persist over time. Others—such as groups supporting ballot initiatives or home owners' groups fighting changes in their neighborhoods—may disband when they have expressed their preferences about a particular issue.

A typical example of the functioning of materialistic interest groups was the response of the major oil companies to President Carter's energy proposals in 1977. Carter proposed a number of conservation measures to cope with an energy crisis that he described as so severe that its resolution required the "moral equivalent to war." The oil industry did not want the issue to focus on conservation, which they regarded as a threat to their business and a blow to future growth. They proposed short-term conservation measures and the deregulation of oil prices to stimulate corporate growth. Among typical efforts by the oil companies to control the development of the energy issue on the systemic agenda were the activities of Union Carbide, outlined by a spokesperson for the company:

The Union Carbide Corporation plans advertisements tomorrow in 25 newspapers to underscore the coming energy message. The ads will argue that the United States needs both an "energy conservation program" and "an energy development program. . . ." Union Carbide, which has had a carefully organized group planning for the energy message since early this year, is developing internal communications as well. On Friday, a discussion of energy by top executives will be videotaped for showing to company employees.[4]

Following the energy crisis of 1979, oil prices were partially deregulated, and the companies shifted their lobbying efforts to the institutional (in this case, congressional) arena to fight proposals to tax the profits they would reap from their victory.

In contrast to the materialistic groups are many interest groups that might be described as "moralistic." Moralistic groups are committed to the advancement of particular values or ideologies, and their members are drawn together by shared beliefs, values, or life styles. Moralistic groups tend to maintain their organization over time, and they may sponsor diverse issues that are seen as means of advancing their causes. For example, in 1977 and 1978 many fundamentalist churches and religious organizations spearheaded efforts to defeat the Equal Rights Amendment to the Constitution. These groups saw the amendment as a threat to religious doctrine pertaining to the role of women and the sanctity of the family. During the same period, many of these groups also mobilized their resources in various parts of the country to fight against so-called gay rights ordinances, which prohibited states and cities from discriminating against employees on the basis of sexual preference.

Although effective political organization and access to resources are crucial aspects of issue formation, these factors alone are not sufficient to determine how an issue will affect public opinion. The ways in which issues are defined and the manner in which they are transmitted by the mass media are probably the major elements in the issue formation process. Factions advocating different positions must convince less interested political spectators that their positions are valid and ought to be represented on the political agenda.

THE DEFINITION
AND MEDIA COVERAGE OF ISSUES

When President Carter began his energy campaign in the spring of 1977, he understood that the issue had to gain a place on the systemic agenda before it would be addressed seriously by Congress. There were a number of reasons for this, including Carter's poor relationship with Congress, the strength of oil company lobbying in Congress, and the absence of an immediate energy crisis to mobilize public concerns and dictate legislative action. Although Carter attempted to define the issue in ways that would generate public involvement, his efforts failed. This failure to place the energy issue high on the national agenda illustrates at once the importance of issue definitions and the limitations of definitions that do not mesh with prevailing public understandings or that run counter to the definitions of other powerful sources of information.

Symbols, Reality, and Public Opinion

Carter's approach to defining the issue was twofold. First, he tried to convince the public that the energy problem was serious. He spoke repeatedly of an energy "crisis" and urged the public to wage a "moral equivalent of war" against the energy problem. These emotional terms would have been more compelling during the "oil crisis" years of 1973 or 1979, when gas prices soared and long lines waited at gas stations for meager allotments of fuel. However, 1977 was not 1973 or 1979, and there were few visible signs of an energy crisis. Gasoline and heating fuel were plentiful. News stories during the spring of 1977 reported massive discoveries of oil in Alaska, the North Sea, and Norway. Moreover, the oil companies were running intensive "public information" campaigns, which claimed that an abundance of energy resources existed if only government policy would allow them to be developed.

The result of Carter's efforts to define the situation as a "crisis" in the midst of such hostile circumstances is striking. Prior to the President's national speeches, only about 40 percent of the public felt that the energy situation was very serious. Although the dramatic speeches and the massive media coverage devoted to them boosted public opinion for a short period, it was not long before public concern about the energy situation began to drop. Within two weeks after Carter's attempts to define the issue, public opinion about energy had returned to its "prespeech" level. During the next months, the decay of public concern continued. By June only slightly more than 40 percent of the public thought the energy situation was serious. In July the percentage slipped below 40. Finally, in August a national poll asked whether the public felt things were as bad as the President claimed. In response to this question only 33 percent said yes; 57 percent said no.[5]

The second thrust of Carter's public opinion strategy was to define the energy issue in terms of conservation rather than energy development. In part this strategy reflected the President's commitment to conservation over resource depletion, but in part it reflected his political advisers' (incorrect) judgment that the public was more likely to support conservation measures than development programs. This perception of the public mood was grounded in what seemed to be strong evidence from the opinion polls. Louis Harris interpreted one of his polls in the spring of 1977 to suggest that 70 percent of the public favored a tough energy conservation program that would affect both consumers and industry. Another Harris Poll showed that 92 percent of the public believed that Americans were wasteful in their energy use. The President's own private pollster, Patrick Caddell, sensed that the public mood was turning away from waste and unrestrained industrial growth and toward conservation of resources. These apparent trends in public thinking seemed to argue for defining the energy situation as a conservation issue.

Lurking beneath the seeming support for conservation, however, were other popular attitudes, which, in light of the eventual public reaction, must have been more important to people. Other polls taken during the same period showed that the American public was tired of being asked to make sacrifices. Moreover, the majority of people felt that conservation was important, but that the development of new resources was equally important. In light of these public dispositions, it is clear that people were more receptive to the oil lobby's suggestions to think of the energy issue in terms of development and prosperity than to think in Carter's terms of conservation and sacrifice.[6] Carter's miscalculations produced the wrong issue definition at the wrong time.

The Shape of the News

The mobilization of opinion during the issue formation process depends on more than just the ability to size up an audience and select the appropriate symbols for the issue. In order for issue definitions to have the desired impact, the messages of elites and interest groups must reach the public in the first place. The news media play a major role communicating between political actors and the public. The media—particularly television—supply most political information to the public. The publishers, producers, editors, and reporters who construct "the news" about important issues make a number of crucial decisions that directly affect how the public sees the political world. News organizations decide what issues to cover and what ones not to cover. They decide to emphasize some issues and to downplay others. They determine who represents the various "official" positions in a conflict and who should be asked to respond to different definitions of an issue. Moreover, news organizations must decide which "angle" or "story line" to run and whether to emphasize stories that might be damaging to the parties involved.

The energy debate of 1977 was given major attention by the national press. The energy program was President Carter's first major policy initiative, and he went to great lengths to dramatize its importance. There were rumors of a falling-out between the President and leadership in Congress. However, the drama had less to do with the problem of energy than with the political plight of the President. This accounted for the media emphasis on Carter's political position, his relations with Congress, and public reactions to his proposals. It also may have accounted for the tendency of news organizations to allow representatives of the oil industry to respond to the Carter program. In contrast to their reporting of the energy crises of 1973 and 1979, the media in 1977 treated the position of the oil lobby as a respectable one. This combined with the emphasis on growth and prosperity in a time of economic uncertainty to give the message of the oil companies a broad popular appeal.

The dominant story line that emerged from media coverage of the energy issue was that the Carter administration was facing its first major policy defeat at the hands of an unruly Congress and a skeptical public. In light of this general trend in media coverage, it is not surprising to find that public approval of Jimmy Carter's overall performance as President followed the path of steep decline set by the growing public disapproval of his handling of energy problems. In April 1977, NBC News/Associated Press polls showed that popular approval of Carter and support for his approach to energy were both around the 50 percent level. By March 1978, opinion on both counts had plummeted along the same steep decline to a dangerously low approval level of about 30 percent.[7]

The news establishment is clearly a force to be contended with in the formation of public issues and the mobilization of opinion about them. Research on the production of news has revealed numerous examples in which news organizations have contributed directly to the definitions of public issues. For example, Epstein reports a case in which television coverage of a teachers' strike in

New York downplayed volatile racial issues when the program producer decided that airing the racial theme was "not the way to play the story."[8] The reporter's story was changed in keeping with this editorial decision. In some cases, the coverage of broad issues may even be influenced by formal organizational policy. An example of this has been documented in a major network's coverage of the Vietnam War. In the late 1960s, public reaction to the war became an increasingly important political consideration. Although Richard Nixon had been elected in 1968 on his promise to end the war, his decision to use military pressure to force the other side into a settlement depended on the willingness of the public to accept several more years of fighting. This depended, in turn, on whether the public saw the war winding down or continuing as before. What the public concluded about the war depended in part on news policy decisions like the one handed down by the executive producer of the ABC evening news to his correspondents in the field: "I think the time has come to shift some of our focus from the battlefield, or more specifically American military involvement with the enemy, to themes and stories under the general heading: We Are on Our Way Out of Vietnam."[9] By so directly selecting and defining issues, the news establishment can play a role in determining the agenda of issues that comes before the public.

In an interesting study of the political aftermath of the urban riots of the 1960s, Lipsky and Olson addressed the problem of why racial problems, riots, and the urban crisis (the most significant domestic issues of the late 1960s) virtually disappeared from the agenda of national concerns in the 1970s. After rejecting the views that the demands expressed through the riots were insubstantial or that legitimate demands raised by blacks had been satisfied by the end of the 1960s, they considered the possibility that public issues are governed by "issue attention cycles."[10] One explanation of these cycles is that issues have varying potentials for drama and impact on the public interest. When issues move in the direction of resolution or reach their dramatic climaxes, they are susceptible to being bumped from public attention by newer issues whose dramas are just unfolding and whose public impact is of greater concern.[11] However, Olson and Lipsky pointed out that this analysis of issue cycles does not account for how issues are brought to the attention of the public, how they are dramatized, or how representations of the public interest are communicated to the general political audience.

Their explanation for declining political concern about pressing problems emphasized the role of elites in defining the issues and the role of the media in shifting their emphasis on the coverage of urban problems. Olson and Lipsky argued that after the violence was over, elites attempted to diminish public concern. They did this through definitional tactics such as emphasizing isolated and local causes of the riots, rather than broad underlying problems, and creating riot commissions that gave assurances that the problems would be solved. These tactics were accompanied by a drop in media coverage of urban unrest. Olson and Lipsky's analysis raises the interesting possibility that the general impression that the riot situation improved after 1969 had more to do with policies of the news media than with any change in the incidence of riots.

> Media influence on reducing perceptions of crises may be illustrated by their role in covering riots in the late 1960s. A widespread belief arose following the Kerner Commission's work that the number of riots diminished in the years after 1967. According to the Lemberg Center for the Study of Violence, however, the number of riots actually increased through 1969. In 1967 the Center reported 257 race-related civil disorders, while in 1968 it recorded 724 riots and in 1969, 835 riots. The Justice Department reported more civil disturbances in 1970 than in 1969 and almost as many in the peak quarter of 1971 as in the peak quarters of the two previous years. . . . The fact that racial violence tended to occur in smaller and medium-sized cities meant those cities receiving substantial media attention were no longer the focal point of its riots. A riot in Los Angeles is more likely to receive media attention than a riot of relatively equal proportions in Pasadena. . . .The disorders were also more spread out over the year, so that the "long hot summer" was considerably cooler but was replaced by a considerably warmer riot "year." More even riot distribution over the calendar year reinforced tendencies to reduce public visibility of the violence because the media tended to underplay events whose newsworthy qualities partially derived from their seasonal concentration.[12]

The apparent collusion between the media and political actors under such circumstances need not be taken as intentional. The factors that may join news organizations and political elites in unwitting cooperation in the shaping of the public agenda is the format for the production of news. News organizations operate within a set of tight constraints that govern the formats of the stories they run. Elites and organized political interests that have the resources and skills to transform their political messages into the appropriate news formats stand the greatest chance of reaching the public with their appeals. The opposite principle also holds: Issues can be packaged in formats that are less newsworthy (such as riot commission hearings) in order to reduce their political salience.

As a general rule, the stories that dominate the news must be short, dramatic, predictable, and coverable. Very few stories warrant more than a column of newsprint or a few seconds of air time. Short stories are cheap to produce; they require little or no investigative reporting; they guarantee a lively and fast-paced news format; they assure that the news will contain "something for everyone"; and they reduce the chances of losing the attention of the audience. As a result, information in political appeals is generally sacrificed for high-impact symbols and familiar stereotypes. As former Secretary of State Dean Acheson once remarked about the public presentation of foreign policy:

> The task of a public officer seeking to explain and gain support for a major policy is not that of the writer of a doctoral thesis. Qualification must give way to simplicity of statement, nicety and nuance to bluntness, almost brutality in carrying home a point. . . .If we did make our points clearer than truth, we did not differ from most other educators and could hardly do otherwise.[13]

These kinds of political appeal make it easy to satisfy the criterion that the news must contain conflict, intrigue, or drama. The producer of the NBC evening news once detailed the requirements of a good story in a memo to his staff: "Every news story should have structure and conflict, problem and denouement, rising action and falling action, a beginning, a middle and an end."[14] Another observer has noted: "The media follow narrative lines. They tell stories—parables—morality plays. . . .In 1968 . . . the story of [Hubert] Humphrey was (a) the story of the underdog and the obstacles besetting him; (b) the story of the underdog gathering courage to confront one obstacle after another; (c) the story of momentum and 'rags-to-near-riches.' "[15]

Since the world seldom comes in such simple, dramatic packages, the drama of politics often has to be created. It is created in part by journalists who impose familiar themes, conflicts, and roles on political issues and their casts of characters. However, in large part the drama of politics is staged by the political actors themselves. The careful staging, timing, and scripting of political performances guarantees that political actors have more control over the symbolic appeals that they transmit to the public. Daniel Boorstin has referred to these dramatizations as "pseudo-events." These performances are appealing to the media because they reduce complex situations to short, simple, and often powerful dramatizations.

They appeal to political actors because they increase the chance that their positions will be reported, and they offer greater political control over the image the public receives. Finally, Boorstin argues, psuedo-events are appealing to the public because they replace complex and hard-to-grasp realities with simple and interesting images that are more compelling than reality.[16]

Pseudo-events also contribute another desirable characteristic to a news story—predictability. At first it may seem contradictory to demand that a news event be predictable before covering it. However, news outlets operate on tight schedules, and they must meet deadlines. Each day, they must fill up their pages or their programs with a certain minimum amount of news. They must assign reporters in advance to cover stories that are expected to develop. Finally, they must organize all this news gathering with a minimum of expense, delay, and lost stories. The portion of the news that is planned, produced, scripted, and dramatized by political elites and interest groups is the ideal solution to media needs for predictable news. Epstein summarizes this situation by simply saying, "The more predictable the event, the more likely it will be covered."[17]

The criteria of brevity, drama, and predictability all enter into the final consideration of whether a story is coverable. Stories stand a greater chance of being reported if they occur at a time, in a location, or in a form that is cheap and easy to cover. Although some people have charged that these practices smack of collusion between journalists and politicians, they appear to be an entrenched feature of political reporting. After an investigation of alleged "staged news" by ABC in its coverage of the 1968 Democratic convention, the Federal Communications Commission cause to this conclusion:

> In a sense, every televised press conference may be said to be staged to some extent; depictions of scenes in a television documentary—on how the poor live on a typical day in the ghetto, for example—also necessarily involve camera directions, lights, action instructions, etc. The term "pseudo-event" describes a whole class of such activities that constitute much of what journalists treat as "news." Few would question the professional propriety of asking public officials to smile again or to repeat handshakes, while the cameras are focused upon them.[18]

Not everyone interested in making a political point can produce a performance that is newsworthy in the terms just outlined.[19] Such political performances typically require money, access to facilities, contacts with news organizations, political organization, and some control over the cast of political actors involved. This does not imply that all the news through which the public forms its opinions about the political world results from the symbiotic relationship between the press and political elites and interest groups. Radical groups may capture the news through movements, demonstrations, violence, or terrorism. In addition, many news events are spontaneous, uncontrolled, and covered through considerable effort, expense, and journalistic skill on the part of news organizations. However, the backbone of the daily news consists of stories that emerge from political performances that are tailored to news formats. Through such stories the public receives its impressions of most political issues.

PUBLIC RESPONSES TO ISSUES

The definitions that emerge around an issue can have dramatic effects on public reaction to it. Public response, in turn, can have a variety of consequences for the resolution of the issue. As suggested in Figure 8-1, public reactions can affect the standing of an issue on the systemic agenda, public expectations about the resolution of an issue, pressure to move an issue onto an institutional agenda, and the eventual legitimation of institutional policies. The impact of public responses can be described in terms of what Schattschneider has called the "scope and bias" of political processes.[20]

Schattschneider argued that American politics is dominated by a "pressure system" in which disadvantaged groups and more powerful interests compete with each other to control the status of issues on the systemic agenda and to move onto the agendas of institutions issues that are biased in their favor. As Schattschneider has noted, the *scope* of public response can determine an issue's status on the systemic agenda, and this in turn affects groups' ability to obtain advantageous institutional solutions for their problems. Each political institution has an *issue bias*, affecting the kinds of issue it can address, the types of solution it can provide, and the types of political pressure to which it is sensitive. Scope and bias are related to each other: Institutions responsive to certain public inputs may be biased in favor of particular political issues. Similarly, institutions and political processes that fail to address particular issues limit the scope and impact of public responses:

> Americans hold more elections than all the rest of the world put together, but there must be millions of issues on which we cannot

vote, or we cannot vote on them when we want to vote on them or we cannot define them as we want to. A conclusive way of checking the rise of conflict is simply to provide no arena for it or to create no public agency with power to do anything about it. There are an incredible number of devices for checking the development of conflict within the system. . . . .All legislative procedure is loaded with devices for controlling the flow of explosive materials into the governmental apparatus. All forms of political organization have a bias in favor of the exploitation of some kinds of conflict and the suppression of others because *organization is the mobilization of bias*. Some issues are organized into politics while others are organized out.[21]

Even if an issue encounters bias in a political setting, the character of the ensuing debate on the issue depends on the ability of the groups involved to control the scope of conflict. The scope of conflict is determined by what proportion of the audience expresses what intensity of opinion, in forms that are appropriate to the setting, over what period of time. As Schattschneider has observed: "The distinctive quality of political conflicts is that the relations between the players and the audience have not been well defined and there is usually nothing to keep the audience from getting into the game."[22] In most cases the scope of audience participation in public debate is determined by the political groups that have defined the issue and moved it into a particular political setting. The definition contributes to the level of public arousal, and the setting limits the range of possible and appropriate public responses. Schattschneider bluntly concluded that the fluid relations between players and audience are governed by the following principle: *"Whoever decides what the game is about decides also who can get into the game."*[23] This idea captures at once the importance of initiating groups, issue definition, communication, and public opinion in the issue formation process.

This perspective on public opinion and issue formation in America has several important implications. First, it suggests that the public strongly affects the emergence, intensity, and duration of debate over public issues. However, the role of the public is not the one typically described in classical theories of democracy. Instead of initiating political issues, the general public is most often called on by interest groups and elites to participate in (and thereby shape) the course of debate about issues that have already been defined. As issues develop, they tend to move from a vague systemic agenda into selected institutional settings, which limit or bias the possible outcomes. As this movement occurs, the options for public response are generally constrained by the rhetoric of partisan factions and the procedures of political institutions. All this, in turn, casts a different interpretation on the standard criticism that the public often fails to become informed about, or participate in, key policy debates. Schattschneider suggested that the image of the mass public as a willfully ignorant and nonparticipatory group is a self-serving myth generated by political elites, whose control over public debate is, in reality, the source of this seeming popular passivity on many issues:

> It is profoundly characteristic of the behavior of the more fortunate strata of the community that responsibility for widespread nonparticipation is attributed wholly to the ignorance, indifference and shiftlessness of the people. This has always been the rationalization used to justify the exclusion of the lower classes from any political system. There is a better explanation. Abstention reflects the suppression of the options and alternatives that reflect the needs of the nonparticipants. . . . *Whoever decides what the game is about decides also who can get into the game.*[24]

ISSUE FORMATION AND PUBLIC
INVOLVEMENT IN POLICY MAKING

As the preceding discussion indicates, forces leading to the formation of issues are difficult to sort out. In many cases it is hard to tell whether an issue takes shape in response to public demands or whether public demands are mobilized behind issues that gain their focus through the communication strategies of elites and interest groups. Both factors probably come into play in most issues. Access to communication channels is more available to elites and interest groups, which initiate issues, but the scope of public response is often a major determinant of an issue's importance on the systemic agenda and its movement through political institutions during policy making.

Thus, issue formation can be thought of as the first stage of policy making. The early history of an issue can pave the way for important features of eventual policies. Following the course of a policy debate from the issue formation stage can reveal a number of interesting hidden dimensions of policy. For example, organizing sustained public support for particular policy preferences can be very costly—especially when the group orchestrating the support is a public agency able to charge the costs of its crusades to the same tax-paying public that must subsidize its programs. In these cases the costs of public policy must be calculated in terms of the price of the program and the expense of generating public support. These hidden costs are often astonishingly high, as was the case when the Defense Department set out to win popular support for its proposed Antiballistic Missile System (ABM) in 1968. The campaign began with the distribution of pictures and stories about the proposed weapons to the print and broadcast media. Journalists were invited to witness missile tests, and they were given briefings designed to counter various criticisms of the program. Scale-model ABM displays were dispatched to cities around the country, and local opinion leaders were flown to military installations to observe impressive defense facilities.[25] These and other aspects of what the Pentagon called "Operation Understanding" are typical components of any policy initiative by the Defense Department. They operate above and beyond the massive routine public relations efforts aimed at creating a favorable public image for the armed services and their activities.

This example illustrates both the hidden costs of engaging public opinion in the policy process and the methods through which the public can be "prepared" to expect and support certain policy goals. Just as the routine public relations efforts of interest groups and government agencies can mobilize support for particular policies, the routine methods for handling conflicts within institutional settings can shape public concerns to fit predictable policy outcomes. The delicate chemistry of controlling the scope of public opinion around a political issue can affect other hidden dimensions of policy such as the time frame in which policy is produced, the public priority assigned to particular policies, and the substitution of manageable and expedient concerns for more fundamental problems.

For example, Lipsky and Olson argued that government procedures for addressing the urban riots of the 1960s had three hidden effects: (1) delaying attention to chronic social problems, (2) diminishing the public's perception of the importance of these social problems on the national agenda, and (3) deflecting eventual policy recommendations away from a concern with the most fundamental underlying social causes of the riots. The hidden characteristics of social policy established during the issue formation process overshadowed the substance of the eventual policies themselves.[26]

A number of key issue formation variables set the stage for the eventual policy outcomes of riot issues. The reduction of media coverage lowered the salience of riots in particular and urban problems in general. This effect was reinforced by the reassurances of public officials that the police had the immediate problems under control and that specially appointed riot commissions would deal with the long-term issues. The perceived significance of the issues raised by the riots was further diminished by the reports of investigating commissions, which found that the riots were inspired to a large extent by "riff-raff," troublemakers, and other irresponsible social elements.[27] Finally, the process of moving the policy questions through the slow and tedious setting of an investigating commission had the multiple effects of delaying recommendations, restricting the scope of further public input (particularly political dissent) about the issues involved, and biasing the final recommendations in favor of the moderate leanings of commission members and their reassuring representations of the problems to the public.

Perhaps the most important hidden effect of the issue formation process is the shaping of public expectations about eventual solutions for pressing problems. Issue formation may lay the groundwork for popular acceptance of political outcomes and the legitimation of political processes. The production of public policy is of little consequence if losing groups refuse to honor the outcomes, or if large segments of the public regard the actions of the government as illegitimate. Many of the factors that shape the expression of public opinion about political issues also contribute to the legitimation of public policy and its implementation by the government.

Among the most subtle, legitimating factors are the symbolic definitions that become associated with issues. These definitions can shape public thinking even though they may bear little relation to the hard details of eventual policy. For example, programs of subsidies and price supports for farm products tend to give overwhelming benefits to large, corporate farming interests, which already operate at a competitive advantage. However, the public debate about these policies tends to be filled with touching images such as the "disappearance of the small farmer" and neutral terms such as "parity" and "fair compensation." As Edelman notes, these symbolic definitions of the issues tend to promote broad public acceptance for policies that benefit narrow interests:

> "Parity" has long invoked an image among political spectators as a fair distribution of costs and benefits among farmers and consumers; but it has legitimized a system of generous government subsidies to

large commercial farms, little or no help for the small family farms, and no effective protection for consumers. But who can oppose "parity"? It encourages quiescence among the mass public as effectively as it provides self-justification for the material benefits of farm policies.[28]

The effects of issue definition are magnified when issues move onto the agenda of particular institutions. We have seen, for example, how the language, the time frame, the procedures, and the constraints on the expression of opinion associated with the riot commissions affected important dimensions of public policy in response to urban unrest in the 1960s. The commissions may also have contributed heavily to the legitimation of the resulting policies. They performed this function first by channeling the political demands of the rioters back into the framework of American political institutions. The resolution of political problems within normal procedural channels increases the likelihood that the public will accept the results.

The issue bias of an institution can further transform issues into publicly acceptable terms. The powers of the riot commissions were too limited to address the most fundamental demands of political dissidents for changes in the political system. Even within the rather limited lists of demands that remained, the commissions were authorized to decide which were legitimate and which were illegitimate. As a result of this discretion, the commissions exercised a great deal of influence on public perceptions about which minority interest groups and leaders were legitimate and which ones were inappropriate representatives of minority interests. As Lipsky and Olson pointed out, the riot commissions attempted to legitimate the positions of established black organizations and leaders even though these groups had lost much of their credibility with the black community itself.[29] It was clear that the legitimacy of government responses to the riots depended on appealing to a much broader segment of the public than to just the black community.

Even the forms in which public opinion is expressed during the issue formation process can affect the legitimation of eventual government action. Most Americans expect to be able to take certain roles in policy debates. This procedural socialization is accompanied by the norm that as long as these roles are available, the policy outcomes should be accepted. For example, as Edelman has noted, various kinds of political participation, such as voting, reinforce general beliefs about legitimate public representation in institutional processes. The simple fact that elites and interest groups appeal to public opinion as issues move through the formation and policy-making processes creates the impression that what the public thinks matters. From there it is only a short jump to the conclusion that policies are based on substantial degrees of public favor. Even the act of expressing opposition to government policies bolsters the belief that competing viewpoints are taken into account and that the losers have had a fair chance to influence policy.[30]

The sense of choice that dominates the popular view of the policy process stems from the presentation of alternative definitions of issues accompanied by the option to support the definition that is most appealing. The common perception that the public has input to the policy process comes from the public's being addressed by competing political interests and encouraged to express opinions in politically effective ways. The image or controversy surrounding policy stems from the development of competing positions through civilized debate, which provides a satisfying sense of expression and generates a tolerance for defeat. In these terms, the mobilization of public opinion during the issue formation process has a direct effect on the eventual formation of policy, and it has an equally important indirect spinoff for the power of government itself. Perhaps Napoleon put this most succinctly when he said: "Power is based on opinion. What is a government not supported by opinion? Nothing."[31]

NOTES

1. For a discussion of issue formation and the "institutional" and "systemic" agendas of the political system, see Roger W. Cobb and Charles D. Elder, *Participation in American Politics* (Boston: Allyn and Bacon, 1972).
2. Earl Latham, "The Group Basis of Politics: Notes for a Theory," in *Pressure Groups in American Politics*, ed. H. R. Mahood (New York: Scribner, 1967), p. 30.
3. Emanuel Celler, "Pressure Groups in Congress," ibid., p. 233.
4. Steven Rattner, "Companies Plan Reaction to Carter," *New York Times*, April 18, 1977, p. 14.
5. These figures are from Gallup and CBS/New York Times polls conducted from April 1977 through August 1977. They were reported in Kevin P. Phillips, "The Energy Battle: Why the White House Misfired," *Public Opinion*, Vol. 1 (May–June 1978), p. 12.
6. The data referred to in the preceding discussion are from ibid., pp. 10–11.

7. Ibid., p. 13.
8. Edward Jay Epstein, *News from Nowhere: Television and the News* (New York: Vintage Books, 1973), p. 27.
9. Quoted ibid., p. 17.
10. Michael Lipsky and David J. Olson, "The Processing of Racial Crisis in America," *Politics and Society*, Vol. 6, No. 1 (1976), pp. 79–103.
11. See Anthony Downs, "Up and Down with Ecology: The Issue-Attention Cycle," *The Public Interest*, No. 28 (Summer 1972), pp. 38–50.
12. Lipsky and Olson, "The Processing of Racial Crisis in America," pp. 89–90.
13. Dean Acheson, *Present at the Creation: My Years in the State Department* (New York: Norton, 1969), p. 375.
14. Quoted in Epstein, *News from Nowhere*, p. 153.
15. Michael Novak, "Notes on the Drama of Politics and Journalism," in *The Politics of Broadcasting: 1971–1972*, ed. Marvin Barrett (New York: Thomas Y. Crowell, 1973), p. 175.
16. Daniel Boorstin, *The Image: A Guide to Pseudoevents in America* (New York: Harper and Row, 1961).
17. Epstein, *News from Nowhere*, p. 145.
18. Quoted ibid., p. 159.
19. For an excellent discussion of the media access problems of resource-poor groups, see Edie N. Goldenberg, *Making the Papers* (Lexington, Mass.: Heath, 1975).
20. See E. E. Schattschneider, *The Semisovereign People* (Hinsdale, Ill.: Dryden Press, 1960), ch. 2.
21. Ibid., p. 71.
22. Ibid., p. 18.
23. Ibid., p. 105.
24. Ibid., pp. 104–05.
25. See J. William Fulbright, *The Pentagon Propaganda Machine* (New York: Vintage Books, 1971), ch. 1.
26. See Lipsky and Olson, "The Processing of Racial Crisis in America."
27. Ibid., p. 91.
28. Murray Edelman, *Politics as Symbolic Action* (Chicago: Markham, 1971), p. 71.
29. Lipsky and Olson, "The Processing of Racial Crisis in America," p. 88.
30. Edelman, *Politics as Symbolic Action*, p. 37.
31. Quoted in Jacques Ellul, *Propaganda* (New York: Vintage Books, 1973), p. 123.

9

Symbolism, Persuasion, and Opinion Formation

POLITICAL EVENTS are often distant, permitting little direct exposure or involvement for the average citizen. The involvement of individuals depends on whether the images sent through mass communications channels trigger their imagination and concern. Similarly, the issues that dominate public debate and occupy political institutions usually involve abstract ideas and complex social consequences. Popular reactions to issues often depend on how the ideas and consequences are symbolized by elites, special interest organizations, and reference groups. The formation of any given issue depends on the gradual replacement of numerous viewpoints by a small number of compelling symbolizations that attract the interest of various individuals. The symbols that emerge during the issue formation process link the issue and individuals' experiences in meaningful ways. Some symbols may condense a wide range of individual concerns and represent broad social understandings. Others may seem alien and lacking in emotional or social reference. The ways in which symbols make reference to individual concerns and social experiences can determine the scope, direction, intensity, distribution, and impact of public opinion.

In light of this, it may be a misguided exercise to try to distinguish too sharply between an "underlying" political reality and the symbolic forms in which that reality is encountered by the public. It is often tempting to dismiss different ways of symbolizing issues as mere window-dressing and to talk about issues as stable packages of political meaning. It is also easier to analyze political events as they "really are" rather than to search for the public version that has been mediated by political symbolism and techniques of mass communication. A better understanding of public opinion and politics will not be produced by analyses that try to debunk political symbolism. To the contrary, as Arnold has pointed out, the familiar symbolic formats of politics convey powerful meanings and focus public responses:

> To illustrate the futility of debunking [consider] the motto which runs across the façade of the New York Post Office. It reads: "Neither snow nor rain nor heat nor gloom of night stays these couriers from the swift completion of their appointed rounds." Debunked, this phrase is changed to "mail will be delivered even in bad weather." Yet one who has so changed it would understand neither the functions of architecture nor the emotional factors which bind organizations together.[1]

POLITICAL SYMBOLS AND PUBLIC UNDERSTANDINGS

The first liberating insight that comes from the study of political symbolism is the idea that issues are not preordained problems that have to emerge in the political arena in particular forms and at particular times. Political issues are constructed by political actors for public consumption. The substance and the public impact of issues depend a great deal on how they are symbolized. This is even true of many grassroots issues, which generally don't trigger broad popular involvement until they have been defined in ways that capture public interest and concern. In order to understand public opinion, therefore, it is necessary to understand the nature and uses of political symbolism.

No matter how concrete and timeless an issue seems, it always consists of a symbolic representation of a problem or state of affairs. Public opinion is always focused on interpretations of problems or conditions and never on the physical phenomenon itself. As Walter Lippmann observed so brilliantly, the images of politics that the public receives are not direct pictures of events, immediate experiences of actions, or provable social and economic theories. Popular images of politics are generated by competing political interests, which choose their symbols on the basis of judgments about what is most significant about the political situation, what values they want to promote, what they think the public is disposed to hear, and what sort of public response will benefit their political cause. Lippmann pointed out that this is both an inevitable state of affairs, due to the public's distance from developing political situations, and a welcome solution for the public, which looks to political leaders for simple interpretations of complex events. It is also a simple fact of mass communications. It is impossible for large numbers of people to communicate meaningfully about anything without first assigning some common symbolism to take the place of the object of concern.

This perspective leads to Lippmann's provocative description of every public issue or political account as a "fiction." A fiction in this sense refers to "a representation of the environment which is in lesser or greater degree made by man himself."[2] In order to understand public opinion, then, one must understand how these political representations work, because, in Lippmann's words, "The only feeling that anyone can have about an event he does not experience is the feeling aroused by his mental image of that event."[3]

Our mental images of political events are produced by the transmission of various symbols. In simple terms, a *symbol* is any communication device that represents or stands for some other thing. Communication occurs when symbols that provide a meaningful image are substituted for the thing a person wants to address. Even if the object of attention is in the physical presence of the people concerned about it, precise and sophisticated communication requires the use of symbols. In the political world, where communication takes place among masses of people about distant objects and abstract ideas, symbols are the foundation of all meaningful interaction.

Symbols stand in a curious relation to reality. On the one hand, they are only indirect means of contact with the real world. The world can take on any number of forms and feelings, depending on how it is symbolized. On the other hand, the actions that symbols lead us to take have a direct impact on the reality they represent. Thus, the initial interpretation of a situation may be subject to great dispute, but the responses to an interpretation have an indelible impact on the situation.

For example, there may be considerable debate about whether a human fetus can be symbolized (represented) as a living thing; but if most people are persuaded to regard it as such and if laws are based on this definition, then the fates of pregnant women and the fetuses they carry will be affected in profound ways. As Lippmann noted, symbols create a "pseudo-environment" between people and their real environment. Although political behavior is a response to the pseudo-environment, its consequences "operate not in the pseudo-environment where the behavior is stimulated, but in the real environment where action eventuates."[4] Firth expressed the same idea a bit differently: "A symbol is 'a device for enabling us to make abstractions,' but with some end in view—a symbol has instrumental value."[5] In other words, symbols produce the pictures of the world on which meaningful action is based.

The capacity of "mere symbols" to unleash actions that change the world is what makes people regard them so seriously. In some ways it seems almost absurd that people can see the world so differently and reach so many different conclusions about the same thing and still take their interpretations of the world seriously. However, people seldom view their differences of opinion as merely idle disagreements about abstract matters. Political experience teaches most people that when political ideas are fueled by political power and public opinion, social reality may be shaped in their image. In a political world in which values often pave the way for truth, what matters most is whether people can represent their worlds in terms that provide a basis for meaningful action and some control over political outcomes.

Here, in essence, is the power of symbols: They enable us to create the world we live in. In some cases, of course, the actions we take in response to certain pictures of the world produce unexpected or undesirable results. This indicates that there are limits to the possible representations of things. However, the striking aspect of symbolization is not the constraint of the real world on possible symbolic interpretations, but the range of possible interpretations that usually operates within the constraints. Each interpretation has the potential to inspire behavior that alters the real and perceived make-up of the material world.

As Kenneth Burke has observed, the simple act of labeling or naming something can affect human behavior toward that thing and, for all practical purposes, transform the nature of the thing itself. He cites the familiar case of the symbolic tactics of an adult trying to reassure a child about a frightening vision.

> Has one seen a child trembling in terror at a vague shape in a corner? One goes impiously into the corner, while the child looks on aghast. One picks an old coat off the clothesrack, and one says, "Look, it is only an old coat." The child breaks into fitful giggles.

> Has one *named* the object which struck terror in the child? On the
> contrary, one has totally *misnamed* it, as regards to its nature in the
> child's precious orientation. To have *named* it would have been to
> call out, "Away, thou hideous monster—thou cackling demon of
> hell, away!" and henceforth that corner would be the very altar of
> terror. One casts out demons by a vocabulary of *conversion*, by an *in-*
> *congruous* naming, by calling them *the very thing in all the world they*
> *are not*: old coats.[6]

As this example suggests, the correct name for something has less
to do with the "true" nature of the thing than with the social context in which the thing exists and the dispositions that people bring
to that context. For example, even though the American public was
frustrated by the Vietnam War toward the end of the 1960s, the
government was able to win popular support for its escalation of
military activity by introducing a vocabulary of conversion that redefined its actions from "waging a war" to "winning the peace."

In view of the impact of skillfully employed symbols, it is not
surprising that the fundamental struggles of politics are over the
symbolization of issues and events. More than most of us would
care to admit, political power accrues to those who control the
symbols of public attention.

SYMBOLS AND MEANING

Two kinds of symbol shape political consciousness: words and
icons. Icons are nonverbal symbols that orient people in social contexts. They operate at a subconscious level to create moods and
themes, to direct attention, to establish relations among actors, and
to encourage a willingness to engage in certain kinds of behavior.
Icons may come in the form of emblems, such as flags, which rivet
people's attention, establish instant bonds of membership and loyalty, or arouse a mood of patriotism at a public gathering. Sometimes icons are dressed in certain colors like the red, white, and
blue that tie together numerous high symbols of state. Other icons
are distinguished by particular forms, shapes, or spatial arrangements, such as the elevated bench of a judge and the throne of a
king, which symbolize the authority of the incumbent over all
those in his presence and remind those present of the respectful
posture they must assume. Still other political icons come in the
form of musical compositions, such as marches, which arouse pride
and expressions of support, national anthems, which strike chords
of citizenship and allegiance, and fanfares, which ready the assem-
bled masses for the appearance of leaders. Political icons form the

backdrop of public life. They can be transported into almost any situation to transform a mundane context into a stage for political action.

Within the contexts established by icons, the work of politics is accomplished largely through the use of *words*. Language symbolism differs from political icons in several important respects. Icons operate mainly on the subliminal level of the senses to create a mood, to release tension, to evoke a feeling, or to strike a social posture. In contrast, language can operate on two levels. Words can produce images that arouse emotional and physical sensations; and at the same time, words create conscious representations that allow people to take new insights away from a situation and to formulate plans for action. Words, unlike icons, can create political issues; icons can affect only how people respond to the issues that emerge. Words are the media for creating the substance of politics. Language can be made to refer to everything imaginable. Words make it possible to transform almost any physical object or abstract idea into a source of political conflict. Language makes any arbitrary distinction between political and nonpolitical concerns meaningless.

Language is a more highly developed system of symbols than is the collection of political icons. Language offers those who wish to create the world in their own image a huge vocabulary of terms with highly developed rules for their use and interpretation. Politics has been defined as "the art of the possible." In many respects what is politically possible depends on the sensible uses of language that the rules of grammar and semantics make possible.

Language is "portable" in ways that icons are not. The effectiveness of icons depends a great deal on conditioned responses and the sustaining of a mood in an immediate situation. The state of arousal produced by sensory symbolism can fade quickly when the symbolism is not present. Language, by contrast, can exert a much more lasting and powerful hold on people. Language, in its spoken and written forms, can create beliefs that people take out of situations and strengthen by using them as a basis for understanding other situations. Moreover, since political audiences and political actors employ the same rules for using and interpreting language, audiences make their own conscious connections and draw their own conclusions as they interpret political rhetoric. The conscious act of drawing a conclusion and judging its plausibility may help to cement certain opinions in the public mind. According to an established principle of learning theory, conclusions that one draws independently are more lasting and satisfying than conclusions imposed by external authorities.[7] Skillful use of language can lead people to conclusions for which they feel (however erroneously) responsible.

Language symbolism, unlike icons, can be transmitted through virtually all media of communication. Language is the consuming symbolism of the print media. It shapes perceptions of the visual images people receive through television. It captures the imagination in radio. It provides the lyrics that focus the mood of music. It is also the dominant means of communication in face-to-face encounters. Icons, by contrast, are usually restricted to a single visual, oral, or representational medium.

If all this is not enough to make language the master symbolism of politics, it is only necessary to point out in addition that language can often serve as a substitute for icons, but icons are usually not adequate substitutes for words. It is not always necessary to be present in a situation to receive the impact of its physical symbolism. The mood created by political icons can often be captured in words by journalists, commentators, politicians, or ordinary spectators and passed along to others who could never have witnessed the actual event. Indeed, one of the principal skills of politicians is the ability to blend physical symbols and words into coherent contexts that focus popular imagination.

Although words are the primary symbols of politics, language and icons operate together to shape public opinion. The power of symbolism to shape public images of political reality depends on how it is used. Meaning is not an inherent property of symbols; it is a result of their use in particular contexts. The idea that symbols have no meaning apart from the contexts in which they are used may seem strange. A common response to this notion is that one can go to a dictionary and look up the meaning of a word without worrying about all its possible uses. This reaction is misguided, however. Most words do, in fact, have more than one definition, and only the way a word is used tells us which meaning applies in a particular case. For example, the word "power" in this book defines a special type of *political* relationship, for the symbol is used in sentences about political relations within the larger context of a book about politics. But if this were a book on religion, nuclear energy, or mathematics, the word "power" would take on quite different meanings.

However, even if we could find a unique definition for a word in the dictionary, it would refer only to the word's literal meaning, or *denotation*, and not to its possible implied meanings, or *connotations*. Connotation is established only through patterns of use. For example, a politician advocating "trimming the excess fat" from a budget is referring to nothing that has to do with the literal meaning of those terms; yet we understand what is meant, or at least we understand something. Such a usage connotes in the taxpayer's mind a sense that some government agency is wasting her or his hard-earned money but the vigilant politician is going to put a stop to it. This way of defining the issue of government wastefulness is much different from explaining exactly where the "fat" lies and how the politician proposes to get rid of it. Some of the most powerful political language operates in this fashion, suppressing the literal meaning of words and giving the objects they refer to familiar (though often inappropriate) connotations.

A final reason for understanding the context in which a word is used is that the denotation or connotation of a word is only one dimension of its significance. Symbols also carry with them an action value. The action that a word represents in a situation depends on how it is used. The philosopher J. L. Austin called the *action value* of language its "performative" aspect. He argued that all sentences or utterances have two potential dimensions of meaning: (1) what they are about (that is, what they define) and (2) what they count as or "do" in the situation.[8] For example, if your friend tells you that she is boarding a particularly large and vicious dog, she has conveyed a bit of descriptive information about herself and the animal. However, if she says this just after you have announced that you plan to visit her home for the first time, then her statement takes on the action value of a warning.

The same dimensions of meaning can be found in the political uses of symbolism. For example, in 1964 Lyndon Johnson told the American public that a U.S. navy ship had been attacked by the North Vietnamese in the Gulf of Tonkin. At one level, this statement had a descriptive value similar to dozens of other historical accounts of attacks on American ships. However, the statement also represented the first clear act of "unprovoked" enemy aggression against American forces in Vietnam. In this sense the statement performed (or had an action value) as a threat designed to trigger public support for Johnson's planned escalation of America's involvement in the war. The symbolic creation of a threat was necessary because the public had to be convinced of the need to intensify the war. Although the Johnson administration already had committed itself to escalating the war, its reasons were not suitable for mobilizing public support. As Barnet observed, "The public passion for war is aroused only in response to a threat. Unless a war is perceived as defensive, the public will regard it as frivolous, dishonorable, or excessively dangerous."[9]

The use of political symbols to convey particular meanings can involve many different communication skills and symbolic formats. Among the most common formats are categorization, simile and metaphor, myth, and political dramatization. Each symbolic format creates a context that affects the possible interpretations of the issues or events in question. These contexts can also affect the emotional impact of political symbols. The degree to which the meaning and emotional impact of symbols are limited is one of the major defining characteristics of political symbolism. When a symbolic format reduces the scope of meaning and emotion associated with a message, we may say that the symbols have been used as *referential symbols*. When a symbolic format expands the scope of symbolism and invites the interpreter to project broad understandings and emotions onto it, we may say that the symbols have been used as *condensational symbols*. These terms were first used by the anthropologist Sapir to indicate that symbols can have two sorts of effects, depending on how they are used.[10]

Referential symbols are economical, concrete, and not prone to attract emotional baggage. They refer to things in specific and precise terms. The symbolic formats that create referential connections make these links so binding that the individual has little room to project private sentiments onto them. Condensational symbols, on the other hand, appear in contexts with abstractions that are often ambiguous in meaning or have a history of powerful emotional associations for the audience. Each of these characteristics invites individuals to transfer past experiences and emotional concerns onto condensational symbols. Symbols that condense powerful meanings obviously make reference to something in the process. The distinction to be made here, however, is that some contexts restrict their central symbols to a much more referential status than do others.

As a rule, when political actors want to defuse public concern and limit public involvement in an issue, they attempt to connect the issue to referential symbols. On the other hand, if the goal is to make public opinion more intense and to escalate public involvement, condensational symbols will be created. In political conflicts it is common for the more powerful party to downplay its actions in the public eye through referential definitions, while weaker opponents may attempt to arouse public concern by defining the matter in condensational terms. For example, it was common during the Vietnam War for the government to define military actions like bombing runs in dry and unemotional terms such as "protective reactions strikes." Opponents of the war, however, often tried to spark public concern by defining the bombing in condensational terms like "inhuman acts of terror."

In explaining how the public responds to political symbolism, it is important to evaluate denotations, connotations, action values, and condensational or referential impacts. These things depend on the formats in which symbols are presented. Therefore, it is helpful to understand the basic principles behind formats such as categorization, simile and metaphor, myth, and political dramatizations.

Categorization

Categorization is one of the most powerful devices in everyday communication. Consider how categorization operates in the process of interpreting this simple pair of utterances: "The baby cried. The mommy picked it up." When presented with this example, most people draw the instant conclusion that the "mommy" and the "baby" are related to each other, even though the relationship between the two actors is not specified. One observer has argued that this inference is the result of placing the actors within the general category of "family."[11] Although a number of categories could connect them (age, sex, race, religion), the "family" category seems to give them the most meaningful relationship in the context of the statements. A central rule of interpretation is to find the category that provides the most sensible connection among symbols in a given context.

Categorical operations are crucial in politics. As Edelman points out, particular definitions of an issue or a problem can lead the public to categorize the problem in ways that increase sensitivity to some aspects and decrease sensitivity to other, more important aspects. For example, he cites campaigns to reduce car accidents that focus only on driver safety, leading the public to think of just one cause of car accidents:

> These campaigns divert public attention from information suggesting that automobile accidents are inevitable regardless of driver habits. . . . Faulty design and engineering make them "unsafe at any speed"; but, beyond that, high horse power, high speed limits, and hills and corners create situations with which the human brain and

nervous system cannot be counted on to cope every time. . . . Whether or not a "drive safely" campaign makes drivers more careful, it creates an assumption about what the problem is and who is responsible for it that can be only partly valid. . . . [Yet] who can question the virtue of safe driving? This form of cognition is helpful to car manufacturers and to the highway lobby, while encouraging public criticism of the driver involved in an accident and creating self doubt and guilt in drivers.[12]

Just as the earlier example does not invite most people to think that the mother and the baby might not be related to one another, it does not occur to most people that safe-driving campaigns might be better directed at car manufacturers, highway engineers, or law-enforcement agencies. The point is that when a particular pattern of symbols leads people to make a categorization that makes sense, people tend to take that interpretation for granted. When the public can be led to take the nature of a problem for granted and to overlook other possible interpretations, the policy outcomes in question are well on their way to being resolved.

Simile and Metaphor

A *metaphor* is a direct comparison of two things that equates one thing with a special feature of the other. The use of metaphor often makes it possible to substitute politically useful meanings for potentially damaging realities. For example, bombing raids on another country may alarm the public if they hit civilian populations or if they worsen a delicate situation. To convey the sense that such attacks are limited, controlled, and precise, the military may label them "surgical operations." During the Vietnam War, the expression "surgical air strikes" was used to describe a mission that encroached on densely populated civilian territory. Even though the bombing and its effects were far from "surgical" in their precision or control, the metaphor carried with it a reassuring image. In another case, during the Cuban missile crisis of 1962, the military proposed "surgical bombing" as a means of getting rid of Soviet missiles in Cuba. The intent of the metaphor was to reassure President Kennedy that the missiles could be destroyed without endangering the Soviet personnel assigned to build, operate, and protect them. However, Kennedy's personal advisers warned him that no bombing mission could be that precise and any attack on Soviet personnel might lead to more serious consequences.

A *simile*, like a metaphor, sets up a comparison between one object and some dominant aspect of another. However, the comparisons set up by similes are less direct and leave more to the imagination. The presence of the words "like" or "as" distinguishes a simile from a metaphor. The idea that inflation is "like a monster eating away at the quality of American life" condenses numerous fears and scattered associations during periods of economic distress, yet it conveys virtually no literal meaning. It is an almost purely condensational use of the symbol "inflation."

Myth

Some political situations call for more sweeping transformations than limited symbolic formats such as categorization and metaphors can provide. Among the most familiar and useful symbolic forms in politics is myth. A *myth* is a sacred story or an interpretation of history that tells how something important came into being or what it stands for.[13] Every political system has a collection of myths that illustrate how the nation was founded, the principles it stands for, the qualities of its heroes, the strengths of its people, and the wisdom of its laws and institutions.

There are hundreds of myths about the American political system. At the top of the list stands the saga of the Revolution. There is the story of the Declaration of Independence and the commitment to freedom of those who drafted it. The legendary bravery of troops in past wars inspires the country to dedicate itself to continue the fight for freedom in future wars. We are told about the drafting of the Constitution and about the genius of the men who designed its institutions. These and other myths illustrate powerful ideals, rights, and values. The themes and story lines in these myths can be adapted easily to ongoing political situations. It is no wonder that when political actors cloak issues and events in myth, the result is almost always to condense strong emotions and understandings that go far beyond the boundaries of the immediate situation. No political group is without a collection of myths, and no successful political leader fails to recognize the power of myth to strike a public nerve and crystallize opinion around an issue.

Even colonial Americans, who had not yet formed a political system or a national mythology, had a set of myths that sparked support for the Revolution. Perhaps the central myth was the story of the courageous founders of the colonies who had fled persecution in Europe and braved untold hardships in order to establish a free society in America. Not only did this myth glorify the cause of the Revolution, but it offered every freedom fighter in 1776 a private image of the noble stock from which he or she descended and the heroic deeds of which he or she was capable. For example, Albanese cites a speech by revolutionary leader Joseph Warren that called up the story of the founders to justify any sacrifice in the name of freedom:

> Our fathers having nobly resolved never to wear the yoke of despotism, and seeing the European world, at that time, through indolence and cowardice, falling prey to tyranny, bravely threw themselves upon the bosom of the ocean, determined to find a place in which they might enjoy their freedom, or perish in the glorious attempt.[14]

Such is the stuff of which revolutions are made—particularly when people have little to throw into the struggle other than their bodies and their spirits.

Political Dramatization

The effective use of most symbolic formats depends on the political actor's control over information related to the issue and the distance of the audience from the actual facts of the matter. When information is tightly controlled and the audience is remote from actual events, the chance that symbolizations will be subjected to careful reality testing is reduced, and the willingness of the audience to regard familiar categories, metaphorical images, and mythic themes as realistic is increased. In many cases the control of information and the distance of the audience permit sweeping dramatic reconstructions of political issues, actions, and events. Much of the political news through which issue definitions are transmitted consists of carefully staged and scripted political events. Similarly, many of the accounts offered by political actors to explain their positions or to justify their behavior involve recasting their acts or motives in more acceptable terms.

The official settings, titles, and norms of political office become powerful resources for public officials to use in dramatizing their political appeals. These so-called official symbols of politics also become means of dressing dubious behaviors or partisan activities in publicly defensible terms. Elites' easy access to official symbolism, in combination with the news media's vulnerability to pseudo-events and dramatizations, means that dramatic reconstructions of events and issues are often the only systematic framework by which the public can evaluate political situations. These reconstructions surround ambiguous issues, disputed actions, or volatile events with new political contexts that may yield more desirable interpretations. One of the remarkable things about politics is that in most scenarios political actors often have control over the definitions of a large number of elements.

Kenneth Burke has argued that the understandings we reach about situations depend on how the actions in them fit with the surrounding dramatic structure of scene, actors (Burke calls them "agents"), the means through which the action is carried out (Burke calls this the "agency"), and the purpose of the actions.[15] We interpret social behavior and make various judgments about its sincerity and motivation according to how these elements fit together. When we encounter a symbolic representation of an action or an event, we make similar judgments about it by looking for the same implicit structure among its symbols. We pay attention to how the symbols fit together within common categories, or through known empirical connections in the real world, or by logical deduction. Determining how the elements of *scene, agent, agency, purpose,* and *act* fit together in a political account may lead to a number of judgments about it.

If each element is not defined in a political dramatization, there may be some ambiguity about the meaning of the act described in the scenario. Ambiguity may occur, for example, when it is discovered that a firm that received a government contract did not submit the lowest bid. The creation of ambiguity about the normal means, or agency, for submitting a bid and winning a contract raises doubt about the very meaning of the actions involved—even though the other elements (scene, agent, and purpose) may be defined in great detail. Unless a consistent and plausible definition of the means used to award the contract can be provided, political opponents may question whether the action reflects fair competition or whether it can be better interpreted as evidence of bribery or political favoritism.

In other cases, the elements in a political context may be specified completely, but their definitions may be inconsistent with one another. Inconsistency can affect the credibility of a political appeal. For example, a politician may claim that an alleged bribe was in fact a campaign contribution but that he did not keep a record of it or acknowledge it in his public disclosure statement. In light of the methods, or agencies, prescribed by the Campaign Practices Act and the public disclosure laws, this inconsistency makes it difficult to interpret the act of taking money as a normal campaign practice.

When the elements of a political scenario[16] are specified completely and consistently, the result is a more interpretable and plausible political appeal. For example, consider Richard Nixon's political situation during the last year of the Watergate ordeal. In a word, it was bleak. Nixon was waging a losing battle on all fronts. He was besieged by the press, barraged by investigators, and inundated with requests for tape recordings of secret conversations that might provide evidence about some of the charges against him. Nixon steadfastly refused to release the tapes; and when he did release a tape it was edited, filled with mysterious gaps, and was often irrelevant to the cases against him. In the early going, his explanations for withholding the information were haphazard and inconsistent. He talked about national security. He cited the need to protect the people who talked to the President. He even objected to harassment by investigators on "fishing expeditions." These and other defenses cost him a good deal of public support and were ineffective in blocking the efforts of those who wanted the tapes. The result of the failure to construct a complete and consistent account of his actions was that the public and key political actors could read virtually any meaning into the incomplete scenario surrounding Nixon:

Actor:	Richard Nixon
Act:	Withholding information
Scene:	?
Agency:	?
Purpose:	?

In what context did Nixon make his moves? Was it out of private political considerations or some legitimate official concern? Speculation was rampant, and Nixon's political position eroded almost daily.

Finally, Nixon set out to construct a public account of his actions. He defined all the basic terms in complete and consistent fashion. First, he established a *scene*. He claimed that the information being withheld pertained only to issues in the *Office of the President*. This element of the scenario was intended to separate his actions from the back rooms of politics and from the business of the committee that had run his reelection campaign. He then defined a *purpose* for his behavior. In place of the private, self-serving motives that others had attributed to him, he claimed that he acted only *to protect the presidency* and uphold the principle of confidentiality of presidential conversations. On what basis did he pursue his lofty goal? He stated that the *agency* that enabled him to take these actions was nothing less than the *Constitution* itself, which contained a *doctrine of executive privilege*, binding all Presidents to defend the confidentiality of their conversations. In this emerging scenario the *actor* was even assigned a new name. It was no longer Richard Nixon who was responsible for withholding the tapes; it was the *President of the United States*. Nixon as President was not acting for himself; he was acting as any President would to protect the office for all future incumbents. In short, Nixon constructed a complete account of his actions that had structural completeness and consistency. The result was to create at least a possible interpretation that his act of withholding information was, in fact, his legal obligation and public duty as President. This rather miraculous transformation was accomplished merely through the use of words and the staging of public speeches and performances in physical settings that reinforced the symbolism. The structural transformation of the new appeal may be shown in this way:

Scene:	?	Office of the President
Agency:	?	Constitutional doctrine
Purpose:	?	Protect the presidency
Actor:	Richard Nixon	The President
Act:	Withholding information	Legal obligation/public duty

Nixon's dramatization of his Watergate behavior is an important example because of two rare qualities. First, unlike most political scenarios, it was testable. Tape recordings existed to verify Nixon's claims about the scene, the agency, and the purpose of his actions. It is extremely rare for political dramatizations to be tested against reliable evidence. It is significant that public support for Nixon dropped as each new tape recording was released. Second, the events that the President reconstructed in his scenario were not as distant from public view as most sensitive political activities are. As the top aides and staff members of the Nixon administration began to provide unheard-of testimony about the secret goings-on in the White House, the public obtained an unprecedented set of acts against which to evaluate an official political account. In these senses, the Watergate scenario was a typical political dramatization that became exceptional only because of the erosion of normal levels of control over information and public distance from the events.

Even though these blows to Nixon's dramatization were fatal to his hopes for public support, the scenario retained some political effectiveness. Although Nixon eventually left office, it is important to consider the fact that he was not impeached, nor was he prosecuted. He also left his opponents in a legal position from which they could not release further evidence against him. In fact, he was able to retain most of the potentially incriminating evidence sought by his adversaries. In light of the alternatives, this resolution of the Watergate affair seems to be a rather favorable one, reflecting the impact that dramatizations can have on the evolution of issues and the responses of opponents.

Even though Nixon's scenario failed to mobilize public opinion, it effectively steered the conflict into a particular institutional setting and shaped its development within that setting. Political appeals do not have to convince everyone in order to be effective. A political actor must assess the political audience and determine what segments of it can be moved by what symbolic appeals to take politically favorable actions. Nixon's prime audience was the judiciary. He needed only to convince the federal courts and the Supreme Court that his explanation was at least plausible and that it defined his actions in terms that required a legal ruling.

Nixon's scenario was not only consistent and complete, but it was categorizable in terms of legal and constitutional issues. The scenario appealed successfully to a most powerful, if small, segment of Nixon's political audience: the Supreme Court. When the Court agreed to hear the Watergate tapes case, Nixon regained a substantial measure of control over his political situation. He bought time. He restricted the political attack, which had spread into numerous arenas, to the single arena of the Supreme Court. There he was able to make the best use of his political resources, and he silenced his opponents, who had to withhold further comment pending the outcome of the case. Perhaps most importantly, the scenario redefined the political issues surrounding the whole Watergate scandal. In place of bribes, cover-ups, espionage, and deleted expletives, the press began to talk of a "constitutional question." The issue was dignified. Even if the majority of the public still believed that Nixon was guilty of wrongdoing, the intensity of public outcry was dampened with the serious matter of a debate over constitutional principles. Even though the original doubts of the majority persisted, there was now the nagging possibility of another interpretation for his actions.

Although the Court eventually ruled against Nixon on the tapes case, the political scenario had defused public outrage, blurred the nature of the issues at stake, and provided Nixon with a more dignified exit opportunity from public life. Given the circumstances confronting Richard Nixon prior to the construction of the tapes scenario, these are no small accomplishments.

Both in its failures and in its successes, this example illustrates the power of symbols to appeal to a selected audience and to shape the course of political events. As the Watergate example implies, much of the enormous power of public officials comes from the fact that the basic symbols of office constitute all the resources necessary to construct convincing symbolic structures around most of their actions. All that Richard Nixon and his legal advisers needed to do was apply a bit of creativity to blend his office, its official purposes, its agencies, and his public persona into a symbolic context around a most sensitive political action. Had the tapes not existed and the loyalty of his aides not failed, the Watergate storm would probably be remembered only as a dark cloud in the Nixon administration.

CONDITIONS OF POLITICAL PERSUASION

There are limits to the power of symbolism to shape public opinion. Although Nixon's Watergate scenario had some impressive political effects, it did not change the opinions held by a majority of persons about the President or his activities. The degree to which political appeals can change mass opinion depends on two factors: (1) the symbolic format of the appeal (as outlined in the last section) and (2) the existence of certain conditions of persuasion.

By the time Nixon presented his final Watergate scenario to the public, conditions favorable to political persuasion had eroded considerably. There were a number of credible competing interpretations of his actions, blocking the clear *reception* of his appeal. A majority of the public had already formed stable attitudes about Nixon's behavior; so his appeal may have come too late to win the hearts of the masses. Research has identified *commitment to initial attitudes* as another major factor in persuasion. Moreover, with the release of the tapes, Richard Nixon had lost much of his credibility as a source of information. Many people were unwilling to believe him no matter what he said or how well he said it. The *credibility of the source* is another major condition of persuasion. Finally, Nixon's statements received a hostile reception from commentators, political opponents, and the opinion polls. Persuasion researchers have determined that the *response of the audience* is another important condition of persuasion. Had these conditions been operating in Nixon's favor, it is likely that he would have removed himself from the Watergate predicament with considerable public support. When the persuasion variables can be introduced effectively, a well-constructed symbolic appeal can have dramatic effects on public opinion.

Reception of the Message

It is obvious that in order to have an impact on opinion, a message must be received by the audience. This means two things: First, the message must get through to the audience. Second, it must get through without being garbled by competing messages (in the lingo of information theorists, the *signal-to-noise ratio* of a message must be high). Access to communications media increases the likelihood that political appeals will be transmitted. Also, groups with access to public officials or to financial support will be more likely to get their messages transmitted. Even if a message is transmitted, however, the public still must pay attention to it if it is going to be received. We know that most people are not very interested in politics and don't go out of their way to gather political information. Debates over routine political issues tend to escape the awareness of large numbers of people. The obvious implication of this is that the more dramatic the issue can be made to appear, the greater is the chance that is will capture the attention and interest of the public.

In most political situations, competing groups attempt to get their appeals across to the public while damaging the claims of the opposition. Thus political appeals often cancel each other out, and key political issues become lost in the "noise" of competing messages. The most effective solution to the clarity problem provides a solution to other reception problems as well. Successful political actors must become practiced at staging "pseudo-events" of the sort that were described briefly in Chapter 8. These simple, planned, dramatic political performances give political actors maximum control over the structure of their symbolic appeals, and they promote receptivity. Since they conform to media news formats, pseudo-events are likely to receive news coverage. Since they are dramatic and memorable, they are likely to capture public attention. Finally, since they encapsulate issues, set them apart from their complex surroundings, and give them a clear focus, pseudo-events are less likely than other sorts of appeal to be disrupted by competing information.[17]

Commitment to Initial Attitudes

Another major finding of persuasion research is that the more committed people are to existing attitudes, the more immune they are to new political appeals.[18] Like most persuasion maxims, this one is fairly obvious. Its implication is obvious as well: People who have unstable political attitudes are more easily led to new opinions in response to political appeals. This condition of persuasion is likely to be operating positively in most political situations most of the time, for even the most generous interpretation of the data on attitude stability in the mass public suggests a fairly high degree of instability.

Even if new converts to one side of an issue or the other don't hold their opinions very long, they may hold them long enough to play a role in the resolution of a conflict or the adoption of a policy. Political candidates are usually aware that the bloc of "undecided" voters may determine the outcome of an election and that producing even short-term opinion changes within this group can be helpful. Wheeler reports an interesting case of this principle in the race between Richard Nixon and Nelson Rockefeller for the Republican presidential nomination in 1968.

Going into the convention, both Nixon and Rockefeller appeared to have nearly equal support in the opinion polls and among the delegates. Among the undecided delegates, the key issue was which of the two candidates seemed to be the most "electable." This question could be settled by a strong showing in the public opinion polls just before the convention began. Wheeler reports that Nixon had access to secret information about the date on which Gallup's pollsters would take to the field for the last national opinion survey prior to the convention. On the eve of this survey Nixon delivered a dramatic speech on prime-time national television. The impact of the speech registered clearly in the subsequent poll, which showed Nixon with a strong advance in popularity over Rockefeller. Even though this jump in public support died within a couple of weeks (as did Carter's surge in public support shortly after his energy speeches), Richard Nixon was able to enter the convention with what seemed to be strong evidence that he was the more electable of the two candidates. Most observers credit this as the major factor in Nixon's nomination.[19]

Credibility of the Source

The credibility of the source of an appeal is a complex and fascinating condition of persuasion. The basic findings from persuasion research are straightforward: The more expert and trustworthy the communicator is, the more persuasive the message will be.[20] The political implications of this maxim are interesting. Recall from the earlier discussion of socialization that most citizens acquire a high level of trust in government and leaders at a very early age.[21] This trust is reinforced by the fact that most Americans regard their leaders as high-status and glamorous individuals possessing special skills and knowledge.[22]

The trusting orientation of the public toward its leaders may be compounded by what Sears has called the "positivity bias" in political judgment. It appears that most people are inclined to view things in a positive way, and they want to believe what they are told. Most people prefer to support one side rather than to oppose the other. Sears and Whitney suggest that the positivity bias is the result of two things.[23] First, most people live in environments filled with positive information and positive appeals. Overtly negative inputs in life are the exception rather than the rule for most people. Second, early socialization accentuates the positive. Even before they learn about politics, most children are taught to be positive. Childhood is filled with maxims such as the one that Sears and Whitney cite: "If you can't say something nice, don't say anything at all."

The combined effects of political trust, the awe of leaders, and the positivity bias are probably quite powerful in most political situations. The implication is that leaders have to do relatively little to establish their credibility with the public. Credibility seems to be more something that is bestowed than something earned (although this has changed somewhat with the new "politics of trust" in the years since Watergate). The dominant public disposition to trust its leaders until they are proven untrustworthy has some obvious implications for public opinion. Leaders and government representatives have enormous power to shape public opinion—as long as their appeals are received by the public, they do not run up against strongly held prior opinions, and their credibility is not damaged by being caught in outright lies.

Time and again in American politics, the enduring credibility of leaders and public officials is demonstrated in forms such as large shifts in public opinion following major speeches by respected leaders, the ability of Presidents to mobilize massive public support in crises, the tendency of the public to quickly support newly elected leaders even if they belong to the opposition party, and the uncritical acceptance of most government analyses of national priorities and policy problems. As Barnet points out, opinion pollsters have long known the impact of a leader's opinion on polling results:

> Analysts of public opinion polling note that the responses differ markedly if they are prefaced with "The President thinks ... Do you agree?" The ordinary citizen is ready to oppose the judgment of the commander-in-chief on a matter of national security only when the credibility of the President has been seriously compromised by events.[24]

It is important to recognize that the legacy of trust from socialization and positivity is not the only basis of political credibility. The structure of power in a society like America produces a huge gap between leaders and the public. In most situations leaders can act and the public can't. This leaves the public without much choice but to trust its leaders, and it creates a strong psychological incentive to think that they are credible. As Edelman has pointed out:

> Alienation, anomie, despair of being able to chart one's own course in a complex, cold, and bewildering world have become characteristic of a large part of the population of advanced countries. As the world can be neither understood nor influenced, attachment to reassuring abstract symbols rather than to one's own efforts becomes chronic. And what symbol can be more reassuring than the incumbent of a high position who knows what to do and is willing to act, especially when others are bewildered and alone? Because such a symbol is so intensely sought, it will predictably be found in the person of any incumbent whose actions can be interpreted as beneficent, whether it is because they are demonstrably beneficent or because their consequences are unknowable.[25]

The effects of public insecurity seem to reinforce the other bases of credibility, with the result that leaders will be trusted and believed until massive evidence is built up to the contrary. Thus it is no wonder that the public and leaders have been concerned about the decline in public trust and leader credibility in the years following Lyndon Johnson's credibility gap, Richard Nixon's Watergate scandal, and Jimmy Carter's fall from public grace. Both political actors and the public have clear, though different, interests in restoring public trust. For the public, the ability to form opinions in response to a trusted leader's appeals is a surrogate for understanding complex realities that are too distant to be grasped except through the vision of leaders. Moreover, for the powerless, opinions become small affirmations of faith that the powerful do understand their problems and look out for their interests. Although for the public, opinions are largely means of reassurance and personal control, for political actors they represent tangible political resources. Loss of public trust in government means that leaders lose control over opinion formation, and the result of that loss is damage to policy making and legitimation. It does not take a crystal ball to see the "politics of trust" as a major political theme of the 1980s.

Response of the Audience

A final condition of persuasion is the impact of other members of the audience on an individual's opinion about an appeal. Most of us are exposed to political appeals as members of *target audiences*. In target audiences, people may be physically present together, as at a speech, or they may simply communicate with one another after being exposed to information through more individualized means of communication, such as television or radio. The attitudes of others who have been exposed to the same information can have profound effects on how an individual perceives and judges the information.

The most dramatic proof of this principle came in Solomon Asch's pioneering experiments on social influences in perception. In the most famous of these experiments, Asch showed a group of subjects a set of lines of different lengths and asked each member of the group to make judgments about the relative lengths of the lines. All members of the group but one (the real subject) were confederates of the experimenter. They were instructed to give the correct answer sometimes and to state incorrect responses at other times. Asch found that the subjects in these experiments tended to see the lines as others in the group saw them, and not as they really were. This was even true when the lines were quite different in length and the other group members insisted that the shortest line was really the longest, or that the medium line was the shortest. After the experiment, when the subjects were interviewed, it became clear that they were not simply giving in to social pressure and saying things that they didn't really believe. They had actually seen the physical objects in the way they described them.[26]

A number of interesting areas of research have followed these experiments. Recent studies indicate that what we ordinarily think of as "hypnotism" has little or nothing to do with putting people into trances and gaining control of the hidden recesses of their minds. One of the major conditions of hypnosis is the mutual support among subjects or audience members for the hypnotist and the shared belief that hypnosis is possible. In fact, one observer has argued that hypnosis is simply the result of having all the conditions of persuasion present in a situation in ideal forms. In addition to audience support, Etheredge argues that hypnosis requires a clear message from the communicator. (This high signal-to-noise ratio is one of the conditions of receptivity mentioned earlier.) Next, the subjects must not be biased against hypnotism or unwilling to believe in the hypnotist. This is an aspect of the commitment condition of persuasion. Finally, the subjects must trust the hypnotist and feel that he or she has highly developed skills or knowledge. This is synonymous with the credibility condition.[27]

Whether or not we want to believe that the conditions of persuasion can set up a hypnotic relationship as they approach their ideal forms, it is clear that under the right conditions even a single factor like audience support can get people to see and believe things that they would not ordinarily see and believe under their own power. The implication for politics and public opinion is obvious: Political actors will have more success shaping the opinions of their publics if they can control audience reaction to some degree.

One of the unwritten rules of politics has long been to carefully select and "prepare" audiences for speeches and public appearances. The art of audience control achieved its greatest heights in Nazi Germany. The great public rallies held by Hitler during the years of the Third Reich were always centered on the audience. The rallies and speeches drew hundreds of thousands of people, often brought in by the regime from all over the country. The settings were carefully selected so that the audience was packed together with no possibility of directing attention anywhere but at the speaker. The audience had roles to play at the rallies. They wore military uniforms, arm bands, or the outfits of various youth corps and citizens brigades to symbolize their common bonds and their support for the regime. The rallies often began and ended with impressive parades of troops carrying banners and saluting *Der Führer*. Often the entire audience would parade past the speaker or interrupt speeches with wild enthusiasm or well-orchestrated salutes and pledges of allegiance to the regime. The key to Nazi propaganda was structuring the behavior of the audience. It is little wonder that the word most often used to describe the atmosphere at these rallies is "hypnotic."

Concern with audience response is a standard item of business in American politics as well. On occasion, the structuring of the audience has taken on extreme proportions. For example, in the presidential election of 1896, William McKinley made virtually all his speeches from the front porch of his home in Canton, Ohio. This "front-porch" campaign drew tens of thousands of voters, who were transported from all over the country at Republican party expense to hear McKinley. The candidate lavished personal attention on each group that passed through town. He prepared selected speeches for different audiences. Needless to say, McKinley spoke to very few unsupportive audiences that year. Moreover, the intimacy and novelty of the campaign captured the imagination of the national press (whose publishers and editors had already been captured by the Republican party). Virtually every story on the campaign carried references to the enthusiastic audiences for McKinley's speeches.

Although few political campaigns go to those lengths, careful attention is always paid to turning out large and enthusiastic crowds that have been well prepared for the candidate's appearance. An interesting problem that developed during Jimmy Carter's campaign in 1976 was that many of the Carter faithful who turned out for his speeches were disappointed by the feeling that the candidate did not really want them to cheer, shout, and engage in normal audience hoopla. Carter seemed embarrassed by this sort of carrying-on by the audience. The result of inhibiting these forms of audience response was that some of Carter's supporters had difficulty maintaining their opinions about him and convincing newcomers of the attractiveness of their candidate.[28]

As the McKinley campaign shows, all members of an audience need not be physically present in order to be affected by a performance. A distant or "secondary" audience can be swayed by the responses of the immediate audience. McKinley's most important audience was the majority of the voting public, which never came to Canton, but whose imagination and vicarious enthusiasm were sparked by the reports of the front-porch performances.

Sometimes the efforts to shape the responses of immediate audiences in order to sway the opinion of distant publics become mind boggling in their complexity. For example, persuasion research has shown that undecided individuals may find a leader more trustworthy or an appeal more credible if a leader's message runs against the dominant sentiment of the immediate audience.[29] Pursuing the tactic of taking a controversial stand before an audience will, of course, risk losing the support of the immediate group, but it may win the trust of secondary audiences. In an age of mass media, a politician can stage a performance before a small audience and have the scene transmitted to a huge audience of millions of viewers and readers. In recent years the public has been confronted with an increasing number of situations in which a politician appears to be taking a "tough" or "courageous" stand on an issue by making a speech that arouses the disfavor of the audience. Political actors may be increasingly willing to alienate small and politically inconsequential immediate audiences in order to win credibility with the distant and larger media audience.

The case study presented in Chapter 10 shows that this is precisely what Gerald Ford did shortly after becoming President in 1974. He needed to generate broad popular support for his proposal for an amnesty program—particularly among liberals suspicious of his conservative record. Therefore, he opened his crusade for amnesty by delivering a major speech before the most hostile and conservative veterans' group he could find. The results of this tactic were predictable: The speech triggered outrage from the immediate audience, making the event a major national news story that conveyed an image of the new President taking a courageous stand on a major policy issue before a hostile audience. Not surprisingly this audience effect generated initial support for the amnesty program among liberals and enhanced Ford's credibility as a leader.

THE IMPACT OF SYMBOLISM AND PERSUASION ON OPINION

The use of symbolism and persuasion can affect a number of important characteristics of opinion discussed earlier. The way in which an issue is defined and presented to the public can affect the intensity, distribution, and expression of opinion. These properties can determine such things as the public's perception of the importance of the issue, the place of the issue on the systemic agenda, and the role of the public in the resolution of the issue.

Intensity of Opinion

The intensity of opinion depends in large part on whether the political actors who set in motion the issue formation process can successfully define the issue in condensational or referential symbols. For example, the public is likely to become intensely concerned about foreign policy issues defined in terms of condensational images about national security, the arms race, or the balance of power. By contrast, public concern is likely to be minimized in situations defined in referential terms such as "routine diplomacy" or "minor misunderstanding." Barnet observes that the symbolism attached to foreign policy issues often changes dramatically as the role of public opinion in the plans of political elites changes. For example, a country like Vietnam may be declared "empty of vital U.S. interests" at one point in time only to be described as a "vital bastion of the whole Free World" when it later figures into military or diplomatic plans. As the communications among elites involved in the Vietnam War (released in the Pentagon papers) showed, such shifts in political rhetoric are standard operating procedure for "preparing public opinion" for wars and crisis.[30]

Similarly, a domestic issue like federal regulation of broadcasting triggers a much more intense public response if the issue is cast in terms of condensational symbols such as freedom of speech or the protection of public morals than if the issue is addressed in technical referential terms involving the application of standards or the review of broadcast practices. As Edelman points out, the Federal Communications Commission has restricted the discussion of public issues on the air to a number of obscure policies, which have had little impact on the behavior of broadcasters. However, these weak regulatory practices have failed to arouse public concern because of their reassuring and seemingly comprehensive nature.[31]

In both foreign policy and domestic policy there are a number of reasons why cycles of condensational and referential symbols that produce alternating states of alarm and reassurance can have such dramatic effects on the intensity of public opinion. People recognize the capacity of political events to affect their lives in profound ways, yet they also tend to see political problems as beyond their capacity to resolve. This increases the tendency (discussed in Chapter 8) to displace private fears and anxieties onto distant public symbols. When these symbols are drawn into the definition of political issues, they can become targets for the release of intense private concerns. Thus the recurring cycles of arousal and reassurance that characterize so many issues are probably sustained by deep individual concerns about security. Edelman calls security the "primal political symbol." The symbolization of threats engages public concerns, and the eventual reassurances of leaders provide welcome relief from anxiety; but this emotional upheaval generally leaves enough lingering concern to draw people into the next cycle of threat and reassurance.[32]

Given sufficient control over information and enough public distance from the reality of events, even the most unlikely situations can be endowed with powerful emotional trappings. Barnet pointed out that the government even overcame the difficulty of mobilizing public concern about the Vietnam situation. It had been easy, by contrast, to mobilize intense feeling about the Soviet Union and the cold war, because the Soviet Union represented a fearsome power that seemed bent on upsetting the world order. However, in the case of Vietnam "it was harder to play on fear, for the stubborn fact always remained that the enemy was a fourth-rate power with no capacity whatsoever for hurting Americans who stayed out of their country. The dominoes 'theory' was designed to transfer Vietnam into a respectably frightening enemy."[33] The "dominoes theory" was the idea pushed by the Kennedy and Johnson administrations that the communists were out to take over small nations in the Third World one by one. The fall of each nation would give the communists an increased chance of "pushing over" its neighbors, until the chain reaction would lead right to the doorstep of the major powers of the free world. Thus, although North Vietnam was not a direct threat to American security, it played a part in a truly terrifying communist plan to take over the world. The picture that the public received of this political situation was constructed with almost total control by political elites, with little check exercised by the public on its accuracy.

As Walter Lippmann pointed out over fifty years ago, the pictures that the public receives of the real world of politics are, for the most part, images put together by elites on the basis of a combination of how they see things, what they regard to be the public interest, and what definitions they feel they must construct in order to get the public to act in its better interests.[34] Not only are most political situations ambiguous to begin with, but the filtering role played by elites who stand between the public and political reality make the "objective" conditions surrounding any issue all the more obscure. The implications of this ambiguity for public opinion have been well described by Edelman:

> The same experience and set of facts can be interpreted by a group of people as meaning either that their legitimate interests are being protected or that the status and benefits due them are being denied or threatened. . . . Does the large scale influx of black people into a northern city mean that the status, the livelihood, or the lives of white residents will ultimately be threatened, or does it signal one more phase in a continuing process of cultural diversification, economic progress, and political coexistence? Do large scale troop movements in a foreign country signal an intention to attack another country, an intention to protect it, or routine maneuvers? It is always the ambiguity, the uncertain and diverse possible implications of news that creates the fears, hopes and the search for authoritative cues that public policy often satisfies.[35]

Distribution of Opinion

Sometimes the arousal of the entire population can have the most effective impact on the formation of an issue involving the resolution of conflicts. This is the case, for example, when the President and Congress resolve to go to war. In other instances it is only necessary (and more manageable) to arouse intense concern among a small part of the public, who will carry the issue forward in an organized and committed fashion. Political success often depends on whether the political factions involved with issue formation can define the issue in ways that control the distribution of public response. It is important for political actors to be sensitive to the various publics that might respond differently to an issue and, therefore, require special consideration in its definition. A typical example of the "audience analysis" that goes into any public opinion campaign is contained in the following staff memo to the Secretary of Defense in the early days of the Vietnam War:

> Special considerations during the next two months. The relevant audiences of U.S. actions are the Communists (who must feel strong pressures), the South Vietnamese (whose morale must be buoyed), our allies (who must trust us as "underwriters"), and the U.S. public (which must support our risk-taking with U.S. lives and prestige). During the next two months, because of the lack of "rebuttal

time" before election to justify particular actions which may be distorted to the U.S. public, we must act with special care.[36]

Presidential candidates often walk a similar symbolic tightrope in their efforts to add narrow bands of public support to their electoral coalitions. For example, in his early primary bids for the presidential nomination in 1976, Jimmy Carter faced an uphill climb against better-known opponents who often had secure followings among different groups in the electorate. Carter and his opinion analysts often had to figure out how to piece together fragments of these different groups through special appeals while being careful not to alienate them through exposure to other groups' messages.

In Florida this task of opinion management entailed a masterful piece of market research through which each target group was exposed to special appeals through information channels that were not likely to be monitored by the other groups. For example, a tape of Carter saying that the Civil Rights Act was "the best thing that ever happened to the South in my lifetime" was run exclusively on black radio stations throughout the state. This message was withheld from other audiences. The reason for the selectivity of the appeal was simple: Carter stood a good chance of attracting black voters, but he did not want to risk losing any conservative whites to George Wallace, who was already the frontrunner in the race. Following a similar rationale, spots showing Carter talking about "togetherness" and the "mood of the country" were aired on "Sara," a television program with a "middle American" audience. Liberal renditions of Carter's stands on welfare and employment were broadcast during episodes of "Maude," a program with a young and liberal following. Other selective appeals were presented to blue-collar audiences on "Hee Haw," to professional viewers on "Today," and to senior citizens on "Lawrence Welk,"[37] The result of this careful engineering of appeals to different bands of the opinion spectrum was a surprisingly strong finish in a primary in which Carter had been picked to do poorly.

Expression of Opinion

Within the constraints on opinion established by its intensity and distribution, there remain different forms in which the public can express its reactions to emerging issues. Strong and widely held views can be expressed through forms ranging from voting, letter writing, and bumper stickers to demonstrations and social movements. Intense but narrowly held opinion can surface in forms ranging from lobbying to riots. In still other cases the most effective expression of opinion may simply be the passive support for a policy or a leader recorded in the opinion polls. These and other expressions of opinion can be affected by the symbolic definition of an issue.

Some efforts to shape the expression of public opinion may go to such extremes as inventing new political support groups and establishing their credibility through the media. For example, Richard Nixon faced massive protests against his war policies in 1969. He felt that the protests could damage his credibility at the peace negotiations that were in progress. They also threatened to undermine the legitimacy of his policies in the eyes of the larger public. In the fall of 1969 Nixon and high-level officials in his administration launched an effective public opinion campaign to create the impression of broad public support for his handling of the war. One objective of the campaign was to create a new political support group and direct its expressions of opinion as much as possible. The other objective was to divert media coverage from protesters and to suppress their expressions of opposition.

The campaign began by claiming that public attitudes about the war involved questions of patriotism and pride in America. Only unpatriotic citizens would oppose the administration's attempts to end the war. Public opposition at the delicate stage of the peace talks was branded as an insult to the thousands of honorable Americans who had fought and died in Vietnam. The administration also charged that opposition played into the hands of the enemy at the negotiating sessions. This definition of the issue was accompanied by the claim that the media had paid more attention to the voices of a few dissidents than to the overwhelming support of the "great silent majority" of patriotic Americans. The attack on the media was spearheaded by Vice President Spiro Agnew, who accused the liberal media of identifying with the political cause of the "nattering nabobs of negativism" and the "effete snobs" who opposed the administration's efforts to end the war.

This language raised the uncomfortable issue of political fairness, which can loom as a formidable obstacle in network dealings with regulatory agencies. Moreover, Agnew's charges contained an embarrassing grain of truth. Media policy is almost always geared to presenting two sides of an issue. Even if a competing viewpoint does not emerge on its own, journalists will often seek one out or state alternative views in their analyses.[38] However, no clear support movement had emerged for the administration's actions. As a result, the most visible and dramatic news coverage had been devoted to the antiwar movement. Suddenly the administration was claiming that there had been an overwhelming support group all along—a group so large that it lacked effective organization, a group whose members were so decent and patriotic that they had refrained from adopting the loud and violent methods of opinion expression used by the dissidents. In the absence of evidence that the hard-to-cover "silent majority" did *not* exist, the media had yet another reason to downplay its coverage of the protests.

As Edelman has noted, the impact of the "silent majority" on the development of the Vietnam issue had little to do with the group's actual existence or actions:

> Politicians' statements about unobservable people are often either impossible to verify or quite clearly invalid. When, in the midst of widespread public objection to the Vietnam War, Richard Nixon referred to a "silent majority" that supported his hawkish war policy, his allegation was dubious in light of pertinent research. Its function was to evoke a reference group other than the plainly visible and nonsilent one for the large number of people who were torn or uncertain regarding their position on the war. For such a purpose a "majority" that cannot be observed because it is "silent" is ideal. For anyone looking for a reason to support the President and the war, the "silent majority" serves its purpose even if it does not exist.[39]

To enhance the illusion of massive support for the war, the administration promoted counterdemonstrations in Washington and around the country. These rallies were led by religious figures and celebrities who claimed to represent the sentiments of the vast majority of Americans. Media coverage of these activities increased, while coverage of antiwar protests decreased. Faced with the greater difficulty of getting its message across to the public and the increased difficulty of turning out demonstrators in the face of apparent public disapproval, the antiwar movement virtually died during the fall of 1969.[40] This example illustrates the degree to which the struggle between elites and pressure groups during the period of issue formation can affect the expression of public opinion and how opinion in turn can affect the outcome of an issue.

CONCLUSION

Symbolic appeals and the conditions of persuasion operate in fascinating combinations to link political actors, issues, and the public in the formation of public opinion. In order to understand how public opinion is formed and what its political impact is in a given situation, it is important *not* to regard issues as fixed political problems or positions that remain the same over time and toward which the public adopts a constant political role. Issues evolve and change, and the public's political relationship to them can change also. An issue may be symbolized much differently in future political contexts than it was in the past. Moreover, what the public "means" by the opinions it expresses on an issue may vary over time. In short, it is virtually meaningless to talk of issues as though they had constant meanings simply because we call them by the same names over time. The political significance of an issue seems to depend on how it is defined in a particular political context. This perspective helps to explain how the significance of issues can change. It also emphasizes the fact that the political role of public opinion can vary, depending on how it is aroused and how it is focused. In some cases public opinion may push an issue toward an important policy resolution. In other cases opinion may have little or no impact on policy.

It is also important to recognize that issues can be deceptive. Their political uses may have little to do with the problem or policies they address. Political issues can have ulterior political uses such as improving the public image of a politician or group, assuaging or arousing public concerns, stirring up old political rivalries or coalitions, building support for a candidate, or bringing public opinion to bear on other political problems that are too sensitive to confront directly. In order to understand that issues and opinions have to be analyzed in terms of how they fit into a political context and not according to static definitions, it is helpful to look at issues that have political uses other than their stated policy goals. In the next chapter we will see how Gerald Ford tried to define the issue of amnesty for Vietnam-era dissidents in a way that was designed to solve a number of other more important problems he faced as a new President.

NOTES

1. Thurman Arnold, quoted in Sidney Hook, *Reason, Social Myths and Democracy* (New York: Harper and Row, 1940), p. 56.

2. Walter Lippmann, *Public Opinion* (New York: Free Press, 1949), p. 10.
3. Ibid., p. 9.
4. Ibid., p. 10.
5. Raymond Firth, *Symbols: Public and Private* (Ithaca, N.Y.: Cornell University Press, 1973), p. 76.
6. Kenneth Burke, *Permanence and Change* (Indianapolis: Bobbs-Merrill, 1954), p. 133.
7. This point is established powerfully in the developmental psychology of Jean Piaget. See Jean Piaget, *The Construction of Reality in the Child* (New York: Basic Books, 1954); and Jean Piaget, *The Moral Judgment of the Child* (New York: Free Press, 1969).
8. J. L. Austin, *How to Do Things with Words* (New York: Oxford University Press, 1962).
9. Richard J. Barnet, *Roots of War* (Baltimore: Penguin Books, 1972), p. 283.
10. Edward Sapir, "Symbolism," *Encyclopedia of the Social Sciences* (New York: Macmillan, 1934), pp. 492–95.
11. Harvey Sacks, "On the Analyzability of Stories by Children," in *Directions in Sociolinguistics: The Ethnography of Communication*, eds. J. Gumperz and D. Hymes (New York: Holt, Rinehart and Winston, 1972).
12. Murray Edelman, *Political Language: Words That Succeed and Policies That Fail* (New York: Academic Press, 1977), p. 36.
13. For the various perspectives on myth from which this definition was distilled, see Jerome S. Bruner, "Myth and Identity," in *Myth and Mythmaking*, ed. Henry A. Murray (New York: Braziller, 1960); Ernst Cassirer, *Language and Myth* (New York: Harper and Row, 1946); Mircea Eliade, *Myth and Reality* (New York: Harper and Row, 1963); Claude Levi-Strauss, *The Savage Mind* (Chicago: University of Chicago Press, 1966); and Victor Turner, *Drama, Field, and Metaphor* (Ithaca, N.Y.: Cornell University Press, 1974).
14. Catherine Albanese, *Sons of the Fathers: The Civil Religion of the American Revolution* (Philadelphia: Temple University Press, 1976), p. 24.
15. See Kenneth Burke, *A Grammar of Motives* (Berkeley: University of California Press, 1969).
16. For a detailed discussion of this concept, see W. Lance Bennett, "Political Scenarios and the Nature of Politics," *Philosophy and Rhetoric*, Vol. 8 (Winter 1975), pp. 23–42.
17. Boorstin argues that pseudo-events blur the connection between an image and the underlying reality of a situation. See Daniel Boorstin, *The Image* (New York: Atheneum, 1961), p. 11.
18. Charles A. Kiesler, Barry E. Collins, and Neal Miller, *Attitude Change: A Critical Analysis of Theoretical Approaches* (New York: Wiley, 1969).
19. Michael Wheeler, *Lies, Damn Lies, and Statistics: The Manipulation of Public Opinion in America* (New York: Dell, 1976), pp. 119–23.
20. Carl I. Hovland, Irving L. Janis, and Harold H. Kelley, *Communication and Persuasion* (New Haven: Yale University Press, 1953).
21. For the major findings of trust in leaders and government, see Fred I. Greenstein, "The Benevolent Leader: Children's Images of Political Authority," *American Political Science Review*, Vol. 54 (December

1960), pp. 934–43; David Easton and Jack Dennis, *Children in the Political System: Origins of Political Legitimacy* (New York: McGraw-Hill, 1969); and Robert D. Hess and Judith V. Torney, *The Development of Political Attitudes in Children* (Garden City, N.Y.: Doubleday, Anchor Books, 1968).

22. See, for example, R. W. Hodge, P. M. Siegel, and P. H. Rossi, "Occupation Prestige in the United States, 1925–1963," *American Journal of Sociology*, Vol. 70 (November 1964), pp. 286–302; and M. Kent Jennings, Milton C. Cummings, Jr., and F. P. Kilpatrick, "Trusted Leaders: Perceptions of Appointed Federal Officials," *Public Opinion Quarterly*, Vol. 30 (Fall 1966), pp. 368–84.

23. See David O. Sears and Richard E. Whitney, *Political Persuasion* (Morristown, N.J.: General Learning Press, 1973).

24. Barnet, *Roots of War*, p. 245.

25. Murray Edelman, *The Symbolic Uses of Politics* (Urbana: University of Illinois Press, 1964), p. 26.

26. Solomon Asch, "The Doctrine of Suggestion, Prestige and Imitation in Social Psychology," *Psychological Review*, Vol. 55 (September 1948), pp. 250–76.

27. Lloyd Etheredge, "Hypnosis and Order," in *Politics and Society*, ed. John Sweeney (forthcoming).

28. See W. Lance Bennett, "The Ritualistic and Pragmatic Bases of Political Campaign Discourse," *Quarterly Journal of Speech*, Vol. 63 (October 1977), pp. 219–38.

29. J. Mills and J. M. Jellison, "Effect on Opinion Change of How Desirable the Communication Is to the Audience the Communicator Addressed," *Journal of Personality and Social Psychology*, Vol. 6 (May 1967), pp. 98–101.

30. Barnet, *Roots of War*, p. 271.

31. Edelman, *The Symbolic Uses of Politics*, p. 39.

32. Edelman, *Political Language*, pp. 4–5.

33. Barnet, *Roots of War*, p. 281.

34. Lippmann, *Public Opinion*.

35. Murray Edelman, *Politics as Symbolic Action* (Chicago: Markham, 1971), pp. 10–11.

36. Quoted in Barnet, *Roots of War*, pp. 266–67.

37. The description of this opinion strategy is from Joseph Lelyveld, "The Selling of a Candidate," *New York Times Magazine*, March 28, 1976. See also Bennett, "The Ritualistic and Pragmatic Bases of Political Campaign Discourse."

38. See Edward Jay Epstein, *News from Nowhere: Television and the News* (New York: Vintage Books, 1973), pp. 64–72, 136.

39. Edelman, *Political Language*, p. 30.

40. For an excellent analysis of this struggle over issue definitions and public attention, see Henry Beck, "Attentional Struggles and Silencing Strategies in a Human Political Conflict: The Case of the Vietnam Moratoria," in *The Structure of Human Attention: Ethological Studies*, eds. M. R. A. Chance and R. R. Larson (New York: Wiley, 1976).

10

Amnesty: A Case Study of Issue Formation

SYMBOLISM AND PERSUASION techniques can have powerful effects on the way public opinion forms around an issue. Some issues may be presented in referential terms designed to inhibit public concern. This was how America's involvement in Vietnam was handled during the early 1960s, when government officials were concerned that the public might object to American's participating in the fighting. America's role was described as "technical assistance" in "noncombat" situations by "civilian advisers." Other issues may be symbolized in ways that arouse broad public concern. Lyndon Johnson's dramatic account of the Gulf of Tonkin incident, for example, mobilized public opinion in favor of subsequent U.S. involvement in the Vietnam War.

In addition to shaping public opinion, the definition of issues can also affect the political uses of opinion. In some cases issues may be presented as unambiguous policy questions designed to channel opinion into legislative or electoral arenas. In other cases, however, issues may be symbolized in much more subtle ways in order to put public opinion to other political uses. For example, a political candidate may promote a popular issue as a means of enlarging his or her political following. Some issues may be defined in ways that arouse public fears or anxieties in order to pave the way for future policy proposals. For example, police departments may make an issue of crime increases to create a mood of concern on the eve of requests for more officers, new equipment, or special programs. In still other cases, an issue may be promoted to distract public attention from problems that may be too volatile or complex to handle. For example, it has become common knowledge that new Presidents search for issues that they can use to demonstrate leadership skills and to establish a performance record in the face of the intractable problems that seem to come with the office.

These two general aspects of issue definition—controlling the characteristics of opinion and shaping the political functions of opinion—are illustrated nicely by the case of Gerald Ford's first major symbolic crusade after becoming President. Within days of taking over the embattled office of the President at the height of the Watergate scandal, Ford announced his support for a limited amnesty program for Vietnam-era draft resisters and military deserters. One of the fascinating questions about the campaign is why Ford made amnesty his first issue in office, when, as a new President, he was facing a number of more important and more immediate problems. The answer to this question requires a careful look at how the amnesty issue was symbolized and how the definitions of amnesty mobilized and channeled public opinion in a number of crucial political directions, some of them having little to do with amnesty itself.

Amnesty was defined on a number of symbolic levels. One set of symbols was used when public attention was directed at the technical aspects of the amnesty program. A different set was employed in the service of Ford's goal to use amnesty as a means of building public confidence in him as a leader and policy maker. Still another set of terms turned amnesty into a vehicle for changing public perceptions about the mood of bitter conflict and mistrust that Watergate and Vietnam had visited on the country. Finally, a number of subtle symbolic references were designed to link the conciliatory mood created by amnesty to Ford's subsequent pardon of Richard Nixon. The depth of the symbolism pertaining to amnesty is a sign of how important political definitions are to the issue formation process and how much the political significance of public opinion is affected by this process. However, the amnesty issue is a particularly interesting case because it also illustrates the limits of the power of symbolism to shape and channel public opinion. The public outcry against the pardoning of Nixon unraveled almost all the political gains that Ford had made with the amnesty campaign.

THE CHANGING USES OF AMNESTY

During the closing years of America's involvement in Vietnam, opponents of the war increased their efforts to restore draft resisters and military deserters to their normal stations in American life. The issue was defined largely as a moral one: The war had been wrong; those men had acted on their moral convictions; and it was wrong to treat them as criminals. This general definition had no room in the Nixon administration's symbolization of the Vietnam War and its dénouement. As early as 1969, the administration had defended its conduct of the war through repeated appeals to the patriotism, moral responsibility, and courage of "the great silent majority" of Americans. The objective at hand was "peace with honor." The price that America would never pay was humiliation: "North Vietnam cannot defeat or humiliate the United States. Only Americans can do that."[1]

The harsh terms in these early definitions of the issue did not leave room for reconciliation. The moral claims of both sides were clearly drawn and clearly in conflict. As amnesty became an increasingly important issue for the left, Nixon began to invoke it as vindication for his moral definition of the war.[2] For example, during a campaign appearance before an Ohio audience on October 27, 1972, the President said, "The draft dodgers are never going to get amnesty when boys like yours died."[3] After the election, he reiterated his position at a press conference held on January 30, 1973: "Those who served paid their price. Those who deserted must pay their price, and the price is not a junket in the Peace Corps, or something like that, as some have suggested. The price is a criminal penalty for disobeying the laws of the United States." Before a gathering of the Veterans of Foreign Wars (VFW) on March 1, 1973, Nixon went so far as to bend history in an effort to crystallize growing public conflict over amnesty: "These men have broken the law, and if at the end of the war we broke every precedent this country has had, this would be the first time in history that anmesty was provided for those who deserted."

However, by the summer of 1974, public sentiment seemed to be shifting in support of some form of amnesty.[4] A large number of amnesty bills were pending in Congress,[5] and public demonstrations in behalf of the issue had been staged in Washington.[6] Despite these factors and the increasing polarization produced by the Watergate scandal, the position of the Nixon administration on amnesty remained unchanged. Gerald Ford became an advocate for this position. In one of his first speeches after assuming the vice-presidency, he evoked an enthusiastic response from the national convention of Disabled American Veterans when he announced his firm opposition to "unconditional blanket amnesty."[7]

Three days after this speech, the political world changed for Gerald Ford. On August 9, Richard Nixon resigned from the presidency. Ford became President—without an electoral mandate, amidst the aftershocks of Vietnam, during a building economic recession, and at the height of one of the most serious crises of government legitimacy in history. Ford needed a way to address these problems. Amnesty was the most obvious vehicle. On August 19, Ford addressed another group of war veterans at the national convention of the VFW. He again produced cheers with his announcement of opposition to "unconditional blanket amnesty."[8] However, the remainder of the speech evoked surprise and protests from members of that audience. Ford confessed that he had changed some of the attitudes he had held about amnesty as Vice President and as a member of Congress. Faced with the task of "binding the nation's wounds" he would now devote his energies to creating a "lenient," "merciful" program to "give these young Americans a second chance."

This shift in Ford's public pronouncements on amnesty is one of several indicators that the issue had political uses quite removed from its stated policy goals. Further support for the idea that amnesty had ulterior political uses comes from exploring the question of why amnesty was chosen as Ford's first issue in office. It was hardly the most pressing public issue of the day. The economy was plunged in a serious recession, and the problems created by the Watergate crisis were legion. In the context of these and other matters, the amount of attention devoted to amnesty seems disproportionate, particularly in view of the fact that the issue was on its way toward resolution in Congress. If Ford's major political goal was simply to produce an amnesty program, he might have supported one of the bills in Congress. This course of action would seem even more natural because of the strong similarity between Ford's eventual program and Senator Robert A. Taft's "earned immunity" act, which had been introduced in Congress nearly a year earlier. Finally, it is difficult to account for Ford's interest in amnesty in terms of a commitment to implementing a strong program. After reading the program, House Speaker Carl Albert commented that "the plan is pretty much what the law is now."[9]

These anomalies are compounded by the length of time (six weeks) that elapsed between Ford's announced interest in the issue and his eventual public proclamation. Throughout this period, statements from the White House repeatedly stressed the complexity of the issue. Staff members made numerous comments about the degree of Ford's personal involvement in drafting the program. Recurrent reports from the White House Press Office stated that amnesty was occupying all the President's time and that "he has been working on it day and night."[10] These are curious statements to make about a program that was nearly worked out when Ford became involved with it.

Finally, it is significant that Ford's amnesty program did so little for amnesty itself. The individuals who were to benefit from the program were far from enthusiastic. At home and abroad, spokespersons for antiwar groups suggested that the program represented little change over existing informal options available to military resisters. Furthermore, groups on the left suggested that the proposed program was punitive and required a tacit admission of wrongdoing or guilt from those who participated in it.[11] In addition to its apparent unpopularity among the beneficiaries, the program was given only marginal resources to work with. Less than five months after it had come into being, the administration considered canceling it. Despite its renewal under pressure from members of the clemency board, the program was never endowed with the material and symbolic support necessary to carry out its alleged purposes. Nine months after the initiation of the plan, only 165 applications from the more than eighteen thousand cases eligible for review by the clemency board had been acted on by the President. Only eleven of these cases had been placed in the alternative-service jobs required as a condition of pardon.[12]

The point here is not to be critical of the program. Rather, it is to identify a number of anomalies that support the general claim that, despite initial appearances, the amnesty campaign had very little to do with amnesty and a great deal to do with more central calculations in Gerald Ford's political situation. The multitude of political problems that confronted Ford in the early days of his presidency required immediate attention. However, many of them were too sensitive to address directly. As a result, he needed an issue that could be used to transmit deeper political images that also made reference to a plausible political problem. Amnesty was such an issue.

THE SYMBOLIZATION OF AMNESTY

Gerald Ford's delicate political situation after becoming President clarifies many of the puzzles surrounding his choice of the amnesty issue. Ford faced four major types of political problem: (1) direct Watergate-related problems such as public distrust and the disruption of government, (2) indirect Watergate-related problems such as his own rise to the presidency in the absence of a clear popular constituency, (3) standard "new President" problems such as making the transition in office and establishing his legitimacy, and (4) serious difficulties with aspects of his political style and image. The symbolization of amnesty was tailored to each of these problems

Restoring Public
Trust After Watergate

The most serious of Ford's political problems stemmed directly from the Watergate scandal. The aftermath of Watergate was further complicated by unresolved moral questions from the Vietnam era. A major challenge facing Ford was the task of releasing public attention from these concerns while generating faith in the new regime and its goals. Amnesty is an issue ideally suited to the symbolic vocabulary of reconciliation and redemption—mercy, forgiveness, leniency, beginning anew, forgetting the past, acceptance, tolerance, unity. Indeed, these are precisely the terms that Ford used to define amnesty when he used the issue to shape public perceptions about government and the nation's future. A typical example of the use of these symbols in the service of larger political goals occurred in the speech of September 16, explaining the details of the program: "Reconciliation calls for an act of mercy to bind the nation's wounds and to heal the scars of divisiveness."

Any concrete sense that such statements may have had seems to disappear under close inspection. The messages were suggestive, not logical. The contexts of "unity," "binding wounds," and "healing" provided a subtle focus for a litany of political absolution for the era. The opening speech of August 19, 1974, introduced this vocabulary of redemption, which would be pronounced repeatedly in the coming month:

> I acknowledged a power higher than the people, who commands not only righteousness but love, not only justice but mercy. . . . I am

> throwing the weight of my Presidency into the scales of justice on the side of leniency. . . . I ask all Americans who ever sought forgiveness for their trespasses to join in rehabilitating all the casualties of all the tragic conflicts that are past.

In order to keep these images at the center of public attention, Ford limited the scope of amnesty as a policy concern by using popular stereotypes to refer to those eligible for the program. They were people who "illegally evaded the draft," "deserted military service," "dodged the draft," "were wrong," "committed the supreme folly of shirking their duty," and so forth. However, when the issue was discussed in the larger political context of the need to "bind wounds" and move the nation beyond "the tragic conflicts of the past," these same persons were symbolized as "some 50,000 of our countrymen," "casualties," "citizens of this country," and "young Americans [who] deserve a second chance." This switch indicates how symbolism can change drastically as an issue is shifted from one political use to another.

In a similar fashion, the symbols used to define the mechanics of the amnesty program as a policy matter were quite restricted. Ford opened many statements during the amnesty campaign with some variation on this statement: "I am firmly opposed to unconditional blanket amnesty."[13] The forthcoming program was always referred to in terms like "earned reentry," and "earned immunity." Such phrases conveyed the subtle assurance to the public that some payment would be exacted for the errors of the past. Throughout the campaign, all direct references to the issue of amnesty itself contained such assurances:

> As minority leader of the House and recently as Vice President, I stated my strong conviction that unconditional blanket amnesty for everyone who illegally evaded [the draft] or fled military service is wrong. It is wrong. Yet . . .[14]

> I want them to come back home if they want to work their way back.[15]

> Individuals who have violated either draft laws or selective service or deserted can earn their way or work their way back.[16]

The effect of such statements was to restrict the scope of the issue and to control its political volatility.[17]

Having constructed narrow boundaries around the surface issue itself, Ford was in a position to begin defining the relations among powerful amnesty-compatible symbols and other, more sensitive, political concerns. The primary political context in which the symbols were to take on meaning was the problem of unifying the country in order to move beyond the crisis of legitimacy following Watergate. Ford opened the amnesty campaign with the clear representation of amnesty as a means of solving "the urgent problem of how to bind up the nation's wounds."[18] This was the dominant context for the presentation and interpretation of symbols throughout the campaign. One of Ford's last statements on the subject during this period stressed the same often-repeated theme: "We are trying to heal the wounds by the action that I took with the signing of the proclamation this morning."[19] Ford frequently made the symbolic equation between amnesty and harmony quite specific: "The primary purpose of this program is the reconciliation of all our people and the restoration of the essential unity of Americans within which honest differences of opinion do not descend to angry discord and mutual problems are not polarized by excessive passion."[20]

Creating a Political
Constituency for Ford

Despite the restricted scope of Ford's definition of amnesty as a policy concern, there was significance in the fact that he chose to address it at all. It is no accident that his first issue in office was one that held considerable intrinsic appeal for liberals. It was also a matter on which Ford could engineer a clear break with the policies of his predecessor in office. These factors contributed to the desired image of independence from the past administration. They also elicited favorable public responses from potential political critics early in the campaign. The very fact that Ford changed his public position on amnesty was explained in terms of his sense of responsibility to a larger constituency. He attributed his "conciliatory" position to the new and special responsibilities he felt as "President of all the people."[21] Other efforts to define amnesty as a consensus-building issue were characterized by remarks like: "I don't think these are views that fall in the political spectrum left or right."[22]

These symbolizations of the amnesty question provided a continuous backdrop against which to view a barrage of constituency-building gestures during Ford's first weeks in office. The gestures included a successful meeting with the Black Caucus in the House of Representatives,[23] establishing rapport with a number of notable Democrats,[24] selecting a "liberal" Vice President,[25] and appointing a "bipartisan" task force on inflation.[26] Amnesty was such a well-controlled issue that the new administration successfully increased or decreased its visibility in coordination with these other consensus-building events. The result of this management of the issue was a period of almost three weeks in which the public received the constant image that Gerald Ford was attempting to represent a broad spectrum of public sentiment in his administration.

Easing the Transition in Office

In addition to the consensus-building needs peculiar to his political situation, Ford faced a related problem common to all new Presidents—the need to establish the continuity of the presidency and to reaffirm the bases of its authority. A new President typically operates in a "grace" or "honeymoon" period, during which he has an opportunity to establish rapport, transcend the partisanship of the election, and consolidate the administration. It is also a period in which the highest symbols of political culture are invoked in a celebration of the office of the President.[27] Ford's obligation to attend to these rites of the presidency was complicated. Not only was his grace period a fragile one, but the crisis of government legitimacy directly challenged the sacred symbols that are usually invoked. Moreover, Gerald Ford had none of the ordinary ceremonial occasions on which to perform the rites of sanctification for his office. Such occasions normally include victory speeches, inaugural addresses, and state of the union messages. In these contexts, a new President typically reaffirms the ideals of the polity, invokes the ultimate symbols of state and office, seeks the blessing of God, glorifies the destiny of the nation, finds inspiration in the wisdom of predecessors in office, defines the electoral victory in terms of impersonal, bipartisan, and democratic values, and praises the strengths of the people and their heritage.[28]

Ford's response to this lack of transition rituals was to display the symbolic trappings of the American "civil religion" in the context of amnesty, an issue of some spiritual proportion. The following statements from the speeches of August 19 and September 16, which opened and closed the amnesty campaign, are indicative of his attention to the sanctification of the office:

The transcendence of partisanship:
Yet, in my first words as President of all the people . . .

Inspiration from a power higher than the people:
... I acknowledged a power higher than the people, who commands not only righteousness but love, not only justice but mercy.

The historic continuity of the office:
like President Truman and President Lincoln before him, I found on my desk ... the urgent problem of how to bind up the nation's wounds.

The wisdom and guidance of predecessors:
I will act promptly, fairly, and firmly, in the same spirit that guided Abraham Lincoln and Harry Truman.

The heritage and ideals of the citizenry:
As men and women whose patriotism has been tested and proved, I want your help. I ask all Americans who ever asked for goodness and mercy in their lives ...

The amnesty campaign opened and closed with reference to the same high sentiments about the polity, the presidency, and the people. In this sense, the symbolic development of amnesty provided a frame for the normal ritual sanctification of the office of the President. Moreover, the development of the campaign occupied public attention for nearly a month. This period of time created a comfortable space in which to accomplish the transition of office.

Strengthening Ford's Political Image

The extended time frame over which the campaign developed gave Ford a means to construct certain elements of political style and public image. Most Presidents have achieved a clear and effective leadership style by the time they take office. Such styles are usually constructed over the course of an extensive national campaign or during years spent as national political figures. Ford's major asset was the reputation of being honest, moral, and straightforward. However, he had few credentials as a policy maker. He had no reputation as an assertive, creative leader. There were even suggestions about the limitations of his basic abilities to grapple with challenging issues. If Ford hoped to operate as an effective leader, these difficulties with public image had to be overcome.

The amnesty issue was an important part of a larger strategy for dealing with problems of political style. Throughout the amnesty period, Ford was the center of attention. Many of the symbolic actions that contributed to the definition of the issue also served to strengthen Ford's posture as a leader. For example, Ford opened the campaign before one of the least supportive audiences he could have found—the seventy-fifth annual convention of the Veterans of Foreign Wars. This setting added an element of controversy that was useful to bolster the surface appearance of amnesty as a serious issue. More importantly, such a persuasion tactic would enhance Ford's credibility as an independent leader who would rather face adversity than court easy favor. As if he were anxious to communicate this desired effect, Ford remarked about his choice of an audience immediately after the speech: "The more I thought of it, the more I thought that the right audience would be an audience that might be difficult rather than some hand-picked audience. . . . It would have been a little cowardice, I think, if I'd picked an audience that was ecstatic."[29]

At a press conference a week later he again underscored the independence of his stand on amnesty: "I intend to make the same kind of judgments in other matters because I think they're right and I think they're for the good of the country."[30] The significant message in such remarks was that Ford was taking an active stand on a policy question. In support of this image, he emphasized repeatedly that he was drafting the amnesty program personally. The month between the VFW speech and the eventual proclamation was devoted to this goal of building Ford's image as an aggressive and creative leader who could take the initiative in developing complex policy. The following examples of press releases are characteristic of the use to which the amnesty issue was put during this period:

August 21: Ford ordered his staff to research amnesty questions and report back to him.

August 25: Ford ordered a Justice Department study of pardon powers.

August 31: Ford met with the Secretary of Defense and the Attorney General on amnesty.

September 1: Ford said that he "has several ideas of his own on amnesty."

September 3: The White House announced that amnesty was taking all of Ford's time. Ford went to Camp David to work on the details of the amnesty plan. Ford was said to have "his own ideas" on amnesty.

September 4:   Ford's Press Secretary said that Ford "has some ideas of his own on amnesty."

September 5:   Mrs. Ford announced that "after rather deep discussion," Ford had "made up his mind" on amnesty.

September 6:   The Press Secretary announced that Ford was still working on the amnesty plan.

September 7:   Ford announced his intention to create a clemency board.

September 8:   The White House announced that Ford was seeking more information on the complex issue of amnesty. Ford announced that he would announce his decision next week.

September 10:   The Press Secretary announced the delay of the announcement on amnesty by saying that it was "more complex than he [Ford] thought initially and that he wants to be personally involved in the entire method."

September 14:   The White House announced that Ford would announce his plan soon.

September 15:   The Press Secretary said that Ford had been working on the amnesty plan "day and night" for the past several days.

The image constructed during this period was of Gerald Ford gathering information about a complex issue in order to deliberate at length in preparation for drafting his own policy statement. Virtually every press release from the White House during that time contained images of clear, independent action. Ford "ordered," "decided," "deliberated," "worked day and night," "had ideas of his own," "made up his mind," "worked on his plan," and "confronted the complex issues." Amnesty was defined as Ford's own issue. He used it to evoke front-page headlines almost at will. The substance of his amnesty-related actions during the middle portion of the campaign involved repeated images of Ford's activity, independent judgment, and leadership skills. It mattered little that the eventual program resembled previous political suggestions or that the plan was poorly executed. What was important was that the amnesty issue provided a sustained format in which to present and control a desirable image of leadership.

THE IMPACT OF AMNESTY

When discussing the political functions of issues like amnesty, it is important to attempt to assess their effectiveness. It goes without saying that such evaluation presents enormous problems. However, there are several criteria against which judgments can be made. The most obvious criterion is the degree of control the political actor exerts over the presentation of the issue to the audience. Since issues like amnesty serve primarily as vehicles for the transmission of deeper political images, it is important for the political actor to maintain control of the message format, the choice of settings in which messages will be delivered, and the times when the issue will be presented to and withdrawn from the audience. Measured against these standards, Ford's amnesty campaign was fairly effective. Figure 10-1 indicates the distribution of amnesty-related news stories in the *New York Times* during the period of August 20 to September 20, 1974.[31]

There are several things worth noting about Ford's control over the issue during most of this period. First, amnesty-related stories provided a fairly constant backdrop for Ford's first month in office. Moreover, it appears that Ford successfully increased or reduced the attention devoted to amnesty in order to accommodate other planned actions (the vice-presidential nomination, meeting with the Black Causus, announcing his candidacy for 1976, meeting with the economic "summit conference," and the other events noted in Figure 10-1). Amnesty captured ten front-page stories between August 20 and September 20. Eight of those stories concerned events or actions whose timing and format were under virtually complete control of Ford and his staff.

Despite this control over the public presentation of the issue, Ford's management of the main political images became increasingly ineffective toward the end of the campaign. By the time the amnesty proclamation was finally delivered, the issue itself was virtually out of his control. The proclamation of September 16 was intended to be a climactic performance that would integrate the various symbolic images of amnesty. In addition to evoking the symbols of leadership, consensus, and legitimacy, the speech called for the end to an era of political disarray:

> I do not want to delay another day in resolving the dilemma of the past, so that we may all get going on the pressing problems of the present. . . . My sincere hope is that this is a constructive step toward

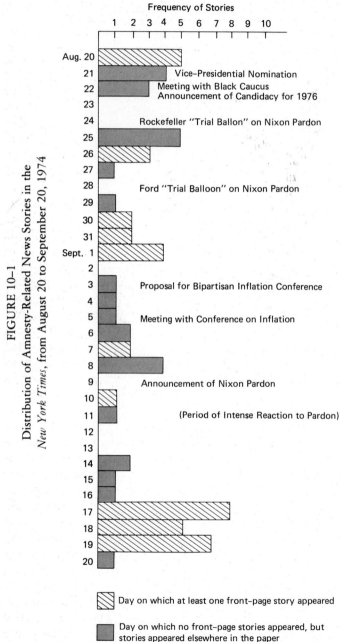

FIGURE 10-1

Distribution of Amnesty-Related News Stories in the *New York Times*, from August 20 to September 20, 1974

a calmer and cooler appreciation of our individual rights and responsibilities and our common purpose as a nation whose future is always more important than its past.

However, rather than ending the era of disarray (or even the amnesty campaign itself), the proclamation was followed by a period of intense public criticism. The criticism came from many of the same groups and leaders who had supported the proposed program a month earlier. Amnesty again became a front-page story. This time, however, the story was not of Ford's making. Ford lost control of public reaction to his issue because of a miscalculated action, which created a major inconsistency between amnesty and the structure of the surrounding political context.

On September 9, Ford granted a full pardon to Richard Nixon. The Nixon pardon disrupted the symbolic development of the amnesty issue, and it set back the progress made on a number of the political problems that the symbolism of amnesty was designed to resolve.[32] Virtually none of the images created during the amnesty campaign was unaffected by the pardon. It is, of course, impossible to say whether any rhetorical strategy could have accommodated the pardon better than the one Ford selected. Perhaps a negative backlash was inevitable, and the amnesty campaign cushioned it as well as could be expected. However, there are indications that White House strategists had expected Ford's amnesty rhetoric to create images that would help the public see the pardon more favorably. On September 12, an aide admitted that Ford had "grossly misjudged" public reaction to the pardon.

It is pointless to debate the question of what Ford intended to accomplish with various rhetorical tactics and whether his expectations were reasonable. However, there is considerable evidence of a strategic link between the pardon and the amnesty campaign. For example, on August 24, Nelson Rockefeller made a statement about the possibility of a pardon for the disgraced President. He expressed the opinion that "Nixon has suffered enough." This statement appears to have been a "trial balloon" on the possibility of a pardon. More importantly, it provided an opportunity for Ford to begin shifting his earlier claims of opposition to a pardon. The White House assumed no responsibility for the statement by the Vice President, but the denial of responsibility was accompanied by the assertion that the President had "not taken a public stand" on the Nixon case. A second trial balloon was released at a press conference on August 28, when Ford said that it was "untimely" to make a commitment on the prospects of a Nixon pardon.

As Figure 10-1 shows, Ford's amnesty pronouncements were scheduled carefully around these trail balloons. Perhaps most importantly, the terms of the symbolic definition of the pardon were virtually identical to the terms of the symbolic definition of amnesty. This similarity served to anchor the pardon within the set of deep images created by the amnesty rhetoric. For example, in his speech of September 9, Ford announced the pardon as a means of moving beyond the chaos of the past. He also introduced a vague reference to his actions on amnesty: "The tranquillity to which this nation has been restored by the events of recent weeks could be irreparably lost by bringing to trial a former President of the United States." Ford then announed the pardon in terms that easily could have been substituted for those in his amnesty speeches of August 19 and September 16:

> my primary concern must always be the greatest good for all the people of the United States. . . . My conscience tells me clearly and certainly that I cannot prolong the bad dreams and continue to reopen a chapter that is closed. My conscience tells me that only I, as President, have Constitutional power to firmly shut and seal the book. . . . I, not as President, but as a humble servant of God, will receive justice without mercy if I fail to show mercy.

At a press conference held on September 17 immediately after the amnesty proclamation, Ford again attempted to symbolize a particular link between the pardon and amnesty: "The only connection between the two cases is the effort that I made in the one to heal the wounds involving the charges made against Mr. Nixon and my honest and conscientious effort to heal the wounds for those who had deserted military service or dodged the draft."

Connecting the two issues did not suppress visible opposition to the pardon, however. The symbolic context created by the amnesty campaign was not powerful enough to control broadly based audience reactions to the pardon. To the contrary, the negative reactions to the pardon seemed to work against many of the images created during the amnesty campaign. It seems that the act of pardoning Nixon fit better within a context larger and more powerful than the context created for it by the amnesty campaign. The larger context was the immorality, illegality, and corruption of the Watergate era. Ford's action took on meaning for the public as a result of the context in which they interpreted it. For the majority of the public, the pardon was inconsistent with the scenario of forgiveness and trust created by the amnesty campaign, but it was perfectly consistent with the scenario of corruption, deception, and misconduct established by Watergate.

In addition to its inconsistency within the structure of the amnesty appeal, the Nixon pardon violated the conditions of persuasion discussed in Chapter 9. What Ford asked the public to believe about the pardon ran directly against the stable, previously held opinions of the majority, who favored criminal prosecution of the former President and opposed a pardon.[33] The symbolism of amnesty did not change these opinions, and it did not create for the pardon a context that was strong enough to enable Ford's claims to compete with them. Not only did the pardon contradict the prior opinions of the majority, but it damaged Ford's credibility as well. It associated him with the discredited President, whose past actions had been a major concern of the amnesty campaign.

Not only did the loss in credibility affect public reaction to Ford's explanation of the pardon, but it stirred considerable doubt about the sincerity of the entire amnesty issue. The credibility that he had established in the amnesty crusade through such tactics as his speech before the hostile VFW audience and his selection of an altruistic issue was not strong enough to withstand the damage done by the pardon. Credibility built through the amnesty appeals, instead of carrying over to the pardon, was undermined by the pardon.

Needless to say, the pardon created a hostile audience response. Not only did the press criticize the action, but many of the leaders who had come out in support of the new President withdrew that support on the heels of the pardon. Moreover, Ford's standing in the opinion polls dropped sharply in a steep decline that lasted well into the next year. White House staff members reported a record deluge of mail that ran overwhelmingly against the action. In this atmosphere of a hostile press and renewed skepticism by the public, most of the political gains that Ford accomplished with his amnesty rhetoric were reversed. The public returned to its concerns about Watergate, political corruption, and trust in leaders. The political constituency that had been built through the conciliatory mood of amnesty fell apart quickly. The short presidential grace period that Ford had established by introducing high symbols of state into his amnesty appeals ended abruptly. Neither the press nor the majority of the public seemed willing to continue the "honeymoon" period. Finally, the image that Ford was building as a leader, a policy maker, and a skilled politician crumbled under a variety of public criticisms, including charges that he had acted in bad faith, had not really drafted the amnesty plan as he claimed, and had seriously miscalculated the public's response to the pardon. Many of the components of Ford's later negative image as a "bumbler" began to fall into place as White House aides leaked stories of the political chaos and miscalculation surrounding the amnesty issue and the pardon.

With the negative audience reaction to the pardon and, in turn, to amnesty came a rapid decline in another condition of persuasion—receptivity. As a result of blocked communication between Ford and his audience, his ability to transmit his amnesty appeals to the public virtually ceased. The public was less open to Ford's political appeals. This was a direct result of his loss in credibility, which was registered in the polls. Other receptivity factors also declined. For example, Ford virtually lost control of the messages transmitted through the media. During the portion of the amnesty campaign charted in Figure 10-1, virtually all the messages were constructed to carry the political images desired by the administration, and they were usually run verbatim as news stories. After the pardon, few official pronouncements on amnesty were given exclusive coverage, and more and more critical and independent stories were produced by the press. In short, the number of transmission channels available for Ford's chosen messages was greatly restricted, and the messages that did reach the public had to compete with a great deal of "noise" in the form of attacks from political opponents and critical news analyses.

The amnesty campaign illustrates a number of important points about the nature of political issues and public opinion. First, its great initial success shows that symbolic appeals and persuasion techniques can have a dramatic impact on public opinion. The handling of the amnesty issue in the early days almost resembles a precision engineering feat: A team of political strategists set out to shape the content, intensity, and expression of public attitudes about a number of political concerns, and they met with remarkable success. The other notable aspect of the amnesty issue was, of course, its ultimate failure, which offers an interesting contrast to the early successes and points out the impact of structural flaws, new events, and a decline in the conditions of persuasion on the effectiveness of political appeals.

The amnesty campaign also demonstrates the wide array of political meanings that seemingly straightforward issues can take on. Although it is true that Gerald Ford did produce an amnesty program and tried to generate some public support for amnesty as a policy question, it would be difficult to argue that the major political purpose of the amnesty campaign was to produce policy in the area. The main thrust of Ford's appeals was designed to affect public orientations about other political matters. This is not to say that issues should never be taken at face value. It simply suggests that issues can vary enormously in their political implications and in the political relationships they establish in the public. In order to grasp this feature of issues, public opinion, and politics, issues must be examined in terms of their political contexts and the way their symbolic definitions put public opinion to various political uses.

Finally, the amnesty issue shows how public opinion can play a variety of political roles in addition to its traditional policy support function. The amnesty campaign illustrates the potential for public opinion to validate national priorities, to legitimize new leaders and embattled governments, and to acknowledge leadership potential. These and other political functions of public opinion can be as important as the policy support role and must be acknowledged in the analysis of popular responses to public issues.

NOTES

1. The quote is from Richard Nixon's masterful speech of November 3, 1969, quoted in Michael Novak, *Choosing Our King* (New York: Macmillan, 1974), p. 85.
2. For an anlaysis of Nixon's symbolization of a moral posture for his Vietnam policies, see ibid., ch. 13.
3. Unless otherwise stipulated, all quotations in this analysis appeared in the *New York Times* on the day following the date of the speech cited in the text.
4. The Gallup Poll of April 1974 showed a full 34 percent of the public in favor of unconditional amnesty. Moreover, of the 58 percent who opposed unconditional amnesty, less than 20 percent favored criminal prosecution of the offenders. See Gallup Report No. 107, May 1974.
5. At the time Gerald Ford assumed the vice-presidency, there were ten different amnesty bills before Congress. See the *New York Times* report of August 21, 1974.
6. On July 3, 1974, the first in a series of planned demonstrations was conducted in front of the White House by a number of groups including Vietnam Veterans Against the War.
7. Speech reported in the *New York Times*, August 6, 1974.
8. Speech reported in the *New York Times*, August 20, 1974.

9. Reported in the *New York Times*, September 18, 1974.
10. See the official White House statements of September 3, 4, and 16, 1974.
11. See interviews appearing in the *New York Times*, June 20, 1975.
12. *New York Times*, June 20, 1975.
13. Variations on this basic statement were made throughout the amnesty campaign. For example, see Ford's speeches and public statements of August 6, 20, and 29, 1974, and September 1, 4, 6, 10, 16, and 17, 1974.
14. Speech reported in the *New York Times*, August 20, 1974.
15. Ibid.
16. Press conference of August 29, 1974.
17. In addition to the functions mentioned, these statements also served to establish continuity between Ford's past actions and his subsequent change of position. Among the political constraints of the Watergate crisis were strong pressures to be accountable for past actions. Prefacing his "change of mind" with a reaffirmation of past political stands served this continuity function well.
18. Speech of August 19, 1974.
19. Press conference of September 17, 1974.
20. Speech of September 16, 1974.
21. Speech of August 19, 1974.
22. Press conference of August 29, 1974.
23. On August 22, Ford met with the Black Caucus in the House of Representatives. Members of the caucus responded to the meeting in terms ranging from "cautious optimism" to "enthusiasm" and "surprise." This important symbolic bond was strengthened on September 1, when the caucus announced that it had voted to endorse the amnesty plan.
24. A number of prominent Democrats expressed early support for Ford's interest in amnesty. The amnesty issue was a focal point for a *New York Times* story under the heading "Democrats Say Ford Hasn't Made a Wrong Move Yet" (August 21, 1974). The story included favorable comments on Ford's first weeks in office from a number of prominent members of Ford's political opposition.
25. On August 21, Ford's selection of a Vice President was another action calculated to expand his constituency. Despite reported pressure from conservative factions within his party to appoint a conservative Vice President, Ford nominated Nelson Rockefeller. Rockefeller was regarded generally as a "liberal" Republican.
26. See *New York Times* articles of September 4, 5, and 6, 1974.
27. For an excellent discussion of the sanctification rites of the presidency, see Robert N. Bellah, "Civil Religion in America," in *Secularization and the Protestant Prospect*, eds. James F. Childress and David B. Harned (Philadelphia: Westminister Press, 1970).
28. For examples of such invocations, see Novak, *Choosing Our King*. See also W. Lance Bennett, "Political Sanctification: The Civil Religion and American Politics," *Social Science Information*, Vol. 14 (December 1975), pp. 79–102.

29. Press conference of August 20, 1974.
30. Press conference of August 29, 1974.
31. This distribution of stories does not include essays, editorials, or letters that appeared in the *New York Times* during this period. Only those "events" that were covered by the working press are included.
32. There is a great deal of evidence that bears on this claim. For example, a Gallup Poll reported on September 6, before the pardon, showed that 66 percent of the public approved of Ford's job in office, while only 13 percent disapproved. Three days after the pardon, a New York Times Poll revealed that only 32 percent of the public thought that Ford was doing a good job in office. More importantly, a full 25 percent of this sample disapproved of Ford's performance. Furthermore, the early enthusiasm of the Democratic leadership (see *New York Times* articles of August 21 and 22, 1974, and September 1, 1974) turned into highly critical reactions to both Ford and his amnesty program after the pardon (see *New York Times* articles of September 17, 18, and 19, 1974). Indicative of the chill in Ford's grace period was a critical editorial in the *New York Times* on the day after the amnesty proclamation. This editorial linked amnesty with the pardon and repudiated two pre-pardon editorials supporting Ford and his programs. Finally, following the pardon, Ford was booed for the first time in public since taking office.
33. Gallup polls reported on August 20 and September 12 showed that a large majority of the public favored some form of conditional amnesty. Furthermore, a Gallup Poll reported on September 2 showed that 56 percent of the public favored the criminal prosecution of the former President. The September 12 poll indicated that 62 percent disapproved of the pardon.

11
Public Opinion
and the
News Media

THE NEWS MEDIA transmit most of the information on which public opinion rests. The way in which this information is selected, symbolized, and emphasized depends on political and organizational factors that have an impact on news operations. Besides transmitting political information to the public, the media also monitor the responses of the public to political issues and events. In this capacity, the media are the primary means of informing government officials, interest organizations, and the public itself about public opinion in ongoing political situations. In short, the media play active parts in the formation of opinion.

The examples discussed in Chapters 8, 9, and 10 all point to the same conclusion: Political success depends on access to the media. In most political situations "access" means one thing: news coverage. Only to a small degree do political groups rely on paid advertising to get their issues on the political agenda. Advertising is not only expensive, but it lacks the credibility that dispassionate news coverage can give to an issue.

The attainment of political goals depends to a large extent on the capacity to control the political images that are transmitted through the news channels. This was illustrated by the political success of the early stages of Gerald Ford's amnesty campaign. As the later developments surrounding amnesty also illustrate, the failure to control news images can result in political failure. The pivotal role of the news media in the issue formation process makes the struggle for control of news content an important factor in American politics in general and public opinion in particular. This struggle not only goes on among political actors, but it also can take the form of a game between political actors and news organizations. At times, news organizations may act as passive communication links from political actors to the public. In other cases, the press may help develop a political issue by searching out a credible opposition or investigating critically the claims of the leading side. Whether the news media play a passive reporting role or an active investigative or advocacy role, the information transmitted through the news is the major variable in the formation of the political agenda.

THE AGENDA-SETTING FUNCTION
OF THE MEDIA

A great deal of research has been done on the agenda-setting function of the media. The general conclusion is that there is a positive correlation between the amount of coverage devoted to political issues by the media and the degree to which the public regards those issues as important.[1] There is also evidence that the more exposure people have to the news media, the more able they are to cite important issues and to suggest solutions for them.[2] Despite these discoveries, it is important not to conclude that the media are the real hidden power centers in American politics. The media's role in setting the political agenda is involved much more with reinforcing dominant social values and legitimizing the positions of elites and respectable groups than with creating new issues or advocating new values. Thus the political impact of the media might be labeled more appropriately "agenda reinforcement" rather than "agenda setting." The reinforcement role is by no means a trivial one. By deciding that some political positions are newsworthy and others are not, news organizations play important parts in issue formation, conflict reduction, political legitimation, and political change.

For several reasons it makes more sense to think of the media as reinforcers of dominant issues and values rather than as independent sources of the issues and values that make up the political agenda. The most obvious reason for this distinction is the fact that the people who are most influenced by media coverage of issues are the members of the public who are least informed about and least interested in politics.[3] The politically powerful individuals and groups who most often define issues and their solutions are the segments of the public least influenced by what the news media say and do. This suggests that the chain of political causality runs from elites through the media to the public rather than from the media to elites and the public

This should not imply that agenda setting and agenda reinforcement are so simple that the chain of causality can run in only one direction. Under certain circumstances public opinion may affect media coverage of issues, with the result that public values may shape the definition of issues on the political agenda. Indeed, media executives often claim that the media are accountable to the public and not to government officials or special interests. If the public were not satisfied with the content of news and entertainment programming, so the argument goes, it would take its viewing business elsewhere. On the surface there is an element of logic in this reasoning, and it is easy to conclude that the public must be getting what it wants from the media. However, research on the formation of specific issues suggests that the dominant causal arrow runs from the media to the public and not from the public to the media. Research on public interest in the Watergate scandal shows that patterns of public concern and involvement were much more responsive to the timing and content of news coverage than news coverage was responsive to public opinion.[4] Similar findings have emerged in research on the formation of issues in elections.[5]

Research on patterns of causality in media coverage is only one source of support for the agenda-reinforcement hypothesis about the media. Another approach to the problem takes a much broader look at patterns of issue coverage. Instead of defining the political agenda as the result of the issues that the media emphasize at any particular time, this broader perspective views the political agenda as the range of social values that receive legitimation through media coverage over long periods of time. This viewpoint downplays the importance of the formation and resolution of any particular issue. The claim is that the emergence and resolution of specific issues may have marginal effects on the short-run fortunes of groups in society; but in the long run, most of the issues emphasized by the media tend to reinforce mainstream social values. Even the political conflicts that dominate the news tend to be conflicts between equally legitimate positions whose implementation would be unlikely to change the social order. The idea here is that the media produces *hegemony* in society. This term refers to the domination of particular values and ideas and the systematic exclusion of competing images of reality. The media operate as "gate-keepers," transmitting "normal" or legitimate issues and ideas to the public and filtering out new, radical, or threatening perspectives.[6]

The causes of political hegemony have less to do with the conscious motives or interests of media executives than with the organization of society, the economy, and mass communications in America. The mass public depends overwhelmingly on mass news sources for political information and on mass entertainment programming for intellectual stimulation and images about society.[7] This captive audience is fed a steady diet of familiar social images and traditional social values because mass communication depends on the mass economic base for its profits.

For example, the wire services, which provide the backbone of newspaper (and much television) national news coverage, must report stories in ways that will make them acceptable to the maximum possible number of subscribers. To do otherwise would be poor business policy.[8] In addition, the television networks that provide the major supply of public information must sell their programs to their affiliates. Unless news and entertainment programs deliver a competitive share of the viewing audience, the networks cannot charge premium prices for advertising time. Perhaps more importantly, unless the value content of programs is acceptable to the widest possible audience, various regional affiliates may not be able to attract viewers. Local stations make a large share of their profits from selling local commercial time on network programs. If the programs are not acceptable to local audiences, the affiliates may drop network programs. This would threaten the economic foundations of the broadcasting industry.[9]

This vicious communication and profit cycle results in the systematic elimination of radical positions, challenging ideas, or alternative values in mass news and entertainment programming. However, the fact that the public is the key link in the cycle should not lead to the familiar conclusion that the mass media are simply giving the people what they want. The economy of the mass communication industry does not rest on pleasing people or satisfying anyone's tastes. It is organized on the principle of not offending anyone. Therefore, the proliferation of "lowest common denominator programming" is not a reflection of public wants or demands; it is aimed at areas of shared indifference.[10]

The mass media tend to appeal to values and opinions that are already widely understood and acceptable.[11] The media also tend to "withdraw from unnecessarily baring structural flaws in the workings of . . . institutions. They are an insulating mechanism in the potential clash between powerful modes of behavior, normatively ideal ways, and persistent, pragmatic ways."[12] As one observer has noted, these tendencies cannot be called censorship of the news, but their practical results are the same.[13] The effects of agenda limitation and agenda reinforcement have been summarized nicely by Janowitz: "The influence of mass media . . . is not in dramatic conversion of public opinion, but rather in setting the limits within which public debate on controversial issues takes place."[14]

As Janowitz's statement suggests, the most important political function of the media is legitimizing certain ideas and excluding others from political debate. This selection process regulates the scope of political conflict and the range of viable political options in situations. The most intriguing aspect of this selectivity is the absence of conspiratorial activities or heavy-handed politics. The everyday messages of the media and the undisputed economic facts of life in the mass communication industry provide cues to political groups about how to present ideas in a newsworthy way. Since political success depends on media access, and since media access depends on the adoption of legitimate values, the media are crucial political mechanisms for transforming threatening or radical demands into mainstream political positions. The media are all the more important as a political variable because they accomplish this transformation in broad daylight, through respected methods, and for widely accepted reasons.

When nonconforming values persist in the demands of groups or in the nature of events, the economic and political pressures operating on wire services or television networks may simply lead to changes in reporting policies. New themes for the treatment of a story may be introduced. This occurred in the case mentioned in Chapter 8, in which a network news producer issued orders to his reporters in Vietnam to downplay the continued fighting and to develop more stories about American withdrawal from the war (a withdrawal that would not take place for several more years). In other circumstances, policy decisions may simply call for coverage of an issue to be phased out. For example, Lipsky and Olson argued that diminished public concern about urban and race problems in the early 1970s had less to do with any reduction in urban unrest than with a reduction in media coverage of urban troubles: "By the mid-1970s the question 'What happened to the 1960s-style riots?' had become a familiar query among scholars and citizens alike. Perhaps a partial answer is provided by focusing on 'What happened to media coverage of the 1960s-style riots?' "[15]

A preliminary answer to the question "What happened to media coverage of the 1960s-style riots?" is that the media tended to represent the later riots as comparatively minor incidents presenting less cause for concern than the earlier riots. The coverage devoted to major urban upheavals in 1964 was both massive and alarming in its emphasis on chronic social problems, volatile race relations, and the potential for future violence. The picture of the riots in 1968 following the assassination of Martin Luther King, Jr., was vastly different:

> The NBC Evening News carried a filmed report about the "relative calm" in the ghettos in New York City. Huntley introduced the story by saying "Los Angeles and New York City, scenes of the first big-city racial riots, were relatively quiet over the week end. Though there were disturbances Thursday night in Harlem, Mayor John Lindsay stepped in quickly, and his intervention has been credited with helping prevent further trouble."[16]

This and other similar stories conveyed the impression that the 1968 riots were comparatively minor incidents, although, as Epstein has noted, there was evidence that the two waves of disturbance differed very little.

It might be argued that the decisions in 1968 to ignore some of the evidence were minor matters of judgment and editing. For example, even though the NBC coverage of New York City emphasized the apparent tranquillity brought on by the mayor's visit to Harlem, it failed to point out that his walk through the city ended abruptly when violence broke out and he narrowly escaped from a nasty situation by speeding away in his limousine.[17] However, in view of the official statistics on the riots, it is difficult to explain why their severity was downplayed. These statistics were available to the media at the time, and they showed the 1968 riots to be equal to, or more serious in most respects than, the 1964 insurrections:[18]

	1964	1968
Reported violent incidents	600	534
Arrests	465	491
Property damages (in millions)	5	15

The decision to run stories that minimized the magnitude of the 1968 riots in place of stories that emphasized their obvious similarity to the 1964 riots may have had a number of important consequences. It may have discouraged people (both black and white) from seeing the later riots as political responses to the assassination of minority political leadership and the persistent frustrations of urban blacks. These kinds of issue could be seen as threats to the political system, and they could bring criticism to the news media for promoting such threats. The reassuring media treatment of the civil disruptions of 1968 also may have minimized concerns about the failure of institutional efforts to solve urban problems.

NEWS OBJECTIVITY AND THE POLITICS OF INFORMATION

On a broad systemic level, the media filter particular values and positions in and out of the political agenda. Once issues have found a place on that agenda, the media take on another political function. Out of the competing interests, charges and countercharges, and endless background information surrounding a political conflict, reporters and editors select a coherent set of facts and weave them into a story. The news story that emerges can have important effects on public opinion and on the political outcome of the situation—particularly when (as is often the case) the stories run by major newspapers and television networks are substantially the same. This similarity tends to give the impression that the story is an accurate and objective picture of political reality. In fact, a news story is one of many possible interpretations of the actual situation.

A number of factors can affect the information that is included and excluded from a piece of political reporting—the reporting practices of the press, the editorial policies of news organizations, political actors' decisions about what information to release and how to present it. The way in which these factors come into play can have important effects on the public's perceptions of political issues and events. For this reason one of the key concerns of politics is to try to control media variables that will result in the most favorable construction of a news story.

The fact that news stories can take different forms depending on how a number of political and journalistic factors come into play does not mean that news organizations intentionally bias the news. Many of the factors that affect the construction of a news story are beyond the control of individual reporters because they originate from either organizational patterns in the news business or from the information strategies of political actors. The fact that most of the news is not biased intentionally does not make the construction of a news story any less significant politically. The news is largely a political construct, and this fact is crucial for understanding the formation of issues and public reactions to them.

In order to grasp the political construction of the news, it is necessary to examine critically a number of preconceptions about information and objectivity. At first, it may seem strange to think of information as being so malleable. Most of us are taught that information is objective; it consists of the "facts" relevant to something. It is easy to imagine that more or less information can expand or limit our comprehension of something, but it is difficult to imagine that information can be constructed so that it affects the very definition of something and our reactions to it.

The last few chapters have shown that a major part of politics has to do with defining issues in ways that produce favorable public reactions. This suggests that the heart of politics is the selection and symbolization of information. It is tempting to think that somewhere behind the self-serving performances of politicians and interest groups there lies a body of facts that would clarify the issue and help us form objective opinions about it if we had access to it. This is a comforting, though misguided, thought. At every step of the way back to its source, information about public issues is an inherently political commodity. It is concealed, revealed, leaked, released, classified, declassified, jargonized, simplified, and packaged symbolically according to the political interests of those ubiquitous "informed sources" who have a stake in the outcome of the issue in question.

Popular beliefs about the objectivity of the news are based on an easy misinterpretation of the claims of journalists. Reporters claim (correctly, for the most part) that they have no stake in a story and no interest in misleading the public. It is common to hear grand assurances like this one from a network news president: "Our reporters do not cover stories from their point of view. They are presenting them from nobody's point of view."[19] Whether it is possible for somebody to be "nobody," the fact is that reporters are trained to report only what they see and to avoid casting their own interpretations on events. This training is regarded by the press and offered to the public as evidence of objectivity in the news, and this rather narrow definition of objectivity is often stretched to fit much broader uses. Because the news is a fragile construction from selected information, reporters are often criticized for bias. In the face of such criticism, claims about objectivity are often expanded to imply that news stories actually do capture some immutable reality. As Tuchman has observed, these uses of the term "objectivity" are more properly regarded as a self-defense ritual than as an accurate description of reporting practices: "To journalists, like social scientists, the term 'objectivity' stands as a bulwark between themselves and critics. Attacked for a controversial presentation of 'facts,' newspapermen invoke their objectivity almost as a Mediterranean peasant might wear a clove of garlic around his neck to ward off evil spirits."[20]

The expanded and misguided use of the concept of objectivity may reinforce the popular belief (or wish) that the world comes packaged in finite clusters of facts that have self-evident meanings. This assumption probably accounts for much of the impact of the news on public opinion and political behavior. As Molotch and Lester have observed:

> The power of the media to create experience rests on what we'll term the "objectivity assumption," to which almost everyone pledges allegiance. This assumption has it that there is indeed a world "out there" and that an account of a given event reflects that world, or a piece of it, with some degree of accuracy.[21]

It is important to distinguish between the use of objectivity to defend reporting practices and enhance credibility and the fact that the news is largely a political construct that depends heavily on the information that political actors deem useful to present to the public. Virtually all political information becomes public through the judgments of political actors about what will advance their political interests. Actors who control politically relevant information tend to regard that information as a valuable political resource, not as a free public good. In a remarkably candid affirmation of this principle, the noted American statesman George Kennan once gave the following reply to a reporter's question about the State Department's failure to inform Congress and the public adequately on an important national security matter: "I entered a profession which I thought had to do with representation of United States vis-à-vis foreign governments . . . and never understood that part of my profession was to represent the U.S. government vis-à-vis Congress."[22]

In his memoirs Kennan elaborated on his belief that information was a prize political resource and not something to which the public has privileged access: "I resented the State Department being put in the position of lobbyists before Congress in favor of the U.S. people. . . . It was up to them to inform themselves just as it is up to us to inform ourselves."[23] When one considers that virtually all information about diplomatic and foreign policy originates in, and is controlled by, the State Department, the idea that the public should fend for itself in the quest for information is an extraordinary one indeed.

When one looks behind the scenes of almost any developing story, there is usually reason to believe, if not documentary evidence to prove, that the source of the information on which the story is based had some political reason for releasing (or leaking) it at the time, in the form, and in the amount in which it was reported. For example, even though the point of classifying information secret or top secret is to protect it from public scrutiny, it is standard practice for "high government officials" to leak classified information to reporters who demand documentation for stories that the officials want to promote. Sometimes an official leak can precipitate a virtual flood of secrets traded back and forth between factions in an organization lining up on different sides of issues or policies.[24]

Political actors' calculations about what to say and when and how to say it can have important effects on the development and resolution of issues. A dramatic illustration of this occurred during the press coverage of the legal struggles of convicted Watergate conspirators. Following their convictions for attempting to cover up Watergate activities, former Nixon administration officials John Mitchell, H. R. Haldemann, and John Erlichman appealed their cases to the Supreme Court. During the period in which the Court was deciding whether to hear the case, Nina Totenberg, a National Public Radio reporter, announced that the Chief Justice was holding up further discussion of the case in hopes of winning the fourth vote necessary to bring the case before the Court.[25] This extraordinary leak from the inner sanctum of the Court probably came from one of the justices who was displeased with the proceedings. It added a major complication to the already difficult issues in the case, and it gave the defendants new grounds for appeal, regardless of the Court's final decision on the pending appeal. Such decisions to make secret information public can give a group or an individual enormous leverage in a political situation and change the very nature of the issues.

Despite the fact that leaks can help define issues, sway political outcomes, or mold public opinion, investigative reporters virtually never reveal the motives behind the leak or the alternative issues that the information source may be trying to suppress. Such revelations would shatter the journalistic code of confidentiality. Perhaps more importantly, they would undermine the credibility of the press—a credibility that is anchored in public faith in an objective world.

An interesting example of the conflict between confidentiality and news objectivity occurred in another piece of Watergate reporting. There has been growing suspicion that the person who kept Pulitzer Prize–winning reporters Bob Woodward and Carl Bernstein on the trail to the Oval Office may have fed them the information to steer their investigation away from possible CIA involvement with some of the Watergate criminals. Memos from the CIA files suggest that a former CIA official who had employed Watergate burglar E. Howard Hunt in espionage work planned to feed Woodward and Bernstein information that implicated the Nixon administration with Hunt. If the source of the information was the CIA, the reporters would have been obligated to steer the story away from the intelligence organization, both out of gratitude and out of ethical concerns to protect the confidentiality of their source.

In a provocative article, Edward Jay Epstein suggested that a high CIA official was the famous "Deep Throat" who fed so much crucial information to the journalists.[26] Epstein argued that the press must create the impression that such information is "accidental." It must do this in order to protect its sources and to preserve the image that a developing story stands on its own as the real objective issue and is not merely a calculated move in some larger political game. By the term "accidental," Epstein means that the information on which a story is based must be represented as natural and objective facts that the reporter stumbled across and pieced together in the normal course of following a story. Although the myth of "accidental information" may be necessary to protect the sources and integrity of the story, it may hide the possibility that larger political issues lurk behind the ones presented in the story: "Even for the best of reasons, if journalists represent news as being accidental when in fact it is deliberate, then they may willy-nilly assist in camouflaging the interest behind the disclosure, and thereby be part of a grander scale of the cover-up of an intra-government power struggle."[27]

The political information on which public opinion rests can have deliberate connections to the political goals for which public opinion is courted. In some instances the involvement of the press in converting politically "loaded" information into news may be a passive one. This happens when, as in the Watergate coverage, standard reporting practices or relationships with sources turn reporters into direct conduits between political actors and the public, while making it impossible to show that the story behind the information is as relevant to the situation as the story created by the information. In other cases, as in the decision to phase out coverage of urban riots, the press may become an active participant in the reconstruction of political information.

It is important to understand the factors that determine what political information will be presented to the public and how it will be presented. Five factors that can affect the selection and presentation of political information are: (1) economic pressures, (2) political pressures, (3) cooperation between reporters and political actors, (4) news-gathering procedures, and (5) professional standards that inhibit the reporting of background information.

ECONOMIC PRESSURES ON THE MEDIA

The most powerful economic factors affecting news reporting have to do with the relations between television networks and their affiliates and between wire services and their subscribers. The need to maintain harmony within these miniature economic systems has a leveling effect on story lines, acceptable value positions, and the presentation of legitimate groups. These pressures are particularly acute in television news. A number of studies indicate that stories are constructed around considerations of drama, visual imagery, and action.[28] The obvious result of these considerations is that the information content of television news is very low. A more serious unintended effect of the response to perceived economic pressures is that the short, dramatic, and planned performances of political actors often receive preferential treatment on television because they satisfy dramatic criteria.

Internal pressures to use particular formats for the presentation of information may be compounded by pressures from advertisers concerning the content and emphasis of stories. Newspapers are less vulnerable than television to economic pressures because their advertising base tends to come from local businesses without direct interests in national issues. Television news, by contrast, is sponsored by large companies that may be directly involved in political

issues such as auto safety, environmental protection, antitrust viola-
tions, political bribery, product defects, and energy development.
There is no way to determine exactly how much impact economic
interests have on political reporting. Network executives vehe-
mently deny that there is any effective pressure to slant the coverage of political stories. Most observers concede that although the
pressures do not operate in simple or direct terms, they exist all the
same. A few examples illustrate the difficulties in documenting and
assessing their impact.

A former president of CBS News has revealed that intense pressures were felt from the tobacco industry following the earliest
news reports of the link between cigarette smoking and lung can-
cer. This pressure was not only channeled through the commercial
sponsorship of cigarette companies, but it also was aimed at related
industries doing business with tobacco firms. For example, Alcoa
Aluminum (which sold aluminum foil for cigarette packages) finally dropped its sponsorship of a CBS news and documentary program after the program ran a number of stories that offended
Alcoa's customers. The program was gradually shifted from a
weekly to a monthly format.[29]

The problem with pinning down such economic influences on
the news is that they can be justified as good business sense as easily as they can be called efforts at political censorship. For example,
it would be poor policy for an airline to encourage customers to
"Come Fly with Us" right after an air tragedy involving one of its
planes. It would be equally damaging to the image of a new car if
the manufacturer were to continue to run ads on the car following
a disclosure that the gas tank of this "spirited little family sedan"
had a design flaw that could lead to fiery death for passengers in
even a minor collision.

News executives use a number of other arguments to discount
the impact of economic pressures. For example, they maintain that
it is seldom the case that pressure from advertisers can completely
stop the flow of information about a story. Thus, there is always
some information that the public can use to form independent
opinions about the political activities of economic interests. It is
also argued that the documented cases of successful intervention by
advertisers in the coverage of news stories are so rare that the practice probably isn't common enough to worry about.

Although these objections have merit, it is important to bear several things in mind when evaluating them. The priority that the
public assigns to an issue generally depends on the amount of news

coverage devoted to it. If pressure from advertisers makes news departments reluctant to launch follow-up investigations of issues damaging to sponsors, a whole array of potentially important problems may never rise to the top of the national agenda. Moreover, the ways in which economic pressures operate make them hard to measure. As a result, the small number of documented cases does not necessarily indicate that economic constraints play a minor role in directing the flow of public information. There is a tendency among social scientists to discount the importance of things that are difficult to observe. This is a dangerous tendency in an area in which those who control the information on which observation depends have both the interest and the capacity to keep the information from public view. Finally, it is important to regard economic constraints as just one element in a large and complex set of factors that can influence the flow of public information about some issues under some circumstances.

POLITICAL CONSTRAINTS ON THE PRESS

Since the government controls the licensing and monitoring of television and radio frequencies through the Federal Communications Commission (FCC), pressures from the President can carry implicit or explicit threats about license removal. The most dramatic example of such pressure in recent times was the attack by the Nixon administration on the broadcasting industry in 1969. After his promise to end the Vietnam War in his victorious election campaign of 1968, Nixon escalated the air war in Vietnam in the summer and fall of 1969. His actions were met with massive protests by a coalition of antiwar groups. The escalation of the war was not news, but the confrontation between the numerous protest groups and the President was. The media devoted a great deal of coverage to the unfolding saga of the monthly protests scheduled throughout the fall of 1969. Nixon regarded this coverage as a threat to his war policy, for it seemed to lend credibility to the protesters and it carried their message directly to the American people.[30] He launched a crusade to boost public support for his policies. A major component of this crusade was an attack on the "bias" of the news media.

In the fall of 1969 Vice President Spiro Agnew began an intensive national speaking tour, the primary theme of which was the liberal bias of the "Eastern establishment" and the "effete snobs" who controlled the press. These "nattering nabobs of negativism" were, according to Agnew, opposed to the Nixon administration's goal to win an honorable peace in Vietnam, and they used their news coverage of the antiwar demonstrations to propagandize their position to the public. In the midst of Agnew's speaking tour, Nixon delivered his masterful "silent majority" speech. He claimed to represent the preferences of the vast majority of Americans, whose voice had been stilled by the clamor of protesters and the neglect of the media.

This campaign had three major components. First, Agnew delivered a number of veiled suggestions that the media had violated their professional and legal standards of objectivity and thus should be investigated by Congress or the FCC. This placed the television networks in a defensive position and forced them to justify much of their political coverage.[31] Throughout the administration's involvement in Vietnam, overt pressure continued and was sustained by such activities as the congressional investigation of the CBS documentary "The Selling of the Pentagon." This program took a critical view of the Defense Department's public relations practices and produced an equally critical investigation of its reporting practices by Representative Harley Staggers.[32] Although Staggers did not succeed in censuring the networks in this investigation, he continued to bring official pressure to bear on them the next year in an investigation of "news staging." This hearing continued throughout most of 1972 and forced all three networks to defend particular news reports. Moreover, the FCC followed up several of the cases covered by Staggers' investigation and ordered the networks to provide detailed information on them.[33]

Although it is impossible to prove that such political pressures have specific political motives, their timing in relation to political events is often highly suggestive. For example, one of the Nixon administration's last direct moves against the media came in 1972. Just prior to the President's decision to resume bombing in North Vietnam, the Justice Department filed antitrust suits against ABC, CBS, and NBC. Although the suits did not involve news policies directly, the broadcasters protested that their intent was political intimidation. This charge was confirmed by an administration media adviser, Patrick Buchanan, who told a public television interviewer:

my own view is . . . that a monopoly like this of any group of people with a single point of view and a single political ideology who tend to continually freeze out opposing points of view and opposing information, that you're going to find something done in the area of antitrust suit action.[34]

Since news bias was not a valid area for antitrust actions, the Justice Department quickly denied that its suits were being filed for these reasons.[35] However, in a later interview Buchanan reaffirmed that the primary political objective of the administration was to secure free media access for the President's views to reach the public: "My primary concern is that the President have the right of untrammeled communication with the American people. You can't compare newspapers to those pictures on television. They can make or break a politician."[36]

The second goal of the campaign against the news media was to generate public disfavor toward the press and, by extension, toward the antiwar movement. The creation of the "silent majority" was a masterful way to crystallize support among a confused public in search of leadership, direction, and positive political commitments. Public support for the administration's war policies rose sharply after the suggestion that the media and the protesters constituted the only opposition to the vast multitudes who supported the administration. The resulting drop in media coverage of the protests combined with the rising tide of public support for the government to virtually destroy the protest movement by the end of 1969.[37]

The third outcome of the attack on the media is in many ways the most interesting consequence of direct political pressure. By claiming that the media are biased on an issue and then getting the media to increase coverage of the "official" position on the issue, the government can create real bias in reporting practices, yet cloak this bias in a semblance of objectivity. Extrapolating from statements like those made by Patrick Buchanan, it becomes clear that the administration not only wanted to block the flow of information favorable to its opponents, but it wanted to turn the press into a passive conduit for transmitting official definitions of the issue.

This was accomplished, in part, by staging news events that appeared to confirm the administration's claims. For example, in late 1969 the White House organized a series of support rallies, prayer days, and patriotic celebrations around the country. When these events were aired on the news programs, they appeared to confirm the existence of support for government policy, and they underscored the charge that the way an issue appeared to the public did, in fact, depend on how the media decided to cover it. The press was compelled to cover these events because they were staged in proper news formats and because failure to cover them would appear to be proof of the charge of bias.

Through the combined use of direct pressure and the natural workings of symbiosis, Nixon's claims about the war, the media, and public opinion became self-fulfilling prophecies. The fascinating aspect of the whole episode is that a charge of press bias was used to create a new press bias. A shift in the flow of information about the war issue was achieved through the very practices that were condemned. This strikes at the heart of political "reality." It demonstrates that the way the public regards information about an issue has less to do with any "objective" properties of the information than with the ability of information sources to control press coverage (and public attitudes about press coverage) in ways that make the information *seem* credible.

COOPERATION BETWEEN
REPORTERS AND NEWS MAKERS

One of the major reasons politically "loaded" information becomes communicated to the public as objective "news" is the mutual dependence of press and politicians. The most common form of this dependence is the parallel format required for news stories and political performances. In order to achieve their political goals, political actors must attract the attention of the public and persuade them of a particular interpretation of a situation. This requires simple and dramatic performances, the symbolic formats of which were described in Chapter 9. These performances generally reach the public because they conform to the media standards for appropriate news stories, outlined in Chapter 8. The symbiosis between press and politicians does not involve the press in any active reconstruction of information; it merely converts the press into a passive conduit for the transmission of competing partisan appeals to the public. In the process, the performances with the most familiar themes, the most simple-to-grasp messages, the most engrossing personalities, the most interesting and inoffensive dramatic conflicts, and the most powerful symbolic presentations become certified as the legitimate perspectives on a political issue.[38] It is no accident that these perspectives usually become attached to major political organizations, famous political personalities, or well-financed interest groups.

The dictates of preferred news formats often reduce the media to transmitters of highly contrived political scenes, as long as the contrivance conforms to the news production needs of the media and glaring evidence of contrivance is carefully hidden off-stage. Sometimes even the most blatant evidence of contrivance is buried beneath the dictates of news format. For example, it has been well documented that the 1972 Republican convention was orchestrated down to the last detail to dramatize routine events, glamorize the party nominee, and instill excitement in the nomination of a candidate whose victory was a foregone conclusion. Much of the Republicans' media strategy in 1972 came to light when a messenger from convention headquarters mistakenly picked up a script for the entire convention and included it in a sheaf of routine press releases that he dropped off at the command post of the British Broadcasting Company. A BBC correspondent read in disbelief the long list of stage directions, including one that called for a spontaneous demonstration to interrupt the convention secretary in the middle of a particular sentence in a speech and another one that called for an elaborate "ten-minute spontaneous demonstration" when Richard Nixon's name was placed in nomination.[39]

Despite the fact that copies of the script soon circulated among all the major newspaper and television contingents at the convention, it did little to alter their coverage of the planned events mentioned in the script. NBC, for example, in order to deliver visually dramatic news to its audience, keyed its coverage to the scripted aspects of the proceedings. An observer at the NBC control room during the demonstration following Richard Nixon's nomination reported the scene:

> The delegates were about to go wild in a ten-minute spontaneous demonstration and 20,000 red, white, and blue balloons were about to drop from nets in the flies of Convention Hall.
> "Watch the balloons up there," [NBC news executive producer George] Murray yelled at Tony. . . . From inside the adjacent trailer, Tony could be heard shouting into a microphone, directing his engineers and cameramen. He referred to the cameramen by number.
> "Five, hold five! Hold three. Hold four!" Suddenly the balloon drop commenced. "Here they come! Here they come!" shouted Murray. . . . "Go! Start the zooms, Tony!" Murray yelled, getting even louder, "in and out, in and out! yo-yo! yo-yo! . . ."

The screen jumped with sudden cuts from one delegation to another. There was a giddy collage of laughing faces, banners standards, balloons, more faces, people dancing in the aisle. Tony was cutting so fast from one camera to another that the scene seemed to whirl.[40]

Dramatic visual scenes are the backbone of television news. A powerful measure of the impact of visual communication on the public was revealed in Patterson and McClure's study of the 1972 election. They reported: "An analysis of the television audience's recall of the 1972 campaign stories indicates that, fully half the time, their memory was primarily about something their eyes had seen. Only twenty percent of the time was viewers' recall clearly dominated by what their ears had heard."[41] The capability of political actors to construct political performances along the lines of news formats greatly increases the chances of establishing direct communication links with the public.

Another form of symbiosis between the press and politicians involves the professional relationships between journalists and political actors. These relationships can take on a number of dimensions that affect the flow of political information. Most obvious is the dependence of journalists on the political actors for their livelihood and (which is the same thing) for future stories. Thus, reporters may have to honor requests to hold up a story, or they may refrain from transmitting information that is overly critical of their news sources.[42] This sort of self-censorship can also operate on a much more personal basis. As one Washington correspondent stated:

> A reporter may hesitate to take a critical view of regularly tapped sources for the very human reason that he prefers to be treated pleasantly when he walks into an office, rather than to be treated as though he were poison. His vested interest is in maintaining a pleasant atmosphere.[43]

Close working relations between the press and their sources of information can lead to an even more complex form of symbiosis: role taking. Reporters may spend long periods of time covering a particular branch of government. They may grow to understand and sympathize with the problems confronting the officials they observe. When this happens, their personal and professional orientations may merge. They may identify with the political interests of the people they cover. This can lead to the subconscious filtering of information in keeping with the reporter's increasingly sympathetic outlook. The role-taking syndrome has been described by Sigal:

> In direct daily contact with officials in one department and out of touch with other parts of the government, the reporter on the beat gradually absorbs the perspectives of the senior officials he is covering. This absorption is not as much due to the attitudes he brings to his job as it is necessary to his performance on it. Much of political conversation employs catch phrases and slight shifts in nuance to convey meaning. The reporter with a long-standing relationship with officials on his beat can develop a finely calibrated sensitivity to even the slightest sign of movement on an issue. When tuned in, he can sometimes detect a nuance, and from it, infer a change in policy. Without role-taking, without putting himself in officials' shoes, a reporter might find it somewhat harder to anticipate the outcomes of controversies, or even to understand what a source's comments mean. Yet repeated role-taking may lead him to adopt the official's perspective on issues. The line between role-taking and absorption is a thin one indeed.[44]

When such symbiotic relations develop, they give political actors access to "objective" news outlets for their partisan political messages. The power to control the flow of information to the public on an issue is, of course, a crucial political advantage. It is important to acknowledge that extreme cases of symbiosis in which an official exercises complete control over reporting practices (or in which a reporter identifies wholeheartedly with an official position) are rare. However, some degree of symbiosis probably operates in most high-level situations in which political actors have a strong, vested interest in the success of their policies and the press has an equally strong interest in obtaining newsworthy information about those policies.

In its milder forms, journalistic symbiosis can lead to the emphasis of some issues over others, the direct transmission of politically "loaded" information, and the subtle injection of political values into news reporting. In its more advanced forms, journalistic symbiosis can result in the suppression of information, the concealment of political motives (such as possible CIA involvement in the Watergate story), and the protection of sources who use the press to circulate strategic but unfounded political information. Former presidential press chief Bill Moyers captured the inherent danger in the willingness of journalists to report the leaks, plants, and "background" reports of "informed" political sources who demand that they remain anonymous. If carried to the extreme,

Moyers observed, one can imagine a powerful official giving his press entourage the following preface to his "deep background" remarks: "The interests of national security dictate that the lie I am about to tell you not be attributed to me."[45]

THE ORGANIZATION OF THE
NEWS BUSINESS

The factors that have been discussed thus far can operate directly on the content of the political information that reaches the public. They can affect the place of various issues on the political agenda, and they may shape the public's perception of those issues. In addition to these conditions directly affecting the definitions of political issues, a cluster of related factors works indirectly to reinforce the effects of symbiosis, political pressure, and economic constraints. These indirect variables are all related to the organization of the news business. They not only reinforce the effects of news reporting on issue definitions, but can have an independent impact on the quality of information that reaches the public.

It is important to recognize that public opinion depends on the quality (as well as on the quantity) of the information that the public receives. All too often the news outlets most available to the public display little if any difference in their coverage of stories. They offer scant detail to fill in the picture of events or the implications of issues. They provide little in the way of descriptive context to establish the significance of a news item or the probable purposes of the political moves behind it. Moreover, few stories are followed to their conclusions. The format of news permits isolated vignettes and scenarios to stand alone, independent of their future developments (which may not be as dramatic as the initial clashes and conflicts, which brought them to the attention of the press). Finally, issues and events are generally presented without adequate discussion of their historical evolution. Thus average individuals have difficulty detecting shifts in policy or changes in the political coalitions involved with an issue. Polsby offered the following overview of these defects:

> To my mind, the performance of the American news media does leave something to be desired. And their worst sins are these: *incoherence*, stemming from a style of news coverage and reporting that is highly mechanical and tailored more to the techniques of presentation than to the needs of citizens or contours of events; *sparseness*, a

characteristic that is mostly a consequence of the pressures on reporters to converge and concentrate on a narrow range of phenomena; and *inexpertise*, a quality that has its roots in journalistic craft norms that value amateurism, the general ability to turn out an undifferentiated product (the "story") and egalitarianism ("we write for the man in the street").[46]

These deficiencies in the quality of public information all have their roots in the internal organization of the news media. The major organizational factors responsible for the uneven quality of information in the news are news-gathering practices, editorial policies, and the informal working relations among journalists. Each of them builds on the weaknesses of others, as the following discussions indicate.

News-Gathering Practices

The dictates of producing news programs and publishing newspapers have introduced a number of efficient and economical routines into the gathering of news.[47] For example, the policy of basing network camera crews in a few large cities means that most news originates from major urban centers. Information and issues relevant to the public beyond the borders of Washington, New York, Chicago, Los Angeles, and Houston often goes unreported because of the convenience of geographically based reporting and the time and money costs of roving news teams. Moreover, the cost of covering complex stories and the need to fill air time and column space with acceptable news items have resulted in a tendency to cover staged political events (like press conferences and rallies) and visually dramatic spontaneous events (like riots and strikes). There is often little payoff in slowly unfolding investigative reporting: The stories may not pan out; they may disrupt tightly scheduled news agendas; and they may lack the dramatic impact of planned events featuring captivating personalities. Moreover, the necessity to file a story before the daily deadline makes it difficult for reporters to discover much background information beyond what is provided by the organizers of the event or what is available at the scene. Even if a reporter turns up background details and contextual information, they may be sacrificed to the news producer's fear of boring the audience with the facts or to the competition among department editors at a newspaper to make room for their respective stories.

In short, virtually all the mechanics of news gathering are geared to the most efficient, reliable, and economical filling of air time and column space with items in standard news formats. Stories that depart from these formats may be costly and may disrupt normal operating procedures in the organization. The obvious benefit of these news-gathering practices lies in their promotion of smooth operations. However, they often prove damaging to the quality of public information, for they may restrict its diversity, detail, and contextual adequacy.

Editorial Practices and
News Content

Editors in news organizations are often in conflicted positions. They must be accountable to the interests of management as well as to the journalistic judgments of their reporters. They must decide how to reach (and hold on to) readers and viewers as well as how to preserve the integrity of reporters' stories. These and other editorial responsibilities dictate that factors other than professionalism and simple information gathering must enter the construction of news.

For example, editors may opt for "generalist" reporting strategies out of the sense that the public isn't equipped to handle a more sophisticated or intensive presentation of the news. This perception can have important effects on the structure of information transmitted to the public. For example, Epstein has demonstrated convincingly that considerations of brevity and interest level outweigh information content in most television news reporting.[48] A study of the 1972 election has shown that the vast majority of television time was devoted to human interest and action stories, while only a fraction of air time involved the serious presentation of campaign issues.[49] A survey of news correspondents conducted in 1972 revealed the early stages of the continuing trend toward the "lightening" of the news. Over half of the correspondents polled reported "an increase in emphasis on humorous items, short jazzy items, or good news."[50]

Even though the images of the audience on which these changes in news format are based may bear little resemblance to the actual audience, the intense competition to win the favor of the mythical news audience "led to fluffier stories, fancier sets, and better-looking and less professional anchormen, but also in some instances had accounted for the elimination of all serious documentary and investigatory projects."[51] One disgruntled reporter described the shifts in local-news policy decisions in this way:

> The basic trends are evident: (1) a panic shift to the so-called "happy news" format, and (2) a panic flight from genuine investigative reporting of hard-to-dig-out, significant original local news. . . . Everyone seems to be . . . uncertain what it is that wins audience. What they never seem to consider is original reporting of significant news.[52]

In addition to lightening the information content of news, editorial practices can affect the substance and diversity of political perspectives appearing in the news. Although the norm of objectivity prohibits overt political endorsements from entering news accounts, most news organizations display implicit preferences for some political themes over others. In general, the political perspectives of editors and publishers are masked by professional standards such as the norm against publishing controversial or sensational news. Professional standards could be used to account for an editorial decision to treat a teachers' strike as a traditional labor conflict over higher wages rather than as a racial struggle over the control of schools. Similarly, "antisensationalism" could be used to explain networks' decisions to downplay the seriousness of urban riots in 1968. However, the fact remains that each of these cases resulted in the inclusion of certain political values and perspectives in the news and the exclusion of others.

In other cases, editorial decisions may simply reflect the undisguised political leanings of editors and publishers. Reporters often regard these decisions as part of the routine policy of their news organizations. Just as reporters may come to identify with their news sources, they may also become socialized into the political values of their own employers. It is obvious that the political preferences of media management are not (and cannot be) transmitted overtly. The socialization process through which the reporter acquires these preferences operates in a much more subtle fashion.

In one of the classic studies of the socialization of reporters in conformity with the policies of management, Breed found that the reporter begins to acquire the "ethos" of his or her paper through the simple activity of reading it every day.[53] This produces a general sense of what the editors are looking for, what kinds of story receive priority, what sorts of language and style are favored, and what story angles dominate various topics. This general introduction to news policy is reinforced by direct contacts with editors who hand out assignments, suggest story lines, edit reporters' copy, and decide what to do with stories. Direct cues from editors have a major impact on the reporter's outlook, for they can directly determine success in a career. The overwhelming tendency is for reporters to adopt political perspectives that maximize occupational success and minimize personal frustration. One reporter interviewed by Breed related the following experience:

> I heard a union was going out on strike, so I kept on it; then the boss said something about it, and well—I took the hint and we had less coverage of the strike forming. It was easier that way. We lost the story, but what can you do?[54]

As Breed points out, the political preferences of management seldom intrude this bluntly into news reporting. However, in most cases the powerful socialization of reporters into the "mentality" of the organization makes the need for overt censorship unnecessary. Thus, its absence may be due more to the effective role of editors as socializing agents than to the absence of subtle political bias in news organizations.

One of the most important effects of editorial policy has less to do with the substance of the information that reaches the public than with its diversity. Although editors generally maintain an image as independent judges of news merit in aggressive pursuit of their own stories, recent studies suggest quite another picture. In most large organizations editors are under pressure to account for their decisions. They must certify the importance of stories and justify cases in which their story lines depart from the themes used by other media outlets in the coverage of an event. These matters are often difficult to explain because there are few hard and fast standards for what constitutes an "important" story or the "correct" story line. In fact, given the endless possibilities in the construction of political information and the development of political events, in some cases it is even difficult to pin down what is "news." The most immediate defense against these kinds of uncertainty is to establish among media policy makers a loose and informal consensus about the proper news treatment of various events. When such a consensus operates, it is necessary only to point to the behavior of other organizations to justify one's own course of action. Moreover, the sometimes difficult question of "What is news?" takes on a more practical answer: "News is what news organizations decide to report as news."

In his study of election coverage by the press, Crouse interviewed a reporter who summed up the possible ill effects of editorial consensus on reporting practices:

> But while these papers want to have a guy there getting all the inside stuff, they don't want reporters who are . . . different enough to make any kind of trouble. It would worry the s——t out of them if their Washington reporter happened to come up with a page one story that was different from what the other guys were getting. And the first goddam thing that happens is they pick up the phone and call this guy and say, "Hey, if this is such a hot story, how come the AP or the *Washington Post* doesn't have it? . . ." Their abiding interest is making sure that nobody else has got anything they don't have, not getting something that nobody else has.[55]

As this reporter implied, the safest way to create a news agenda is to follow the lead of some common news source. The wire services are the most obvious consensus builders in the news industry. Virtually all news organizations subscribe to them. Morever, the wire services are in the business of disseminating the first information about events. This makes them an obvious source of guidance in deciding what to cover. Finally, wire-service stories generally adopt the least controversial story line on an event because they must "sell" their stories to subscribers with different political leanings and different audiences. This makes the wire-service story line the common denominator in most developing stories. This principle even holds in broadcast journalism.

Epstein found that wire-service stories were the basis for 70 percent of the reporting assignments handed out by the assignment editors of NBC News.[56] An interview with an ABC news executive produced this comment: "Without the wire services, we'd be dead."[57] Newspaper studies have shown that "the wires" virtually set the agenda of news run by a paper. Even more interesting is the finding that the services can dictate the importance of an event simply as a result of the number of stories they send out over the wires. Editors in the newspapers studied tended to print stories on a topic in proportion of the number of stories appearing on the wire copy.[58]

The only exception to this rule of wire-service promotion of editorial consensus seems to be major national newspapers such as the *New York Times*, the *Washington Post*, and the *Los Angeles Times*. In his study of the first two of these major dailies, Sigal found that there was some resistance to using wire-service stories because of the papers' commitments to large stables of reporters.[59] However, other aspects of editorial consensus were found to operate in the making of assignments and the handling of stories. These editorial practices combine with the factors just discussed to contribute to perhaps the most immediate constraint on the structure of political information: the dynamics of "pack journalism."

The Working Habits of Reporters: Pack Journalism

The above-mentioned news-gathering and editorial practices reinforce in reporters certain working habits that further fragment political information and limit its range of content. Reporters who cover a particular "beat" or who are assigned to a story tend to feed indirectly off one another when writing their stories. There are two reasons for this. First, it is only natural that consensus about an event would emerge among a group of individuals who live and breathe the same experiences and share the common need to make sense of the information to which they have been exposed. Second, and more importantly, reporters share the same working conditions, the same relations to news sources, the same professional norms, and the same editorial constraints. In an environment in which there are few incentives or opportunities to engage in original investigations, and in which deviant stories have to be justified, the pressures point to the sharing of ideas and the convergence of story lines.

This phenomenon has come to be known as *pack journalism*. It was first described in detail by Cohen in a study of foreign affairs correspondents. He discovered that they tended to read each others' work, discuss possible story lines among themselves, and find justification for their own angles if they appeared in other reports about the event.[60] This finding gained considerable support (and stirred up some controversy) when it was reflected in Crouse's observations of press coverage of the 1972 election. He argued that close association, the pressures toward conformity, the need to justify stories, and the weight of wire-service lead stories combined to impose a fairly narrow range of information around most campaign events.[61]

Different explanations of pack journalism have been offered by different observers. When these explanations are combined, they begin to resemble a list of all the factors described so far in this chapter. The implication of this is that the vast pyramid of factors that can affect the construction and transmission of political information exerts its greatest pressure at the interface between political information and its recording instrument, the reporter. For example, Sigal cites the objectivity norm, the inadequacy of investigative staffs, and the dominance of wire services as explanations of pack journalism (or "news consensus").[62] Crouse stresses the role of the wire services and the related impact of editorial pressures to justify stories.[63] Epstein attributes the restricted scope of information to the wires, editorial consensus, and the norm of generalism.[64] Cirino cites pressures on editors to run noncontroversial, "lowest common denominator" stories.[65]

Despite the diversity of causes, the effect of pack journalism is singular: It limits the flow of information about an event. Even though information in the real situation may be voluminous, interpretations may be ambiguous, and the political motives behind an event may be patently obvious, the filtration of information through the "pack" (and on up the editorial ladder) tends to produce the appearance of simple situations with clear meanings and few ties to ulterior political motives. In short, information becomes transformed from complex, diverse, ambiguous, and politically "loaded" data into simple, uniform, clear, and "objective" images.

THE CONSTRAINTS OF PROFESSIONAL JOURNALISM STANDARDS

Among the most interesting factors that affect the flow of political information are the standards of journalism that give the press its professional standing. These norms of the profession are designed to improve the quality of the news and protect the independence of the press. However, they often work in just the opposite way. Sometimes, professional norms prevent reporters from divulging background information. At other times, political actors may take advantage of the professional code, knowing that certain key bits of available information will not be reported to the public. The professional norms that most often become involved in the unintended restraint of political information are the journalistic standards of taste, objectivity, and generalism.

Standards of Good Taste

One of the hallmarks of a major news organization is the observance by reporters and editors of standards of good taste. Reputable organizations avoid sensational stories, gossip, compromising reports on the private lives of public figures, and the verbatim reporting of obscene language used by public personalities in informal conversations. These taboos serve a number of beneficial functions. They help keep the focus of news on public issues rather than on the personalities behind them. They reduce the likelihood that gossip, slander, and blackmail will become dominant factors in the resolution of political issues. They also make the news palatable to the moral sensibilities of the majority of the public.

However, these standards of taste also can endow news stories and political actors with an unblemished surface that distorts important incidents and protects wayward politicians from serious public criticism. The things that people do and the way in which they speak may or may not be important bits of information in judging their political actions. However, judgments about whether private behavior and personal speech are politically relevent are seldom left up to the public. They are generally preempted by members of the press, who use broadly shared standards of taste to screen out some personally sensitive matters and to phrase others in euphemisms.

At times, the uses of these standards of taste is fairly harmless. For example, during a press briefing, the Press Secretary for the Carter administration became upset about a reporter's suggestion that the President's national security adviser (Zbigniew Brzezinski) was upstaging the Secretary of State (Cyrus Vance) on important foreign policy matters. The Press Secretary (Jody Powell) angrily dismissed the suggestion with an obscene expression. Even though the lead paragraph in the *New York Times* article on Powell's reaction was concerned with the use of the obscenity, his verbatim remarks were replaced with an inoffensive euphemism: "The White House press secretary, Jody Powell, used a barnyard vulgarity today to describe what he called the 'implication' of a *New York Times* article that speculated about the power relationships in the foreign policy establishment."[66]

In this case it would be difficult to argue that the priority assigned to standards of good taste over verbatim reporting did serious damage to the impression that the public received about the episode. However, in other cases the norm of good taste may serve to cover up serious political revelations and soften the public image of an incident. For example, during the close presidential race of 1976, Secretary of Agriculture Earl Butz was an active campaigner for Gerald Ford's reelection. During an informal chat with reporters between campaign appearances, Butz was asked about the prospects for the black vote. The Agriculture Secretary dismissed the black vote with a crude and disturbing racist remark about "coloreds." In order to illustrate the point here, it is necessary to suspend the normal standards of taste that apply to academic writing and quote the Butz remark: "I'll tell you what coloreds want. It's three things: first, a tight _____; second, loose shoes; and third, a warm place to _____."*

Needless to say, a statement like this coming from a high governmental official is most significant. Not only might the public find such a statement useful in forming opinions about its author, but it could be used in judging the man running for President, who had appointed Butz to a high government post. However, the overwhelming majority of the public never received a verbatim account of the statement.

At first, no major reputable news outlet would even run the story. The story broke in *Rolling Stone*, a paper regarded by many news professionals and by the public as an organization with low professional standards and a fringe readership. After *Rolling Stone* made the incident public, the professionally minded news organizations that feed information to a majority of the public were faced with the dilemma of how to treat the story. A growing furor surrounded the remarks, and Butz issued an apology for his "unfortunate choice of language." However, the misleading nature of the apology, along with the reasons for the outrage of people who knew of the remarks, would never reach the public unless mainstream news outlets ran the statement. The Associated Press decided that the matter should be left to the judgments of individual editors, and it sent a verbatim transcription out over the wires. However, out of the hundreds of major newspaper and broadcasting organizations that subscribe to the AP news feed, only one newspaper printed the actual statement.[67] All the other news organizations that ran the story found euphemistic phrases to represent Butz's actual words.

For example, the *New York Times* said Butz referred to black

---

*The actual words spoken by Butz were included in the original version of this chapter. However, the very point I am making about the news media also seems to apply to publishers. The publisher found Butz's language too offensive to be printed. The interested reader can reconstruct the verbatim remarks by consulting *Rolling Stone*, October 7, 1976, p. 57.

people as "coloreds" who wanted only three things. The article said he listed these things, in order, "in obscene, derogatory and scatological terms."[68] Needless to say, it requires a virtually impossible leap of imagination to infer the actual remarks from the euphemisms "obscene," "derogatory," and "scatological." (The *Times* apparently had learned to sharpen the inferential power of its euphemisms by the time it covered Press Secretary Powell's "barnyard vulgarity.") Some papers came closer to the actual sentence structure but refused to print the offensive words. For example, the *Des Moines Register* ran the following version: "I'll tell you what the coloreds want. It's these three things: first, a tight (obscenity); second, loose shoes; and third, a warm place to (vulgarism)."[69] Although this treatment comes closer, it still fails to deliver the astounding impact of the actual statement.

Although most newspaper editors acknowledged the political significance of Butz's remarks, all except one upheld the supremacy of standards of good taste. The managing editor of the *New York Times* rationalized: "But we recognize that if we use this series of filthy obscenities then we'll probably use the next."[70] The editor of the *Des Moines Register* explained that he "found the [Butz] quote so offensive and so atrocious 'I couldn't bring myself to give it to people with their breakfast.'"[71] In a complex train of reasoning, the *Washington Post* editor explained that he would bend the standards of good taste only if the offensive remarks were made by the President. The outrages of lesser officials like cabinet members were apparently less damaging to the image of goverment or to issues such as official regard for minorities.[72]

The point here is that journalistic standards of good taste can result in the virtual blanket censorship of some remarks or activities that might otherwise affect the political thinking of the public. The Butz remarks were potentially volatile on several fronts. They reflected not only on the Secretary of Agriculture, but on the President as well. Perhaps more importantly, the failure of the media to transmit the actual words blunted the possible crystallization of an important issue: the significance of a high public official holding the most blatant and inexcusable racial prejudices. In the end, these issues faded away with Butz's bland and off-the-point apology for his "unfortunate choice of words" and his forced resignation in the interests of protecting Ford's presidential chances. In cases like this, it is clear that the standards of good taste clash with the second major professional standard: objectivity.

The Limits of Objective
Reporting

Although there has been a recent upswing in the practice of so-called advocacy journalism, most news organizations and reporters still maintain an allegiance to traditional standards of objectivity. As mentioned earlier, journalists who observe this professional norm see themselves as simple conduits of information to the public. They view their job as collecting observable facts about an event, organizing the facts into a coherent and readable form (a story), and transmitting them without comment or judgment to their audiences. The norm of objectivity prohibits reporters from taking a special interest in a story, biasing a story to favor the perspective of one of its characters, or passing along undocumented suspicions that the reporter may have about the event or actors in it.

These consequences of the objectivity norm have positive effects. They minimize the distortion of information. They reduce the chances that the press will knowingly advance the interests of one side over another in a political conflict. They also prevent the spread of possibly inaccurate information based solely on a reporter's unfounded hunches about behind-the-scenes activities. For the most part, professional objectivity is maintained often enough to give the press a good deal of credibility in the eyes of citizens and politicians alike. There is little that is of higher value to a reporter or a news organization than credibility.

However, the norm of objectivity can operate in several unintended ways to promote the transmission of politically "loaded" information. Three unintended consequences of the objectivity norm may affect the flow of political information. First, since objectivity dictates that things that can't be verified completely will not be reported, the overwhelming pressure on reporters is to cover detailed, accessible, and documentable events. Complex investigative reporting often runs into dead ends which may damage a story's credibility or prevent it from being released altogether. For example, much of the intrigue and excitement of Woodward and Bernstein's Pulitzer Prize-winning investigation of Watergate involved the constant prospect of not being able to turn up a key piece of information or to document it once it had been leaked.[73]

As prior discussions of symbiosis and political performances have indicated, planned political productions solve this problem of objective reporting. Staged events like speeches, press conferences, briefings, and official conferences provide ready-made stories, completely displayed information, and built-in official sources to document reporters' questions. As a result, the norm of objectivity reinforces the tendency (set in motion by news format criteria) to give disproportionate coverage to political pseudo-events. Sigal's study of the content of the front-page news of the *New York Times* and the *Washington Post* showed that about 60 percent of the news came from planned official events like press conferences, ceremonies, speeches, hearings, and official press releases. In contrast, only about 25 percent could be traced to reporter-developed stories through private interviews or investigations.[74] These are startling figures for two papers that prize their investments in investigative reporting and their independent political stances.

The second unintended consequence of objectivity is related to the first. Not only does objectivity lead reporters to cover planned events, but it leads them to rely heavily on official sources of information and confirmation. Information must have a reliable source. The planned events that make up most of the news come equipped with the officials who act in them. These officials become the primary sources for interpreting the events and documenting reporters' stories.[75] Even when news does not originate from planned events, most political stories have some implications for the government. As a result, government officials are often placed in a position of confirming or denying political charges or contributing new information to a developing issue. These officials thus become the "objectifying" agents for news stories. Since officials seldom promote information that runs counter to their political interests, the situation often arises in which the reporter's objective style transforms a source of politically expedient information into the validation for the same information.

The final unintended effect of objectivity is also a spinoff from the first factor. Because the dictates of objectivity prevent reporters from reporting things that they cannot document completely, they are often placed in a position of transmitting information that they suspect to be biased. However, since they cannot document their suspicions, they must pass along the information (in its cloak of objectivity) and conceal their suspicions. A classic case of this occurred during the 1968 presidential campaign between Richard Nixon and Hubert Humphrey.

Nixon had long suspected that the press had contributed to his somewhat negative public image, which his media advisers desperately wanted to improve. Nixon's advisers designed for their candidate a sophisticated image campaign, which forced the press to stand at a distance and transmit to the public without comment highly contrived images of the candidate. The heart of the campaign was a series of "unrehearsed" discussions with townspeople and reporters from different cities around the country. Panelists were carefully selected to represent the sort of people with whom Nixon wanted to be seen (by the voters) having a dialogue. The setting was carefully arranged to show off the candidate in his best light. He was well rested, relaxed, alert, and carefully made up. He appeared to be having a confident and concerned exchange of ideas with average Americans. These impressions were punctuated by the responses of the studio audience, which applauded his answers and cheered his campaign rhetoric.

What the public did not see was the rousing "warm-up" designed to stir the hand-picked audience into a frenzy of enthusiasm for the candidate. Nor did the public see the editing of the sessions to select the best camera angles and to screen out politically volatile questions. Finally, the voters did not witness the careful stage preparations, rehearsed responses, or the acting lessons, all designed to communicate desirable images of Nixon to the public. These things were not part of the information transmitted by the press. The reason is simple: The press was not admitted to watch any of the "discussions" at first hand. They were only permitted to watch the tapings on television monitors in another room.

To the extent that they reported on the campaign, reporters were constrained by the objectivity norm to report what the candidate said and not how he had staged his statements for particular impacts.[76] Thus "objective" press reports became anchored in the dramatized visual images of the media campaign when the taped discussions were run as paid political commercials following the evening news programs. Although a few reports appeared in newspapers detailing the image mechanics of the campaign, they occupied the comparatively minor status of "special features" and could not be discussed in the same context with serious coverage of campaign issues.[77] The connection between the issues and their dramatic format was frustrated by the objectivity norm, for all that the press could observe directly were the dialogue and the audience responses at these sessions. The elaborate behind-the-scenes preparations were not directly observable.

Reporters as Generalists

The tendency to report planned events at face value is further reinforced by the norm of generalism. Reporters are trained to be generalists. They are taught to be ready to handle virtually any assignment. The career patterns of journalists generally reflect this norm. In the course of a career it is common for a reporter to hold a number of different posts and to cover a wide range of stories while in each post. This is particularly true in broadcast journalism, where a long-term assignment to a particular news area is the exception rather than the rule. The professional rationale for this norm is sound. First of all, reporting is a general skill based on observational and writing talents, not on specialized knowledge.[78] This image of the journalist is reinforced by the myth of objectivity, which represents the reporter as a transmitter of information, not an expert interpreter of events. The combined goals of generalism and objectivity may be at least a partial deterrent to the role-taking tendencies of reporters assigned to specialized areas for long periods of time.

In these and other respects, the norm of generalism has a positive intent. However, like standards of taste and objectivity, it can also exert unintended disruptions in the flow of information. For example, the practice of pulling reporters off one story and assigning them to another can fragment information, disrupt the development of stories, and make reporters reluctant to dig beneath the surface of a situation. Morever, the relative ignorance of many reporters about the topics they cover further reduces the presentation of contextual and background information about political events. Nonetheless, the profession continues to take a dim view of specialization. For example, in response to a Justice Department suggestion that the television networks use correspondents with special knowledge of ghetto problems to cover riots, an NBC news executive said: "Any good journalist should be able to cover a riot in an unfamiliar setting. . . . A veneer of knowledgeability in a situation like this could be less than useless."[79]

Underlying the information-diluting effects of generalism is the general editorial opinion that the news must be simple enough to be understood by the average (and not very intelligent) citizen. The generalist, according to most editors and producers, is more likely to hit the level of the average news consumer and not complicate stories with technical detail. This image of the news audience is further reinforced by the "star system," which the generalism norm has helped perpetuate in the news business. Newspapers and (especially) television tend to pipe their major news through a small number of familiar names and faces with whom their audiences come to identify. These "stars" are shuffled from one story to another in order to endow the stories with the by-lines of big-name reporters. It is generally felt—particularly in broadcast journalism—that the familiarity of a star reporter may be as important to the news consumer as the information contained in the story.[80] As this discussion suggests, the professional standards that affect the flow of public information overlap with the earlier-mentioned organizational practices involved in the construction of news.

CONCLUSION

The columnist Russell Baker once wrote a biting parody of the incoherence of a typical newscast. The following is a fragment of Baker's "All-Purpose Newscast for a Dull Season":

> Meanwhile, in Washington, the Carter Administration was reported today as firemen still sifted through the ruins of a six alarm blaze in Brooklyn that left two Congressmen, who were said to have accepted cash contributions from Korean agents, despite their fifth defeat in a row at the hands of the Boston Celtics. . . .
> Seventeen were dead and scores injured by the testimony that two Senators, whom he declined to name, rioted in the streets of Cairo following her son's expulsion from school for shooting a teacher who had referred to him in the easy-going style of the Carter White House, as exemplified by the dispute over the B-1 bomber.[81]

Baker's humor is sobered considerably by a study showing that over 50 percent of the viewers could not recall a single story only a few minutes after a television newscast was off the air.[82] If we return to the debate in Chapters 2 and 3 about the structure of mass belief systems, these findings make it tempting to wonder whether possible states of unstable opinion and low information reflect properties of individuals or properties of the information they encounter. Factors such as the absence of investigative reporting, the use of self-contained story formats, and the political selection of information often leave stories without clear connections to past or future events. This makes it difficult to trace the development of an issue, and it turns shifts in policy and issue definition into mysteries that the public must puzzle over. Thus it should not be surprising when opinion constraint does not run high in the mass public.

Whether the subject is the structure of information or the content of the news, the standard response of media executives to criticism, of course, is that the media are simple transmitters of objective information. One version of this refrain is stated in this way:

> Most of the resources of newspapers and news staffs of television and radio stations are devoted to information transmittal, not persuasion. The reporter covering the city council meeting may help his or her readers form certain opinions as the result of the information placed in the news story, but the purpose of the story is to provide the information. The sports desk editor who sets aside space for baseball standings cares little what evaluations the reader makes of the teams, or the sport itself, based on the statistics. . . . Providing the audience members with information, as any introductory reporting text will say, is the primary function of the modern journalistic profession.[83]

In a strict sense this perspective is quite true. However, it should be obvious by now that the press can avoid conscious efforts to persuade its audience and still play a political role.

Even if the media are mere transmitters of information, the information they transmit is often politically "loaded." The impact of such information can be all-the-more significant if it is delivered in a context of objectivity. Moreover, the issue of "intent to persuade" does not exhaust the possible ways in which the media can play an active role in structuring and symbolizing information. Each step in the construction of news by the media can affect how the public sees an issue. Thus it matters little whether the media set out consciously to persuade their audiences. The unintended effects can be just as serious.

The important point here is that the way in which "objectivity" is used to characterize reporting practices does not, in the words of one team of observers, mean that "the media reflect the world around them":[84]

> media coverage of such crucial stories of the 1960s as the Vietnam War, crime, and urban disorders did not relate well to objective criteria indexing development of these stories. News coverage of the war peaked two years before the number of American troops in Southeast Asia. Similarly, coverage of urban disorders peaked in 1967, while the actual number of disturbances was highest a year later. And crime coverage failed to increase while the number of

crimes committed per capita did. The media seem not to mirror perfectly the events of the day.[85]

As mentioned earlier, the concept of objectivity can be used to make the news concrete for journalists and credible for the public. However, the processes through which political information is constructed and reported make the notion of objectivity irrelevant. The factors that affect the flow of political information may not systematically introduce an ideological bias into the news, but they do produce important political effects. The political impact of the media may vary from time to time and from issue to issue; but on any given issue, the media can become a key factor in shaping the political perceptions, opinions, and actions of the public.

NOTES

1. See, for example, B. C. Cohen, *The Press, the Public, and Foreign Policy* (Princeton, N.J.: Princeton University Press, 1963); Maxwell E. McCombs and Donald L. Shaw, "The Agenda-setting Function of the Media," *Public Opinion Quarterly*, Vol. 36 (Summer 1972), pp. 176–87; Jack M. McLeod, Lee B. Becker, and J. E. Byrnes, "Another Look at the Agenda-setting Function of the Press," *Communication Research*, Vol. 1 (April 1974), pp. 131–66; G. R. Funkhouser, "The Issues of the Sixties: An Exploratory Study in the Dynamics of Public Opinion," *Public Opinion Quarterly*, Vol. 37 (Spring 1973), pp. 62–75; and W. T. Gormley, "Newspaper Agendas and Political Elites," *Journalism Quarterly*, Vol. 52 (Summer 1975), pp. 304–08.
2. Alex S. Edelstein, *The Uses of Communication in Decision-making* (New York: Praeger, 1974).
3. See Lee B. Becker, Maxwell E. McCombs, and Jack M. McLeod, "The Development of Political Cognitions," in *Political Communication: Issues and Strategies for Research*, ed. Steven H. Chaffee (Beverly Hills, Calif.: Sage, 1975, pp. 49–51.
4. David Weaver, Maxwell E. McCombs, and Charles Spellman, "Watergate and the Media: A Case Study of Agenda-setting," *American Politics Quarterly*, Vol. 3 (October 1975), pp. 458–72.
5. See Leonard P. Tipton, Roger D. Haney, and John R. Baseheart, "Media Agenda Setting in City and State Campaigns," *Journalism Quarterly*, Vol. 52 (Spring 1975), pp. 15–22; and Robert D. McClure and Thomas E. Patterson, *The Unseeing Eye* (New York: Putnam, 1976).
6. See Gaye Tuchman, *The TV Establishment: Programming for Power and Profit* (Englewood Cliffs, N.J.: Prentice-Hall, 1974), pp. 1–39.
7. See, among others, Harold L. Wilensky, "Mass Society and Mass Culture: Interdependence or Independence?" *American Sociological Review*, Vol. 29 (April 1964), pp. 173–96; and George Gerbner and Nancy Signorielli, "The World of Television News," in *Television Network News*, eds. William Adams and Fay Schreibman (Washington,

D.C.: George Washington University, School of Public and International Affairs, 1978), pp. 189–96.

8. Edward Jay Epstein, *News from Nowhere: Television and the News* (New York: Vintage Books, 1973), pp. 141–43; Timothy Crouse, *The Boys on the Bus* (New York: Ballantine Books, 1973); Walter Gieber, "Across the Desk: A Study of 16 Telegraph Editors," *Journalism Quarterly*, Vol. 33 (Fall 1956), pp. 423–32.

9. See Tuchman, *The TV Establishment*; David L. Sallach, "Class Domination and Ideological Hegemony," *The Sociological Quarterly*, Vol. 15 (Winter 1974), pp. 38–50; and Muriel G. Cantor, *The Hollywood TV Producer* (New York: Basic Books, 1971).

10. The argument that television programming or newspaper news formats reflect popular tastes is based on an ecological fallacy. The values promoted in mass media programming reflect a strategy of minimizing the defection of subgroups in the viewing population. However, the sum of values across all such subgroups does not necessarily have to "add up to" or "average out at" the value positions established in popular programming.

11. See Joseph Klapper, *The Effects of Mass Communication* (New York: Free Press, 1960); and Gerbner and Signorielli, "The World of Television News."

12. Warren Breed, "Mass Communication and Socio-Cultural Integration," *Social Forces*, Vol. 37 (December 1958), p. 109. This idea is quoted and discussed in Alex S. Edelstein, *Perspectives in Mass Communication* (Copenhagen: Einar Harcks Forlag, 1966), pp. 59–61.

13. Harry J. Skornia, *Television and the News* (Palo Alto, Calif.: Pacific Books, 1968).

14. Morris Janowitz, *The Professional Soldier* (New York: Free Press, 1960), p. 402.

15. Michael Lipsky and David J. Olson, "The Processing of Racial Crisis in America," *Politics and Society*, Vol. 6, No. 1 (1976), p. 90.

16. Epstein, *News from Nowhere*, p. 23.

17. Ibid., p. 24.

18. Ibid., pp. 23–24.

19. Richard Salant, quoted in David L. Altheide, *Creating Reality: How TV News Distorts Events* (Beverly Hills, Calif.: Sage, 1976), p. 17.

20. Gaye Tuchman, "Objectivity as a Strategic Ritual: An Examination of Newsmen's Notions of Objectivity," *American Journal of Sociology*, Vol. 77 (January 1972), p. 660.

21. Harvey Molotch and Marilyn Lester, "Accidents, Scandals, and Routines: Resources for Insurgent Methodology," in Tuchman, *The TV Establishment*, p. 53.

22. Quoted in Richard J. Barnet, *Roots of War* (Baltimore: Penguin Books, 1972), pp. 268–69.

23. Ibid., p. 269.

24. Ibid., p. 290.

25. For the implications of this leak for the cases of the defendants, see *New York Times*, April 28, 1977, p. 14.

26. Edward J. Epstein, "The Grand Cover-Up," *Wall Street Journal*, April 19, 1976, p. 10.

27. Ibid., p. 10.
28. See, among others, Erik Barnouw, *The Sponsor: Notes on a Modern Potentate* (New York: Oxford University Press, 1978); Les Brown, *Television: The Business Behind the Box* (New York: Harcourt Brace Jovanovich, 1971); and Richard Bunce, *Television in the Corporate Interest* (New York: Praeger, 1976).
29. See Fred Friendly, *Due to Circumstances Beyond Our Control* (New York: Random House, 1967), pp. 69–80.
30. See Gary Wills, *Nixon Agonistes* (Boston: Houghton Mifflin, 1970).
31. See *Survey of Broadcast Journalism: 1969–1970*, ed. Marvin Barrett (New York: Thomas Y. Crowell, 1971).
32. See *Survey of Broadcast Journalism: 1970–1971*, ed. Marvin Barrett (New York: Grosset and Dunlap, 1971).
33. See *The Politics of Broadcasting*, ed. Marvin Barrett (New York: Thomas Y. Crowell, 1973).
34. Quoted ibid., p. 61.
35. See ibid., p. 62.
36. Quoted ibid., p. 62.
37. See Henry Beck, "Attentional Struggles and Silencing Strategies in a Human Political Conflict: The Case of the Vietnam Moratoria," in *The Structure of Social Attention: Ethological Studies*, eds. M. R. A. Chance and R. R. Larson (New York: Wiley, 1976).
38. For an application of these principles to the coverage of political campaigns, see F. Christopher Arterton, "The Media Politics of Presidential Campaigns: A Study of the Carter Nomination Drive," in *Race for the Presidency: The Media and the Nominating Process*, ed. James David Barber (Englewood Cliffs, N.J.: Prentice-Hall, 1978), pp. 25–54.
39. See Crouse, *The Boys on the Bus*, p. 177.
40. Ibid., pp. 179–80.
41. Thomas E. Patterson and Robert D. McClure, *The Unseeing Eye: The Myth of Television Power in National Elections* (New York: Putnam, 1976), p. 87.
42. See Barnet, *Roots of War*, p. 297.
43. Reported in Leon V. Sigal, *Reporters and Officials: The Organization and Politics of Newsmaking* (Lexington, Mass.: Heath, 1973), p. 47.
44. Ibid., p. 47.
45. Quoted in *The Politics of Broadcasting*, ed. Barrett, p. 45. Moyers pursued his Orwellian vision of politician-press relations to the bitter end with this picture of symbiosis: "Reporters will be there to report dutifully what isn't officially said by a source that can't be held officially accountable at an event that doesn't officially happen for a public that can't officially be told because it can't officially be trusted to know."
46. Quoted in *The Politics of Broadcasting*, ed. Barrett, p. 47.
47. For more-detailed discussions of these news-gathering routines, see Epstein, *News from Nowhere*; Crouse, *The Boys on the Bus*; Sigal, *Reporters and Officials*; and Altheide, *Creating Reality*.
48. Epstein, *News from Nowhere*.
49. McClure and Patterson, *The Unseeing Eye*.
50. Reported in *The Politics of Broadcasting*, ed. Marvin Barrett, p. 35.
51. Ibid., p. 35.

52. Reported ibid., pp. 35–36.
53. Warren Breed, "Social Control in the News Room: A Functional Analysis," in *Conformity, Resistance, and Self-Determination: The Individual and Authority,* ed. Richard Flacks (Boston: Little, Brown, 1973), pp. 153–60.
54. Ibid., p. 155.
55. Quoted in Crouse, *The Boys on the Bus*, pp. 9–10.
56. Epstein, *News from Nowhere*, pp. 141–43.
57. Ibid., p. 141.
58. See Gieber "Across the Desk"; D. Gold and J. L. Simmons, "News Selection Patterns Among Iowa Dailies," *Public Opinion Quarterly,* Vol. 29 (Fall 1965), pp. 425–30; and Becker, McCombs, and McLeod, "The Development of Political Cognitions," pp. 39–41.
59. Sigal, *Reporters and Officials*, p. 22.
60. Cohen, *The Press, the Public and Foreign Policy.*
61. Crouse, *The Boys on the Bus.*
62. See Sigal, *Reporters and Officials*, pp. 66, 67, 11.
63. See Crouse, *The Boys on the Bus*, chs. 1 and 2.
64. Epstein, *News from Nowhere*, pp. 141–43.
65. Cirino, *Power to Persuade*, (N.Y.: Bantam, 1974) pp. 32–37.
66. Reported in the *New York Times*, March 23, 1977, p. A11.
67. This paper was the Madison, Wisconsin, *Capital Times*. See Priscilla S. Meyer, "Hello, Rolling Stone? What Did Butz Say?" in *Wall Street Journal*, October 7, 1976, p. 18.
68. Ibid., p. 18.
69. Ibid., p. 18.
70. Ibid., p. 18.
71. Ibid., p. 18.
72. Ibid., p. 18.
73. Carl Bernstein and Bob Woodward, *All the President's Men* (New York: Warner Communications, 1974).
74. Sigal, *Reporters and Officials*, p. 121.
75. In a study reported ibid., Sigal found that nearly 80 percent of the information in news stories came from government officials. See ibid., p. 124.
76. See Joe McGinniss, *The Selling of the President: 1968* (New York: Pocket Books, 1969).
77. See Crouse, *The Boys on the Bus*, pp. 198–200.
78. See Epstein, *News from Nowhere*, p. 136.
79. Quoted ibid., p. 137.
80. For example, Epstein's analysis shows that the "top ten" correspondents handle anywhere from 50 to 70 percent of the news stories at the major television networks. Ibid., p. 138.
81. Russell Baker, "Meanwhile, in Zanzibar . . . ," *New York Times Magazine*, February 6, 1977, p. 12.
82. See *The Politics of Broadcasting*, ed. Marvin Barrett, p. 7.
83. Becker, McCombs, and McLeod, "The Development of Political Cognitions," pp. 22–23.
84. Ibid., p. 41.
85. Ibid.

PART FOUR

The Domain of Political Institutions and Culture

Opinion and Political
Institutions:
The Policy Connection

AFTER ISSUES PASS through the formation stage and take their places on the agendas of political institutions, public opinion becomes involved in two other political relationships. The most obvious connection between opinion and political institutions is the impact of opinion on policy. For example, pressure from constituents can affect the way members of Congress vote on legislation. Public protests or low levels of approval in the opinion polls may alter the way the President handles a sensitive issue. Broad shifts in social values or in the public mood may be recorded in subtle ways in the decisions of the courts. These opinion-policy linkages are not constant. They vary, as a situational perspective would suggest, with changing political conditions and shifts in public concerns.

It is also important to recognize that opinion can be shaped by the ways in which institutions process policy questions. Institutions such as the Congress, the presidency, and the courts symbolize the core beliefs and values of the American political system. The symbols of law, authority, party opposition, national security, rights, liberties, free enterprise, social welfare, and the public interest create the boundaries of official concern around policy problems. They cast issues in simple, familiar, and reassuring terms, bringing to complex problems a comforting simplicity. New circumstances bend to the pressure of old formulations. The symbolic aspects of policy making become means of reeducating the public about primary social values, and they establish the limits of legitimate debate. As a result, the same processes that produce policy also serve to reinforce social values and limit political conflict.

The two-way relationship between opinion and institutions will be broken down to explore opinion-policy linkage in this chapter and the culture-opinion connection in Chapter 13.

OPINION AND THE POLICIES OF GOVERNMENT

Even though public opinion may play major roles in political integration and issue formation, many analysts think that the most important measure of opinion is its connection to government policy. One of the most active areas of research has been the question of whether public opinion affects the political output of institutions. The general question can be stated simply: After an issue has moved from the broad systemic agenda onto the policy agenda of a specific institution, how can public opinion affect the outcome of the issue? Because the formal links between policy making and the public differ from one institution to another, the means of answering this question also vary from institution to institution. Moreover, within any institution or policy process, the situational perspective cautions us to look for conditions that strengthen or weaken the role of public opinion.

The Courts

It may seem out of place to talk about the impact of public opinion on decisions made by the courts. There is, after all, no formal mechanism through which popular sentiment can reach the judges who deliberate on legal issues. This is in keeping with the fundamental American belief that the law is a force above social whim and broader than any single case. As every schoolchild knows, the American political system is "a government of laws, not men."

The myth of the independence of law and public opinion combines with the absence of obvious linkages between opinion and the courts to make the impact of opinion on judicial policy difficult to assess. However, it is clear that public opinion does become a factor in the way in which some questions of law are decided. A number of well-established theories of jurisprudence even argue that judges must take social values and the public mood into account when making their decisions on cases.[1] Part of this argument rests on the idea that because the law is an instrument of social change and social order, it cannot work effectively without some basis in social values. In addition, it can be argued that the popular acceptance of legal rulings depends on whether people can understand them and see their relevance. Acceptability requires some use of public opinion as a guide in both judicial reasoning and in the presentation of decisions. Finally, judges are also members of society, holding values and beliefs just like the rest of us; they are aware of public concerns and may be sensitive to the pressure of public opinion.

These factors suggest that public opinion enters the process of legal judgment in some cases; it is clear, however, that the impact of opinion by no means affects all legal decisions at all times. This variability calls for a situational analysis of legal decisions: A number of factors must be taken into account in order to explain when the application of the law is likely to be guided by public opinion. For example, judicial biographies and autobiographies tell us that certain judges subscribe more than others to "sociological" theories of jurisprudence. In addition, certain judges may "overrepresent" particular values or beliefs in their attitudes about the law. Some legal issues may serve more as lightening rods for social concern and public pressure than do others. Some historical periods may involve the courts more centrally in volatile social problems and the process of social change. Finally, the level at which an issue is decided in the legal system may provide different channels for public input. Each factor can be explored in an analysis of the role of public opinion in any particular legal decision.

Some of these factors are associated more often with some legal questions than with others, and it is possible to point to some general patterns in the "social conscience" of the courts. For example, in the areas of civil rights and civil liberties the decisions of the courts have often reflected social values. It is not uncommon for popular social arguments to be incorporated along with legal precedent in the presentation of decisions. This was true in the landmark civil rights case of *Plessy* v. *Ferguson* at the turn of the century. In this case the Supreme Court denied a black man's claim to the right to use "whites only" public facilities by arguing that social equality could not be legislated. The decision stated that although political equality was guaranteed by the Constitution, social equality was another matter; social equality could be achieved only when social groups treated each other as equals. As a result of separating social and political equality, the Court ruled that blacks had no *social* right to ride with whites on trains. The notion expressed in this decision—that true equality was a social and not a legal matter—was consistent with many popular social doctrines of the day.

The next major civil rights case decided by the Court also reflected a strong element of public opinion. In the 1954 case of *Brown* v. *The Board of Education (Topeka, Kansas)*, the "separate but equal" ruling of the *Plessy* case was overturned. The Court argued that racial segregation was not a passive reflection of social inequality, but an active cause of it. This reversal of legal principle corresponded to a reversal of public opinion on racial matters. Polls in 1940 showed that only 40 percent of white northerners (and a much smaller percentage of white southerners) favored racial integration. However, by 1956 the idea of racial integration was endorsed by a strong majority of 60 percent of northern whites.[2]

In the absence of formal linkages between the public and the courts, it may be impossible to pin down the general patterns in the impact of opinion on legal policy. Indeed, there may be disputes even about the impact of opinion in separate cases. For example, Casper argues that the 1954 ruling of the Court in the *Brown* case was much more a forward-looking move than a response to existing social sentiment.[3] It is true that the coalition of public support for racial equality in the 1950s was a fragile one. However, it is also clear that the Supreme Court's decision followed sharp increases in public support for the idea. Perhaps the best resolution for the problem of causalty is to regard the law during periods of social change both as a response to noticeable shifts in public values and as a mechanism for expanding the emerging value consensus.

Congress

The impact of opinion on legislation in Congress is a bit easier to sort out. The linkages between the public and Congress through the electoral process and direct communication are more clear-cut than are the channels of public input in the legal system. More importantly, it is possible to determine who the constituents of a member of Congress are. (At least it is possible to determine the members of the voting constituency.) Once the population of constituents has been identified, it is possible to sample their opinions on various issues and compare them to their representatives' votes on corresponding legislation.

Two pioneering studies found an interesting connection between opinion and the behavior of members of Congress.[4] Elected representatives tend to vote according to the preferences of their constituents on some issues and to ignore completely their constituents' feelings on other issues. The factor that seems to determine whether public opinion counts in the legislative process is the salience of the issue. Issues that arouse intense public concern tend to be handled on the legislative agenda with an eye to the wishes of the people. For example, civil rights issues were among the hottest public concerns at the time the linkage studies were done, and it was found that civil rights legislation yielded the highest correlation between constituents' opinions and representatives' votes. In fact, members of Congress were more likely to register the will of the people on these issues than to vote according to their own consciences. In the case of less salient issues, such as foreign aid, members of Congress did not follow public opinion in their voting. In fact, they tended to have poor or inaccurate perceptions of what their constituents even wanted in these areas.

The best explanation for this pattern has been provided by Mayhew's study of congressional behavior.[5] He argued persuasively that the thing that best explains how representatives vote on legislation is the perceived impact of their votes on future electoral support. Representatives seldom vote against the will of their constituents on salient issues because people are more likely to follow these issues through Congress and remember at election time the performance of their representatives. Moreover, opponents of incumbent representatives are likely to make effective campaign issues out of legislative voting records that deviate from popular sentiment on major issues. Issues that are not major concerns for the electorate do not present such a compelling reason for following the dictates of public opinion.

This explanation of opinion-policy linkages in Congress shatters the democratic ideal that representatives ought to be bound by the will of the people. In place of the ideal we receive a picture of representatives who act to maximize their self-interest. They may on occasion behave in ways that seem consistent with the democratic ideal, but this behavior may be inspired by the wrong motives. Perhaps the most important feature of this analysis is that it removes the onus for the failure of democratic representation from the public and places a share of the responsibility on elected representatives. In place of the argument that public opinion on some issues is not coherent enough to be interpreted, we have the intriguing possibility that some issues do not provide elected officials with enough incentive to find out what the public wants.

The Presidency

When thinking about public opinion and the presidency, it is easy to focus only on elections. However, it is important to recognize that most of what a President does takes place in between elections, when the vote is not available as a means of expressing opinion. Also, since the vote cannot really bind a President to campaign promises, it is necessary to consider the existence of other connections between opinion and the behavior of the chief executive.

The concerns of Presidents about pubic opinion are well known. Lyndon Johnson is reported to have carried the latest public opinion polls around in his pockets wherever he went. When the tide of opinion was running in his favor, he would cite it as justification for his actions. When he fell in disfavor with the public, he would lament the fact that he was maligned by the press and misunderstood by the people.[6] Richard Nixon was concerned that the pollsters were wording their questions in ways that cost him precious points in the popularity column. He registered this complaint with a major pollster, and one observer has claimed that the question formats were changed and Nixon's level of popular support increased as a result.[7] Jimmy Carter and his advisers often expressed their interest in the use of symbols to mobilize public support. Although their openness about this may have cost Carter some degree of public approval, the continued use of blatant symbolic appeals prompted one political cartoonist to add an "Office of Symbolism" to the President's cabinet.

Presidents are sensitive to public opinion for several reasons. The most obvious is that public opinion is probably a President's greatest political resource. It has been said that most of the executive's political power depends on the "power to persuade."[8] Public opinion is a very persuasive force. It is becoming clear that modern chief executives must convince Congress that the people support their legislative programs. President Carter's failure to get Congress to act on his 1977 energy package is strong evidence of the importance of public opinion to presidential effectiveness. In addition, the ability of the President to mobilize his own party behind his programs also depends on his level of popular support. Even loyal party members may avoid the electoral costs of being associated with the programs of an unpopular President.

The need for public support applies to the President's actions in the world arena also. Other nations may be unwilling to negotiate with Presidents who appear doomed at the next election or who may not be able to get Congress to approve of their actions. It often has been rumored that other nations have struck hard bargains with Presidents whose opinion levels could not stand another failure of leadership. Being at odds with the public may force a President to accept less favorable terms simply to bring home a treaty.

In addition to these direct policy-related areas in which opinion matters to Presidents, it is also important to bear in mind that the President is the symbolic leader of the country. The President is the nation's most visible political figure. He acts in the name of all the people. He embodies public concerns and hopes for the future.[9] When support for the President declines, an important measure of national discontent has been registered.

The decade of the 1970s was a period of intense public questioning of national institutions, and no institution suffered more public criticism than the presidency. One of the low points of public support for a President and his office came in 1974 following Richard Nixon's resignation and Gerald Ford's pardon of the disgraced President. A poll was conducted in which the public was asked to rate the performance of fifteen American institutions. The institutions on the list included the military, colleges and universities, churches, the news media, labor unions, the courts, and Congress. By a wide margin, the President and his administration were ranked right at the bottom of the list.[10] If there is any doubt that such a lack of public support affects what Presidents do, even a casual reading of the newspapers of that period shows that the administration regarded the loss of public confidence as its major political problem and devoted a large part of its energy to winning public favor. It is also no accident that Jimmy Carter's central campaign issue in 1976 was the loss of public faith in government.

In addition to long-term trends in popular support for the presidency, short-term cycles of opinion occur within the reign of every President. The capacity to survive and alter these cycles is an important mark of leadership ability in a President. All new Presidents enter office on a crest of public support and approval. Critics lower their voices, and voters who supported losing candidates usually support the new leader in a gesture of good faith. However, the so-called honeymoon period does not last long. Normally within six months after taking office the popularity of a new President goes into a decline.

In some cases, the decline levels off when the "overreactions" of well-wishers stabilize into normal levels of party opposition and ideological division. In other cases, the decline in support seems to haunt a President throughout his term in office. For example, both Truman and Johnson entered office with overwhelming levels of public approval; yet because of steep declines in popularity, both men eventually decided against running for reelection. The reasons for falling into public disfavor can vary. Richard Nixon emerged from his 1972 election victory with a strong approval rating only to see his popularity plummet into the "low twenties" in less than two years because of a succession of damaging Watergate disclosures. Jimmy Carter also watched strong public support following his 1976 election slip to dangerously low levels on the heels of failures in several major policy areas.

It is important to account for these cycles of opinion because they can have such telling effects on the President's leadership ability. In light of the complexity of the office and the role of the President as a condensational symbol, there may be little that any office holder can do to win sustained public support. In fact, one opinion analyst has concluded that the cycles of presidential popularity have operated independently of any particular incumbent or anything that he might have done.[11] According to this analysis, opinion cycles may be a response to opinion dynamics in between elections or a response to the popular use of the office as a symbolic outlet for private concerns and frustrations. Indeed, this analysis fits with the common understanding that the President is "damned if he does and damned if he doesn't"—that is, any action a President takes may cost him supporters, yet the failure to take action may generate the public perception that he is ineffective.

Contrary to this common understanding about the office is evidence suggesting that the President is more damned if he fails to act than if he takes action. One analyst has gone so far as to claim that it is better for a President to act ineptly than to fail to act at all.[12] In support of this argument, poll data show that John Kennedy's popularity rose nearly as much following his dismal handling of the Bay of Pigs invasion as after his successful management of the Cuban missile crisis. It is also instructive to note that Gerald Ford's most popular days in office following his honeymoon period came after his decision to send in the marines to rescue the crew of the *Mayazguez*, the American ship captured by Cambodian troops in 1975. Despite considerable evidence that the action was ill conceived and poorly executed, the public gave Ford high marks on his decisiveness and his defense of American honor.

As these examples suggest, the responsiveness of the public to bold and decisive political action seems to have little basis in rational calculations about the effectiveness of the action. Public support may stem from much deeper psychological concerns. In a complex world of seemingly uncontrollable political forces, decisive actions by leaders may reassure people that their lives are not entirely at the mercy of "accident, ignorance, and unplanned processes."[13]

Until recently, whether the public engaged in any rational calculations when supporting the President was an open question. It was simply not clear whether a President's day-to-day routine performance on policy matters affected the judgment of the public about him. However, more sophisticated measures of political output and public response show that the public does react in predictable ways to some routine policy areas over which the President has some control.

Monroe has discovered that changes in economic variables such as inflation and military spending affect levels of presidential support.[14] As one would expect with such complex economic factors, the relationship is not a simple linear one: Levels of support do not fall as soon as new inflation figures are released, nor do they rise with the announcement of new defense contracts. It appears that the negative effects of inflation and the positive effects of government spending take time to filter through society. The maximum impact of an increase in inflation does not come until about six months after the increase has been recorded by the government's official indicators. As this time lag implies, the pattern of support is a wavelike cycle, with little immediate reaction to economic indicators. Support peaks several months after the economic change is first documented and drops off a few months after that. The overall impact of the economy on presidential popularity is, however, quite substantial. Monroe concludes that "an increase of 1 percentage point in the annual rate of inflation which is maintained for one year . . . will result in a decrease in presidential popularity of 3.75 percentage points."[15]

Are Presidents aware of this complicated opinion-policy linkage, and do they respond to it? Presidents can do a number of things to affect the economy, even though the international monetary system, foreign trade dependencies, and the problems of domestic credit are making the economy ever more difficult to manipulate. Traditionally, Presidents have been able to intervene in the economy by changing the money supply, altering the prime lending rate, proposing tax increases or decreases, creating business incentives, implementing wage and price controls, or simply shifting the timing of federal spending.

The economy would be thrown into chaos if the President reacted to every increase or decrease in public support. However, it does appear that Presidents respond to the public when it is in their strongest political interest to do so—at election time. Tufte has compiled a fascinating set of economic data for the period since the Great Depression. He has compared unemployment and inflation figures in presidential election years and nonelection years. A striking trend emerges.[16] A full 50 percent of election years shows reductions in unemployment and inflation, which compares to drops in both indicators in only 9 percent of the nonelection years. The other half of the election years shows an increase in one of the undesirable economic statistics; but this compares to 73 percent of the nonelection years, in which either inflation or unemployment became worse than in the previous year. Perhaps the most impressive feature of Tufte's data is the fact that in no modern election year did both inflation and unemployment worsen. This "double whammy" in the economy occurred in a full 17 percent of the nonelection years, however. It seems that the President delivers the economic goods to his constituents when it matters the most. One wonders what would happen to the economy (and to levels of public satisfaction) if the American election cycle were changed.

In the areas of congressional and presidential behavior it is becoming increasingly clear that the dominant linkage between opinion and political outcomes is the electoral process. Congressional representatives seem to pay attention to public opinion on issues that could come back to haunt them at election time. Presidents seem to engage in efforts to pump up the economy every four years. This may not guarantee them reelection, but it may keep them from losing valuable electoral support. As a result of new research on voting behavior, electoral linkages between policy and public opinion are beginning to take on a systematic explanation.

OPINION AND VOTING BEHAVIOR

Voting research has long been concerned with the question of whether the vote tends to be based on rational calculations or whether it is more a blind expression of patriotism or party loyalty. This question is important for two reasons. First, our theories of democracy are based on the assumption that citizens are rational. Second, opinion cannot act as a binding political force unless individuals deliver predictable rewards and punishments to candidates and parties that act in their interests.

Early voting studies seemed to show that the opinion expressed through the vote was far from being informed or rational. The first voter surveys in the 1940s showed that many voters made up their minds before the campaign began and, therefore, before the candidates and parties had taken clear stands on the issues.[17] In fact, most voters didn't have a clear idea about what the candidates stood for even after the campaign was well under way. People seemed to identify with a political party on the basis of their social and economic position; and once they identified with a party, they voted for candidates from that party regardless of the issues they endorsed. So strong was party identification that many voters tended to think that their candidates agreed with them on the issues even in cases where the voter and the candidate were some distance apart in their positions.[18]

These early conclusions were confirmed and expanded by more sophisticated survey research techniques developed in the 1950s and 1960s. In 1952 the Survey Research Center at the University of Michigan began a series of National Election Studies, which is ongoing. The main concern of these studies has been to explain why people vote and how they make their voting choices. The early evidence seemed pretty conclusive. In study after study people were unaware of the major issues facing the nation, and they were unable to explain the significant ideological differences between the parties. Despite (or perhaps because of) this ignorance, voters held stable attachments to one party or the other and used this party identification as the major basis of voting choice. It was widely accepted that party identification and not issue awareness or ideological judgments provided the best explanation of the vote.[19] The inescapable conclusion seemed to be that, by any reasonable standard, "voters were fools."[20]

The shock wave from this conclusion was intensified by another early blast at the most hallowed of American democratic myths. Using a persuasive application of economic choice theory, Downs showed that it might be irrational for people to vote "rationally."[21] He reasoned that if voters were rational they would seek to maximize the payoff from the voting act. This would involve weighing the benefits of making a careful voting decision against the costs in time and energy. The only instance in which a vote would count, according to Downs' logic, was the case in which a person could be reasonably sure that his or her vote would be the deciding factor in the election. Since this is an extremely unlikely event and since it would be very difficult (that is, costly) to calculate accurate probabilities for it, there is little rational basis for voting in most cases. Moreover, Downs concluded that if voters insisted on voting in the face of the slim chance that their votes would matter, then it didn't make rational sense to spend much time or energy in making an informed choice. In fact, it might make a good deal of sense to use a shorthand method such as party identification as a basis for the voting decision.

By the early 1960s it appeared that long-standing myths about opinion, elections, and democracy were seriously misguided. Not only did most people seem to shirk their duties as citizens, but it could be argued that they had rational grounds for doing so. Although these "revisionist" ideas became accepted for a time as standard knowledge about elections and voting in America, they were based on a flaw, which eventually led to their downfall. They stemmed from the state-of-consciousness fallacy, reflected in the tendencies to overgeneralize from a small number of cases and to attribute too much weight to individual variables at the expense of situational factors.

One of the few theorists who recognized these problems was V. O. Key, Jr. He argued that people will behave as rationally in elections as their interests and the circumstances of the election permit.[22] He advocated that voting research should pay attention to the issues that concerned the voters rather than to the issues that the "experts" thought were important. In this way voting analysis could determine whether the candidates took noticeably different stands on the issues that mattered to the electorate. Only if elections provided voters with clear choices on relevant issues could rational voting behavior be expected. Key's general argument can be summarized by the statement that voters will be as rational as the circumstances warrant and permit. However, Key was widely ignored in the early days of voting research, for his data were not very convincing and the data from the major survey research organizations seemed conclusive.

Eventually, two changes in the National Election Studies tended to confirm Key's view of things and to revise earlier views of voters as simple "interest maximizers" or as out-and-out fools. The first change was in the design of the surveys. In addition to asking voters to discuss the issues that the survey researchers regarded as important, voters were allowed to provide issues that they thought were important. Not surprisingly, when voters talked about their own issues, they tended to be more concerned, more informed, and better able to compare candidates' positions. This prompted one analyst to draw the tentative conclusion that the public has "at least a few substantive issues in mind at the time of an election, and the voters seem to be acting more responsibly than had previously been thought."[23]

The second change in the National Election Studies that moved voting theories further in the direction of Key's argument was more a matter of happenstance than of survey design. Over the years the National Election Studies compiled a large number of cases and, not surprisingly, surveyed a number of different kinds of election. It began to occur to analysts that elections could be different from one another in terms of issue emphasis, candidate divergence on the issues, and the degree of overlap between the interests of voters and the concerns of the candidates.

In a pair of articles analyzing the 1968 election, Brody and Page showed that voters did not discriminate very well between the candidates' positions on the major issue in the contest, the Vietnam War.[24] However, they argued that this probably reflected the simple fact that the positions of the two major party candidates (Richard Nixon and Hubert Humphrey) were so similar on this issue that they could not be distinguished meaningfully. Their conclusion (which may be recalled from the discussion of the state-of-consciousness fallacy in Chapter 2) was: "Our picture of the ignorant voter may be . . . largely a reflection of the choices he is offered."[25] In their theoretical discussion of the bases of voting choice, Brody and Page suggested that when substantive differences are blurred, voters may make their voting choices on other grounds (such as party identification) and then project their own positions on issues onto their chosen candidates as a means of rationalizing the legitimacy or the seriousness of the choice.[26] This argument casts quite a different interpretation on the early studies that found voters often felt their candidates supported their positions even when there seemed to be substantial evidence to the contrary.

These conclusions were carried even further in another analysis of the 1968 election, which showed that the only real pocket of "issue voting" in that contest occurred among supporters of the third-party candidate, George Wallace. Wallace's positions on all the major issues were notably different from the stands taken by the other two candidates, and his supporters responded accordingly.[27] These findings produced an acknowledgment of Key's earlier thesis from some of the analysts whose earlier work seemed to contradict it: "It is obvious, as Key himself recognized, that flat assertions about the electorate being rational or not are of scant value."[28]

The general consensus in contemporary voting research is that public opinion can be a rational force in elections and can reward or punish candidates according to calculations of rational choice and interest.[29] However, for opinion to operate in this way in the electoral context, a number of situational factors must be present. It is increasingly obvious that the rationality of voters depends on the presence of serious concerns and the willingness of candidates to take divergent stands on issues related to those concerns. All this may have been fairly obvious from a situational perspective such as the one adopted by Key. However, the general appeal of the state-of-conciousness fallacy led many analysts to overlook a "conditional" model of voter rationality until an overwhelming array of evidence began to collect in its favor. As discussed in earlier chapters, the danger of this sort of misguided empiricism is that it produces general conclusions from small numbers of studies. Once these conclusions have gained general favor, they are difficult to dislodge. Moreover, they are replaced with more accurate models of opinion only through the slow and haphazard process in which the real world offers up enough different cases to create contradictions in the previously oversimplified conclusions. Despite over thirty years of empirical research on voting, only recently have the leading experts in the field recognized the importance of situational factors. On the basis of this recognition, a number of the central elements of voting and elections have been reformulated.

CHANGING CONCEPTIONS OF
VOTING BEHAVIOR

New conceptions have emerged in the areas of issue voting, voter rationality, party identification, and candidate behavior. The revisions in each suggest that public opinion can take on a variety of characteristics and play a number of political roles in elections, depending on the mix of issues, voter calculations, party loyalties, and candidate strategies at work in a particular electoral context. It is now clear that people tend to vote on the issues when meaningful issues are available to be voted on. This finding has led to new conceptions of the rationality of voters. Limited information and the shifting emphasis on issues from one election to another make it virtually impossible for voters to operate as simple "interest maximizers." The best they can do is to employ sensible decision-making routines that make the most of the constraints they have to contend with. Simon called this limited form of rational behavior "satisficing."[30] March has used the term "bounded rationality" to refer to this sort of behavior.[31]

Once it is recognized that voters operate in electoral contexts that can impose a variety of limits on their calculations (and perhaps even on their preferences), it becomes reasonable to expect voters' opinions about candidates and issues in different elections to display different levels of information, constraint, and stability. To expect anything else would be to ignore the changing parameters within which voters must make their decisions.

One of the most interesting implications of this is that things like party identification, once regarded as fixed states of consciousness, are beginning to be understood as shifting decision-making tools that respond to different voting conditions. Fiorina, for example, has argued that party identification is probably not an enduring political affiliation yielding blind allegiance to parties and their candidates.[32] He defined party identification as a "perceptual screen" that filters, compares, and summarizes a wide range of politically relevant information. This idea implies that, within any election, an individual's level of party identification may change from one point in time to another. It also suggests that party identification, far from being the opposite of a rational basis for voting, may in fact be a result of rational calculations.

In light of these radical changes in thinking about party identification, it is a safe bet that the next major development will be the discovery that the characteristics of party identification can change for individuals from one election to another. In elections featuring candidates who differ only slightly on the issues, it is likely that party identification will resemble the traditional conception of an emotional and unchanging commitment to a political party and its candidates. However, in issue-oriented elections, party identification should become a much more rational and constantly changing mechanism for organizing the information on which voting decisions are based.

The idea that party identification may change because of the situational properties of the election resolves much of the mystery about how the early election studies could have produced such a misguided but well-documented picture of voting choice. They sampled only a small slice of the possible situational patterns that can operate in elections. As a result, they discovered in voters only one pattern of behavior. Moreover, since the analysts were not looking for situational differences in elections, they placed the data in an interpretive context that was much too general.

The reformulation of the concept of party identification is likely to be accompanied by changes in thinking about a number of other aspects of voter choice. For example, it was once thought that voter's concerns with the image of a candidate involved a preoccupation with irrelevancies such as looks, style, and personality. In some elections these aspects of image may be the only "information" available to voters. However, recent research reveals that what voters are looking for when they evaluate a candidate's image is much more substantial information—about experience, poise, capacity to handle stress, and leadership potential.[33] Thus it seems that the incorporation of candidate image in the voting choice also involves different types of information under different circumstances.

The conclusion seems to be that whether issue position, party identification, or candidate image forms the basis of the voting choice, the meaning of these factors depends on the kind of information available in the election. In some elections any of these dimensions of judgment can produce well-reasoned and sensible choices. In other contests, voters' best efforts to explore the rational side of issues, candidates, or parties may be a waste of time and effort.

The growing conclusion in voting research is that voters tend to rise to whatever standards of careful decision making the situation will permit. This reformulation of voting behavior is likely to be followed by less emphasis on what individual voters do and more concern with how candidates and parties behave. If voters respond within the constraints set down in the election context, then it becomes important to know more about the nature and causes of those constraints. This broadening of focus may be a major step toward the acceptance of situational approaches to voting and opinion.

There already exist some promising ideas about how candidates behave and how issues are defined. For example, Downs explained that candidates in a two-party system will tend to minimize their differences in order to capture the broadest possible range of the vote.[34] This idea has been formalized by Page, who refers to it as the "theory of political ambiguity."[35] Under most circumstances, so the theory goes, candidates will attempt to make their issue appeals ambiguous in order to eliminate the most direct cause of lost votes.

These preliminary ideas about the behavior of candidates need further clarification and expansion. For example, it is important to explain exceptions to the theory of political ambiguity—such as the issue-oriented campaigns of Barry Goldwater in 1964 and George McGovern in 1972. Are they cases of candidate irrationality? If so, perhaps a conclusion reminiscent of early voting studies is in order: Candidates can be fools too. On the other hand, there may be deeper explanations for issue-oriented campaigns, having to do with voter realignments or party reorganization. These factors would provide a more satisfying theory of elections.

It is also important to draw some of our earlier conclusions about symbolism into a theory of voting behavior. It should be clear from the previous analysis of issue formation that the impact of issues on opinion depends on how the issues are symbolized. The symbolic content of campaign issues will affect the way in which voters can process information about them. An important area of future research lies in this interaction between issue definitions and the decision-making routines of voters.

CONCLUSION

The gradual shift toward situational analysis is evident in research on the courts, the Congress, the presidency, and voting. In these crucial areas it is clear that opinion takes on different characteristics according to the political conditions operating in particular situations. It is also evident that the impact of opinion can vary from one situation to another. In some cases the decisions of the courts reflect public concerns and morals. Members of Congress vote according to the will of their constituents on some types of legislation. Presidents respond to public input on economic matters and try to mobilize popular support for their programs. Elections can be conducted as issue-oriented affairs in which opinion is expressed rationally through the vote. The challenge for the future in each area is to determine more precisely what political conditions result in more sophisticated and more effective expressions of opinion in institutions. An equally challenging task is understanding the importance of opinion in institutional settings even when it may not operate as an obvious causal force in making policy. This is the subject of the next chapter.

NOTES

1. See, for example, Benjamin N. Cardozo, *The Nature of the Judicial Process* (New Haven: Yale University Press, 1949), ch. 3; Roscoe Pound, *An Introduction to the Philosophy of Law* (New Haven: Yale University Press, 1922); and Edwin M. Schur, *Law and Society* (New York: Random House, 1968).
2. See Andrew M. Greeley and Paul B. Sheatsley, "Changing Attitudes of Whites Toward Blacks," *Scientific American*, Vol. 225 (December 1971), pp. 13–19.
3. Jonathan D. Casper, *The Politics of Civil Liberties* (New York: Harper and Row, 1972).
4. See Warren E. Miller and Donald E. Stokes, "Constituency Influence in Congress," *American Political Science Review*, Vol. 57 (March 1963), pp. 45–56; and Charles F. Cnudde and Donald F. McCrone, "The Linkage Between Constituency Attitudes and Congressional Voting Behavior: A Causal Model," *American Political Science Review*, Vol. 60 (March 1966), pp. 66–72.
5. David R. Mayhew, *Congress: The Electoral Connection* (New Haven: Yale University Press, 1974).
6. On LBJ and the polls, see James David Barber, *The Presidential Character* (Englewood Cliffs, N.J.: Prentice-Hall, 1977); and Doris Kearns, *Lyndon Johnson and the American Dream* (New York: Harper and Row, 1976), pp. 309–52.
7. See Michael Wheeler, *Lies, Damn Lies, and Statistics: The Manipulation of Public Opinion in America* (New York: Dell, 1976), pp. 17–29.
8. See Richard Neustadt, *Presidential Power* (New York: Wiley, 1976).
9. For an excellent discussion of the symbolic functions of the presidency, see Michael Novak, *Choosing Our King* (New York: Macmillan, 1974).

10. Reported in the *Institute of Social Research Newsletter* (Winter 1974), p. 8; cited in Stuart Oskamp, *Attitudes and Opinion* (Englewood Cliffs, N.J.: Prentice-Hall, 1977), p. 256.
11. James A. Stimson, "Public Support for American Presidents: A Cyclical Model," *Public Opinion Quarterly*, Vol 40 (Winter 1976), pp. 1–21.
12. John F. Mueller, *War, Presidents, and Public Opinion* (New York: Wiley, 1973).
13. Murray Edelman, *The Symbolic Uses of Politics* (Urbana: University of Illinois Press, 1964), p. 78.
14. Kristen R. Monroe, "Economic Influences on Presidential Popularity," *Public Opinion Quarterly*, Vol. 41 (Fall 1978), pp. 360–69.
15. Ibid., p. 336.
16. The data reported here are from Edward R. Tufte, *Political Control of the Economy* (Princeton, N.J.: Princeton University Press, 1978).
17. See, for example, Bernard R. Berelson, Paul F. Lazarsfeld, and William N. McPhee, *Voting* (Chicago: University of Chicago Press, 1954).
18. See Paul F. Lazarsfeld, Bernard R. Berelson, and Hazel Gaudet, *The People's Choice* (New York: Columbia University Press, 1968).
19. Angus Campbell, Philip E. Converse, Warren E. Miller, and Donald E. Stokes, *The American Voter* (New York: Wiley, 1960).
20. Richard G. Niemi and Herbert F. Weisberg, *Controversies in American Voting Behavior* (San Francisco: Freeman, 1976), p. 164.
21. Anthony Downs, *An Economic Theory of Democracy* (New York: Harper and Row, 1957).
22. V. O. Key, Jr., *The Responsible Electorate* (Cambridge, Mass.: Harvard University Press, 1966).
23. David E. RePass, "Issue Salience and Party Choice," *American Political Science Review*, Vol. 65 (June 1971), pp. 389–400.
24. See Richard A. Brody and Benjamin I. Page, "The Assessment of Policy Voting," *American Political Science Review*, Vol. 66 (June 1972), pp. 450–58; and Benjamin I. Page and Richard A. Brody, "Policy Voting and the Electoral Process: The Vietnam War Issue," *American Political Science Review*, Vol. 66 (September 1972), pp. 979–95.
25. Page and Brody, "Policy Voting and the Electoral Process," p. 995.
26. Brody and Page, "The Assessment of Policy Voting."
27. Philip E. Converse, Warren E. Miller, Jerrold G. Rusk, and Arthur C. Wolfe, "The 'Responsible Electorate' of 1968," *American Political Science Review*, Vol. 63 (December 1969), pp. 1095–1101.
28. Ibid., p. 1095.
29. For other statements on situational factors affecting voter choice, see Arthur H. Miller, Warren E. Miller, Alden S. Raine, and Thad A. Brown, "A Majority Party in Disarray: Policy Polarization in the 1972 Election," *American Political Science Review*, Vol. 70 (September 1976), pp. 753–78; and Norman H. Nie, Sidney Verba, and John R. Petrocik, *The Changing American Voter* (Cambridge, Mass.: Harvard University Press, 1976).
30. Herbert A. Simon, "Rational Choice and the Structure of the Environment," *Psychological Review*, Vol. 63 (March 1956), pp. 129–38.

31. James G. March, "Bounded Rationality, Ambiguity, and the Engineering of Choice," *The Bell Journal of Economics*, Vol. 9 (Autumn 1978), pp. 587–608.
32. Morris P. Fiorina, "An Outline for a Model of Party Choice," *American Journal of Political Science*, Vol. 21 (August 1977), pp. 601–25.
33. Dan Nimmo, *Political Communication and Public Opinion in America* (Santa Monica, Calif.: Goodyear, 1978), p. 380.
34. Downs, *An Economic Theory of Democracy.*
35. Benjamin I. Page, "The Theory of Political Ambiguity," *American Political Science Review*, Vol. 70 (September 1976), pp. 742–52.

13

Political Institutions, Culture, and the Structure of Public Opinion

ONE IMPORTANT STEP in the public opinion process still must be explained: How do competing political demands, the disorganized information in news reports, and the diverse interests of individual members of the public interact with the policy processes of institutions to produce coherent public understandings about most issues? Even though individuals, for various personal reasons, may follow an issue during its formation period, the way an institution presents an issue tends to generate consensus about what political principles are involved and what the alternative solutions are. It is difficult to watch the development of new public issues without experiencing a powerful sense of *déjà vu*. New political situations seem to fall quickly into old symbolic molds.[1] Not only does the public seem content with these recurring patterns of issue definition and debate, but there is no reason to believe that most people find them meaningless or unimportant.

How does the coherence in public understandings emerge from the underlying complexity and chaos of political conflict? In order for issues to be fit so quickly into familiar molds in the absence of precise or formal communication among members of the public, some underlying frame of reference must be organizing public understandings into broad areas of agreement and disagreement. Some of the elements in this frame of reference were introduced in the discussion of the domain of the individual and society in Chapters 5, 6, and 7. For example, the distribution of basic political beliefs and values in society affects the interpretation of issues and the emergence of shared public understandings.

The mere existence of certain beliefs and values, however, does not explain how individuals use them to interpret issues. The linkage between individual political orientations and public opinion on issues is a particularly difficult problem in light of the fact that the United States is widely conceded to be a nonideological polity. Ideologies are formal devices for analyzing issues in terms of particular beliefs and values. In the absence of widely shared ideologies, some other mechanism must exist to explain how beliefs and values become assigned to particular political issues in the opinion formation process.

The framework that best explains the emergence of public understandings about issues in American politics is culture. *Culture* consists of the enduring beliefs, values, and behaviors that organize social communication and make common interpretations of life experience possible. The beliefs, values, and behaviors that make up a culture are organized into widely shared institutional processes and activities that create common social understandings and guide people in responding meaningfuly to new social conditions. The two most important aspects of culture are (1) the fundamental models of society that give practical meaning to values and beliefs and (2) the behavior routines through which these models are applied to everyday experience. The basic models of society are called *myths*, and the behavioral routines through which individuals and institutions use these models to interpret concrete social concerns are called *rituals*.

The procedures that institutions routinely use to resolve policy questions contain rituals that lead the public to apply commonly held myths to practical political problems. The cultural foundation of the policy process tends to limit the solutions to alternatives consistent with traditional values. The cultural basis of institutions also transforms conflict into familiar and manageable terms. Most political conflicts in institutional settings are ritualized in the sense that roles are well established (for example, Republicans versus Democrats), competing positions are anticipated and well understood, and possible outcomes are usually limited to a range of more or less acceptable alternatives. In short, the institutional uses of myth and ritual operate on public opinion to minimize conflict and maximize the popular acceptance of political outcomes.

THE NATURE OF POLITICAL MYTH

Political myths are difficult to analyze because they are such basic elements of our everyday perceptions. They are rather like the lenses in a pair of glasses: They are not the things we see when we look at the world; they are the things we see with. Since myths structure ordinary social perception, we are seldom aware of them at a conscious level. They are the truths about society that we take for granted. Most people possess a rich set of these "self-evident" truths and rely heavily on them to make sense of their lives and the world. These basic cultural principles are woven throughout everyday experience, from conversations at the dinner table, to the morals of soap operas, to the lofty policy debates of Congress.

Myths and Political Socialization

The presence of myth-related symbols throughout everyday life reinforces the belief in basic myths and expands their social applications. In the process, the ever-present symbolism infuses ordinary experience with the enduring themes of political culture. This system of learning and reinforcement has important effects on the thinking of individuals. The universal appeal and pervasive occurrence of cultural perspectives encountered at an early age make them the supreme set of unquestionable truths operating in society. Mythic themes and symbols are learned along with language skills and the child's first awareness of the external world. They become the implicit categories in which thinking about society and politics takes place.

The pervasiveness of myths as a result of their role in socialization helps explain why the range of policy debate in America is so fixed, why the alternatives so predictable, and why the outcomes are so tolerable. Even citizens who oppose a particular policy can tolerate it by virtue of their myth-induced understandings of its principles. As Weissberg has observed, this broad socialization pattern in American politics makes it likely that in most public policy debates

virtually all the alternatives usually considered will be at least *tolerable* though not necessarily preferred by the vast majority. Thus, although the precise preferences of 50 percent plus one may not be satisfied by the policy outcome, the losers would not regard the results as completely unacceptable. Put another way, the underlying broad consensus on the range of permissible choices probably guarantees that almost everyone will get no lower than, say, their third or fourth choices (as opposed to, say, their twenty-fifth choice).[2]

In this fashion, policy making reinforces the themes of myths, and the myths selected out of specific policy cycles shape the political preoccupations of society. The presence of certain dominant themes, in turn, makes people sensitive to the official pronouncements of government. Even when people disagree with the outcomes, they almost always find them tolerable and legitimate.

Categories of Political Myth

The universal political concerns of authority, security, order, and community make some general categories of myth common in most societies. Members of most societies learn about the exploits of great heroes and leaders.[3] They also hear about the great fools and failures that illustrate weakness in leadership and authority.[4] Concerns about security are embodied in myths about internal and external enemies that threaten the status quo. These myths are designed to keep individuals vigilant and to point out political threats in their various forms.[5] Myths about law and order maintain social expectations about justice and provide models for the behavior of individuals who feel they have been wronged.[6] Myths concerning desirable social values and group relations are important guides for maintaining community and working out competing demands.[7]

Although certain broad political categories may be universal, the themes of myths differ from society to society. The values, beliefs, and symbols used to represent political understandings must fit the unique history, economy, social structure, and religious traditions of a particular society. Thus, American myths about authority emphasize reluctant leaders who come from ordinary stock and earn the respect of the people by conquering adversity through raw stamina and common sense. The model of the American hero differs from the Persian image of distant but watchful religious elites who can be counted on to bring divine guidance to politics during times of turmoil in Iran.[8] American myths of community emphasize the virtues of individual freedom tempered with equal rights and opportunities.[9] This is nearly the opposite of the Kung Bushmen's notion that community depends on the subordination of the individual to the equal interests of all.[10] Most American legends of justice emphasize the triumph of impersonal legal codes and fair procedures that allow the law to be applied uniformly to all cases. Perhaps the central theme of American myths of justice is that "no person is above the law." This stands in sharp contrast to the Zapotec ideal of justice, in which legal codes and procedures are tailored to each case so that the outcome will promote harmony in the community.[11]

A Sampling of American Myths

The basic themes in American political myths are passed down from one generation to another in the form of legends, folk tales, songs, movies, television series, and the lessons in history books. As individuals grow up, they encounter hundreds of myths, which gradually slip into their subconscious thinking, carrying important social and political understandings along with them. For example, young children hear and read folk tales that recount the exploits of great American heroes like George Washington, Daniel Boone, Davy Crockett, Andrew Jackson, Abraham Lincoln, Susan B. Anthony, Charles Lindbergh, John Kennedy, Martin Luther King, Jr., and Muhammad Ali. Whether these heroes are black or white, rich or poor, elected leaders or simple citizens, their exploits illustrate similar virtues for the respective groups who perpetuate their myths. Through these cultural models people first encounter the ideals of honesty, industry, bravery, perseverance, and individualism. The range of myths available to make essentially the same points makes it possible for political values and beliefs to be transmitted in forms that make sense to different social groups.

Another set of important political lessons is learned through myths about the pilgrimages of different groups to America. Whether the myths pertain to the experiences of seventeenth-century Puritans or twentieth-century Italian immigrants, the lessons are essentially the same: American stock consists of brave individuals who resisted oppression in their homeland and set out for a new, promised land in which they endured great hardships in order to live in peace and freedom and make a better life for future generations. Prior to the American Revolution, this myth helped crystallize public opinion.[12] A version of the same myth sparked the demonstrations and patriotic displays of ethnic groups and "hard-hats" during the Vietnam War.[13] In the 1970s, a variation of this myth even shaped public understandings about the black experience in America. That version of the American-heritage myth was represented best by the popular book and television series called *Roots*. Even though in the story blacks' struggle against oppression occurred within America, the familiar American qualities of courage and perseverance were displayed by the protagonists, and the group emerged triumphant.

Other myths illustrate the values of free enterprise, competition, and self-reliance. For example, from the first years in school, students learn about the origins of America's industrial might. The story is told through the lives of the men whose genius, hard work, and belief in free enterprise made them successful and made America great. Every American history book recounts the exploits of Eli Whitney, Andrew Carnegie, Henry Ford, John D. Rockefeller, and others who have come to epitomize the complex values on which American economy and society rest. Their stories illustrate the virtues of inventiveness, drive, competitiveness, and private enterprise. These men (and it is significant that most American cultural heroes are men) also exhibited the traits of public concern, generosity, and philanthropy, which constitute the other side of every great American success story.

These and other myths are usually encountered first in the form of stories with characters, plots, conflicts, and climaxes. However, as the lessons from these stories filter into our unconscious thinking, the stories themselves become more diffuse. The dominant themes in myths may be set apart and reinforced by practical life experiences. For example, history-book lessons about individual effort and competition are reinforced through the everyday classroom experiences of schoolchildren who are impressed with the fact (whether true or not) that they have an equal chance to compete and excel with everyone else. Daily experiences in school become lessons about the rewards of hard work and ingenuity. Winners are identified in the classroom as surely as they are recorded in the pages of history. The losers are left to draw the bitter conclusion that their lesser fortunes must be justified by some lack of personal strength or ability.

Myths thus become flexible components of consciousness. They contribute associations, themes, and an occasional plot outline to the task of organizing the data of everyday life. The business of understanding the outer world is largely a matter of recognizing patterns, and the most powerful patterns emerge from myths. One of the most remarkable features of myths is their capacity to be adapted to new circumstances and to crystallize public opinion out of diverse experiences.

MYTH AND THE RECONSTRUCTION
OF SOCIAL EXPERIENCE

When basic values and beliefs are placed in tension by rapid and confusing social changes, myths can be adapted by authors, song-writers, movie makers, journalists, and politicians to explain the new social conditions and to help people respond to them. For example, at the end of the nineteenth century, millions of Americans were confronted with the sweeping changes of the industrial revolution. People left the farms, moved to the cities, entered new occupations, experienced new conditions of life and work, and encountered new social, economic, and political problems. It is not surprising that the songs, jokes, books, political speeches, and posters of the day provided new references for old values and beliefs so that traditional myths could be translated into forms that helped make sense of the new experiences. The most popular of these mythic adaptations were stories by Horatio Alger. Alger wrote dozens of short stories and novels that dealt with the plight of the new urban dweller in the new moral and economic conditions of industrial society.

A typical Alger story is the saga of *Ragged Dick*. This tale told of a young orphaned boy who came to the big city without money, friends, shelter, food, or education. He fended for himself by shining shoes and saving every penny. He lived frugally and spent every night (after long days of work) teaching himself to read and write. Unlike his compatriots, he resisted the temptation to drink and gamble away his money, and he persisted in his efforts to improve his lot in life. He shined the shoes of many rich and successful businessmen who gradually noticed how Dick seemed to be a cut above the other lads in enterprise, wit, and manners. He was given a real job and a chance to prove himself. His talents and drive paid off, and he became a success in the business world. Even after he had become successful, he continued his earlier practice of helping others and living a morally correct life.

Millions of Americans searching for solace from their hardships, guidance for their actions, and hope for their futures read stories like *Ragged Dick*. Whatever solace, guidance, and hope they found in such works was the result of using the models of society contained in them as guides to applying to their practical everyday affairs traditional beliefs and values such as individualism, honesty, and enterprise. In this fashion, the traditional mythology of society is continually renewed to form convincing guides for contemporary experience. In this fascinating cycle, social experience creates myths, which become in turn guides to future experience. Bruner described this relationship in his classic formulation: "Life . . . produces myth and finally imitates it."[14] This thought captures the reason myths are such important foundations of opinion. Myths create for opinion a content and an expression anchored in observable events and experiences. When myths become part of individuals' consciousness, they provide the most likely bases for common reactions to familiar aspects of new situations.

The Formation of Myth and the Formation of Opinion

When existing myths are inadequate for interpreting and shaping life experience, people begin to look to life itself for the seeds of new myths. Any historical event has in it the potential to be taken as an omen, a "sign of the times," or the inspiration for a new tradition. Any human being from the most humble citizen to the greatest leader may, under the right circumstances, commit an act that becomes a legend in its own time and a model for social behavior. When a public is anxious, uncertain, or simply lacking guidance, it begins to look for deeper significances in the events and people around it. These often mystical interpretations of historical episodes can become condensed into lasting myths that once again give the public the capacity to understand social experiences and exert a check on political processes.

A classic example of this process of myth formation (in which life produced myth and finally imitated it) occurred during the period that historians have labeled the Age of Jackson. This period, from 1812 to 1836, contained some of the most significant social and political changes in American history—the emergence of a stable two-party system, the development of a clear national mythology and symbols of state, the serious entry of the mass public into politics, the tradition of the common man as hero and leader (along with the prototype for the common man's hero, Andrew Jackson), and the emergence of a national commitment to settle the West.

At the beginning of the Age of Jackson, the most important actors were the settlers along the western frontier running from Georgia in the south, through Tennessee and Kentucky, to Ohio in the north. The hardships and marginal existence endured by the majority of these settlers are well established. In addition to the ordinary hardships of life, however, these pioneers suffered strains that the dominant mythology of the day was ill equipped to handle. These strains included the separation of the settlers from eastern society, law, and political processes, and the perception that they were regarded by many of their northeastern countrymen as untutored rustics. A politically uncertain existence was thus compounded by the common—but as yet unexpressed—strains of social stigma, hardship, and uncertainty. In addition to the problems that were unique to the frontier, the nation as a whole suffered a number of more general troubles: The country had yet to establish a clear political identity or a secure economy, and it was engaged in a land and sea war on fronts ranging from Canada to Florida and from the Atlantic to the Mississippi. These more general difficulties compounded the problems on the frontier. In short, the western public of 1812 was ripe to discover some common theme of identity, pride, and political guidance.

To this mixture of local western concerns and national crisis was added an event of dramatic proportions: the victory of Andrew Jackson at the Battle of New Orleans in 1815. By any empirical standard this episode in the War of 1812 should have been of little consequence. An agreement to end the war had been signed prior to the battle, thereby rendering the encounter of no diplomatic or military importance. Moreover, the news of the signing of the Treaty of Ghent, arriving in America right on the heels of the battle, might have turned the victory sour, particularly in light of the treaty's less-than-satisfactory economic terms. Perhaps most importantly, the battle was hardly a military masterpiece. Indeed, it is ironic that an American victory so celebrated should have resulted from such blunders by the opposition, such providence of terrain, and the mercy of an impenetrable cloud of smoke that obscured the battlefield and the combatants for the duration of the clash. Even the popularly acclaimed heroes of the battle (the frontier volunteer "sharpshooters") were, according to Andrew Jackson's own account, sadly lacking in equipment and organization.[15]

Such nagging details, however, were easily overlooked by the vast majority of the American public—particularly in the West—because of a number of dramatic and symbolic characteristics of the victory. First, a slim majority of the American troops were western volunteers. This fact stimulated images that the nation had been rescued by its fearless western settlers and that a band of American citizen-volunteers had routed the well-trained British regulars. Second, the war had seemed endless and the assault on the frontier was viewed as a crucial test of the morale and security of the United States. Third, the war had been declared, at least in part, as an assertion of national integrity, yet it had taken a disastrous turn in 1814 with the burning of the Capitol in Washington and the resulting destruction of many symbols of state. The degrading attack on Washington placed a high symbolic importance on the remaining encounters with the British. Fourth, the nation's banner was carried into the battle by Andrew Jackson, perhaps America's most noted military hero, because of his extended campaign against the Creek Indians. In that campaign, Jackson had preempted President James Monroe's authority by organizing his own army. His initiative was generally credited for the victory against the Creeks, the first land victory of the War of 1812. Finally, the Battle of New Orleans had the remarkable outcome (widely regarded as miraculous) that American casualties numbered approximately twenty while British losses are estimated at well over two thousand.[16]

These dramatic features seemed to focus the private concerns and the depleted spirit of the entire nation. A sustained national celebration was begun. Testimonials to Jackson abounded. Newspaper headlines heralded the "Incredible Victory," the "Unparalleled Victory," and the "Rising Glory of the American Republic."[17] The event was captured immediately in posters, cartoons, tall tales, written accounts, and song.

Popular songs were among the most important mass communications media of the day. Minstrels toured the countryside singing the praises of the western volunteers, the reclaimed virtue of the nation, and Andrew Jackson (the embodiment of both). Easily the most popular song was "The Hunters of Kentucky." The symbolic transformation of Jackson and the western volunteers at New Orleans into the substance for myths of patriotism, citizen duty, and the character of the pioneers was accomplished over the years by the addition of dozens of verses to the song as the magnitude of the legend grew in the minds of the people. Performances of "The Hunters of Kentucky" were mandatory at gatherings, fairs, and theatrical events throughout the West for the next ten or fifteen years. A measure of the song's public impact is contained in the following account by a performer who sang it before a New Orleans audience:

> I found the pit, or parquett, of the theatre *crowded full* of "river men,"—that is, keel boat and flat boat men. There were very few

steamship men. These men were easily known by their linsey-wool-sey clothing and blanket coats. As soon as the comedy of the night was over, I dressed myself in a buckskin hunting shirt and leggins, which I had borrowed of a river man and with *moccasins* on my feet, and an old slouched hat on my head, and a rifle on my shoulder, I presented myself before the audience. I was saluted with loud applause of hands and feet, and a prolonged whoop, or howl, such as Indians give when they are especially pleased. I sang the first verse, and these extraordinary manifestations of delight were louder and longer than before; but when I came to the following lines:

> But Jackson he was wide awake, and
>   Wasn't scared with trifles,
> For well he knew what aim we take
>   With our Kentucky rifles;
> So he marched us down to "Cyprus Swamp";
>   The ground was low and mucky;
> There stood "John Bull" in martial pomp,
>   *But here was old Kentucky.*

As I delivered the last five words, I took my old hat off my head, threw it upon the ground, and brought my rifle to the position of taking aim. At that instant came a shout and an Indian yell from the inmates of the pit, and a tremendous applause from other portions of the house, the whole lasting for nearly a minute. . . . The whole pit was standing up and shouting. I had to sing the song three times that night before they would let me off.[18]

This typical historical scene illustrates the process through which the seeds of myth are drawn from real events and dramatized beyond all proportion in songs, stories, legends, and even in news accounts. These and other media of popular communications transmit the symbols of the new myths to an attentive public. People assimilate the myths through exposure to key myth-related symbols in everyday life, the association of the symbols with positive emotions and experiences, and the attraction of the new myths as dramatic stories providing release from mundane reality and inspiring hope for the future.

After new myths take root, they become available for use in interpreting social conditions, guiding behavior, and shaping political action. For example, the myth of the western hero and patriot grew in popularity over the next decade and gradually found a political outlet in the presidential candidacy of Andrew Jackson in 1824, 1828, and 1832. Jackson became a rallying symbol for political action in the West. He not only helped make the West a dominant force in national politics, but he rekindled the spark of popular sovereignty in the American public. He represented (through the body of myths that grew around him) the virtue of the common man. He symbolized the possibility that greatness could be achieved by average folk. He rekindled the ideal that leaders could know and represent the interests of their followers.

The idea that Jackson "did" all these things is really somewhat off the mark. In many respects the public created Andrew Jackson and the myths that made him important. A public in search of meaning, guidance, and expression found deep significance in Jackson and his timely actions. Out of this public attention rose a compelling body of myths containing the script of Jackson's destiny and the political future of the West. It is certainly true that Jackson played out his part graciously; but the stimulus for his actions, the base of his support, and the significance of his accomplishments came from the popular mythology that created Jackson and his deeds in its own image.

Existing Myths as Windows on the Future

As the continuing public uses of the Jackson myths imply, myths establish a common basis for reactions to new events and conditions. Myths provide a common framework in the search for familiar patterns of meaning in life experience. Myths help people take certain events, ideas, and symbols out of the blur of ongoing history and transform them into powerful objects of opinion. This process often produces in people the uncanny feeling that some primordial insight or understanding has occurred spontaneously to masses of individuals. Cases in which the public seems to focus on common objects of attention and to find remarkably uniform significance in them can provide important insights about the underlying structure of public opinion. Consider, for example, the way in which the transatlantic flight of Charles Lindbergh in 1927 sparked the imagination of the American public.

The 1920s had sorely tested the individualism ethic. It was a period in which individualism and achievement myths had been carried to extremes. Political corruption and collusion between government and industry had clouded the virtues of free enterprise. The values of economic self-sufficiency and the acquisition of wealth crossed the line into dark areas of greed and avarice. A stock market boom swept the nation, prompting millions of individuals to invest their savings in the market in hopes of reaping windfall profits (hardly the model of hard work, honest labor, and restraint that Jefferson had identified as the strengths of American individualism). This drama of individualism-run-amok was played out against the backdrop of prohibition. The ratification of the prohibition amendment to the Constitution reflected better than anything else the conflicts at work in the morals and values of the day. On the surface, prohibition was a proclamation of moral rigor, temperance, and individual purity. However, in practice prohibition encouraged tawdry and hypocritical behavior. Many supposedly law-abiding citizens purchased illegal liquor, frequented illegal speakeasies, and revelled in the alluring fashions, uninhibited dances, and liberated music of the day. Such tension between fundamental values and life experiences is the prime condition that leads diverse people who view the world around them through a framework of common myths to search for new models for behavior.

Enter Lindbergh. The year was 1927. The major event of the time was an air race across the Atlantic Ocean. It drew the major aviators of the day, competing for a huge prize to become the first to make a solo flight across the great ocean. Against a field of skilled pilots with expensive equipment appeared Charles Lindbergh, a virtual unknown. His modest plane was built at a fraction of the cost of the other planes. His inexperience was a tremendous handicap. In comparison to the others in the race, he seemed a mere innocent lad from the heartland of America. In the weeks before the race, the drama heightened. Freak accidents and crashes killed or injured all the other American entries, leaving only Lindbergh to compete for the nation's honor. Foul weather delayed the flight and finally threatened to cancel the race. However, the intrepid American aviator made a heroic decision to take off. The *New York Herald Tribune* reported that he lifted the small, overloaded plane into the sky against the force of wind and rain "by his indomitable will alone."[19]

During the next day and night the world waited for word of the brave pilot and the *Spirit of St. Louis*, his fragile craft. When the plane touched down in Paris some thirty-three hours later, an international celebration was begun. Lindbergh became the greatest American celebrity of the decade. It was as if the public had been waiting impatiently for affirmation of the values and myths that had been threatened by the developments of the 1920s. Lindbergh galvanized public anticipation into a wild and spontaneous proclamation of America's innocence and individualism. In Ward's words, "Lindbergh gave the American people a glimpse of what they liked to think themselves to be at a time when they feared they had deserted their own vision of themselves. . . . America celebrated itself more than it celebrated Lindbergh."[20]

Just as a public inspired by a common vision had made a hero of Andrew Jackson and a legend of the Battle of New Orleans, another public facing other common concerns turned the Lindbergh flight into a reaffirmation of suppressed understandings and threatened values. Such examples lend substance to otherwise vague opinion concepts like public mood and collective consciousness. They also illustrate the possibility that public opinion, under the right conditions, can operate as an independent social or political force. Moreover, these episodes occur with enough regularity to make them worthy of serious attention. A more recent incident involved public reaction to a dramatic action taken by President Gerald Ford in 1975.

In the spring of 1975 the news was predominantly bleak, and the public mood was grim. The country was plunged into a serious recession. Unemployment was high. The specter of Vietnam lingered on. The government that the United States had struggled so long to support appeared lost to the communists. The status of the Vietnam-era military resisters was clouded by the failure of the amnesty program and Ford's apparent ploy to use amnesty to soften the blow of the Nixon pardon. Public disapproval of the pardon had spiraled into overwhelming lack of support for Gerald Ford. In short, the "national spirit" was low. Pride in government (America's most valued national asset) was in need of renewal. Ford needed to reassert his capacity for positive and decisive action. There was need for confirmation of the traditional American belief that direct action could cure almost any problem.

Enter the *Mayaguez*. The *Mayaguez* was an American ship en route from Hong Kong to Thailand. On May 12, the ship was sixty miles off the coast of Cambodia near a group of islands that were the subject of a dispute between Cambodia and Vietnam. Cambodian forces fired on the ship and captured the vessel and its forty-man crew. After two days of deliberations, Gerald Ford sent in the marines to rescue the ship and its crew. It was a dramatic but costly move. Forty-one of the marines in the rescue mission were killed.

It later was revealed that the ship's crew was not even on the island at the time of the American attack. Another government investigation disclosed that the crew had been released by the Cambodians prior to the attack.[21] The same report concluded that the Cambodian government appeared willing to work out a political solution but that diplomatic channels had not been utilized fully by the Ford administration.

These and other details were lost on the public, however. The public was once again in the process of creatively reconstructing history to affirm fundamental values and principles. Under such circumstances, events are not judged according to narrow detail; they are measured by their capacity to represent and illustrate social myth. At these times, opinion does not function to incorporate objective events into consciousness; it projects consciousness onto external events, however much they may need to be rearranged in the process. Public approval for Ford's action was overwhelming. Support for him as President rose sharply. The incident was described as a bold move, a show of principle, and a demonstration of American strength. More than any other event in the 1970s, the *Mayaguez* incident affirmed principles that had been damaged in the ordeals of Watergate and Vietnam, and it expressed the hopes and sentiments of the public about its government and leaders.

As these examples indicate, myths give life to the values and beliefs from which public opinion emerges. They give rise to the powers of symbols used by politicians. They set the boundaries of most public policy debate. They legitimize the status quo in times of tranquility, and they chart the course of change in times of stress. These powerful roles of myth in public opinion processes help fill out MacIver's definition, which identifies myth as one of the key elements of government and society:

> By *myths* we mean the value-impregnated beliefs and notions that men hold, that they live by and for. Every society is held together by a myth-system, a complex of dominating thought-forms that determines and sustains all its activities. All social relations, the very texture of human society, are myth-born and myth-sustained.... We use the word in an entirely neutral sense. Whether its content be revelation or superstition, insight or prejudice is not here in question. We need a term that abjures all reference to truth or falsity. ... Whatever valuational responses men give to circumstances and trials of their lot, whatever conceptions guide their behavior, spur their ambitions or render existence tolerable—all alike fall within our ample category of myth.[22]

RITUALS AND THE INSTITUTIONAL
ROLE OF MYTH

Cases in which public opinion seems to emerge spontaneously in response to political events provide dramatic evidence for the existence of common myths shared by a broad segment of the public. The right social and psychological conditions can lead people to select and interpret familiar patterns in real-world events. Despite the dramatic quality of public opinion in response to events like the Battle of New Orleans or the *Mayaguez* incident, such cases do not represent the most common or even the most important connection between myth and opinion. As suggested at the beginning of this chapter, the most significant uses of myths occur in political institutions.

All institutions have rituals to display procedures, deliberations, or decisions to the public. In some cases the public may participate in the ritual. In other cases the public may be a passive audience whose approval is necessary for the legitimate operation of the institution. In either case, rituals present the workings of political institutions in ways designed to capture the public's attention, promote understanding, limit conflict, and structure the public's responses. Rituals accomplish these tasks by symbolic references to the themes, images, and values of enduring political myths. Symbolic cues invite individuals to use myths when they think about the specific political issues and procedures that occupy the institution. As a result, institutional expressions of opinion are almost always filtered through a "perceptual screen" of myths and enduring political values.

How Rituals Work

A *ritual* is a set of formal rules or procedures used routinely by participants who hold well-defined roles in a situation. Three functions of rituals are to: (1) establish and display the social understandings (values and beliefs) that the participants agree to observe in the situation, (2) show how these understandings will be applied to specific issues in the situation, and (3) demonstrate the reasonableness of the application.

The everyday business of politics depends on hundreds of rituals that structure dealings between the public and the institutions of government. The rituals introduce the political beliefs and values that can be applied to the issue or conflict in question. This is accomplished by cues in the physical setting and in the pronouncements of participants who invoke the themes of popular myths. For example, the judge in a courtroom symbolizes important themes in legal myths. Cues indicating judges' special status are the long black robes they wear, the positioning of their "bench" above the level on which the lawyers work, and the respectful way the lawyers address them ("your honor"; "may it please the court"). In a similar fashion, the principles of popular sovereignty and free choice are introduced in elections by various behaviors of the candidates. For example, they speak of the will of the people, and they ardently claim to differ on "the issues."[23] The public also has a part in introducing high political values into the election ritual by going to the polls and making choices, thus acting out the myth of popular sovereignty.

Political rituals also contain methods for applying general political understandings to the resolution of the specific problems or conflicts on the agenda of the institution. In a trial, for example, lawyers have available to them a number of legal moves that can affect the specific evidence introduced into a case. In addition, the judge explains the law pertaining to the case to the jurors in a way that enables them to apply it to the issues in the case. The deliberation procedures of the jury are designed to connect the law to the case. In another institutional context, a central part of an election ritual is the candidates' interpretations of public problems and their proposals for dealing with them. These interpretations are almost always stated in terms of values and beliefs anchored in traditional political myths. In response, the voters select the general mythic frame that best suits their understanding of the specific issues that concern them.

Political rituals contain ways of demonstrating the validity of these political understandings even to people who may not agree with them. In a trial, for example, the method of selecting the jurors, the privacy of their deliberation, and their isolation from outside influences help create the image of a fair and objective judgment. The right of appeal also increases acceptance of outcomes in the justice system. Similarly, dozens of mechanisms in elections promote acceptance of the results even among the losers. For example, procedures for recording and tabulating votes are monitored by impartial officials. Losers almost always concede graciously and wish the winners well. Moreover, the reliance on myths to define electoral issues means that the issue positions of winners and losers alike are generally staked out within the range of publicly acceptable (if not preferable) values.

The fact that rituals connect the specific issues that pass through institutions with enduring political myths means that in every institutional context public opinion takes on a dual political significance. Opinion is at once a response to specific legal rulings, candidate proposals, or legislation, and at the same time an affirmation of enduring understandings about security, order, authority, and community values. This dualism has some interesting implications for the study of public opinion. The analysis of policy making must be reformulated to go beyond a concern with narrow policy categories and specific opinion-policy linkages. The study of institutions and policy must take into account the symbolic presentation of issues and the role of opinion in legitimating political outcomes and affirming the larger social values they represent. The next two sections of this chapter explore the different views of elections and policy making that emerge when the cultural foundations of opinion are taken into account.

Elections as Rituals

A cultural analysis of opinion and elections suggests that the formation and expression of public opinion in elections are as much statements of traditional popular concerns and images of the political system as they are focused responses to candidates' proposals or specific issues. Exploring this hypothesis requires a reformulation of the conventional view of elections. Most observers of elections, whether journalists or political scientists, acknowledge and criticize the limited debate and the contrived behavior by candidates that goes on. Instead of looking for the possible significance of these dominant features of elections, however, most analysts dismiss them as politically irrelevant defects in the political system. This dismissal is a result of focusing on only one level of the relationship between opinion and institutional processes. The widespread concern with only the specific policy functions of voting ignores the ritualistic aspects of elections that produce banal candidate behavior and that account for the broader political significance of voting.

The failure to understand how ritual focuses opinion on broader political concerns results in brushing aside the low issue content of elections as the result of ineffective party competition, irresponsible press coverage, citizens' ignorance, or candidates' efforts to maximize their votes. There may be some truth to these explanations, but they fail to explain several interesting facts.

First, no matter how much detail the candidates provide about "the issues," elections contain no mechanism for translating votes for candidates into policies. Perhaps it does not make sense to continue to analyze elections in a policy context. This implication is reinforced by a second consideration. Although issues are only incidentally related to policy, they do occupy a solid place in elections in the context of talk about leadership, national priorities, and the shape of the future. Perhaps these are the primary political concerns of elections (especially national elections). If so, then it may make little sense for issues to be defined as concrete and detailed policy proposals. To do so confuses their political functions. The standard issue definitions in elections may be much better suited to obvious electoral concerns about choice, leadership, popular sovereignty, creating a broad systemic agenda, and gaining a sense of control over the future. For these purposes, issues need not be innovative or precisely defined. In fact, too much attention to well-specified and ideologically polarized issues could damage these cultural themes in elections.[24]

A final problem with criticisms of elections that are based only on policy considerations is that the objects of the criticism (such as too much emphasis on personalities and too little attention to the issues) have been constant features of American elections. Since these "shortcomings" seem to be permanent characteristics of American politics, it may not make sense to dismiss them as defects or mutations of the democratic ideal. Rather, if they are examined in the right analytical context, they may tell us a good deal about the foundations of American politics. It is illuminating to rethink some of the taken-for-granted criticisms of elections in the context of elections as rituals.

In recent times one of the most popular criticisms of elections has been that the media (with a little help from the candidates) have turned them into simple-minded melodramas with no substance. This criticism argues that elections are no longer forums for the serious discussion of issues; they have been dramatized to represent the life-and-death struggles of fictionalized candidates. The media and the candidates seek to downplay the issues because they do not make for lively reporting in the first instance and tend to of-fend potential voters in the second. In place of the issues, the public receives dynamic and entertaining images like "the horserace." In this political melodrama one of the presidential hopefuls takes an early lead in the primaries, and the race is on, with the rest of the pack in pursuit of the frontrunner. Suspense is heightened when the leader stumbles (that is, loses a primary) or when a "dark horse" threatens to make a strong run on the outside. A recent critic of melodramatic elections described another equally fluffy scenario:

> The voters and politicians stand at the center of this world, as is appropriate to news coverage of democratic elections. But these are politicians and voters with a difference. In real life, the two groups are so diverse and complex that an observer can never have more than the sketchiest knowledge of their actions, motives, and the like. . . . In the world of television news, by contrast, the diversity, complexity, and uncertainty of the real world become all but invisible. They are replaced by the false simplicity and clarity of what TV news, assuming a posture of omniscience, pretends to know, in sharp detail, about the politician's every important action, secret hope, fear, plan and motive. Instead of participating in a long, confusing, and often inchoate political process, as he does in the real world, television's politician acts out a clear and gripping melodrama—call it "The People's Choice." It opens in the snows of New Hampshire; the plot develops, election by election, until it reaches its denouement before the national conventions. . . . Intensified peril is the basic ingredient of melodrama. Television presents the candidates, not as people who are running for elective office, but as figures deeply and totally embroiled in an all-out struggle.[25]

Studies of the content of news coverage of elections tend to add weight to this criticism. For example, Patterson and McClure's study of television coverage of the 1972 election found that only a minuscule portion of time was devoted to "the issues"; the majority of coverage dealt with rallies, crowds, personal attacks, and other dramatic material.

There is little doubt that these criticisms and their supporting evidence are correct as far as they go. Elections do seem to be mostly melodrama and little else. (In our heart of hearts many of us probably admit that this is what we find most fascinating about them.) However, neither the critics nor the researchers whose data support the criticisms have developed a theoretical framework for their observations. Since most of their criticism is based on common-sense understandings of elections, they fail to consider the possibility that elections, as rituals, must be melodramatic affairs in order to transmit political messages effectively. The absence of theoretical and historical perspectives thus makes the election-as-melodrama criticisms trivially obvious on the one hand but thoroughly misguided on the other.

Even the most casual reading of American history suggests that elections have always been treated by voters and candidates, as well as by the press, as melodramatic affairs. For example, the "horserace" metaphor goes back at least as far as 1824, when Andrew Jackson was referred to as "Tennessee's stud" in the presidential horserace of that year. Long before the advent of television, the "inchoate" process of an election was transformed by popular communications media into melodramatic themes of struggle, conflict, peril, and momentous choice centered on the exploits of heroes, villains, and fools, with a cast of millions. In the present day, the medium that best accomplishes this dramatic transformation happens to be television. In the past, the dramatization has been accomplished by newspapers, cartoons, legends, touring performers, and popular songs.[26]

In short, the dramatizations that have become part of American elections are common to all rituals. Rituals use dramatic themes and actions to attract attention, simplify problems, emphasize particular principles, and structure the responses of participants.[27] To criticize elections for being melodramatic is only to criticize them for being what they are: rituals. To demand that they become serious policy-making forums is to disregard the fact that they contain no policy-making mechanism. To claim that drama overshadows serious ideological debate overlooks the fact that in most political situations both debate and public thinking rest on myth, not on ideology. Thus, the election ritual merely serves as a device to focus and heighten ordinary political communications within a special setting.

Underlying the election-as-melodrama criticism is the related charge that elections do not offer the public meaningful choices. Like the melodrama criticism, this assertion is both true and beside the point. Elections seldom present clear policy alternatives and virtually never contain policy formulations that fall beyond the range of standard myths. When this does occur, the candidates who propose such unconventional ideas are usually defeated resoundingly, thus returning the party system and elections to their normal range of content.[28]

In place of substantive choices, elections are structured to create the appearance of grand choices before the voters. Any number of themes of conflict and choice may run through elections. For example, there is the eternal struggle between the parties. There is the personal struggle between the candidates. In one election the choice may seem to be between someone who favors "the big guys" versus someone who supports "the little guys." In other contests, the choice may be between "guns and butter," "welfare or free enterprise," "austerity or expansion," "easterners versus westerners," and so on.

Each election is fraught with such thematic choices. To disregard their existence and persistence is to ignore an important clue about the nature of elections in America. Yet they seem too insubstantial to be significant. Even in important elections such as those during the Age of Jackson, in 1824, 1828, and 1832, the political pronouncements have tended to be grand and dramatic but with little connection to specific problems or workable solutions. One analyst has observed that "Jacksonian rhetoric . . . conjured up half-imaginary villains—'monarchists,' 'aristocrats,' 'speculators'—which it then slaughtered in pantomime."[29] In this fashion, choices seem compelling and involving, yet after the election they melt back into the form of vague images and forgotten phrases.

In a similar way, the differences between the candidates are dramatized and exaggerated so that they often seem quite real and convincing, but a close comparison reveals that they rest on very little substance. For example, the election of 1824 is often regarded as a watershed election in American politics. Both at the time and in subsequent political accounts, the three candidates in the race—Henry Clay, John Quincy Adams, and Andrew Jackson—seemed to represent clear, momentous political choices. However, on closer inspection one is hard pressed to identify in any systematic, ideological terms the obvious differences among them. As Cunliffe has observed:

> In the 1824 election, discounting personalities, there was little to choose between Clay, Adams, and Jackson. The first two stood for a somewhat greater degree of federal intervention in order to develop the Union: for "internal improvements" and for a tariff to provide adequate revenue and to protect small manufacturers or producers. But their intentions were not basically different from Jackson's.[30]

Despite the difficulty of sorting out clear differences among the three candidates, the election was one of the most contested in

American history. (It was finally decided in the House of Representatives.) Voters regarded the choices as substantial and important. Not only was there a huge turnout, but the hostilities over the disputed outcome lingered for the next four years.

The paradox of seemingly insubstantial but compellingly meaningful electoral choices can be resolved by considering the political uses of myths and the role of rituals in mobilizing them. Recall in the earlier cases of the industrial revolution, the Lindbergh flight, and the Battle of New Orleans how individuals used myths to interpret their life experiences, to forge new social identities, and to react to social change. Rituals are simply means of introducing myths into public communication on a regular basis. The presence of myths in political communication acts as a constant device to absorb social tensions and express ongoing concerns. The implication of the role of myths in political processes is that debate and issue formation in American elections reflect the nature of myth-based communication: Definitions of issues tend to be vague and insubstantial, yet they can evoke recognition and meaningful response from voters who employ myths to make sense of them. Myth-based political processes stand in sharp contrast to more ideological patterns of issue definition and electoral choice in which issues endure because they are understood to be permanent social conditions that account for persistent deprivation and social conflict.

A companion criticism to the absence of meaningful choice in American elections is that in place of serious issues the public is offered little more than personalities. In its most popular form this criticism states that elections have become mere "personality contests." However, it is evident that the cult of personality has always been the dominant force in American politics. For example, failing to find substantial ideological differences in the 1824 election, Cunliffe concluded: "The candidate's reputation and personality . . . counted for much. . . . To some the integrity of Adams commended itself, to others the charms of Clay, to others the bravura of Jackson."[31]

The emphasis on personality has degraded campaign appeals, so the criticism goes, to personal ingratiation and attacks on the character of opponents. This may indeed be the case, but this style of campaigning was ushered in long before the advent of Madison Avenue. As the earlier Madison, James, lamented after the first American elections, it was customary "for the candidates to recommend themselves to the voters . . . by personal solicitation."[32] It seems that this style of campaigning was not beneath even the greatest of America's early leaders:

> On election day the flow of liquor reached high tide.... During a July election day in Frederick County in the year 1758, George Washington's agent supplied 160 gallons to 390 voters and "unnumbered" hangers-on. This amounted to more than a quart and a half a voter.[33]

That sort of campaigning led Madison to raise the first version of a complaint that has been expressed in various forms to the present day. He remarked that "the corrupting influence of spiritous liquors and other treats [was] inconsistent with the purity of moral and republican principles."[34] Today we hear that lavish spending on image campaigns is corrupting the ideals of American democracy. This is the same complaint, updated to refer to the particular campaign practices of modern times.

The cult of personality has been branded as a perverted substitute for the ideals of democratic elections. This may be true; but when viewed historically as an aspect of the American election ritual, it emerges as a permanent feature serving an important political function. The focus on powerful human images (whether they be heroic leaders or gods) is an element of any ritual in which the concerns of private life are translated into shared public images and formulations.

Mythic thinking is projective and condensational. It is a process in which private concerns become translated into public images that acquire meaning on multiple levels. The transformation is facilitated in rituals conducted by powerful figures with whom the individual can identify. The pronouncements of an attractive or respected figure become models for the individual's thinking. More importantly, the actors in rituals literally act out the possible concerns of the audience. The struggle between candidates becomes the struggle between groups, or the battle of good and evil, or the representation of life concerns such as economic security and social harmony. Many of the public's most powerful perceptions are formed in response to dramatic performances symbolizing social concerns and their resolution, not in response to formal intellectual presentations of these concerns. Rituals are means of acting out such concerns in dramatic fashion. The cult of personality in politics is a powerful means of producing audience identification with the actors, thereby creating vicarious involvement with their struggles and the larger concerns they represent.

This form of public political involvement may not satisfy our ideal image of self-government and democratic elections. However, to fail to recognize the central place that such practices hold in enduring political rituals risks a fundamental misunderstanding of elections and the role of the public in them. Moreover, the tendency to treat these practices as some sort of accidental departure from the norm leads to superficial suggestions for reform that are unworkable as a result of their misreading of the nature of the problem. As a result, reform proposals (for example, better journalism, more citizen education) tend to perpetuate the problems they identify by distracting attention from the underlying realities of the election process and representing the problems as incidental defects that can be remedied by minor tinkering with the system.

Perhaps the most significant consequence of the failure to acknowledge the ritualistic nature of elections is the tendency to dismiss the most enduring and significant features of elections as trivial or unimportant. A ritual framework suggests that the real issues in elections are the redundant themes and recurring slogans that seem so tired and unimportant.[35] By contrast, conventional criticisms tend to dismiss these features as unworthy of attention. Whereas a ritual perspective argues that voters' choices are limited to the vague and fleeting alternatives that appear in campaign rhetoric and disappear after the election, conventional criticism insists on looking elsewhere for the "real" choices. Whereas a theory of elections as rituals identifies the cult of personality as a central means of dramatizing popular concerns and structuring voters' choices, standard criticisms dismiss the attention paid to the personal images and posturings of candidates as perversions of true campaign standards.

In short, the standard view of elections as policy processes ignores the functions of campaign practices in the context of the election ritual. As a result, it is easy to overlook the possibility that the public opinion expressed in response to campaign issues has less to do with making policy than with reducing social tensions and reinforcing enduring images of the political order.

THE OPINION-POLICY LINKAGE
REVISITED

In order to understand how rituals and myths affect policy making in general, it is important to recognize the unique characteristics of myth-based thinking. When people rely on myths to interpret the world around them, they engage in what psychologists call *primary-process thinking*. Primary-process thinking is based on subconscious associations, fantasies, and unquestioned assumptions. The absence of well-specified logic and testable propositions stands in sharp contrast to what we know as rational or *secondary-process thought*. One of the reasons political arguments are often so difficult to pin down and refute convincingly is that they frequently rest on myth and primary-process thinking.

In specific terms, primary-process thought has three major characteristics. First, it lacks clearly defined logic and testable connections between beliefs and values and specific opinions. Second, it uses recurring themes and condensational symbols to transform specific issues into enduring understandings about politics and society. Third, it gives individuals the capacity to hold divergent and even contradictory myths with nearly equal intensity. The presence of competing political perspectives makes people receptive to different policy formulations under different circumstances; it also promotes tolerance for opposing viewpoints. Most importantly, the spectrum of myth imposes the limits on acceptable political debate.

The introduction of myths into institutional rituals accounts for a number of important aspects of policy processes that go beyond the simple production of policy. For example, the presentation of policy alternatives in terms of myths and condensational symbols generates about the nature of problems and their solutions a consensus that would not exist if public problems were approached as unique issues with complex causes and undetermined consequences. The fact that most problems are defined in simple and familiar terms suggests that the definition of the problem may be as important an outcome of policy processes as any serious consideration about whether the solutions actually work. When the mythic themes and myth-related language are stripped away from most policy debates, very little of substance remains. Most political controversy centers on disagreement over which myths apply to a particular problem.

The fact that myth-based thinking tolerates logical contradictions and competing values is also politically significant. This tolerance makes the public better able to accept ambiguous political definitions, shifts in leaders' positions, and changes in official explanations. In fact, changes in policy formulations that occur within the spectrum of popular myth may create the illusion of progress in efforts to solve chronic problems. Even though official solutions seldom depart from the theme of competing myths, the "new" approaches seem sensible because the logical contradictions in policy cycles are hard to detect and the recurrence of familiar formulations is reassuring.

Policy processes may have political significance because they reinforce myths and popular images of political problems as well as because they attack the causes of problems. This can be explained largely by the fact that myth-based thinking is circular and not easily tested or disproved. Rituals introduce myths in ways that fit ongoing reality into the myths, rather than in ways that promote recognition of the complex and changing nature of real situations. As Moore notes, the interactions of myths and rituals with real-world problems "represent stability and continuity acted out and re-enacted: visible continuity. By dint of repetition they deny the passage of time, the nature of change, and the implicit extent of potential indeterminacy in social relations."[36]

In this light, the public opinion that emerges in response to policy processes becomes both a response to specific proposals and an affirmation of enduring values and beliefs. For all practical purposes, the limits of political reality and political possibilities are determined by the myths on which public understandings rest. This means that institutional rituals tend to limit the range of possible political solutions for the problems on their agendas. This "limiting effect" is accomplished in an interesting way.

Myths determine the limits of public understanding, and the public plays an important role in almost all institutional processes. Thus popular acceptance or rejection of official actions and policy proposals becomes the ultimate check on policy. In other words, public opinion is the "gatekeeper" in the American political system. As issues pass through policy rituals, they are defined in ways that cue popular myths. These myths, in turn, constitute the dominant basis for popular judgments and reactions. Finally, the important role of opinion in institutional processes results in the legitimation of policies that are consistent with dominant myths and the rejection of policy options that fall beyond the range of popular myths.

An interesting example of the gate-keeping function of political myth and public opinion is provided by diverse public reaction to two different proposals (one by Richard Nixon, the other by George McGovern) for welfare reform in the early 1970s. Shortly after taking office, President Nixon proposed a Family Assistance Plan to the public and to Congress. The plan called for a guaranteed annual income of modest proportions ($1,600) for poor families. In his presentation of the plan to the public, Nixon did not use the words "guaranteed income." Instead, he emphasized the incentives and conditions attached to the annual grant. The program, he said, was designed to break the cycle of welfare dependency by requiring recipients to accept job training or a job while they were in the program. As an incentive to work they would be allowed to continue to receive their welfare stipend until their earned wages brought them above the poverty level. Thus, Nixon's language incorporated the symbolism of individual achievement: initiative, incentive, self-improvement, ambition, and pride. As a result, his Family Assistance Plan was tied to myths of individualism and equality. It was aimed directly at the center of the political and mythological spectrum. From a political standpoint, the result was rather impressive. A conservative politician who had campaigned for office in opposition to any form of a guaranteed annual income won the overwhelming support of 78 percent of the public for a welfare plan that included a form of guaranteed annual income.[37]

In an interesting study of the political orientations of a sample of California "middle Americans," Lamb recorded a number of responses to the plan. Whether liberal or conservative, all the reactions revealed the strong role of myth in selecting viable policy options on an issue. For example, one supporter of the program rejected a purely egalitarian approach to welfare and stressed the importance of individual achievement:

> The idea of redistribution of wealth can't accomplish this in the strictest sense, and still maintain democracy. You have to have some form of encouragement, incentive for people to develop, and right now in the ghettos, that facility does not exist. These people are absolutely without hope. . . . Some of them are chronic unemployed, and why is that? I suspect it's because they were raised that way.[38]

That reaction to Nixon's program was shared in one way or another by most of Lamb's sample. Notice the references to encouragement, incentive, and hope in the foregoing remarks. These are the same symbols that Nixon used in presenting his program. The way they are used makes it clear that they are anchored in a set of myths about the importance of achievement and its social conditions. For example, the reference to the way people are "raised" reflects the widespread belief that socialization, training, and family life account for many important individual tendencies, including the work ethic and motivation. In this view of things, problems like poverty or poor health are generally regarded as having individual causes (such as poor family life, lack of health information, no job skills) that can be corrected by solutions aimed at improvement of the individual. This pervasive understanding was drawn into the Nixon program with the claim that the incentive system would not only restore self-respect but it would keep poor families together.

The restrictions in the old welfare system against holding a job and receiving welfare payments were cited as forces that led to the breakup of many families, who could not support themselves fully either on welfare or on the small incomes received from menial jobs. The work incentive combined with the restoration of the family was billed as a means of creating a better environment for the children of the poor. These offspring would be given a model to follow in their own later efforts to conquer poverty. Thus, the program claimed to restore dignity and incentives to adults and create better living conditions for children. These goals were designed to help the poor lift themselves out of poverty.

The outlines of the Family Assistance Plan (or, more to the point, the content of its symbolism) conjur up the themes of the great American success story: the triumph of individuals over adversity. This was the story of the Puritans, the Founding Fathers, the western settlers, the workers of the new industrial revolution, the European immigrants, the slaves, and even the successful entrepreneurs of the 1980s, who made it on their own and have both material rewards and a measure of pride to show for it. In short, the Nixon program fit poor people into the classic American mold of being responsible for their adversities and equally responsible for overcoming them. Under the Nixon plan, they would be given the same opportunity to make it on their own that had been given to other groups who have staked out their own versions of the myth. The high level of public support for the Nixon plan indicates both the pervasive nature of the myth and the importance of myths as a foundation for policy.

None of this implies, of course, that myths are necessarily the best ways of understanding social problems or that the policies based on them lead to effective solutions. It is not helpful to think of myths as true or false. Doing so can get in the way of recognizing that myths are accepted by their believers as though they were true. As Geertz has observed, one of the main handicaps in thinking about myths is the tendency to evaluate them as though they ought to conform to scientific or rational standards of thinking.[39] Such standards assume that the nature of reality (or of a problem) is a given and that the intellectual task is to derive some theory or explanation that represents an objective view of that reality. When myths are thought of in this way, they often appear to be simplistic, misguided, or out-and-out wrong. This conclusion misses two important points.

First, in a changing society the nature of reality is not given or fixed; it is changing and ambiguous. It is more important for people to find fast, familiar, and simplifying frameworks in which to place ongoing situations than to become plagued by philosophical questions of objectivity and truth. Myths quickly reduce complex problems to simple and sensible terms. Second, the scientific outlook assumes that an explanation is the goal and the end result of inquiry. When this assumption is applied to myths, it misses the point that myths are not just an explanation of reality, but they also take an active part in constructing the very reality they claim to explain.

If people use myths to explain a problem and propose a solution for it, the solution can alter the very nature of the problem. For example, if poverty is assumed to be the result of individual failings and the proposed solutions are aimed at correcting these individual difficulties, then for all practical purposes the assumptions about poverty become the reality. Unlike the world of the scientific laboratory, where theories are rejected if the hypotheses they generate don't work, the hypotheses generated by social myths tend to be sustained as long as they are useful ways of thinking. Once programs and policies are cast in a mythic mold, they need not be rejected if they don't work.

There are any number of ways to explain failure in public policy. It is often enough to simply point out the complexity of the problem. When more substantial rationalizations are called for, the very substance of the myth can be employed in circular reasoning. For example, if the roots of poverty lie in the failings and character defects of the poor, then even the best programs may fail because the people themselves are incorrigible. The reasons people are in their predicament in the first place can be cited for their characteristic failure to respond to help. Because the myth identified variables as the cause of the problem, and these same variables can be cited in the failure of the solution, the failure of public policies can be taken as proof of the myths on which they were based!

FIGURE 13-1
A Conventional or Rational Model of Policy

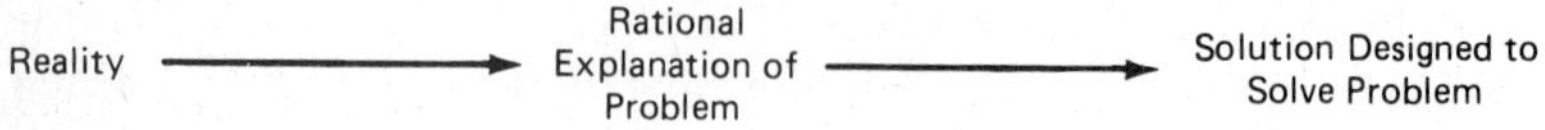

Reality ⟶ Rational Explanation of Problem ⟶ Solution Designed to Solve Problem

Thus, in mythical thinking, the explanation for something can re-create the thing itself, and the seeming rejection of hypotheses can be taken as proof of the explanation. These reversals of ordinary scientific or logical thought processes suggest that there may be other ways of thinking about the nature of public policy. The naive "rational" assumption about policy is that it is a proposed cure for problems that have been identified through some independent or detached view of reality. In this scheme (see Figure 13-1), we begin with reality as a given and proceed to an explanation of the problem that leads to some solution (policy) designed to correct the perceived problem.

However, looking at policy from the standpoint of myth offers quite a different perspective. According to this view, there is no reason to believe that the point of many policies is really to solve problems. This is not to imply that there is a conscious conspiracy at work to prevent the solution of major problems. It merely suggests that policy simply serves a function different from the one described in the rational model. There is no reason to believe that serious social problems need to be eradicated in order for the society to function smoothly. The enduring presence of poverty on the American scene would seem to support this possibility. Moreover, there is no reason to think that typical approaches to a problem are rational or effective. The endurance of a problem in the face of the best efforts of government to solve it lends support to this proposition. In light of these two facts, it may make sense to think of policies as political means rather than as ends. They are not means to the solution of problems, however; they are means to the creation of public images of society and politics. It may make sense to consider the possibility that public thinking about social problems in particular and about the nature of society in general begins with myths. These myths lead to explanations and proposed solutions (see Figure 13-2). These solutions, in turn, help create and stabilize social reality in terms that conform to the dominant myths that produced them.

This perspective suggests that public policy operates as much to

FIGURE 13–2
A Model of Policy as Myth

Explanation	*Solution*	*Reality*
Mythical Explanation of Problem	⟶ Solution Designed to Solve Problem	⟶ Results in Social Conditions in Keeping with Myths

shape society around certain values as it serves to solve specific problems. Policies become means of affirming the larger images of the world on which they are based. In most policy areas it is more acceptable to suffer failure based on correct theories than it would be to achieve success at the price of sacrificing social values. In this sense, persistent social problems become examples that illustrate the correctness of myths to upstanding members of society. Public policy becomes a set of lessons about how people should act and how they should apply values to social dilemmas.

The strength of the gate-keeping function of myth and public opinion is demonstrated most convincingly when policy proposals fall outside the range of acceptable alternatives dictated by social myth. A good example of this occurred with a welfare-reform plan presented to the public shortly after the Nixon plan was introduced. In 1972 the Democratic candidate for President, George McGovern, also suggested a guaranteed annual income for poor families. McGovern branded poverty in America a national disgrace. He argued that all Americans have a right to a decent standard of living. He did not demand work in exchange for assistance. He suggested that dignity could be restored to poor people simply by removing the stigma of poverty. In a sense, the key practical ingredient of McGovern's plan (giving money to the poor) was the same as Nixon's. However, Nixon's program would have implemented that policy in a symbolic context designed to reenact and reinforce prevailing myths about poverty; McGovern's plan seemed to take direct aim at the myths themselves.

Public response to McGovern's proposal was as intensely negative as it had been intensely positive for the Nixon plan. Lamb asked members of his sample to describe their reactions to McGovern's idea. Whereas the Nixon prescription for assistance in exchange for work made sense to these people, they seemed confused about McGovern's concept of just giving money to people with no strings attached. McGovern's program simply guaranteed that each American would have an income of $1,000 a year, and those who did not need the stipend would help subsidize it through the income tax. Some of Lamb's subjects, however, expressed confusion about "giving everybody in the country a thousand dollars, whether he needs it or not."[40] One even asked, "What would Howard Hughes need a thousand dollars for?"[41]

These reactions indicate that policies that are not defined and implemented in terms of familiar political myths generate confusion and misunderstanding. So powerful is the role of myth that policies that do not conform to standard myths may not even make sense to the majority of the public. To the extent that the public cannot comprehend proposals, they tend to regard them as fearful and threatening ideas. Needless to say, these views stimulate public rejection.[42]

This way of understanding policy processes requires a reformulation of the perspective presented in Chapter 12, in which opinion was viewed as a force in generating policy outcomes. It seems that the relationship between opinion and policy works in two directions. Public policy is also a mechanism for generating public opinion in support of dominant political values and images of society.

NOTES

1. For an excellent discussion of this idea, see Murray Edelman, *Political Language: Words That Succeed and Policies That Fail* (New York: Academic Press, 1977).
2. Robert Weissberg, *Public Opinion and Popular Government* (Englewood Cliffs, N.J.: Prentice-Hall, 1976), p. 213.
3. See, for example, Joseph Campbell, *The Hero with a Thousand Faces* (New York: Meridian, 1949).
4. See Henry Beck, "Spiro Agnew the Fool" (paper delivered at the Annual Meeting of the American Political Science Association, Washington, D.C., 1977).
5. See Marvin Harris, *Cows, Pigs, Wars, and Witches: The Riddles of Culture* (New York: Random House, 1974).
6. See Stuart A. Scheingold, *The Politics of Rights* (New Haven: Yale University Press, 1974).
7. See, among others, John Dollard, *Caste and Class in a Southern Town* (New York: Doubleday, 1949); Edward Banfield, *The Moral Basis of a Backward Society* (New York: Free Press, 1958); and Kay B. Warren, *The Symbolism of Subordination: Indian Identity in a Guatemalan Town* (Austin: University of Texas Press, 1978).
8. See A. Reza Sheïkholeslami, "Religion and Politics: Islamic Political Ideology in Contemporary Iran" (Unpublished manuscript, University of Washington, 1979).

9. See Alexis de Tocqueville, *Democracy in America* (New York: New American Library, 1956).
10. See Lorna Marshall, "Kung Bushman Bands," *Africa*, No. 4 (1960), pp. 325–54.
11. Laura Nader, "Styles of Court Procedure: To Make the Balance," in *Law in Culture and Society*, ed. Laura Nader (Chicago: Aldine, 1969).
12. See Catherine Albanese, *Sons of the Fathers: The Civil Religion of the American Revolution* (Philadelphia: Temple University Press, 1976).
13. See Michael Novak, *The Rise of the Unmeltable Ethnics* (New York: Macmillan, 1973).
14. Jerome Bruner, "Myth and Identity," in *Myth and Mythmaking*, ed. Henry A. Murray (New York: Braziller, 1960), p. 283.
15. For an excellent account of the Battle of New Orleans and its historical impact, see John William Ward, *Andrew Jackson: Symbol for an Age* (New York: Oxford University Press, 1955).
16. Ibid., p. 17.
17. Ibid., p. 5.
18. Quoted ibid., pp. 14–15.
19. John William Ward, "The Meaning of Lindbergh's Flight," in Ward, *Red, White, and Blue: Men, Books, and Ideas in American Culture* (New York: Oxford University Press, 1969), p. 24.
20. Ibid., p. 26.
21. See the *New York Times*, October 6, 1976, p. 1.
22. Robert MacIver, *The Web of Government* (New York: Macmillan, 1947), pp. 4–5.
23. For an argument concerning the basis of these aspects of elections in obligatory and ritualistic candidate behaviors, see W. Lance Bennett, "Ritualistic and Pragmatic Bases of Political Campaign Discourse," *Quarterly Journal of Speech*, Vol. 63 (October 1977), pp. 219–38.
24. See ibid.
25. Paul H. Weaver, "Captives of Melodrama," *New York Times Magazine*, August 29, 1976, p. 6.
26. See, for example, Thomas C. Blaisdell, Jr., and Peter Selz, *The American Presidency in Political Cartoons: 1776–1976* (Salt Lake City: Peregrine Smith, 1976); and Vera B. Lawrence, *Music for Patriots, Politicians and Presidents* (New York: Macmillan, 1975).
27. Victor Turner, *Dramas, Fields, and Metaphors* (Ithaca, N.Y.: Cornell University Press, 1974).
28. See Bennett, "Ritualistic and Pragmatic Bases of Political Campaign Discourse."
29. Marcus Cunliffe, *The Nation Takes Shape: 1787–1837* (Chicago: University of Chicago Press, 1959), p. 167.
30. Ibid., pp. 157–58.
31. Ibid., p. 158.
32. Quoted in Charles Snydor, *American Revolutionaries in the Making* (New York: Free Press, 1952), p. 48.
33. Ibid., p. 55.
34. Quoted ibid., p. 57.
35. For an excellent extension of this idea to a wide range of political situations, see Edelman, *Political Language*.

36. Sally Falk Moore, "Epilogue," in *Symbol and Politics in Communal Ideology*, eds. Sally Moore and Barbara Myerhoff (Ithaca, N.Y.: Cornell University Press, 1975), p. 221.
37. Based on a Harris Poll reported in Karl A. Lamb, *As Orange Goes: Twelve California Families and the Future of American Politics* (New York: Norton, 1974), p. 187. Despite this overwhelming public support, Nixon eventually abandoned the Family Assistance Plan when George McGovern later advocated his own version of a guaranteed income in the 1972 presidential election. It would have been politically difficult for Nixon to support his own plan and attack McGovern's at the same time.
38. Lamb, *As Orange Goes*, pp. 185–86.
39. Clifford Geertz, "Ideology as a Cultural System," in Geertz, *The Interpretation of Cultures* (New York: Basic Books, 1973), pp. 208–13.
40. Lamb, *As Orange Goes*, p. 189.
41. Ibid., p. 189.
42. It is interesting to note that even the national press corps assigned to cover the McGovern campaign (a predominantly liberal group supportive of McGovern) tended to dismiss his welfare program as silly, naive, or unworkable. See Timothy Crouse, *The Boys on the Bus* (New York: Ballantine Books, 1973).

14

Culture, Opinion, and the Individual: Toward an Integration of Theory and Method

THE FIELD OF PUBLIC OPINION has been plagued by the difficulty of integrating diverse aspects of opinion such as socialization, personality, mass communications, and institutions and policy. The absence of an integrated theory has left the methodology for studying opinion fragmented and lacking in solid grounding. Throughout this book the emphasis has been to show how each domain of opinion contributes to the operation of the others. For example, socialization and personality development within the domain of the individual and society produce political orientations that occupy central roles in the areas of issue formation and political communication. The development of the political agenda and public expectations about the issues on the agenda affect the operations of institutions and public reactions to official definitions of issues. Along the way, each domain of opinion contributes a separate political effect to the operation of the political system: integration, agenda setting, and policy and legitimation. Taken together, the domains of opinion account for how the political system links the concerns and behaviors of individuals with the distant and abstract processes of government.

These connections between individuals, the public, and political processes need to be spelled out more clearly in order to complete the theoretical framework. The easiest way to understand the linkage between individuals, the public, and politics is to address this question: Where does the substance of political socialization come from, and do the origins of socialization help explain the connection between the general policy processes of institutions and the specific beliefs of individuals?

One way of thinking about the driving force of socialization is simply to say that it arises from culture and therefore the content of socialization is "in the air." It is true that the core values and beliefs transmitted to each generation are encountered and reinforced in every imaginable social situation and life experience. However, there must be something that focuses and selects the socialization content over time and can be identified as a source of change. If the policy process operates in part as described in Chapter 13, then the formal institutional processes of politics provide the guiding structure for political socialization. What political scientists normally regard as "outputs" of the political system also must be regarded as inputs to the development of individual political orientations.

In addition to producing material political payoffs, the formal policy processes of government also promote particular political values. This reinforcement of values is accomplished because policy alternatives and political outcomes are usually defined politically in terms of enduring political myths. Myth-based formulations limit the scope of conflict and the range of imaginable solutions to political problems. They also provide the public with the most salient models of society and the sources of its problems. The models are powerful because they are constructed in symbolic terms that refer to individuals' most deeply held beliefs and values. Moreover, their association with high institutions of government makes them both visible and authoritative. Perhaps most importantly, the fact that myths are applied to specific problems through the policy process makes them compelling and understandable. In this fashion, the selective use of myth to deal with the demands facing institutions during a particular historical period provides the most important source of political socialization for new generations. The role of these cultural models in the development of individual thinking requires new thinking about belief systems and the ways of measuring them.

MYTH AND SOCIALIZATION

The broad, myth-based understandings that have such important impacts on political thought and action are reinforced in hundreds of ways in everyday experiences. The value concerns brought into focus by the policy agendas of institutions also become mirrored in everyday life. This is because the myths that organize public opinion and public debate can be broken down into their key symbols, and these symbols can link powerful political themes to ordinary social action. As Rosenberg has noted, these myth-linked symbols come in many forms:

> [They] need not be verbal: war toys, the ABM display which tours local shopping centers, the converted jet used as a jungle gym at the playground—all begin to construct a pattern of mythic symbols. Other examples could be drawn from the media, from schools, from music. Rituals like parades or patriotic days or flag saluting are important parts of myth and subject to their own special rhetorical devices—rhythm, repetition, color—to heighten some aspect of their meaning. Even where this meaning has lost its emotional intensity, the mere act of making noises at one another . . . can be socially cohesive. Thus, it is not true, despite the apparent decline of old fashioned patriotism, that the symbols of the American myth no longer have meaning. For even where the national anthem has become merely a ritualistic grunt before the ball game, it is a symbol whose proper interpretation can tell us something about our society.[1]

Socialization is not just an isolated learning process that takes place in childhood. The political themes that are introduced early in life through the family, the school, and the peer group can be reinforced or altered in later life as a result of exposure to the political messages in numerous everyday situations. The most important agencies of continuing political socialization are the political institutions whose rituals link enduring political beliefs and values to the most important political issues of the day. Through the continuing linkage of enduring myths to immediate policy problems, myths retain their status as the most widely shared categories of political thought.[2] The role of institutions in continuing socialization also promotes the remarkable degree of tolerance for political outcomes mentioned by Weissberg in Chapter 13.[3]

The socialization function of institutions not only reinforces the political learning that started in the individual domain of opinion, but institutions can produce large-scale changes in the content of socialization. Shifts in the nature of political conflicts, public demands, and policy issues often result in shifts in the institutional emphasis placed on various myths and the underlying values and beliefs that the myths represent.

The causal role of institutions in the socialization process completes the cycle of political relationships among the individual, issue formation, and institutional domains of opinion. Throughout the book we have seen how the political experiences of individuals provide a foundation for the public opinion that emerges through issue formation and mass communication processes, and how emerging public opinion, in turn, becomes an important variable in the policy and legitimation processes of political institutions. Now it is clear that this cycle of political connections is completed by the return link between policy processes in the institutional domain and socialization processes in the individual domain. Not only do the results of socialization and other individual political experiences flow upward to affect institutional operations, but the policy and legitimation processes of institutions flow downward to affect the nature of individual political experiences.

Policy processes are guided by the themes of political myths, and the myths introduced into specific policy debates shape the political preoccupations of individuals in society. The presence of familiar political themes in institutional processes, in turn, makes people more responsive to the directives of government. Even when people disagree with the outcomes of a political process, the symbolism involved in the policy debate may transmit to the public a reassuring picture of social reality. This relationship between the domain of the individual and the domain of culture and political institutions can be summarized in a two-stage model of political socialization as a conditioning process. In the first stage, the proliferation of politically significant symbols throughout life experiences leads the individual to associate intense private meaning and emotion with them. As Merelman pointed out, such association makes it possible in the next stage for citizens to become "conditioned" to respond favorably to the mere use of the symbols by the government.[4] This phenomenon may account for the fact that political rhetoric can be so banal and repetitive and yet continue to hold some apparent meaning for the public. This conditioning may also explain why the public often regards government policies and actions as legitimate even when few material benefits flow from them: Since certain symbols are valued in themselves, citizens may gain gratification from their use even in the absence of more tangible benefits or payoffs.

In some cases the apparent gratification that derives from the use of myth-related symbols may be the result of a simple classical conditioning process. The public, having learned to associate a political symbol with some tangible gratification in everyday experience, continues to respond favorably to the symbol even in the abstract context of government institutions. In other cases, the basic conditioning may be accompanied by the efforts of individuals to reduce cognitive dissonance produced by the failure of government to implement policies or fulfill promises. When a supportive public is confronted by little tangible return for its support, dissonance may result. One means of reducing the dissonance is to downplay the significance of material conditions and to regard symbolic pronouncements as ends in themselves.[5] When this is the case, the symbolic claims of government become self-fulfilling.[6] This important impact of policy on continuing socialization illustrates why it is not clear whether material payoffs or the symbolic reconstruction of myths should be regarded as the most important aspect of the policy process.

NEW IDEAS ABOUT THE STRUCTURE OF OPINION

As explained in Chapter 13, myth-based thinking is different from rational secondary-process thought. It is often fragmentary, contradictory, and immune to testing or logical proof. The fact that in everyday political discourse myths are often represented by key symbols or abbreviated themes also makes myth-based thinking seem terribly shallow and incomplete. People often seem to speak about political matters in a kind of symbolic code or political shorthand. This common pattern of political thinking may account for the frequent conclusion from opinion poll and interview data that most people are politically ignorant. Although it is true that myth-based thinking lacks the sophistication of ideological thought, it does provide some underlying structure for individual and public opinions—a structure more difficult to detect than formal logical structure because much of it remains hidden from view. References to elaborate myths and recurring political themes may be contained in a single symbol or in a cryptic phrase. Moreover, the political understandings that they generate may exist as much on a subconscious level as in formal, conscious terms.

The fact that myths operate at such deep—even subconscious—levels means that individuals may think and act in terms of them without fully realizing the rationale for the underlying structure of their behavior. This often produces the impression that no constraint is operating in mass belief systems. This impression has been reinforced by many survey research studies such as the ones described in Chapters 2 and 3. These studies generally look for evidence of ideological thinking in the public. Ideological thinking is characterized by the systematic and consistent connection of values and beliefs, the articulation of formal principles that govern their application, and the ability to hold stable opinions on a variety of issues. By these standards, the political thinking of the public generally seems disorganized and simple-minded. However, if we listen to people, it is often possible to detect that the thoughts they express on a subject reflect some deeper but poorly articulated structure of political understanding. An interesting example of this characteristic of myth-linked thinking occurs in an interview with a veteran of the Revolutionary War battles of Concord and Lexington. The interview was conducted by a historian some sixty years after the event. The interviewer was interested in the question of what motivated the patriot to risk his life in the struggle for freedom:

Q: Why did you? . . . My histories tell me that you men of the Revolution took up arms against intolerable oppressions.
A: What were they? Oppressions? I didn't feel them.
Q: What, were you not oppressed by the Stamp Act?
A: I never saw one of those stamps. . . . I am certain I never paid a penny for one of them.
Q: Well, what about the tea tax?
A: Tea tax, I never drank a drop of the stuff. The boys threw it all overboard.
Q: Then, I suppose you had been reading Harrington, or Sidney or Locke, about the eternal principles of liberty?
A: Never heard of 'em.
Q: Well, then, what was the matter, what did you mean in going into the fight?
A: Young man, what we meant in going for those red-coats, was this: we always had governed ourselves and we always meant to. They didn't mean we should.[7]

That cryptic remark about self-government reflects the myth of liberty that Albanese has cited as the spark that crystallized public opinion in favor of the Revolution.[8] However, this myth was not understood by the eighteenth-century public in sophisticated ideological terms such as the ones suggested by the nineteenth-century interviewer. The public seldom encountered the myth in complete form. The dominant form of exposure was to key symbols, which infused every aspect of society in prerevolutionary America. Symbols like the Liberty Tree appeared in poems, songs, posters, emblems, statues, and religious sermons. When the myth of liberty was presented in complete fashion, it generally took the form of dramatic ceremonies. Church bells gathered the townsfolk to witness the mock funeral procession of Liberty and to cheer at the last minute the rescue of Liberty from the death grip of oppression. Such dramatic images, reinforced by the proliferation of key symbols, left impressions that became powerful guides for public thought and action. These impressions were mythological, not ideological. They did not consist of articulate positions on issues like the Stamp Act or current philosophies of freedom. Such philosophical perspectives were the domain of the leaders of the Revolution: Adams, Jefferson, Hamilton, Paine, Jay, Washington, and others. However, the absence of widespread ideology was more than compensated for by the strength of mythology, which served as a basis for opinion, a focus for public debate, and a stimulus for action.

In short, the absence of ideological thinking in the mass public need not imply an absence of structure, consistency, or stability. However, as the questions asked by the above-mentioned interviewer indicate, it is tempting to evaluate political thinking in terms of overt signs of systematic organization. If one looks for evidence of formal ideology in the thinking of the American public, it will not be found. Moreover, concentration on overt belief structure increases the chances of overlooking deeper mythological themes that serve many individuals in place of ideology. For example, it is clear that the interviewer was searching for some signs of ideological commitment to the Revolution on the part of the soldier. In the process, he missed the obvious connection between the man's stated reason for joining the struggle for freedom and the dominant myth of the day. However crude it may seem, the man's explanation of the Revolution was virtually a direct summary of the dramatized liberty myth, which was blazed into the consciousness of nearly every citizen.

If one listens carefully for symbolic cues in the opinions expressed by ordinary people, it is possible to detect this pattern of seemingly vague thoughts and ideas that have their origins (and their meanings) in deep but unarticulated political myths. This is part of the basis on which many of the people studied by Lane managed to "contextualize" political issues and ideas even though they used no formal ideology. The "contextualizers," as Lane called them, located issues in terms of underlying values, political themes, historical patterns, and simple philosophies of life.[9] These organizing principles are characteristic of myth-related thought.

Lamb's more recent Lane-type study of the political thinking of residents in a wealthy, conservative California community revealed the presence of similar patterns of thought. The normal range of American thought about the welfare problem was captured nicely by three of Lamb's respondents. One woman supported assistance to the needy and condemned those who were well-off and yet turned their backs on the poor: "I have no use for these kind of people. They made it easy, without taxes, but they don't want *you* to live. And these people are going to have to get that out of their system, because everybody has to live."[10]

A more middle-of-the-road position, which combined a sense of equality with the values of individualism and competition, was expressed by another respondent: "I believe they're created equal with the right to progress, not the equal right to lay down and have fruit drop off the tree to them."[11] A third respondent staked out the conservative end of the normal spectrum of opinion on the welfare problem with this strong assertion of the traditional individualism myth:

> "There's nothing wrong with the fact that some people just barely exist. . . . The main goal of life is to get to heaven, and a guy who has to work like a dog all his life on this earth, maybe he's gonna get to heaven—faster than a lot of us."[12]

As Lamb pointed out, the policy debates that divide the public and the political parties on most social and economic issues result from the application of different myths to the same issue. When this occurs, traditional notions about individualism may be engaged by one segment of the public, and the equality value will be activated in other groups.

Each of the foregoing political statements reflects the influence of a dominant myth (or combination of myths) on the thinking of the individual. As long as political positions fall somewhere along this myth-anchored spectrum, people can understand one another, tolerate diverging viewpoints, and accept policies that emerge in response to them. Perhaps most importantly, the limits of political mythology also determine the limits of political reality for most people. Even the most liberal of Lamb's respondents could not imagine political solutions that fell outside the range of possibilities supported by dominant myths. Lamb observed that these people "cannot really imagine a society that would provide substantial material equality."[13] One of the people interviewed responded to the idea of guaranteed economic equality incredulously: "It would be like everyone going out for a track race and saying, 'Okay, everyone can run this race in the same time,' so eventually there would be no more records to be gone after."[14]

In addition to providing a context for political judgment and a structure for public opinion, myths also explain a good deal about the characteristics of opinion. Since individuals are capable of holding competing myths (and competing values and beliefs), their opinions on an issue may vary according to the symbolic cues in a situation. Cues that appeal to multiple myths can expand the scope of opinion. Cues that focus on single myths may evoke intense expressions of opinion from smaller publics.

Perhaps the most interesting effect of myth-based thinking has to do with the stability of opinion. Some individuals who hold competing values may emphasize one value over the other, while other individuals may hold competing beliefs and values with nearly equal intensity. The implication of this is that opinion instability may not be a product of "random" political thinking, but a systematic result of value and belief alignments. To the extent that individuals emphasize one value in a value-belief pair, their opinions on related issues should be relatively stable. The dominance of one set of values over another is often a characteristic of ideological thinking. Therefore, this prediction is consistent with common understandings about ideologues. However, when individuals emphasize competing values and beliefs with equal or nearly equal intensity, they can be expected to alternate their opinions on issues in response to changing symbolic cues or shifting political concerns.

This pattern of thinking probably applies in one degree or another to the majority of individuals. The implication is that the stability of an individual's opinion should be predicted fairly well as a function of value conflict, short-term political concerns, and the symbolic definition of issues. This opens up the possibility that ordinary individuals do think systematically about most political issues, but their underlying belief structure simply may not be logical or linear. These and other spinoffs from a cultural perspective on opinion call for a reformulation of theories about the structure of opinion and a rethinking of the traditional methods of research and analysis.

CONCLUSION

Patterns of belief, as theorists from Marx to Durkheim and Freud have told us, generally reflect the nature of life experience. In societies like the United States, which display a comparatively high degree of shared experience and political interest, the public can be expected to display a fairly undifferentiated style of political thinking. The dominant pattern of myth-based thought merely reflects the flexibility, tolerance, and value consensus present in a society in which most people (whether they are right or wrong) perceive that they hold more interests and experiences in common than in conflict. The result of having mythology as the structuring device for public opinion is the introduction of high levels of flexibility to policy making and tolerance for the results.

It seems unreasonable to evaluate public opinion against standards of formal ideological thinking when even the political elite in America tends to define issues in terms of symbols and themes from traditional political myths. For examples, Gary Wills cited the following economic pronouncements of the presidential contenders in 1968:

> Here is Ronald Reagan on the subject: "We offer equal opportunity at the starting line of life, but no compulsory tie for everyone at the finish." Here is Nixon: "I see a day when every child in this land has . . . an equal chance to go just as high as his talents will take him." Here is Rockefeller: "I see . . . the welfare concept . . . as a floor below which nobody will be allowed to fall, but with no ceiling to prevent any one from rising as high as he wants to rise." Here is Humphrey: "I'll take my stand, as I always have, on equal opportunity. . . . Our goal is an environment within which all types of business rivalry can flourish."[15]

It is difficult to judge the mass public against ideological standards of thought in a society in which the statements of the political elite are more myth oriented than ideological in their symbolism and themes. Moreover, to continue to discuss public opinion in America using concepts related to formal ideological thinking reflects a basic misunderstanding of the nature of ideology and the conditions that produce it. Ideologies tend to emerge when groups come into constant conflict, or realize that they have opposing interests, or encounter severe psychological strains due to social changes that the prevailing myths cannot explain fully. So much is obvious. However, what is not so obvious is where ideologies come from. In his illuminating contribution to this question Geertz argued that ideologies derive from underlying cultural mythologies. They emerge when more complete formulations of the social order are needed for thinking about complex problems or when the experiences of particular groups increasingly reflect a narrow set of myths and fail to validate others.[16] Thus, ideologies grow out of the seeds of myth in response to particular social conditions.

This perspective suggests that ideology should not be regarded as the standard for judging belief organization, for to do so would ignore political realities. Political thinking is a reflection of social conditions. In times of relative affluence and social stability, there will be a broad sharing of myths and a concentration of individuals at the center of the political spectrum (where competing myths like individualism and equality are balanced equally in the individual's belief system). These conditions inhibit the formation of ideologies. However, in times of stress, change, and economic uncertainty, there will be a tendency for increasing inequality and disparity in life experiences among groups. Under these circumstances, different groups will tend to see different myths as the best frames of reference for their situations.

Ideologies emerge from the use of consistent frames of reference under conditions of political conflict. For example, in times of economic crisis, middle- and upper-class groups may move increasingly toward an individualist orientation and blame their problems on the excessive public spending of government and the demands of labor and the unemployed. The same conditions may push the working class increasingly toward equality-oriented understandings of their problems and corresponding demands for government programs and an increasing share of the wealth. In historical periods like the Age of Jackson, the Civil War, the industrial revolution, and the Great Depression, there have been marked increases in ideological thinking based on the polarization of underlying social myths. Ideological positions grew out of the consolidation of myths held by different groups, the rise of political organizations around these myths, the increasing recognition of social cleavages that needed formal explanations, and the upswing in political action that required formal political categories for coordination and guidance. Just as these ideological positions arise from existing myths, they tend to recede into more broadly shared mythologies when social crises are resolved.

The interplay of culture, individuals, and political institutions explains a good deal about patterns of political integration, conflict, and issue formation. When viewed from this perspective, the characteristics of public opinion appear to be sensible responses to changing political conditions. Through the formation of opinion individuals understand their society. Through the expression of opinion political outcomes are validated and social values are perpetuated. As these aspects of opinion suggest, public opinion is the key variable in the American political system.

NOTES

1. Douglas H. Rosenberg, "Arms and the American Way: The Ideological Dimension of Military Growth," in *Military Force and American Society*, eds. Bruce M. Russett and Alred Stepan (New York: Harper and Row, 1973), p. 167.
2. For a discussion of this point, see Reinhard Bendix, "The Age of Ideology: Persistent and Changing," in *Ideology and Discontent*, ed. David Apter (New York: Free Press, 1964).
3. Robert Weissberg, *Public Opinion and Popular Government* (Englewood Cliffs, N.J.: Prentice-Hall, 1976), p. 213.
4. See Richard Merelman, "Learning and Legitimacy," *American Political Science Review*, Vol. 60 (September 1966), pp. 548-61.
5. Ibid. See also Rosenberg, "Arms and the American Way."
6. See Murray Edelman, *The Symbolic Uses of Politics* (Urbana: University of Illinois Press, 1964); and Murray Edelman, *Political Language: Words That Succeed and Policies That Fail* (New York: Academic Press, 1977).
7. Reported in Charles Warren, *The Making of the Constitution* (Cambridge, Mass.: Harvard University Press, 1928), p. 1.
8. See the discussion in Chapter 9. Also, see Catherine Albanese, *Sons of the Fathers: The Civil Religion of the American Revolution* (Philadelphia: Temple University Press, 1976).
9. Robert E. Lane, *Political Ideology* (New York: Free Press, 1962).
10. Reported in Karl A. Lamb, *As Orange Goes: Twelve California Families and the Future of American Politics* (New York: Norton, 1974), p. 176.
11. Ibid., p. 176.
12. Ibid., p. 177.

13. Ibid., p. 178.
14. Ibid.
15. Gary Wills, *Nixon Agonistes* (Boston: Houghton Mifflin, 1970).
16. Clifford Geertz, "Ideology as a Cultural System," in Geertz, *The Interpretation of Cultures* (New York: Basic Books, 1973), pp. 193–233.

Copyrights
and
Acknowledgments

For permission to use the excerpts reprinted in this book, the author is grateful to the following publishers and copyright holders:

ACADEMIC PRESS for *Politics as Symbolic Action* and for *Political Language: Words That Succeed and Policies That Fail,* both by Murray Edelman. Reprinted by permission.

ATHENEUM PUBLISHERS for *Roots of War* by Richard Barnet. Copyright 1973 by Atheneum Publishers. Reprinted by permission.

JAMES DAVID BARBER for *The Interplay of Presidential Character and Style: A Paradigm and Five Illustrations.* Reprinted by permission.

THE DRYDEN PRESS for *The Semisoverign People: A Realist's View of Democracy in America* by E. E. Schattschneider. Copyright © 1960 by E. E. Schattschneider and The Dryden Press. Reprinted by permission of Holt, Rinehart and Winston.

ALFRED A. KNOPF, INC. for *Democracy Under Pressure* Vol. 2, by Alexis de Toqueville. Copyright 1945 and renewed 1973 by Alfred A. Knopf, Inc. Reprinted by permission of the publisher.

THE NEW AMERICAN LIBRARY for *Thomas Jefferson on Democracy* by Saul K. Padover. Reprinted by permission.

RANDOM HOUSE, INC. for *Boys on the Bus* by Timothy Crouse. Copyright © 1972, 1973 by Timothy Crouse. Reprinted by permission of Random House, Inc.

Index

5335 172

A 0
B 1
C 2
D 3
E 4
F 5
G 6
H 7
I 8
J 9